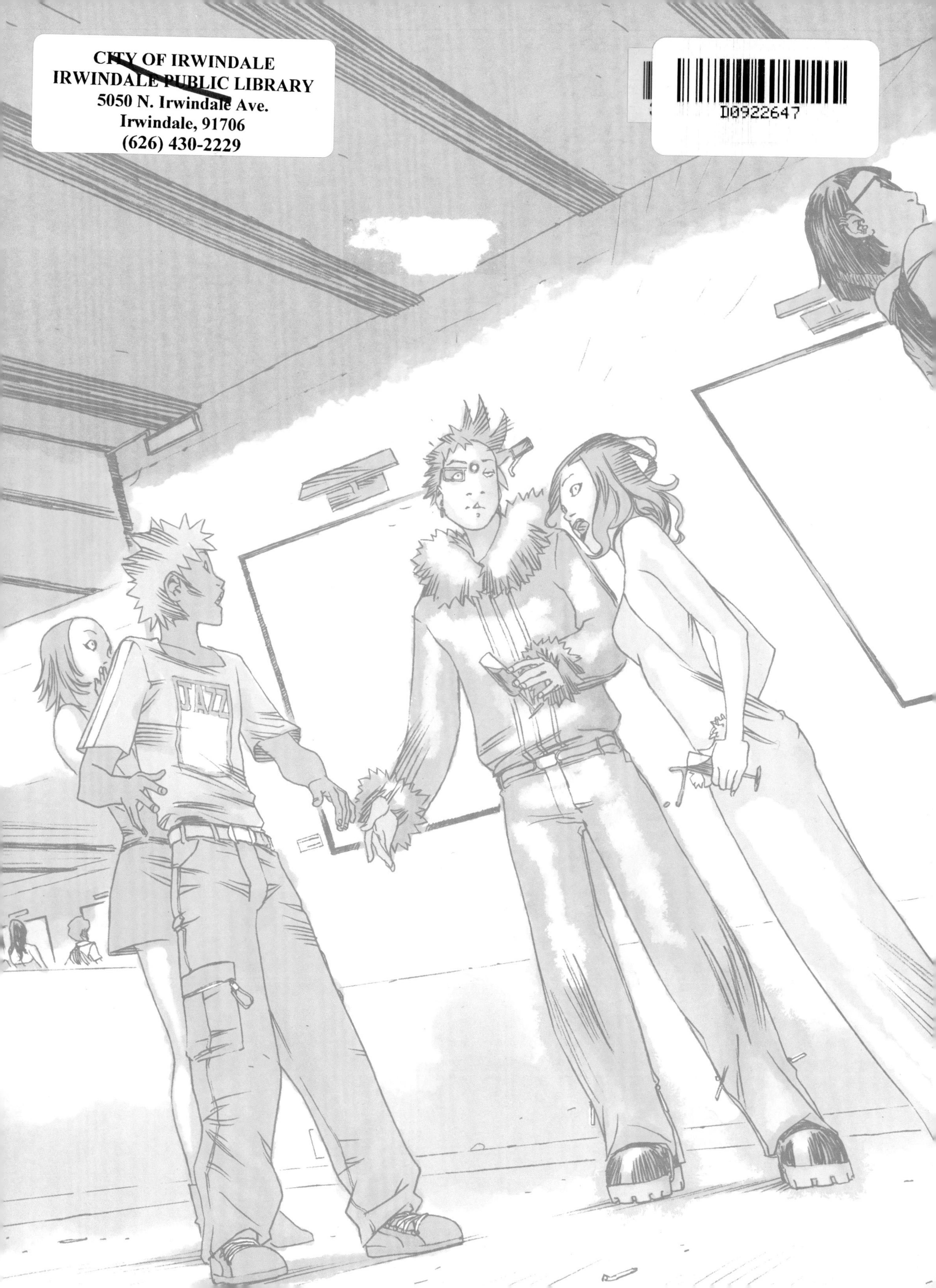
JAZZ

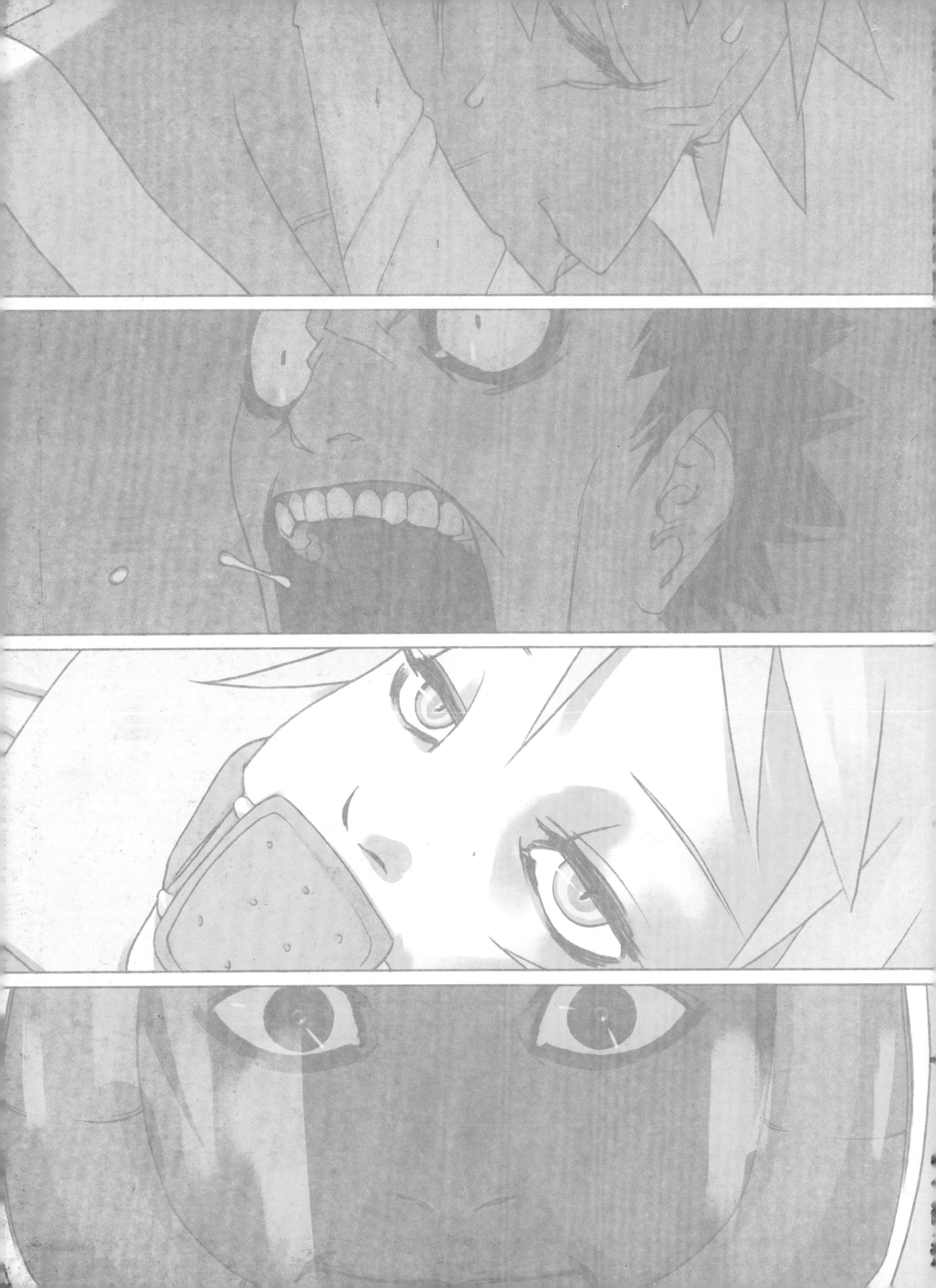

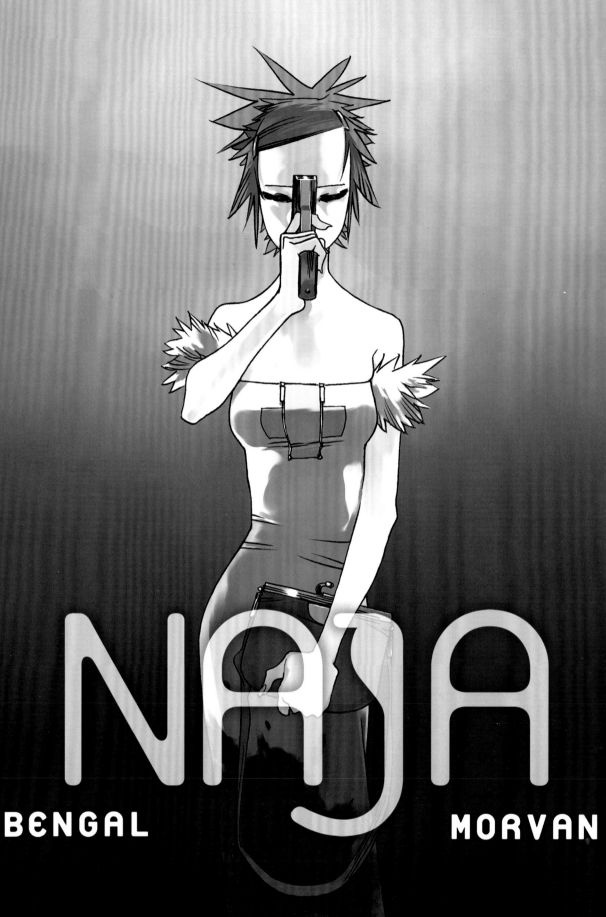

NAJA

BENGAL   MORVAN

MAGNETIC PRESS
www.MAGNETIC-PRESS.com

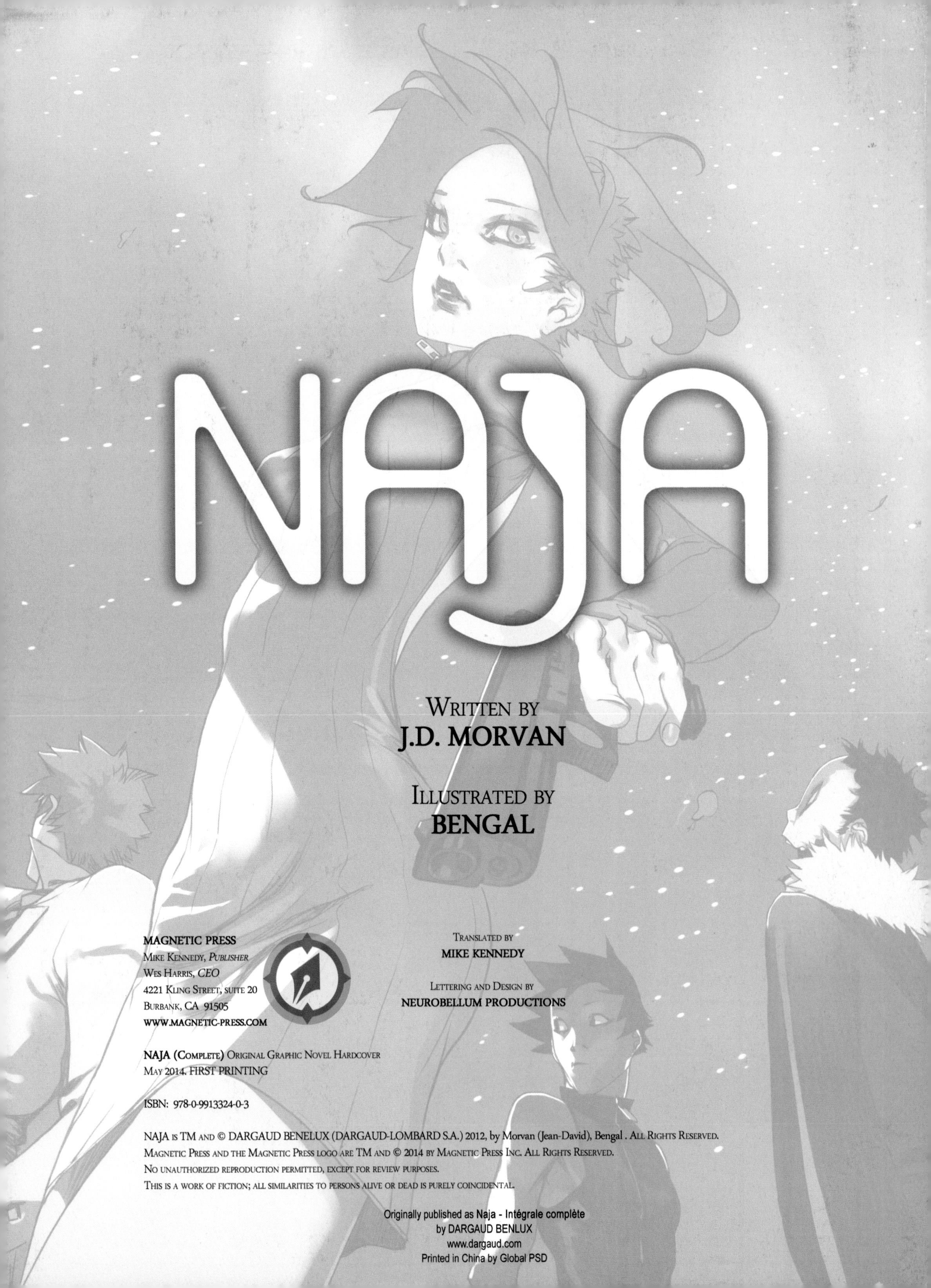

NAJA

WRITTEN BY
J.D. MORVAN

ILLUSTRATED BY
BENGAL

MAGNETIC PRESS
MIKE KENNEDY, *PUBLISHER*
WES HARRIS, *CEO*
4221 KLING STREET, SUITE 20
BURBANK, CA 91505
WWW.MAGNETIC-PRESS.COM

TRANSLATED BY
MIKE KENNEDY

LETTERING AND DESIGN BY
NEUROBELLUM PRODUCTIONS

NAJA (COMPLETE) ORIGINAL GRAPHIC NOVEL HARDCOVER
MAY 2014. FIRST PRINTING

ISBN: 978-0-9913324-0-3

Originally published as Naja - Intégrale complète
by DARGAUD BENLUX
www.dargaud.com
Printed in China by Global PSD

FOREWORD

I write comics because I love to look at sequential artwork.

Well, and to pay bills, but that's really second place. I love few things more than thumbing through pages of art created by a master craftsman. To see still images come to life panel by panel. There are few who make me smile nearly as much as Bengal.

For many years I made my living as an illustrator and animator of cartoons and comic books. During these years, most of them while living in San Francisco, I'd often take breaks from drawing to fill notebooks with ideas for stories and things that I wanted to do. Most of them took shape in my mind in ways my talents would have trouble translating, but I couldn't stop writing the ideas. By the time I was inching towards my 34th birthday I recognized I had about thirteen journals full of story ideas that I wanted to tell, scenarios I needed to see happen, preferably through the lenses of artists better than myself.

During this time, I compiled files full of my favorite illustrators and comic book artists to inspire me to write more stories, in hopes that I could one day write stories for them. A friend of mine, with whom I was sharing a studio, introduced me to Bengal's work during this period. I was immediately enamored by it. The artist in me found him intimidating, somebody who could capture such beauty and depth with so few lines. Everything he does has an airy sense, as if it was just a thrown-off sketch, but any artist can tell you that the foundation and knowledge inherent in his artwork is anything but. More line work usually/often indicates somebody who is trying to mask a failing. Bengal uses a minimal amount of line work because his form and storytelling don't need to be overly rendered to fool the layman into thinking there is something more there. The effortless form of his figures, the motion he captures in every panel, the quiet depths established in more somber moments... he is a master storyteller and illustrator.

And I'm envious of his powers.

And I'm envious of you as you crack this book open for the first time.

This is my first experience with writer J.D. Morvan, and I'm impressed. He allows Bengal's fluid and stunning storytelling to carry you through the pages, he understands that the art that he's working with doesn't need a heavy handed writing approach; the art perfectly captures everything that I imagine was in his script. His dialogue is terse and to the point, and the captions equally so. The book has a velocity in the page-turns themselves. This is the mark of a seasoned professional with total confidence. And the result is a motion picture on paper.

These two men together are a force to be reckoned with. Looking at Bengal's spectacular pages is a reminder to me that I'd rather write stories for those rare humans who can tell them with such exceptional results than to bang my head against the drawing table. Artists like Bengal remind me that I made the right decision to focus on my writing.

It's the rare book that I crack open and immediately feel jealous that I wasn't a part of creating it. NAJA is just that. I think you're going to really enjoy this.

*- **Rick Remender** is the writer/creator of FEAR AGENT, LAST DAYS OF AMERICAN CRIME, STRANGE GIRL, and BLACK SCIENCE. He has also written X-MEN, PUNISHER, SECRET AVENGERS, and CAPTAIN AMERICA, as well as numerous video games, including DEAD SPACE and BULLETSTORM.*

February 2014

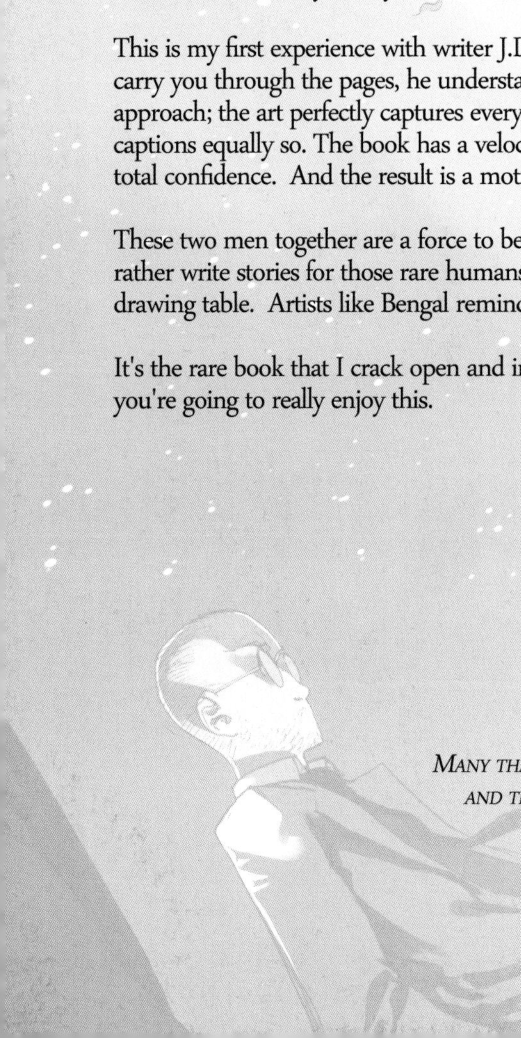

MANY THANKS TO DARGAUD FOR LETTING US GIVE BIRTH TO OUR NAJA, AND THANKS TO MIKE FOR BRINGING HER TO AMERICAN READERS!
- B.

A BIG HUG TO YVESS, CHRISTELH, AND OLIVIERJ.
- JDM.

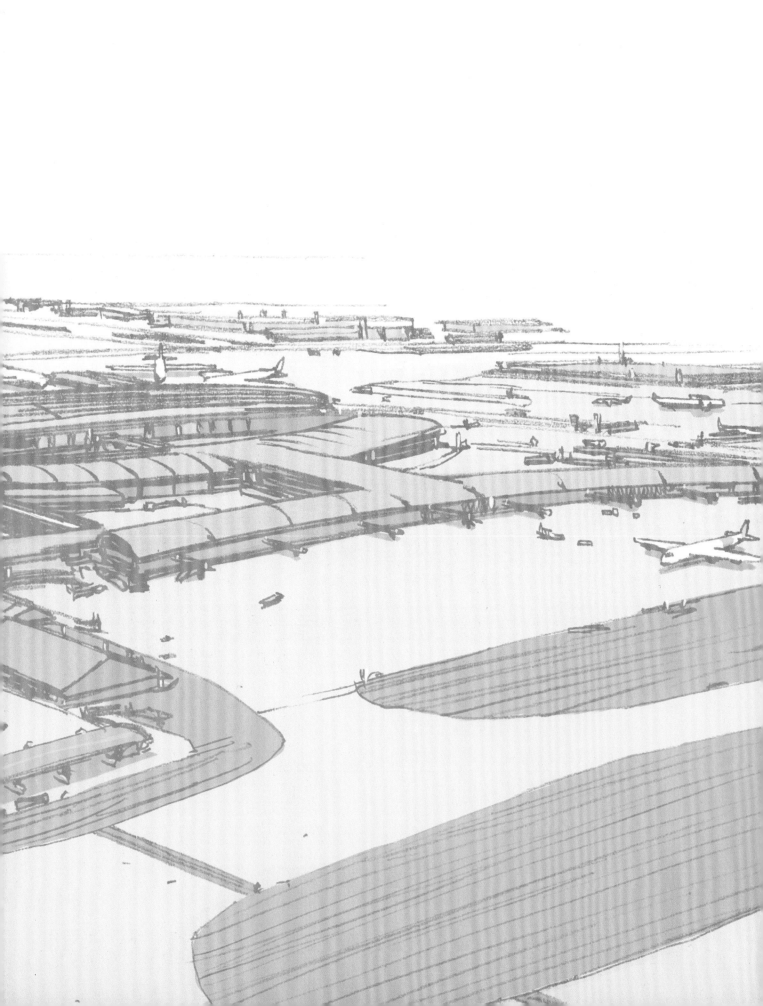

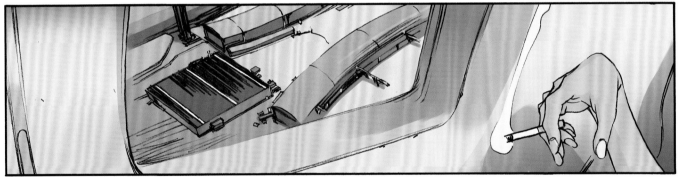

HER NAME IS NAJA.

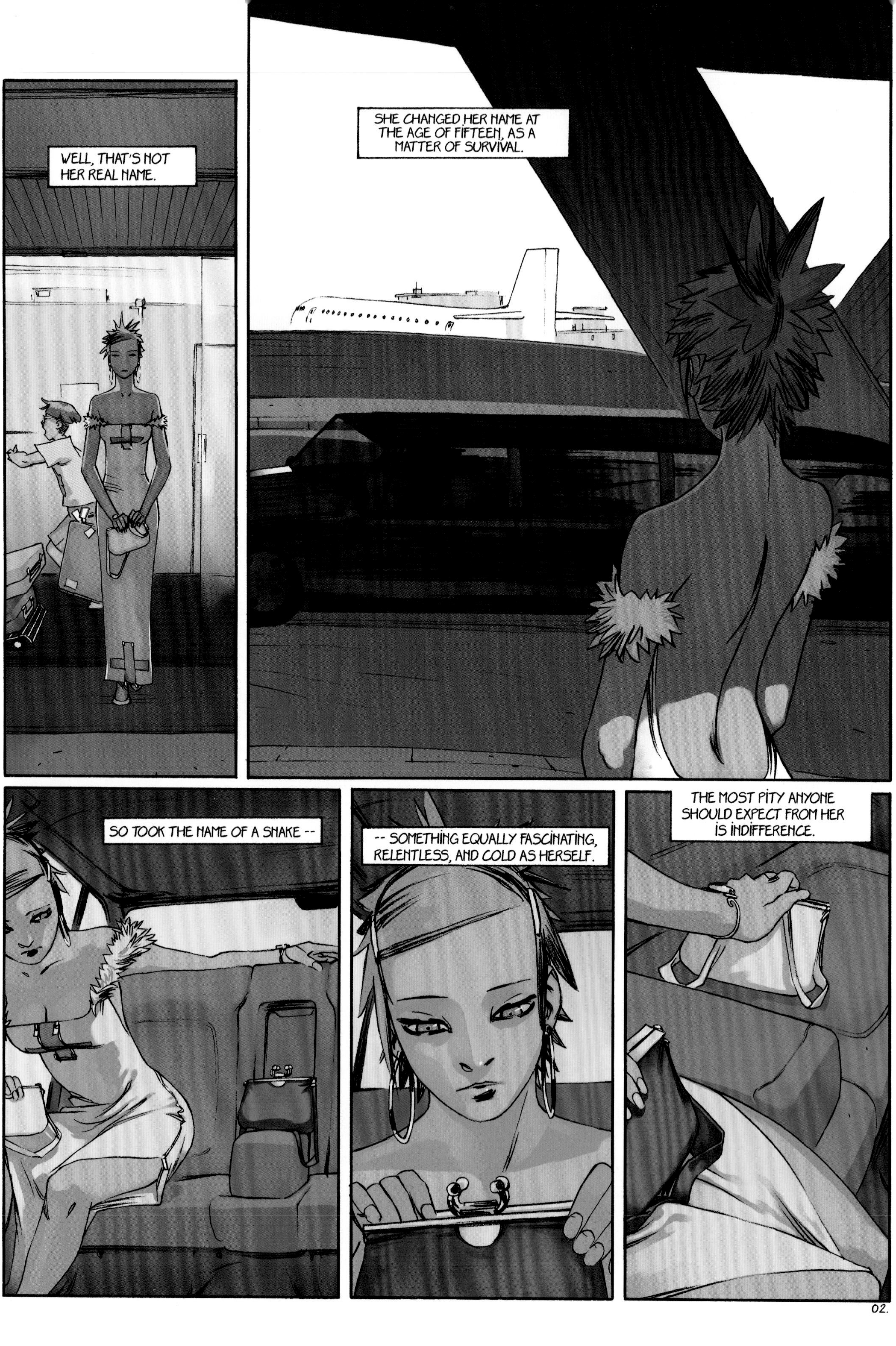
WELL, THAT'S NOT HER REAL NAME.
SHE CHANGED HER NAME AT THE AGE OF FIFTEEN, AS A MATTER OF SURVIVAL.
SO TOOK THE NAME OF A SNAKE --
-- SOMETHING EQUALLY FASCINATING, RELENTLESS, AND COLD AS HERSELF.
THE MOST PITY ANYONE SHOULD EXPECT FROM HER IS INDIFFERENCE.

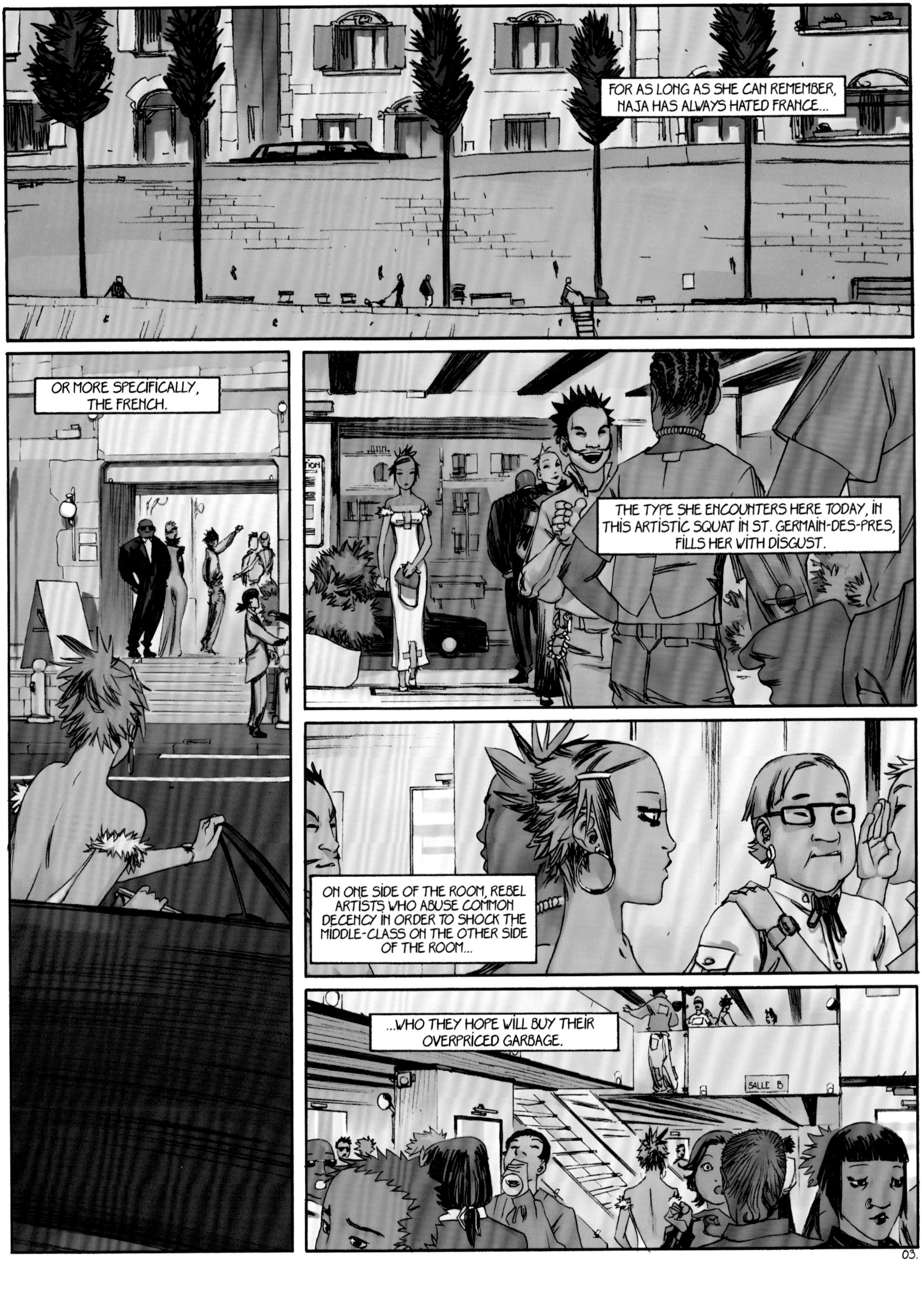
FOR AS LONG AS SHE CAN REMEMBER, NAJA HAS ALWAYS HATED FRANCE...
OR MORE SPECIFICALLY, THE FRENCH.
THE TYPE SHE ENCOUNTERS HERE TODAY, IN THIS ARTISTIC SQUAT IN ST. GERMAIN-DES-PRES, FILLS HER WITH DISGUST.
ON ONE SIDE OF THE ROOM, REBEL ARTISTS WHO ABUSE COMMON DECENCY IN ORDER TO SHOCK THE MIDDLE-CLASS ON THE OTHER SIDE OF THE ROOM...
...WHO THEY HOPE WILL BUY THEIR OVERPRICED GARBAGE.
SALLE B

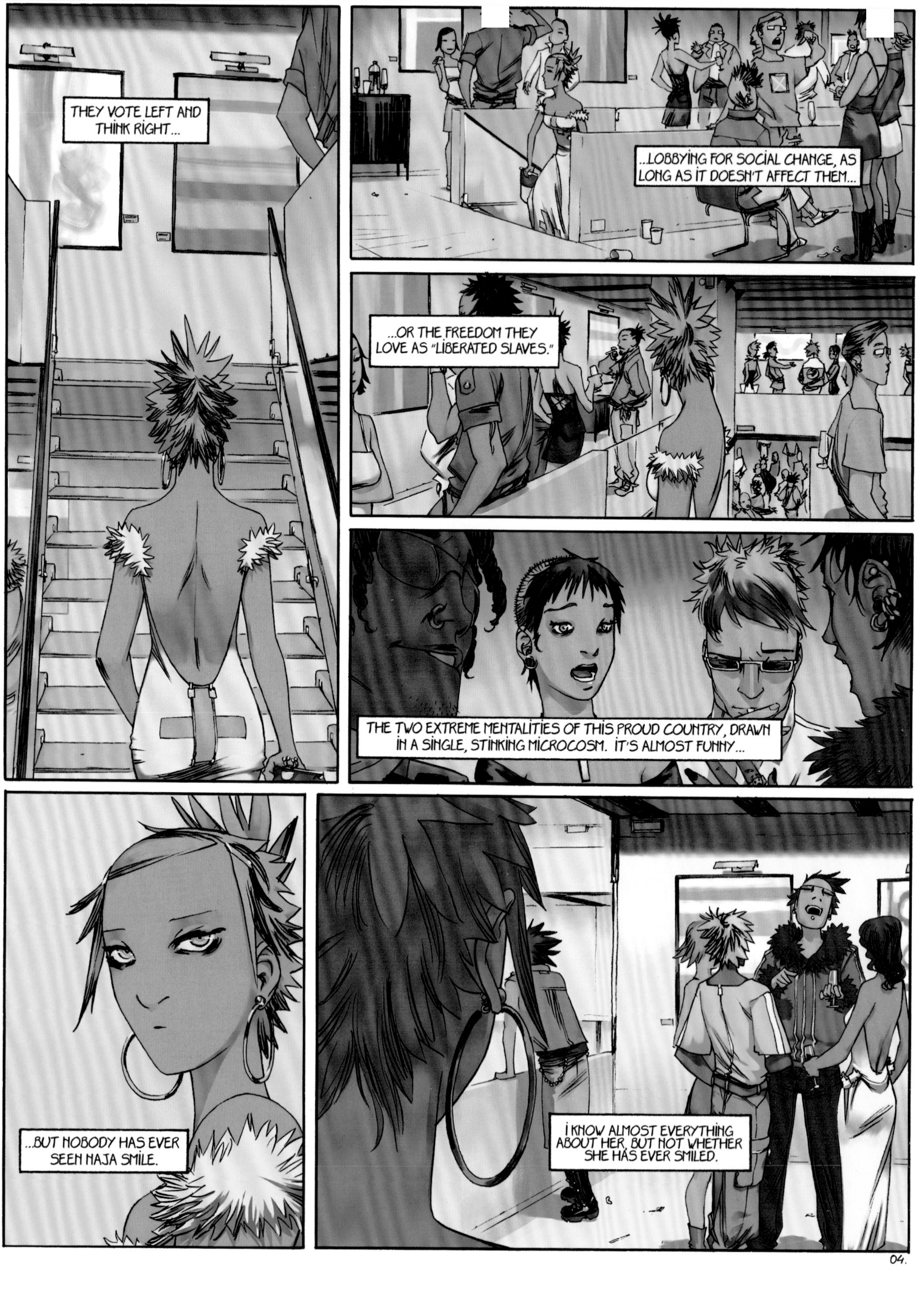
THEY VOTE LEFT AND THINK RIGHT...
...LOBBYING FOR SOCIAL CHANGE, AS LONG AS IT DOESN'T AFFECT THEM...
...OR THE FREEDOM THEY LOVE AS "LIBERATED SLAVES."
THE TWO EXTREME MENTALITIES OF THIS PROUD COUNTRY, DRAWN IN A SINGLE, STINKING MICROCOSM. IT'S ALMOST FUNNY...
...BUT NOBODY HAS EVER SEEN NAJA SMILE.
I KNOW ALMOST EVERYTHING ABOUT HER, BUT NOT WHETHER SHE HAS EVER SMILED.

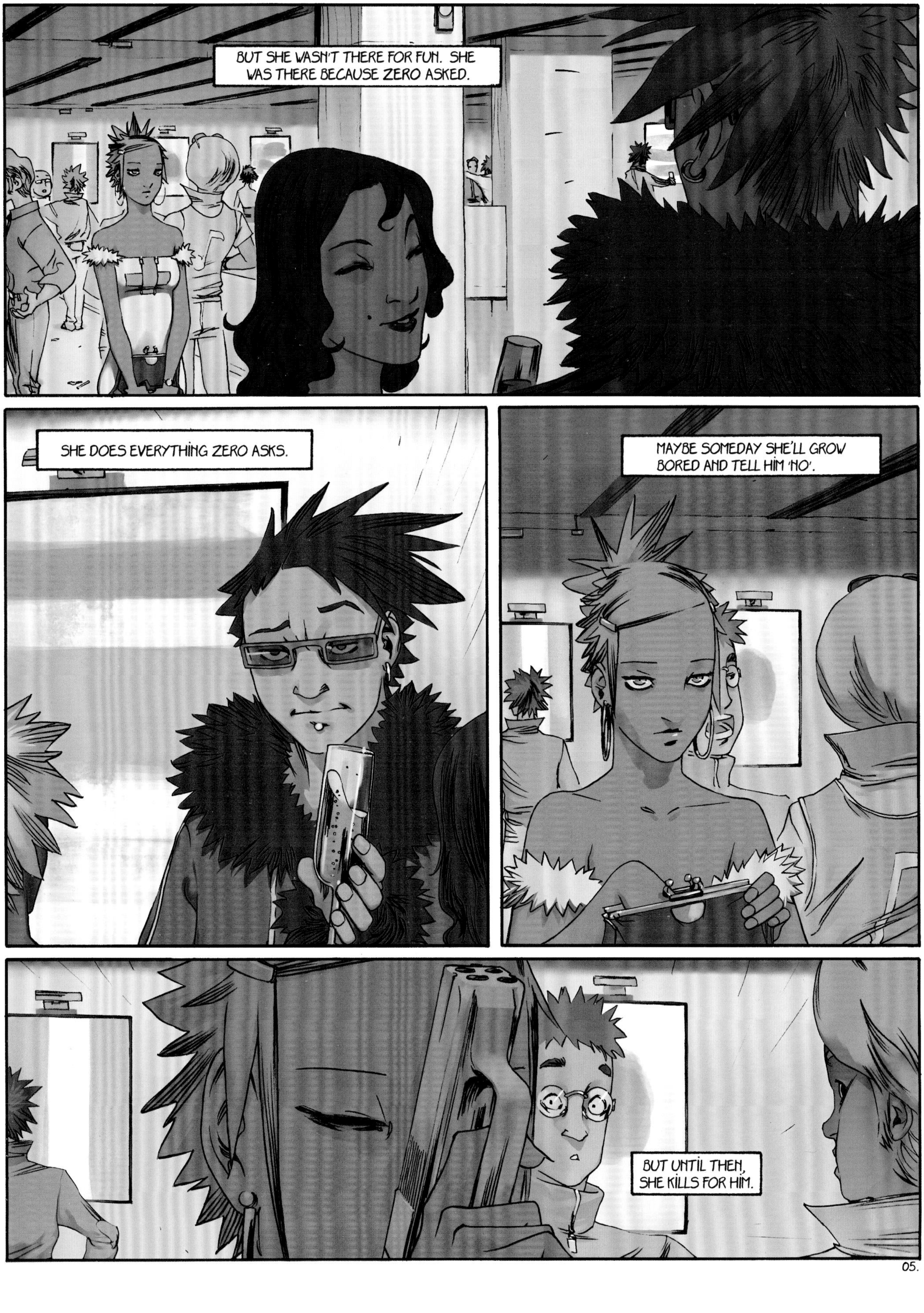
BUT SHE WASN'T THERE FOR FUN. SHE WAS THERE BECAUSE ZERO ASKED.
SHE DOES EVERYTHING ZERO ASKS.
MAYBE SOMEDAY SHE'LL GROW BORED AND TELL HIM 'NO'.
BUT UNTIL THEN, SHE KILLS FOR HIM.

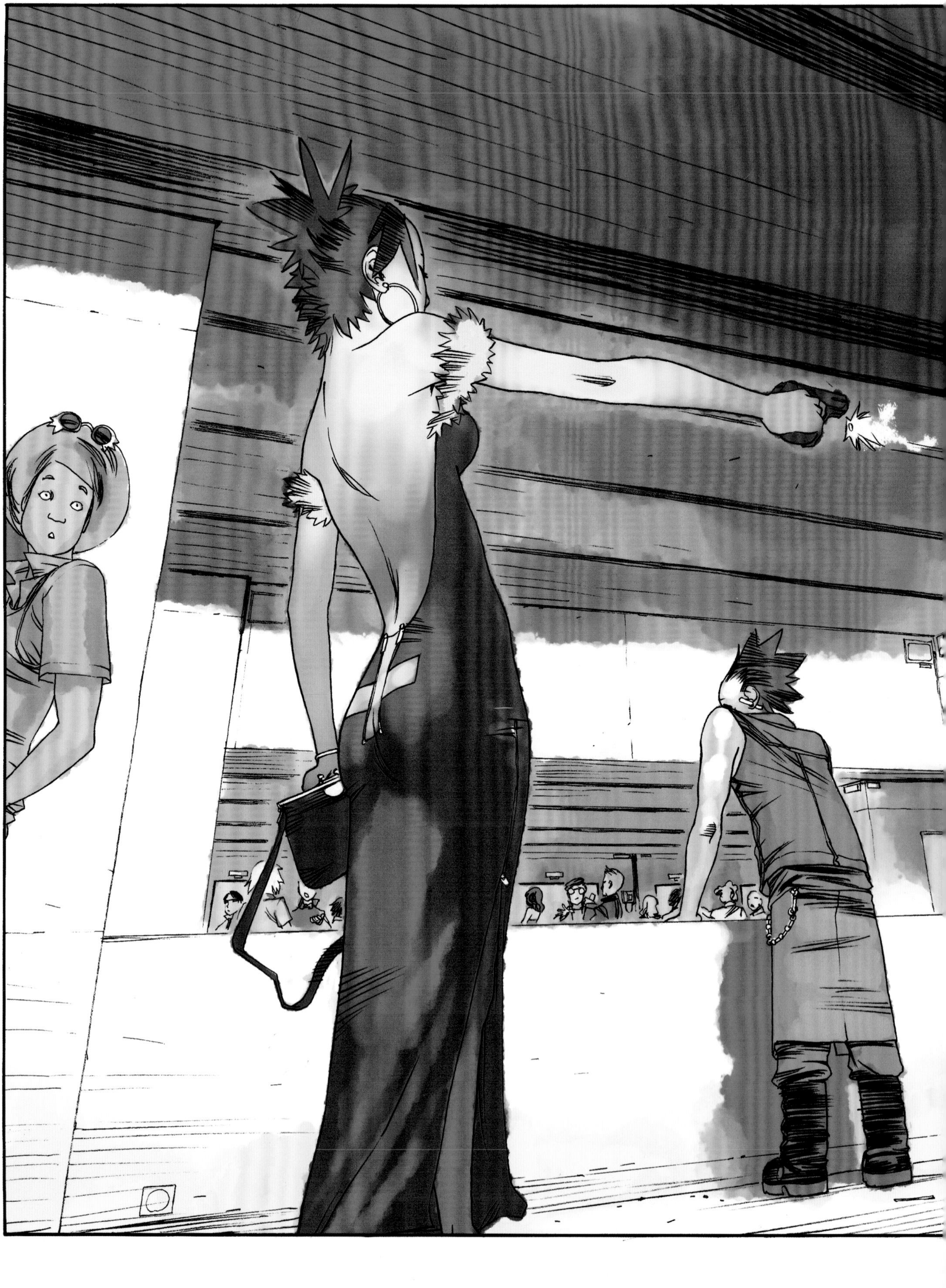

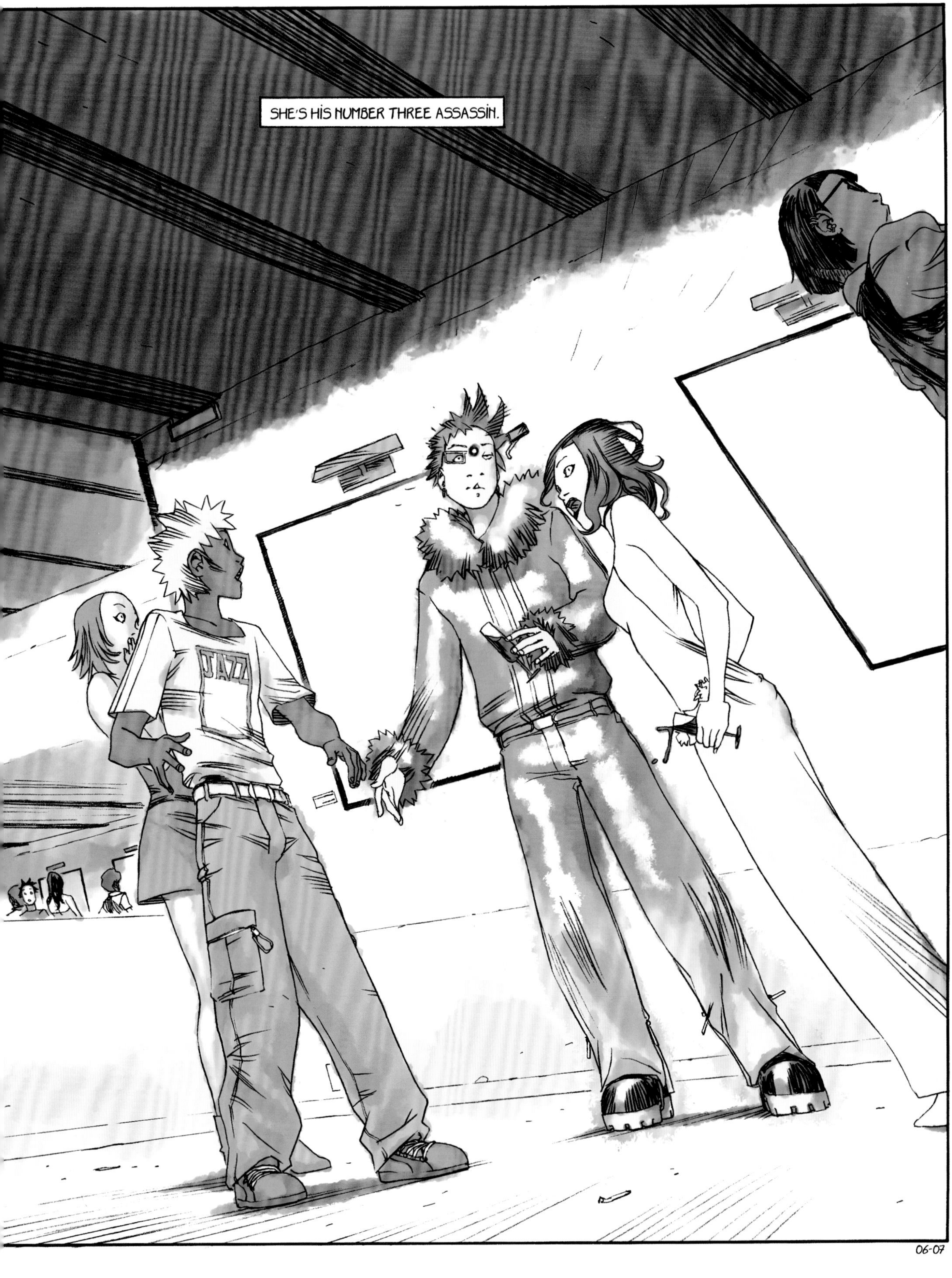
SHE'S HIS NUMBER THREE ASSASSIN.
JAZZ

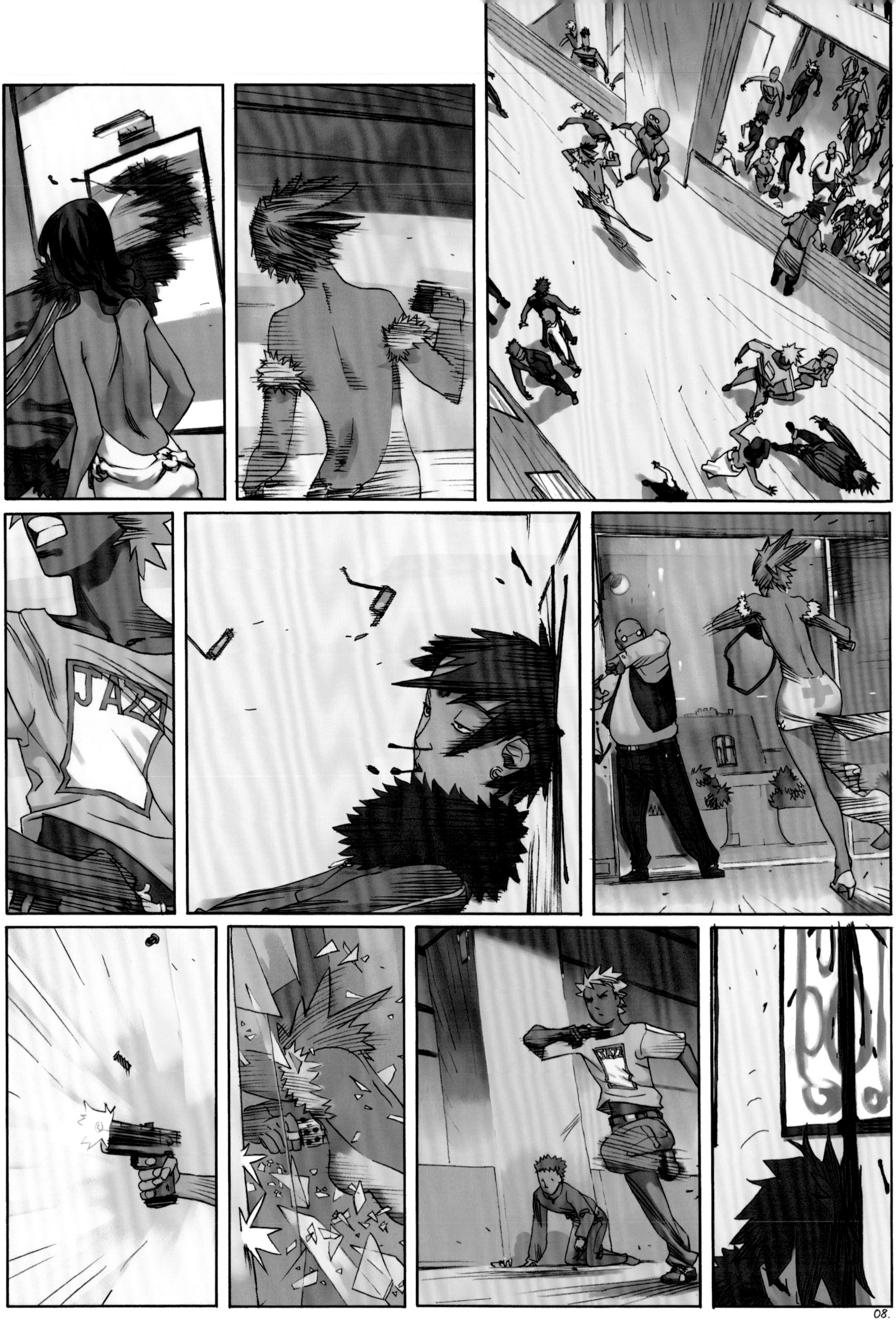
JAZZ

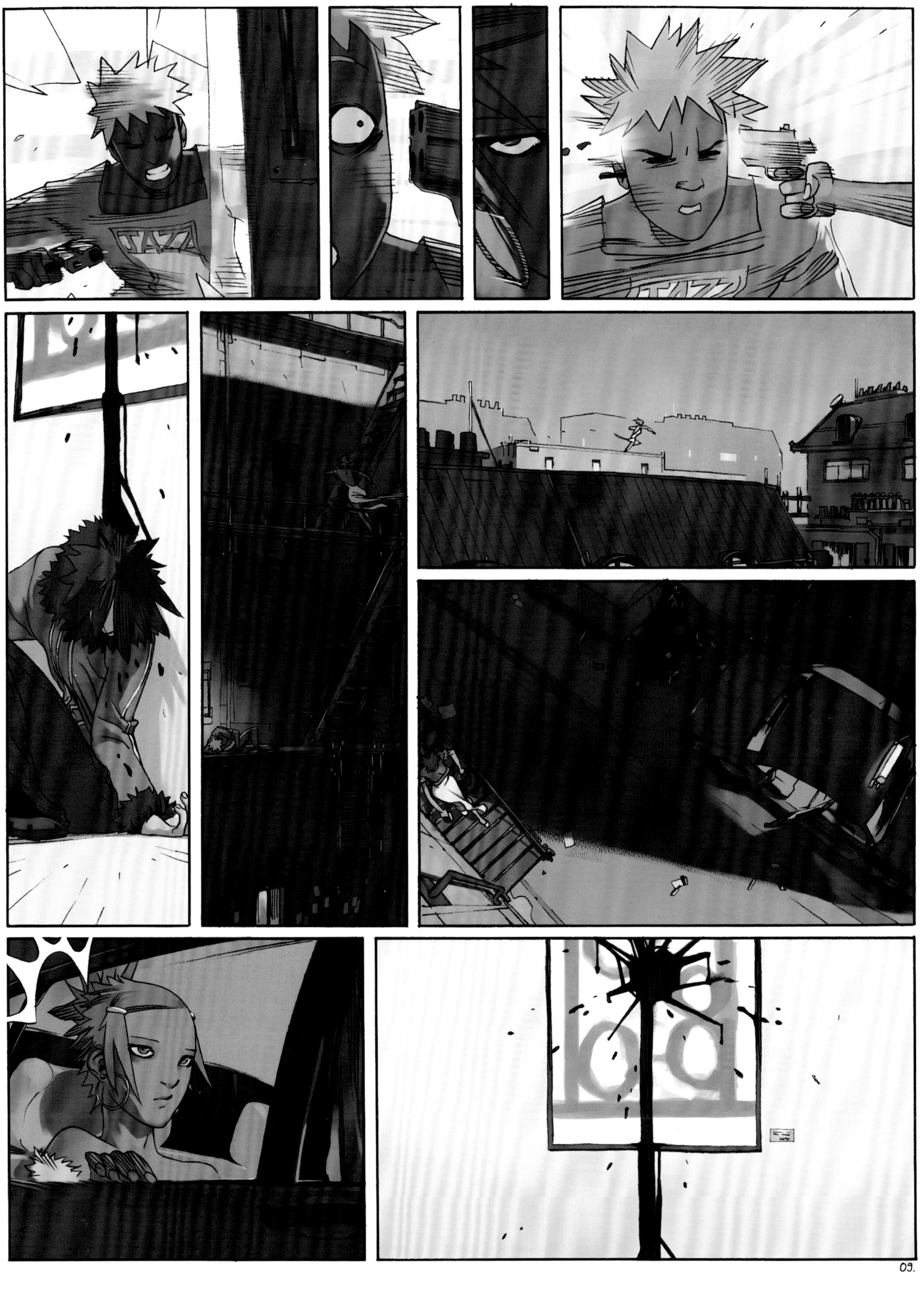
JAZZ

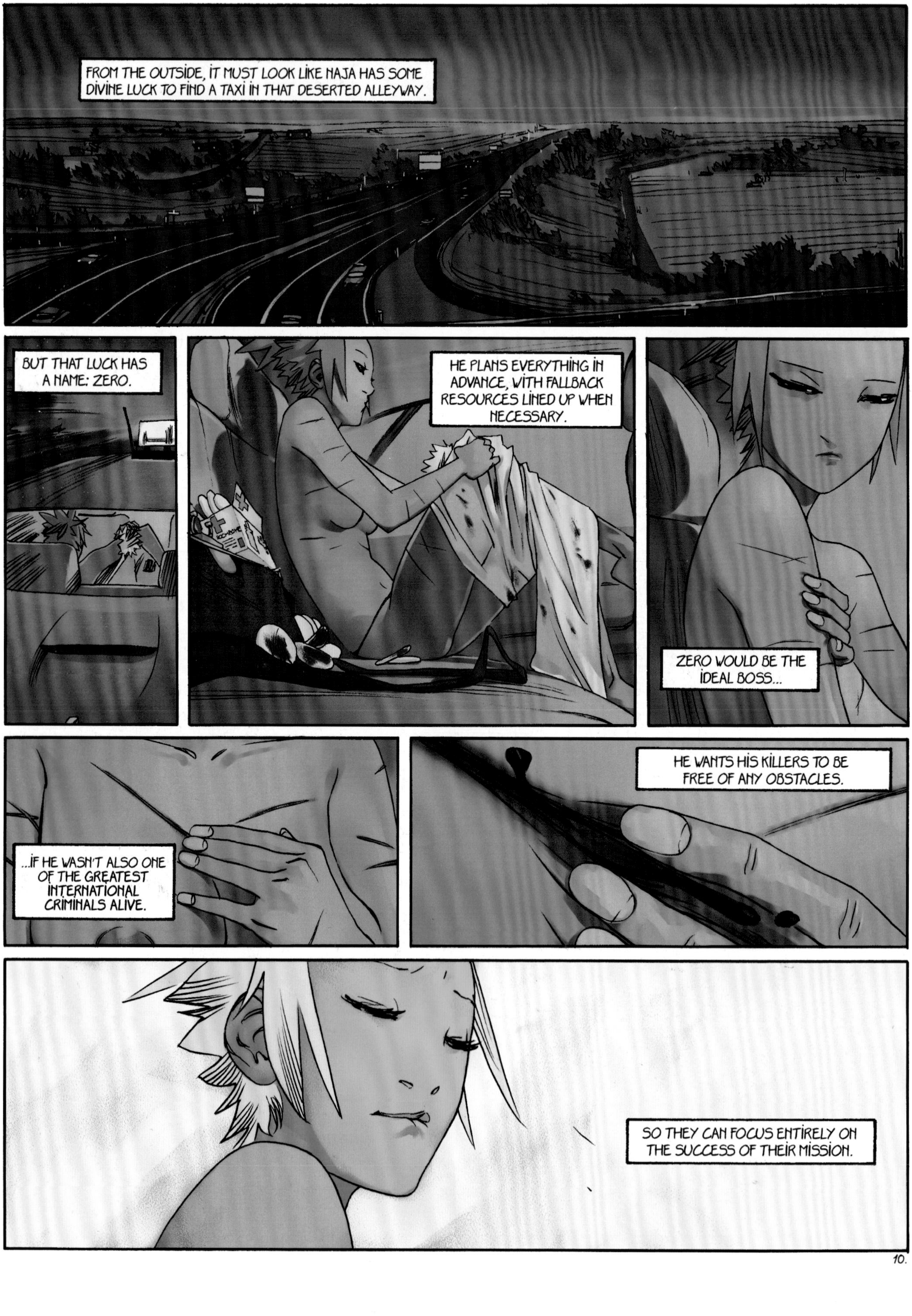
FROM THE OUTSIDE, IT MUST LOOK LIKE NAJA HAS SOME DIVINE LUCK TO FIND A TAXI IN THAT DESERTED ALLEYWAY.
BUT THAT LUCK HAS A NAME: ZERO.
HE PLANS EVERYTHING IN ADVANCE, WITH FALLBACK RESOURCES LINED UP WHEN NECESSARY.
ZERO WOULD BE THE IDEAL BOSS...
...IF HE WASN'T ALSO ONE OF THE GREATEST INTERNATIONAL CRIMINALS ALIVE.
HE WANTS HIS KILLERS TO BE FREE OF ANY OBSTACLES.
SO THEY CAN FOCUS ENTIRELY ON THE SUCCESS OF THEIR MISSION.

THE NEXT PERSON TO TAKE THAT TAXI AFTER HER WILL RECOVER HER ITEMS AND MAKE THEM DISAPPEAR.

LIKE I SAID, ZERO TAKES CARE OF EVERYTHING. THERE IS A CAREFUL STRUCTURE TO IT ALL.

MULTIPLE PARTIES, EACH PERFECT IN THEIR RESPECTIVE ROLE...

... IT'S MASTERFUL.

YOU MIGHT THINK THERE WOULD BE CHAOS IN THIS BEAUTIFUL MACHINE.

MAYBE THERE IS, BUT YOU'D HAVE TO SEARCH FOR IT.

FOR NOW, HOWEVER, LET'S RETURN TO NUMBER THREE.

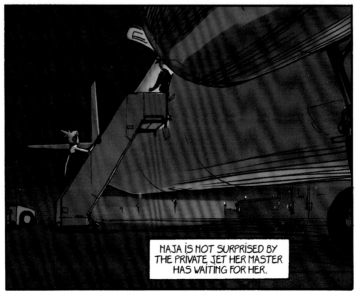

NAJA IS NOT SURPRISED BY THE PRIVATE JET HER MASTER HAS WAITING FOR HER.

NOTHING EVER SURPRISES NAJA.

NOT EVEN INJURY.

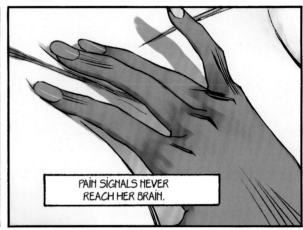

PAIN SIGNALS NEVER REACH HER BRAIN.

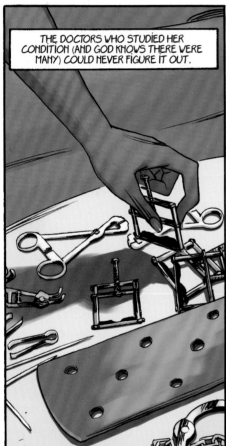

THE DOCTORS WHO STUDIED HER CONDITION (AND GOD KNOWS THERE WERE MANY) COULD NEVER FIGURE IT OUT.

FRANKLY, NAJA DOESN'T CARE WHY SHE DOESN'T FEEL.

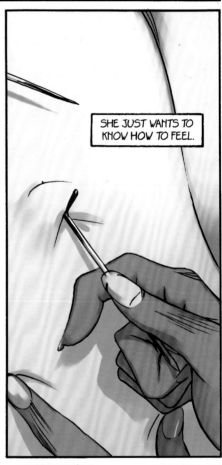

SHE JUST WANTS TO KNOW HOW TO FEEL.

UNTIL SHE EXPERIENCES THAT EVIL PLEASURE, SHE WILL CONTINUE TO PURSUE IT.

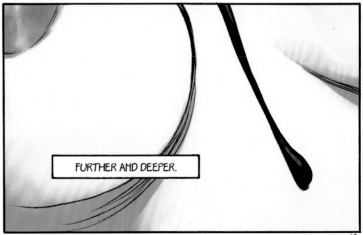

FURTHER AND DEEPER.

AS FAR AS SHE HAS TO GO.

SHE'LL SUCCEED EVENTUALLY, NO MATTER WHAT...

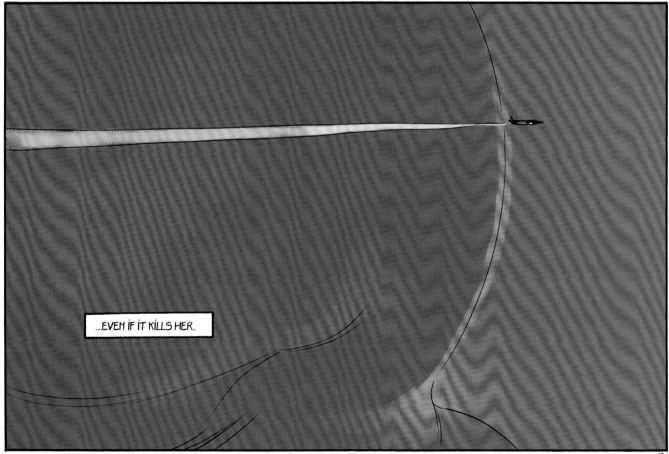

...EVEN IF IT KILLS HER.

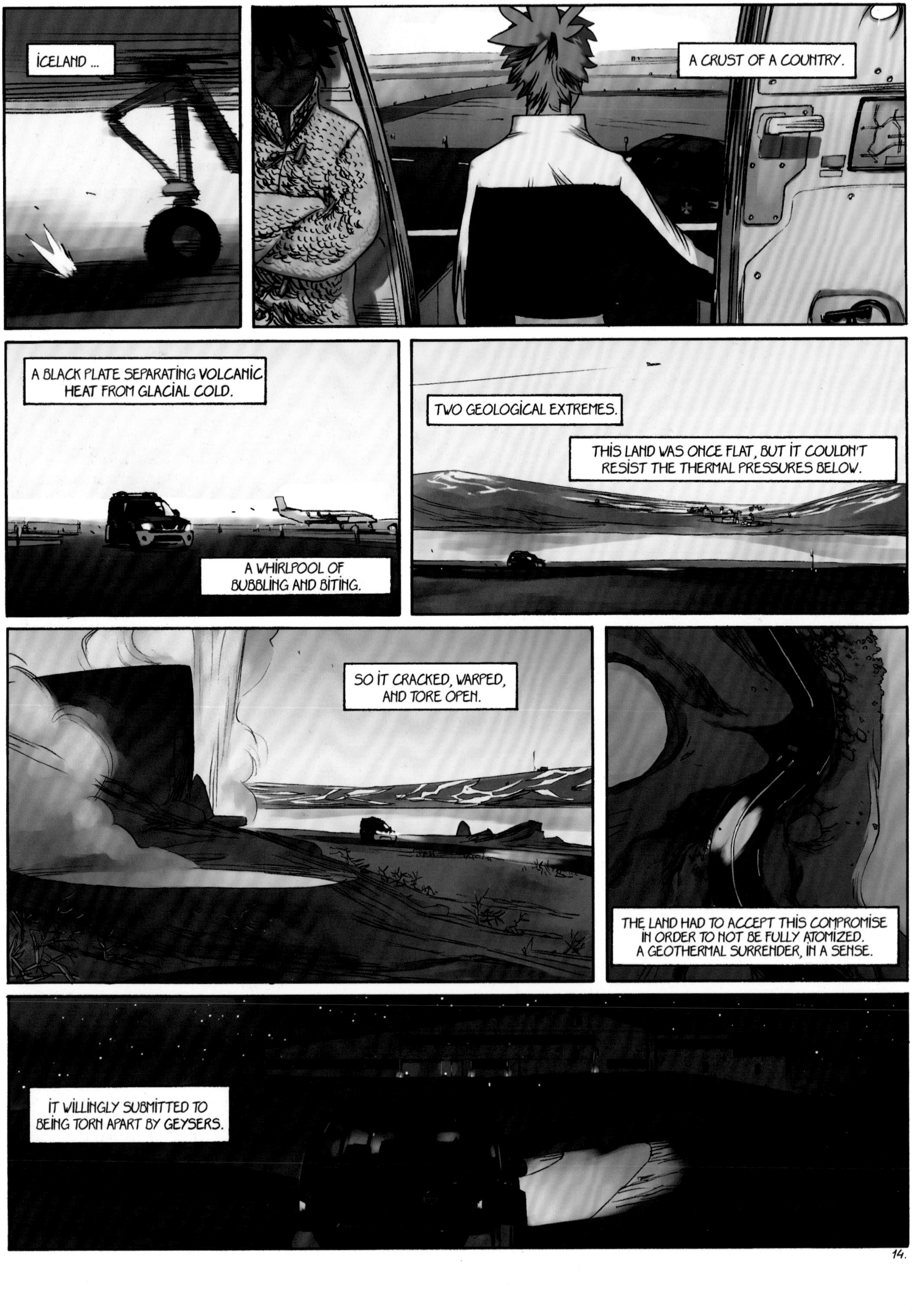
ICELAND ...
A CRUST OF A COUNTRY.
A BLACK PLATE SEPARATING VOLCANIC HEAT FROM GLACIAL COLD.
A WHIRLPOOL OF BUBBLING AND BITING.
TWO GEOLOGICAL EXTREMES.
THIS LAND WAS ONCE FLAT, BUT IT COULDN'T RESIST THE THERMAL PRESSURES BELOW.
SO IT CRACKED, WARPED, AND TORE OPEN.
THE LAND HAD TO ACCEPT THIS COMPROMISE IN ORDER TO NOT BE FULLY ATOMIZED. A GEOTHERMAL SURRENDER, IN A SENSE.
IT WILLINGLY SUBMITTED TO BEING TORN APART BY GEYSERS.

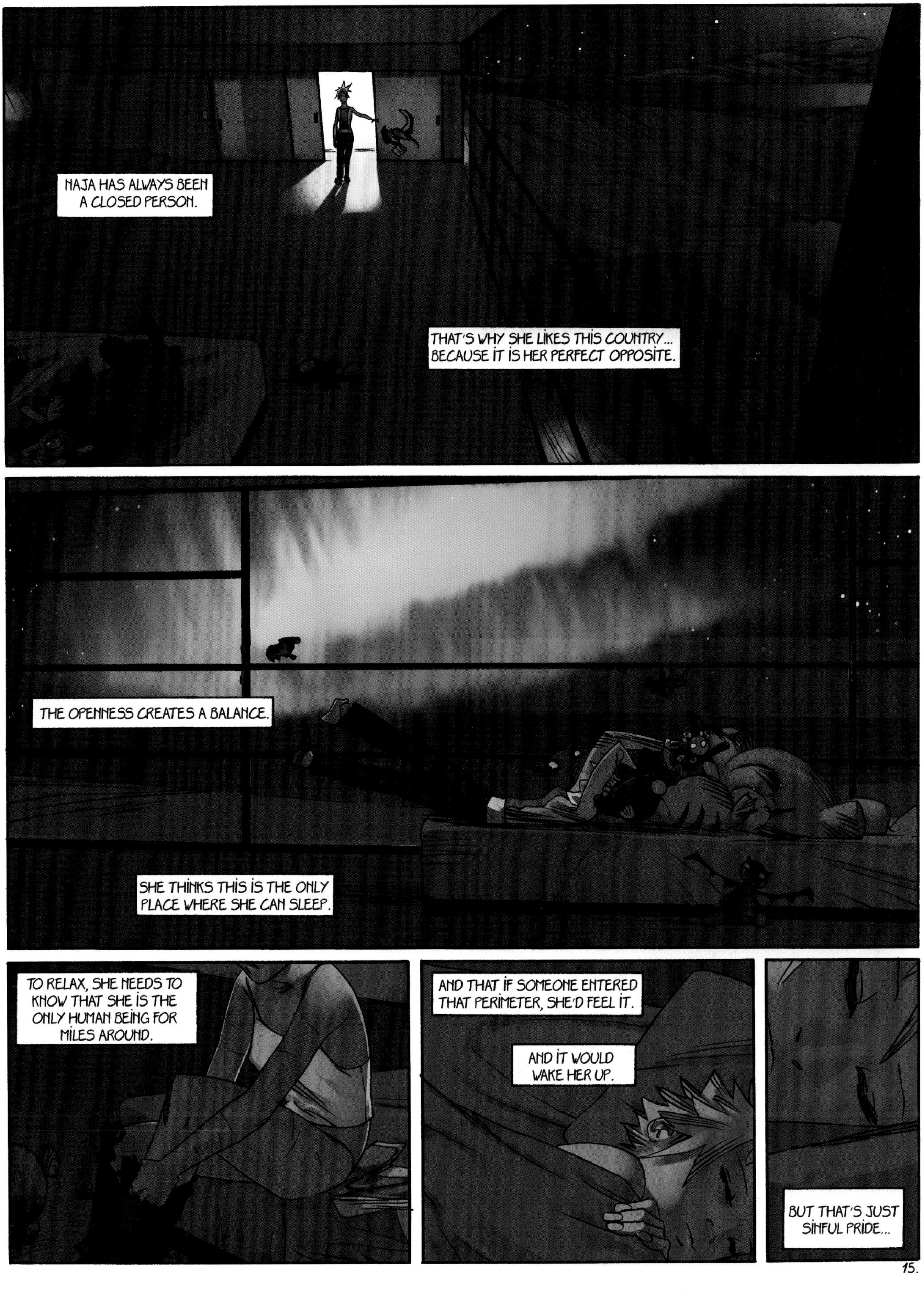
NAJA HAS ALWAYS BEEN A CLOSED PERSON.
THAT'S WHY SHE LIKES THIS COUNTRY... BECAUSE IT IS HER PERFECT OPPOSITE.
THE OPENNESS CREATES A BALANCE.
SHE THINKS THIS IS THE ONLY PLACE WHERE SHE CAN SLEEP.
TO RELAX, SHE NEEDS TO KNOW THAT SHE IS THE ONLY HUMAN BEING FOR MILES AROUND.
AND THAT IF SOMEONE ENTERED THAT PERIMETER, SHE'D FEEL IT.
AND IT WOULD WAKE HER UP.
BUT THAT'S JUST SINFUL PRIDE...

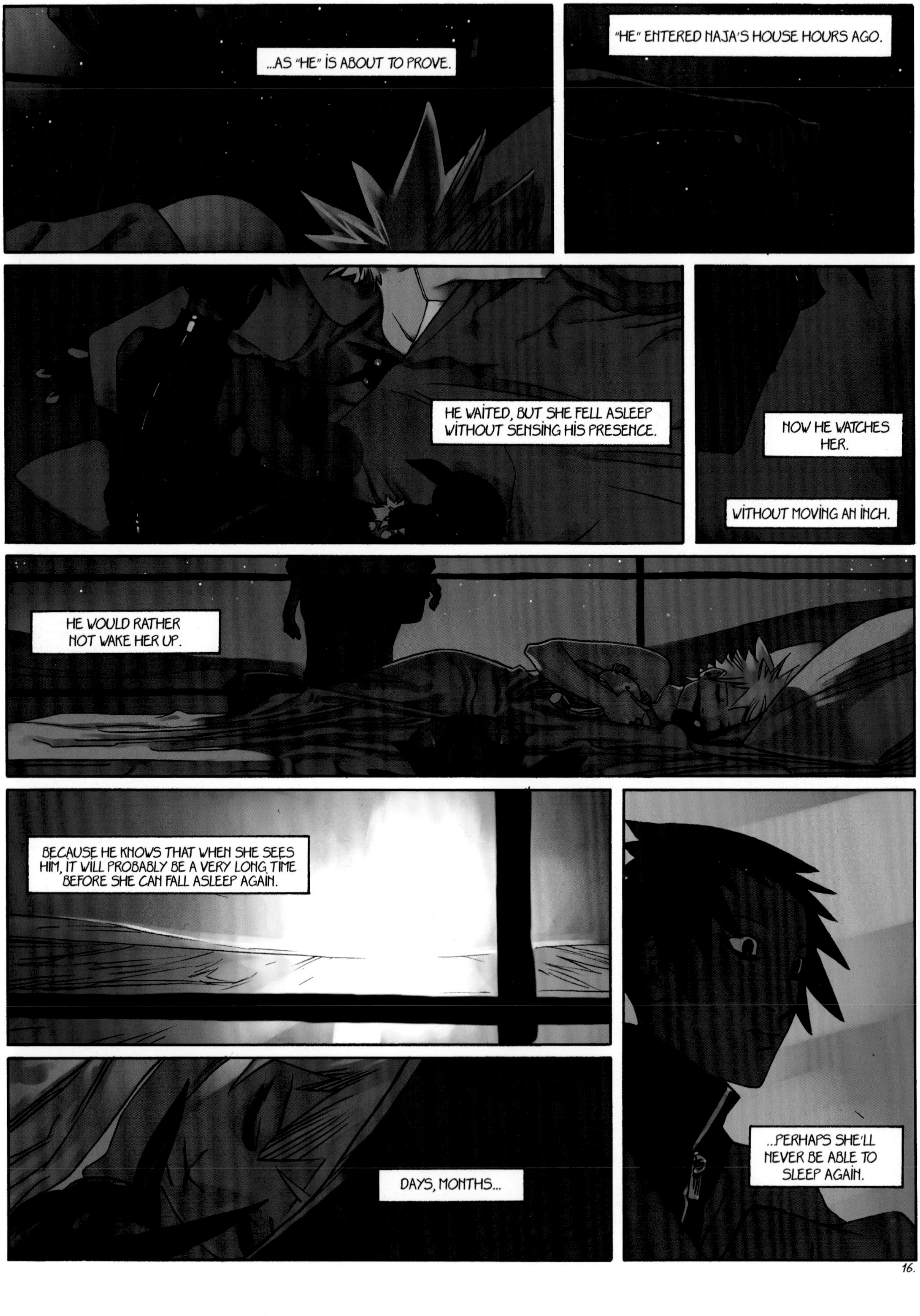
...AS "HE" IS ABOUT TO PROVE.
"HE" ENTERED NAJA'S HOUSE HOURS AGO.
HE WAITED, BUT SHE FELL ASLEEP WITHOUT SENSING HIS PRESENCE.
NOW HE WATCHES HER.
WITHOUT MOVING AN INCH.
HE WOULD RATHER NOT WAKE HER UP.
BECAUSE HE KNOWS THAT WHEN SHE SEES HIM, IT WILL PROBABLY BE A VERY LONG TIME BEFORE SHE CAN FALL ASLEEP AGAIN.
DAYS, MONTHS...
...PERHAPS SHE'LL NEVER BE ABLE TO SLEEP AGAIN.

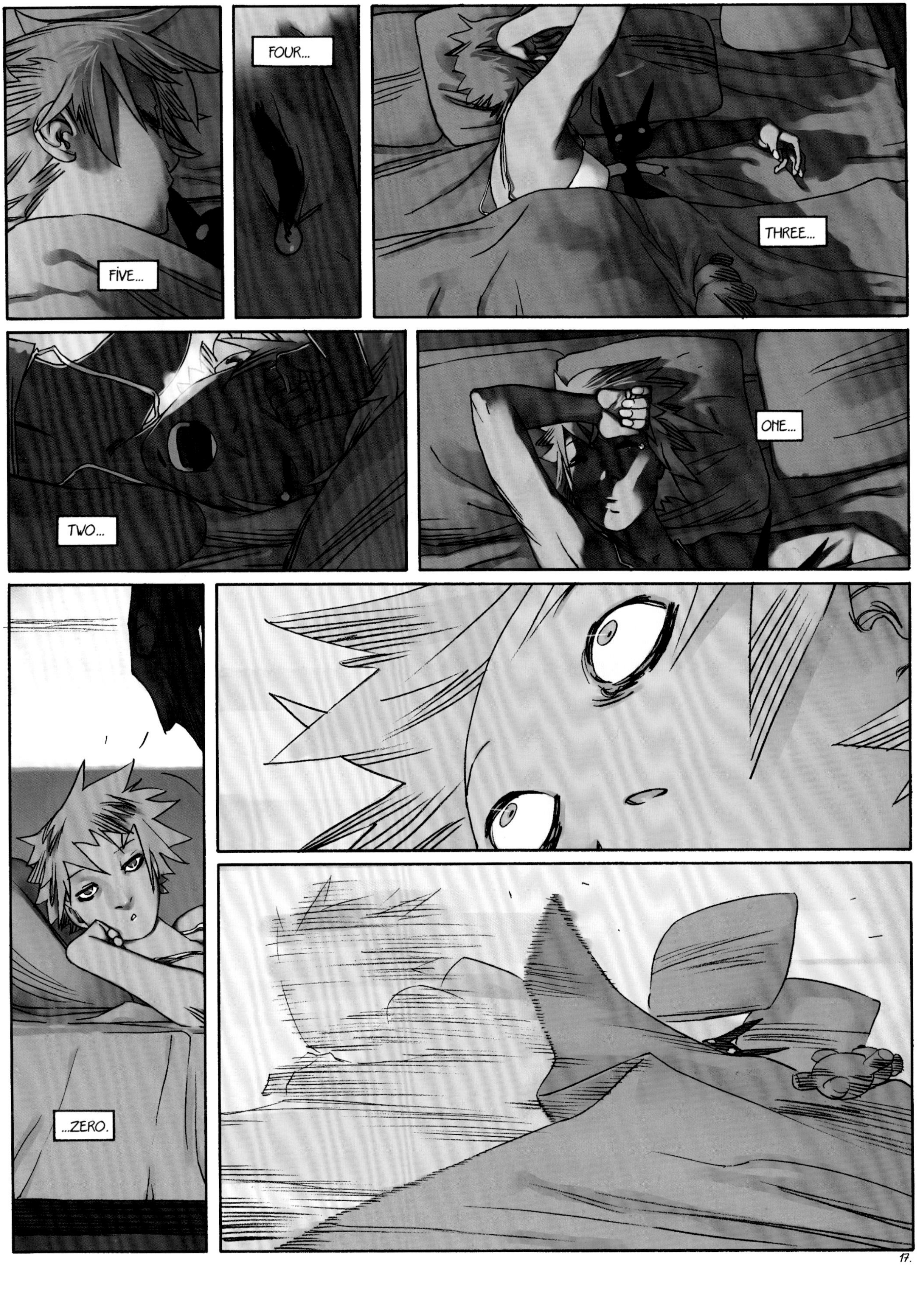
FIVE...
FOUR...
THREE...
TWO...
ONE...
...ZERO.

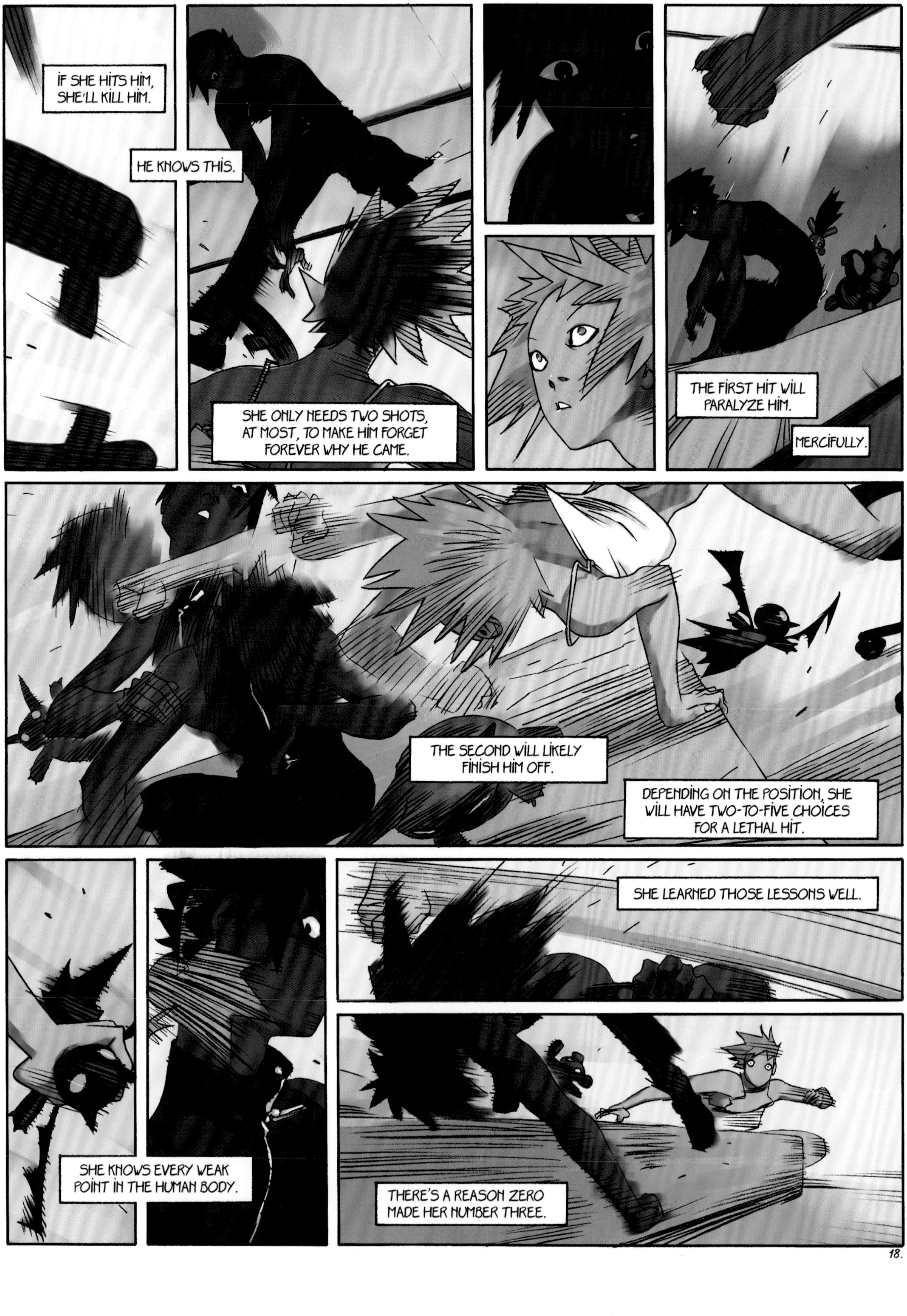
IF SHE HITS HIM, SHE'LL KILL HIM.
HE KNOWS THIS.
SHE ONLY NEEDS TWO SHOTS, AT MOST, TO MAKE HIM FORGET FOREVER WHY HE CAME.
THE FIRST HIT WILL PARALYZE HIM.
MERCIFULLY.
THE SECOND WILL LIKELY FINISH HIM OFF.
DEPENDING ON THE POSITION, SHE WILL HAVE TWO-TO-FIVE CHOICES FOR A LETHAL HIT.
SHE KNOWS EVERY WEAK POINT IN THE HUMAN BODY.
SHE LEARNED THOSE LESSONS WELL.
THERE'S A REASON ZERO MADE HER NUMBER THREE.

BUT "HE" DOESN'T WANT TO HURT HER.

"HE" IS NOT A HITMAN.

THE PROOF?

LOOK HOW BADLY SHE'S TRYING TO HURT HIM.

YET HE HAD EVERY OPPORTUNITY TO TURN HER SHEETS INTO A SHROUD.

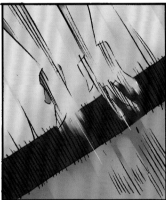

SHE HASN'T EVEN ASKED WHAT HE'S DOING THERE...

I'M HERE TO SAVE YOU.

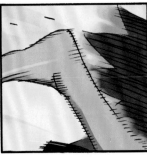

SHE CAN HARDLY
MOVE...

...BUT SHE
DOESN'T GIVE UP.

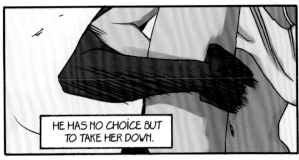

HE HAS NO CHOICE BUT
TO TAKE HER DOWN.

AND HE'S A PRO...

...HE CAME PREPARED.

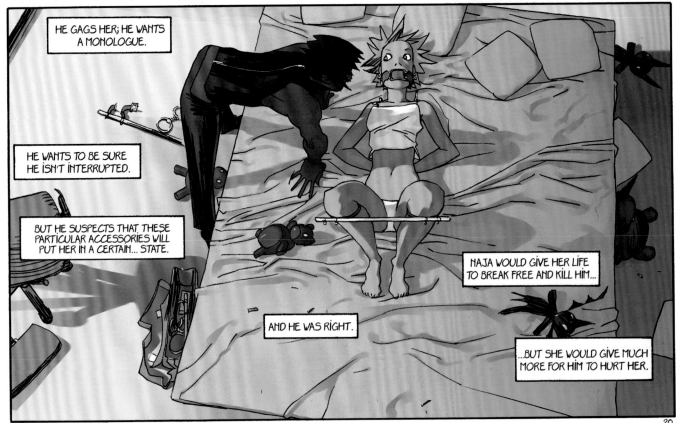

HE GAGS HER; HE WANTS
A MONOLOGUE.

HE WANTS TO BE SURE
HE ISN'T INTERRUPTED.

BUT HE SUSPECTS THAT THESE
PARTICULAR ACCESSORIES WILL
PUT HER IN A CERTAIN... STATE.

AND HE WAS RIGHT.

NAJA WOULD GIVE HER LIFE
TO BREAK FREE AND KILL HIM...

...BUT SHE WOULD GIVE MUCH
MORE FOR HIM TO HURT HER.

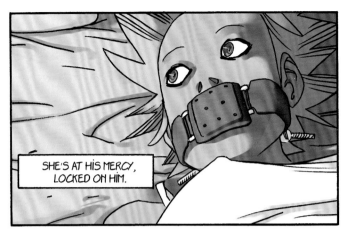

SHE'S AT HIS MERCY, LOCKED ON HIM.

HE KNOWS HIS WORDS WILL CUT LIKE SCALPEL BLADES.

BUT SHE'S BEGGING FOR IT.

STOP TRYING TO REMEMBER -- YOU DON'T KNOW ME. NOBODY DOES.

BUT I KNOW YOU QUITE WELL.

I KNOW ZERO'S ENTIRE ORGANIZATION.

ALL OF IT, FROM THE LOOK-OUT ON THE CORNER TO HIS HIERARCHY OF KILLERS.

THAT'S HOW I HEARD YOU WERE GOING TO DIE SOON.

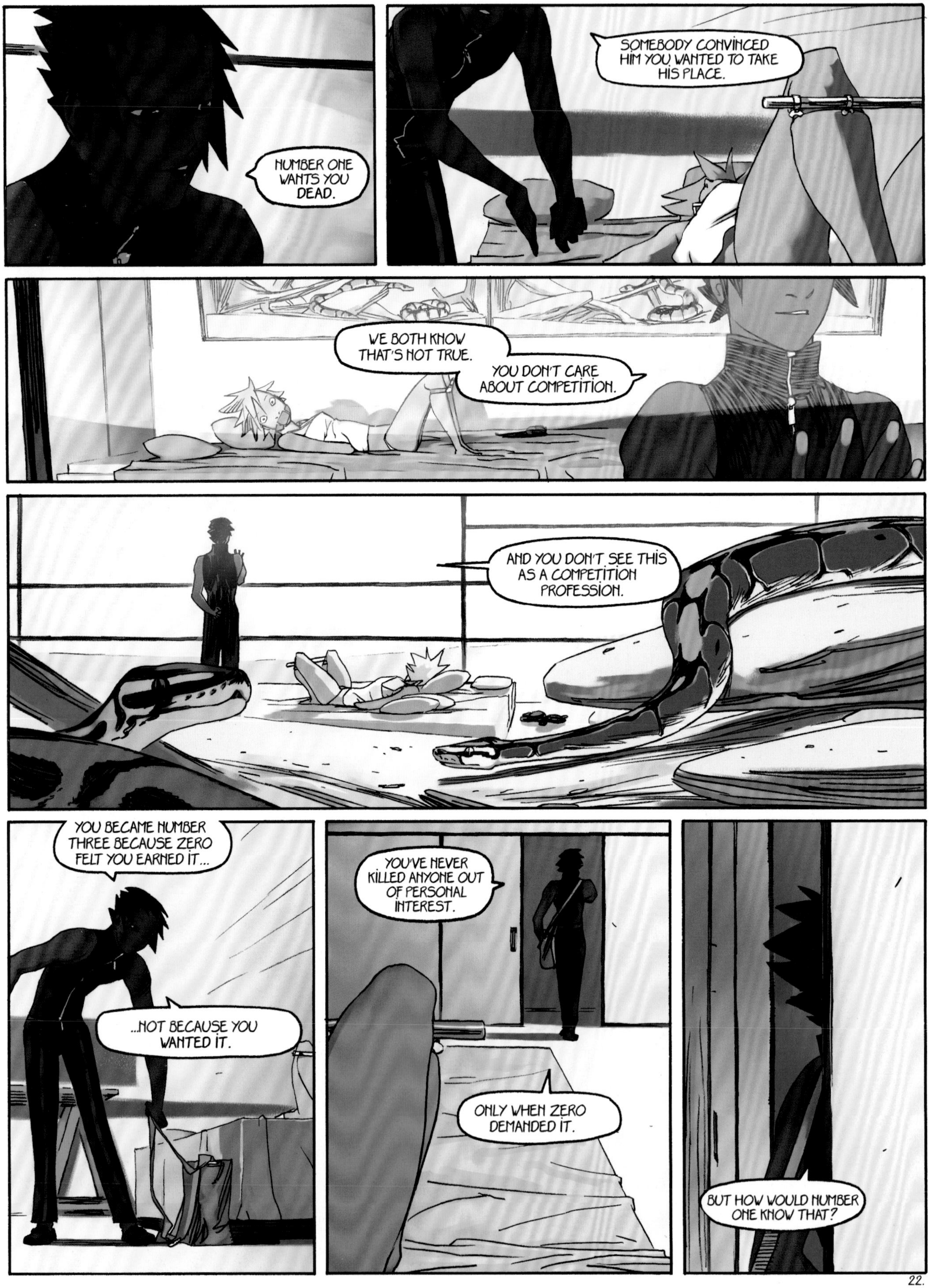
NUMBER ONE WANTS YOU DEAD.
SOMEBODY CONVINCED HIM YOU WANTED TO TAKE HIS PLACE.
WE BOTH KNOW THAT'S NOT TRUE.
YOU DON'T CARE ABOUT COMPETITION.
AND YOU DON'T SEE THIS AS A COMPETITION PROFESSION.
YOU BECAME NUMBER THREE BECAUSE ZERO FELT YOU EARNED IT...
...NOT BECAUSE YOU WANTED IT.
YOU'VE NEVER KILLED ANYONE OUT OF PERSONAL INTEREST.
ONLY WHEN ZERO DEMANDED IT.
BUT HOW WOULD NUMBER ONE KNOW THAT?

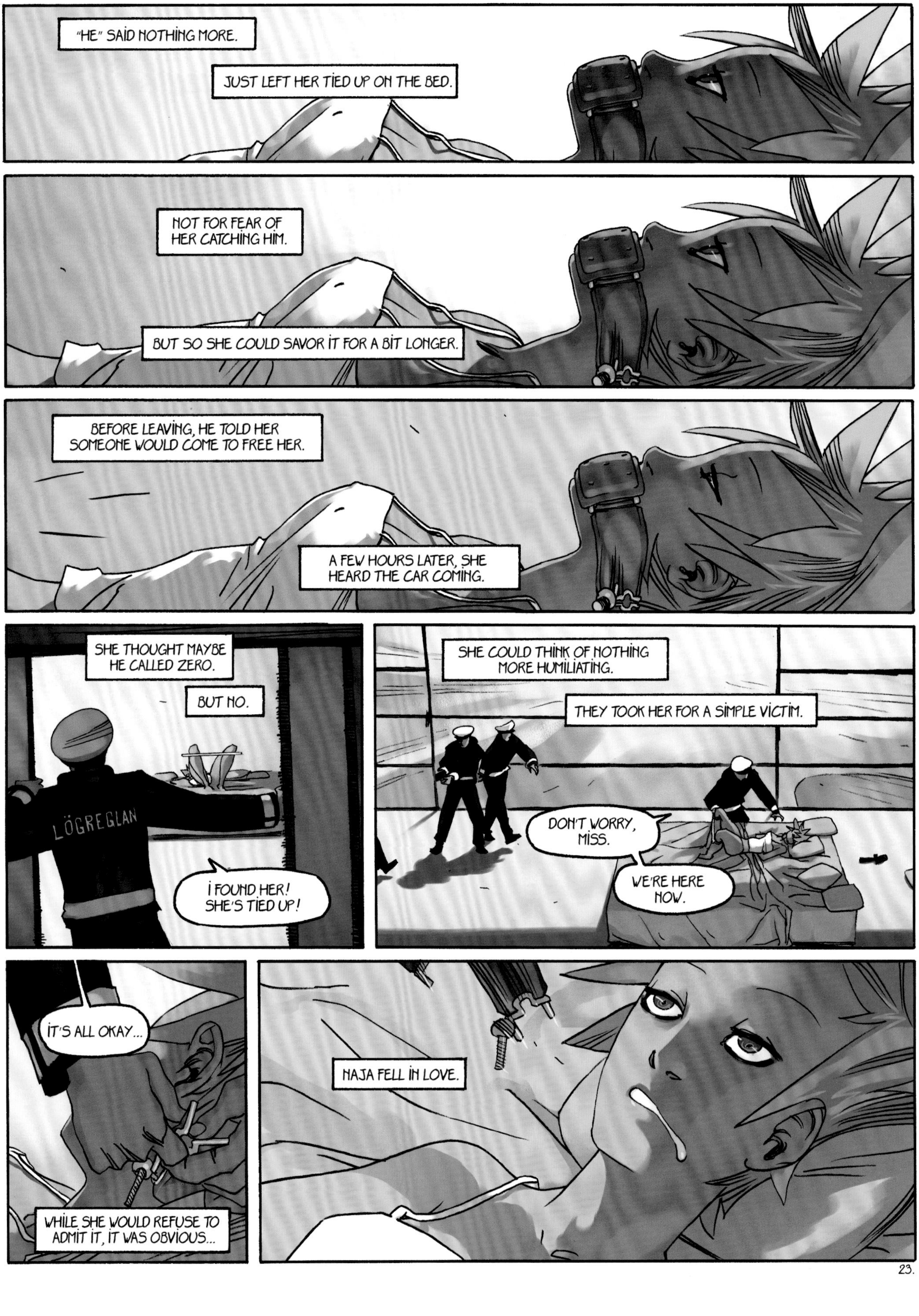

"HE" SAID NOTHING MORE.
JUST LEFT HER TIED UP ON THE BED.
NOT FOR FEAR OF HER CATCHING HIM.
BUT SO SHE COULD SAVOR IT FOR A BIT LONGER.
BEFORE LEAVING, HE TOLD HER SOMEONE WOULD COME TO FREE HER.
A FEW HOURS LATER, SHE HEARD THE CAR COMING.
SHE THOUGHT MAYBE HE CALLED ZERO.
BUT NO.
LÖGREGLAN
I FOUND HER! SHE'S TIED UP!
SHE COULD THINK OF NOTHING MORE HUMILIATING.
THEY TOOK HER FOR A SIMPLE VICTIM.
DON'T WORRY, MISS.
WE'RE HERE NOW.
IT'S ALL OKAY...
WHILE SHE WOULD REFUSE TO ADMIT IT, IT WAS OBVIOUS...
NAJA FELL IN LOVE.

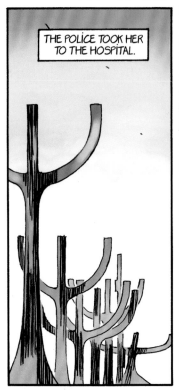

THE POLICE TOOK HER TO THE HOSPITAL.

SHE DIDN'T WANT TO GO, BUT IT WAS PROCEDURE.

NO WAY TO GET OUT OF IT WITHOUT QUESTIONS.

THE DOCTORS AT SJUKRAHUS REYKJAVIKUR REASSURED HER...

...THAT EXCEPT FOR THE BRUISES ON HER LEGS, HER ATTACKER DID NO REAL PHYSICAL DAMAGE.

SHE KNEW THAT.

MUCH TO HER REGRET.

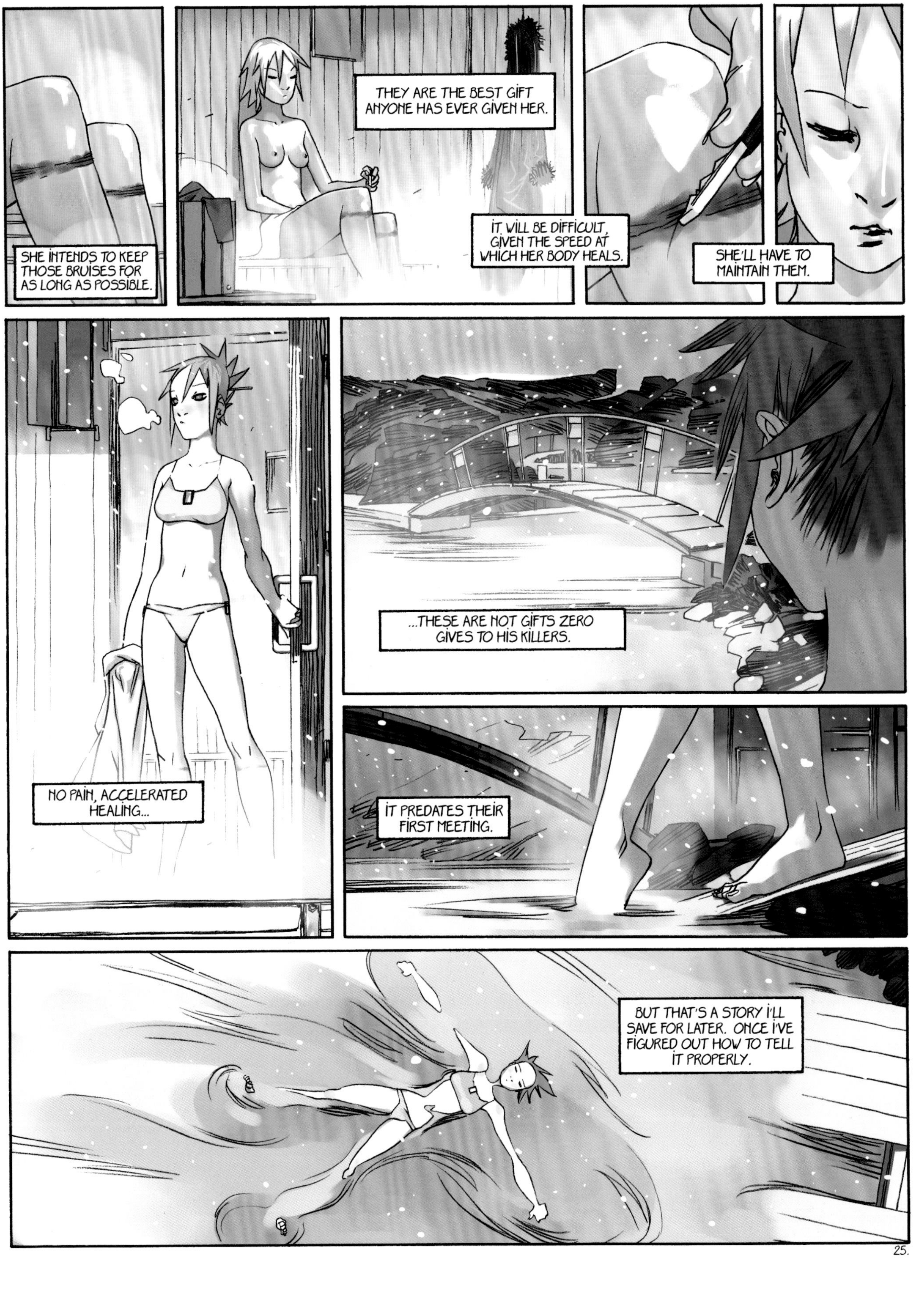
SHE INTENDS TO KEEP THOSE BRUISES FOR AS LONG AS POSSIBLE.
THEY ARE THE BEST GIFT ANYONE HAS EVER GIVEN HER.
IT WILL BE DIFFICULT, GIVEN THE SPEED AT WHICH HER BODY HEALS.
SHE'LL HAVE TO MAINTAIN THEM.
NO PAIN, ACCELERATED HEALING...
...THESE ARE NOT GIFTS ZERO GIVES TO HIS KILLERS.
IT PREDATES THEIR FIRST MEETING.
BUT THAT'S A STORY I'LL SAVE FOR LATER. ONCE I'VE FIGURED OUT HOW TO TELL IT PROPERLY.

BESIDES, RIGHT NOW, NAJA'S MIND IS RACING.

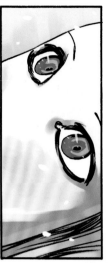

AND IT'S A SHAME TO MISS THE PRESENT...

...BY SPENDING TOO MUCH TIME IN THE PAST.

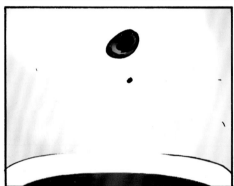

AT FIRST, SHE THOUGHT ABOUT GOING TO ZERO, ASKING FOR HIS HELP.

BUT SHE CHANGED HER MIND.

WHAT IF HE WAS THE ONE WHO PUT THE CONTRACT ON HER HEAD?

BUT WHY WOULD HE DO THAT?

SHE DOESN'T KNOW ANYTHING OF VALUE.

CERTAINLY NO IDEA WHY SHE KILLS FOR HIM.

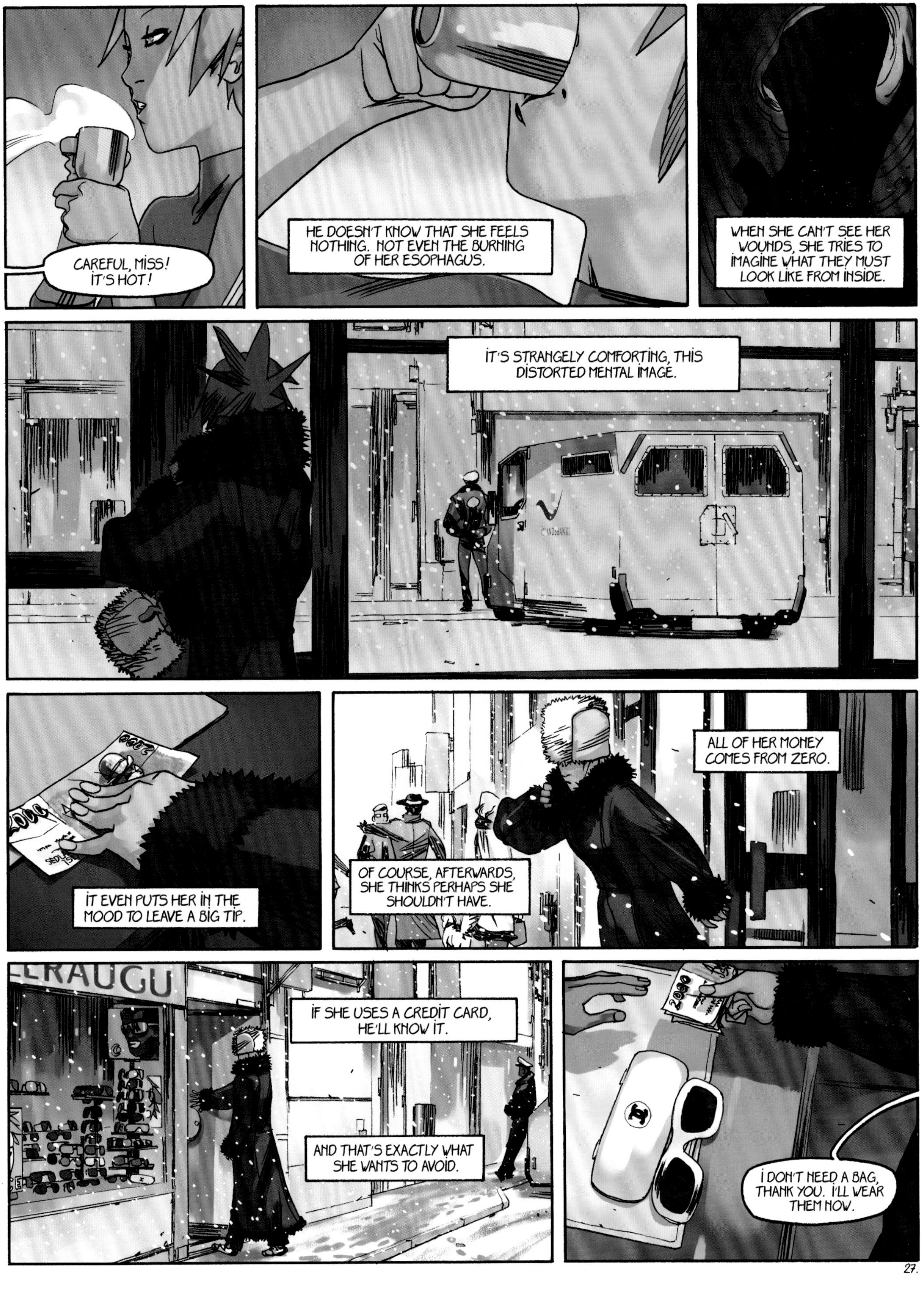
CAREFUL, MISS! IT'S HOT!
HE DOESN'T KNOW THAT SHE FEELS NOTHING. NOT EVEN THE BURNING OF HER ESOPHAGUS.
WHEN SHE CAN'T SEE HER WOUNDS, SHE TRIES TO IMAGINE WHAT THEY MUST LOOK LIKE FROM INSIDE.
IT'S STRANGELY COMFORTING, THIS DISTORTED MENTAL IMAGE.
IT EVEN PUTS HER IN THE MOOD TO LEAVE A BIG TIP.
ALL OF HER MONEY COMES FROM ZERO.
OF COURSE, AFTERWARDS, SHE THINKS PERHAPS SHE SHOULDN'T HAVE.
ELRAUGU
IF SHE USES A CREDIT CARD, HE'LL KNOW IT.
AND THAT'S EXACTLY WHAT SHE WANTS TO AVOID.
I DON'T NEED A BAG, THANK YOU. I'LL WEAR THEM NOW.

SHE MUST LEARN TO BE SELF-SUFFICIENT.

SHE WILL NEED RESOURCES.

AND THEY WON'T COME CHEAP.

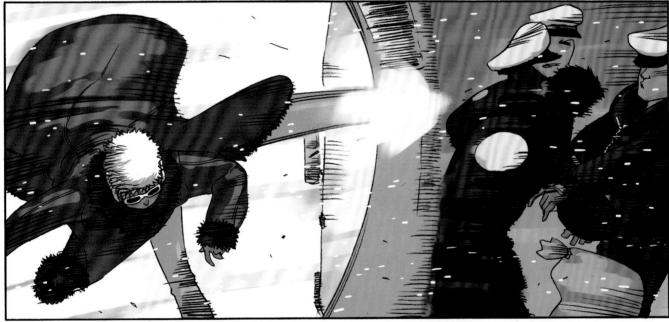

28.

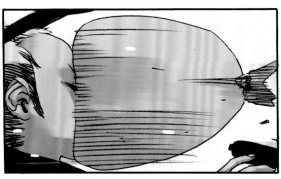

NAJA NEVER KILLED UNLESS ZERO DEMANDED IT. NEVER OUT OF PERSONAL INTEREST.

BUT I TOLD YOU THAT ALREADY...

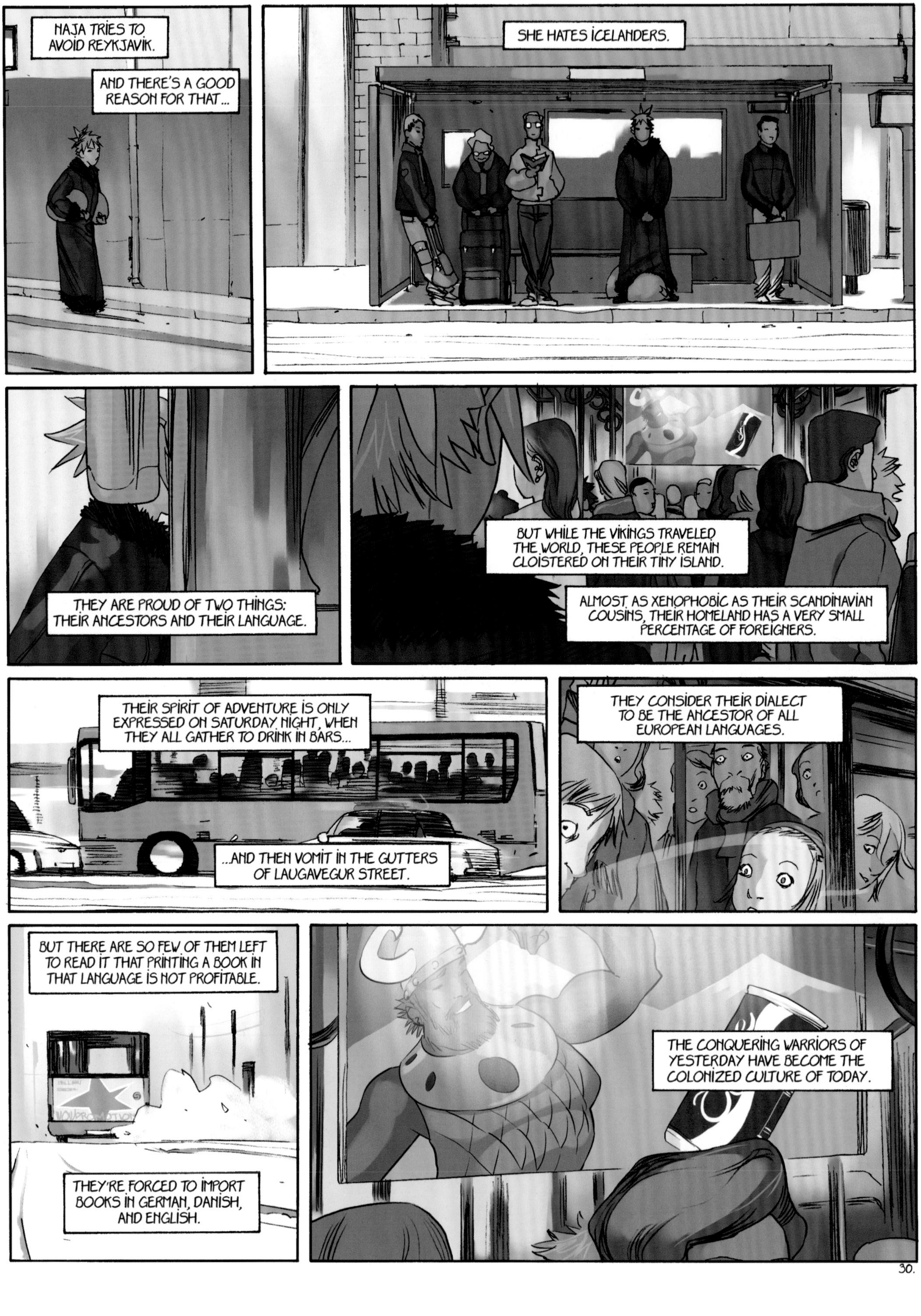
NAJA TRIES TO AVOID REYKJAVIK.
AND THERE'S A GOOD REASON FOR THAT...
SHE HATES ICELANDERS.
THEY ARE PROUD OF TWO THINGS: THEIR ANCESTORS AND THEIR LANGUAGE.
BUT WHILE THE VIKINGS TRAVELED THE WORLD, THESE PEOPLE REMAIN CLOISTERED ON THEIR TINY ISLAND.
ALMOST AS XENOPHOBIC AS THEIR SCANDINAVIAN COUSINS, THEIR HOMELAND HAS A VERY SMALL PERCENTAGE OF FOREIGNERS.
THEIR SPIRIT OF ADVENTURE IS ONLY EXPRESSED ON SATURDAY NIGHT, WHEN THEY ALL GATHER TO DRINK IN BARS...
...AND THEN VOMIT IN THE GUTTERS OF LAUGAVEGUR STREET.
THEY CONSIDER THEIR DIALECT TO BE THE ANCESTOR OF ALL EUROPEAN LANGUAGES.
BUT THERE ARE SO FEW OF THEM LEFT TO READ IT THAT PRINTING A BOOK IN THAT LANGUAGE IS NOT PROFITABLE.
THEY'RE FORCED TO IMPORT BOOKS IN GERMAN, DANISH, AND ENGLISH.
THE CONQUERING WARRIORS OF YESTERDAY HAVE BECOME THE COLONIZED CULTURE OF TODAY.

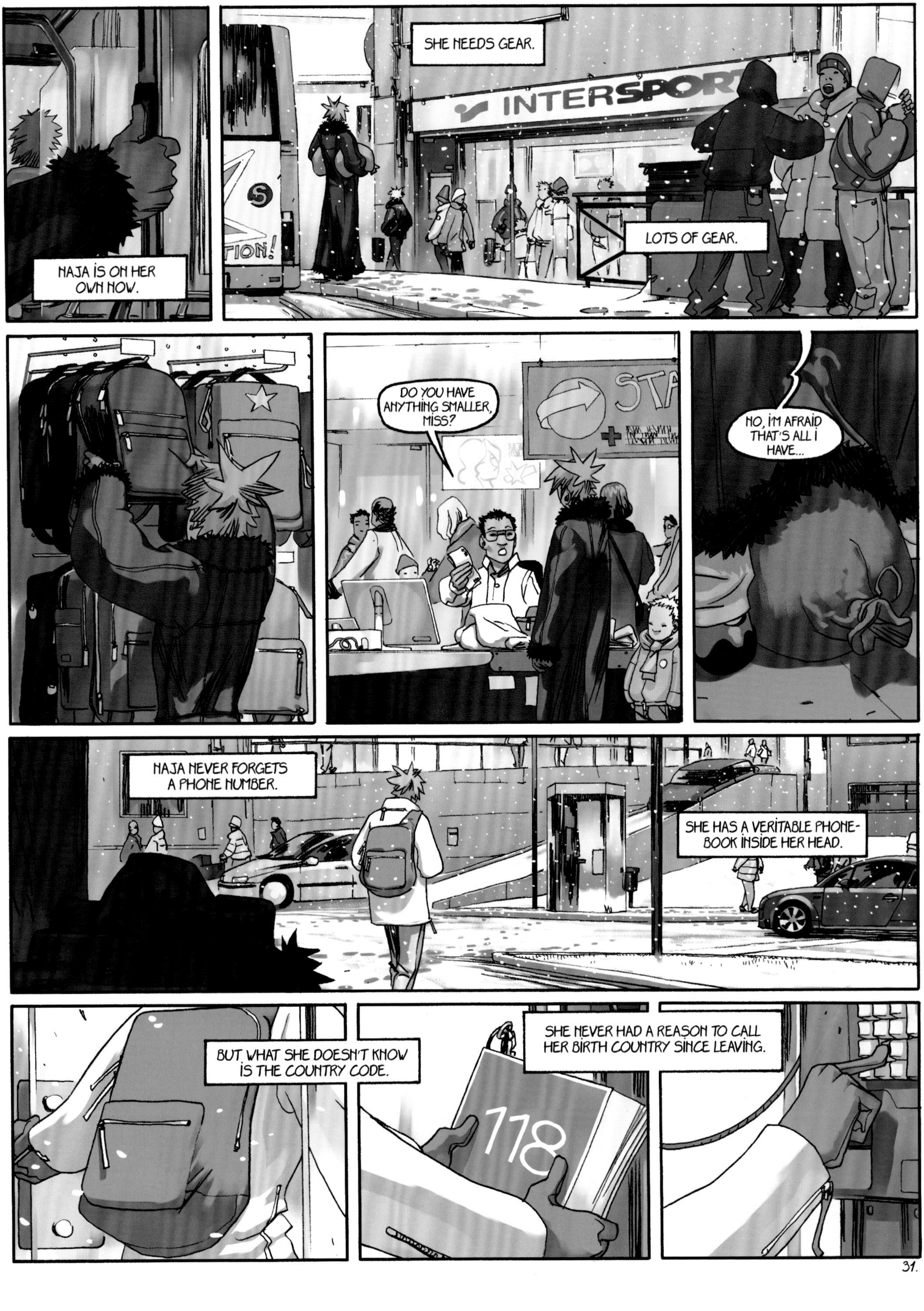
NAJA IS ON HER OWN NOW.
SHE NEEDS GEAR.
INTERSPORT
LOTS OF GEAR.
DO YOU HAVE ANYTHING SMALLER, MISS?
NO, I'M AFRAID THAT'S ALL I HAVE...
NAJA NEVER FORGETS A PHONE NUMBER.
SHE HAS A VERITABLE PHONE-BOOK INSIDE HER HEAD.
BUT WHAT SHE DOESN'T KNOW IS THE COUNTRY CODE.
SHE NEVER HAD A REASON TO CALL HER BIRTH COUNTRY SINCE LEAVING.
118

ZERO NEVER SENT HER ON ANY MISSIONS THERE.

COINCIDENCE, OR ON PURPOSE?

SHE CERTAINLY WASN'T GOING TO RETURN FOR PLEASURE...

...BECAUSE NAJA ALSO HATES THE BRITISH.

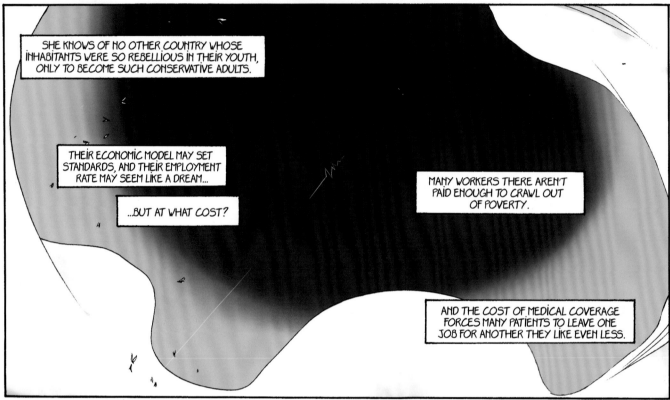

SHE KNOWS OF NO OTHER COUNTRY WHOSE INHABITANTS WERE SO REBELLIOUS IN THEIR YOUTH, ONLY TO BECOME SUCH CONSERVATIVE ADULTS.

THEIR ECONOMIC MODEL MAY SET STANDARDS, AND THEIR EMPLOYMENT RATE MAY SEEM LIKE A DREAM...

...BUT AT WHAT COST?

MANY WORKERS THERE AREN'T PAID ENOUGH TO CRAWL OUT OF POVERTY.

AND THE COST OF MEDICAL COVERAGE FORCES MANY PATIENTS TO LEAVE ONE JOB FOR ANOTHER THEY LIKE EVEN LESS.

THEY'RE UGLY, THEIR FOOD IS BLAND, AND WHEN THEY TRAVEL ABROAD, THEY BEHAVE LIKE IDIOTS.

ALL...

...BUT ONE.

AND HIS MUM.

BUT NAJA WAS ALWAYS AFRAID THAT VISITING THEM WOULD INVITE TROUBLE.

RIIIIING...

RIIIIING...

RIIIIING...

RIIIIING...

RIIIIING...

RIIIIING...

I'M COMING, I'M COMING!

HELLO? WHO'S THIS?

HELLO MRS. STAIRDEY. IT'S -BEEEP-.

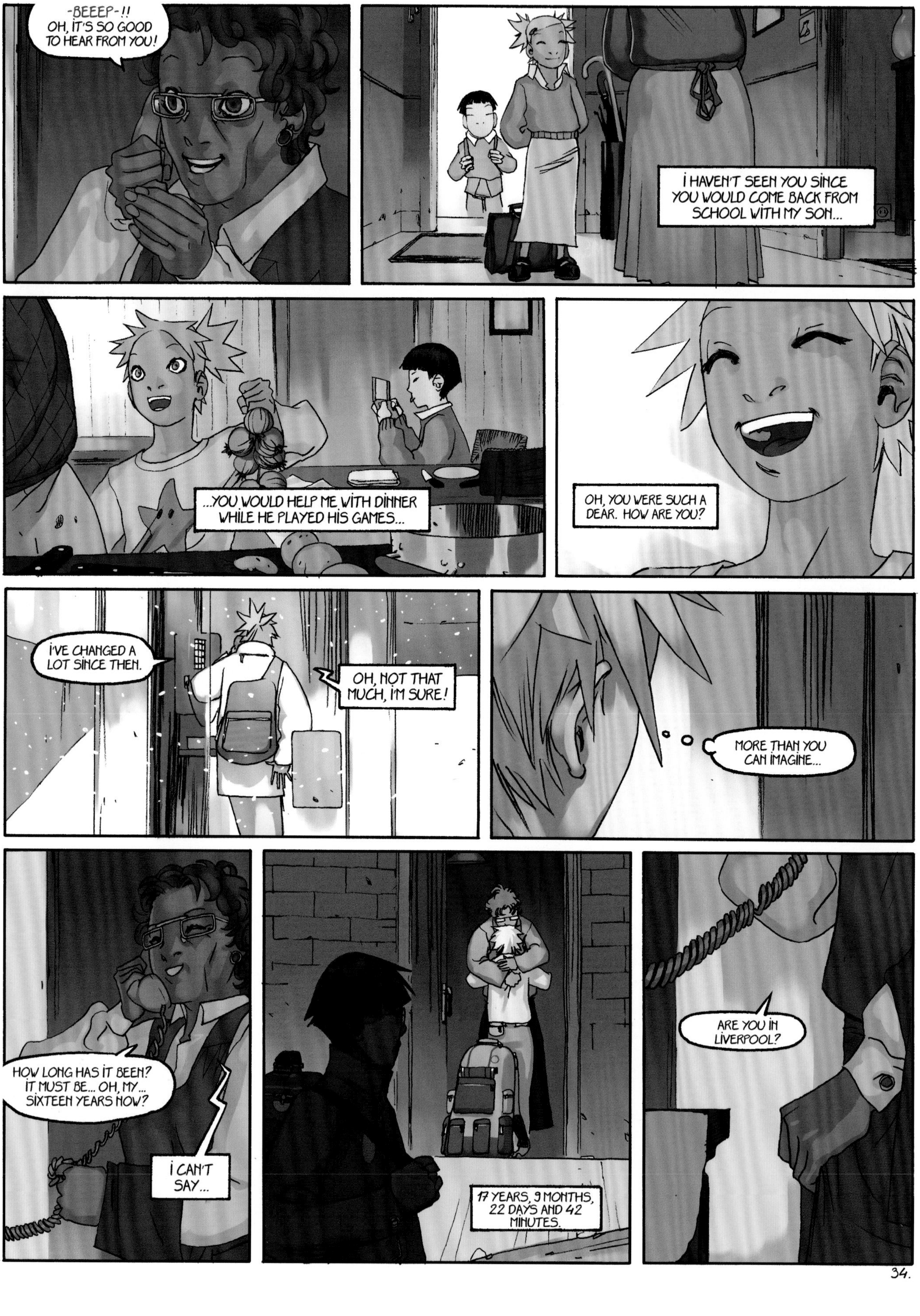
-BEEEP-!!
OH, IT'S SO GOOD TO HEAR FROM YOU!
I HAVEN'T SEEN YOU SINCE YOU WOULD COME BACK FROM SCHOOL WITH MY SON...
...YOU WOULD HELP ME WITH DINNER WHILE HE PLAYED HIS GAMES...
OH, YOU WERE SUCH A DEAR. HOW ARE YOU?
I'VE CHANGED A LOT SINCE THEN.
OH, NOT THAT MUCH, I'M SURE!
MORE THAN YOU CAN IMAGINE...
HOW LONG HAS IT BEEN? IT MUST BE... OH, MY... SIXTEEN YEARS NOW?
I CAN'T SAY...
17 YEARS, 9 MONTHS, 22 DAYS AND 42 MINUTES.
ARE YOU IN LIVERPOOL?

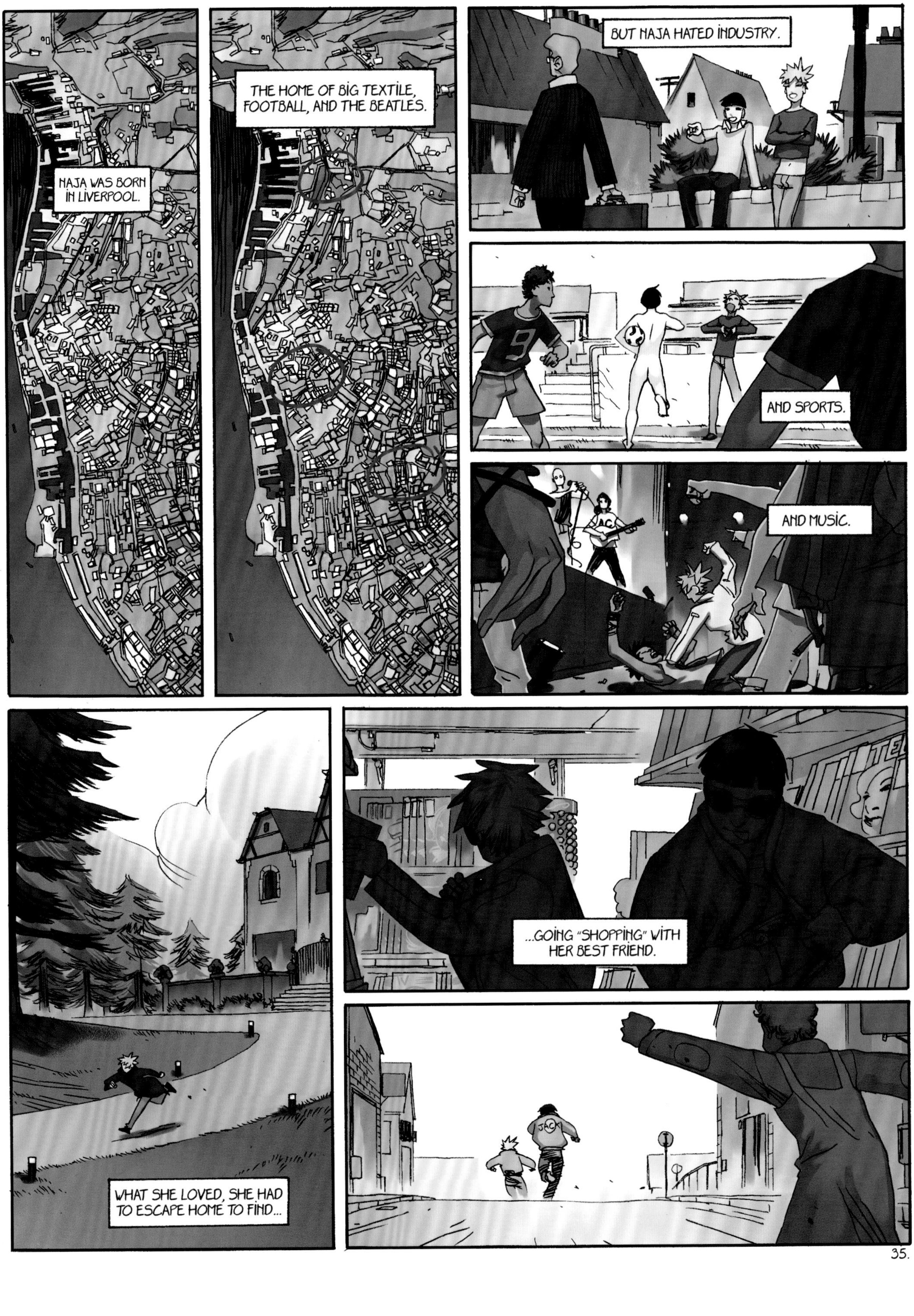
NAJA WAS BORN
IN LIVERPOOL.
THE HOME OF BIG TEXTILE,
FOOTBALL, AND THE BEATLES.
BUT NAJA HATED INDUSTRY.
AND SPORTS.
AND MUSIC.
WHAT SHE LOVED, SHE HAD
TO ESCAPE HOME TO FIND...
...GOING "SHOPPING" WITH
HER BEST FRIEND.

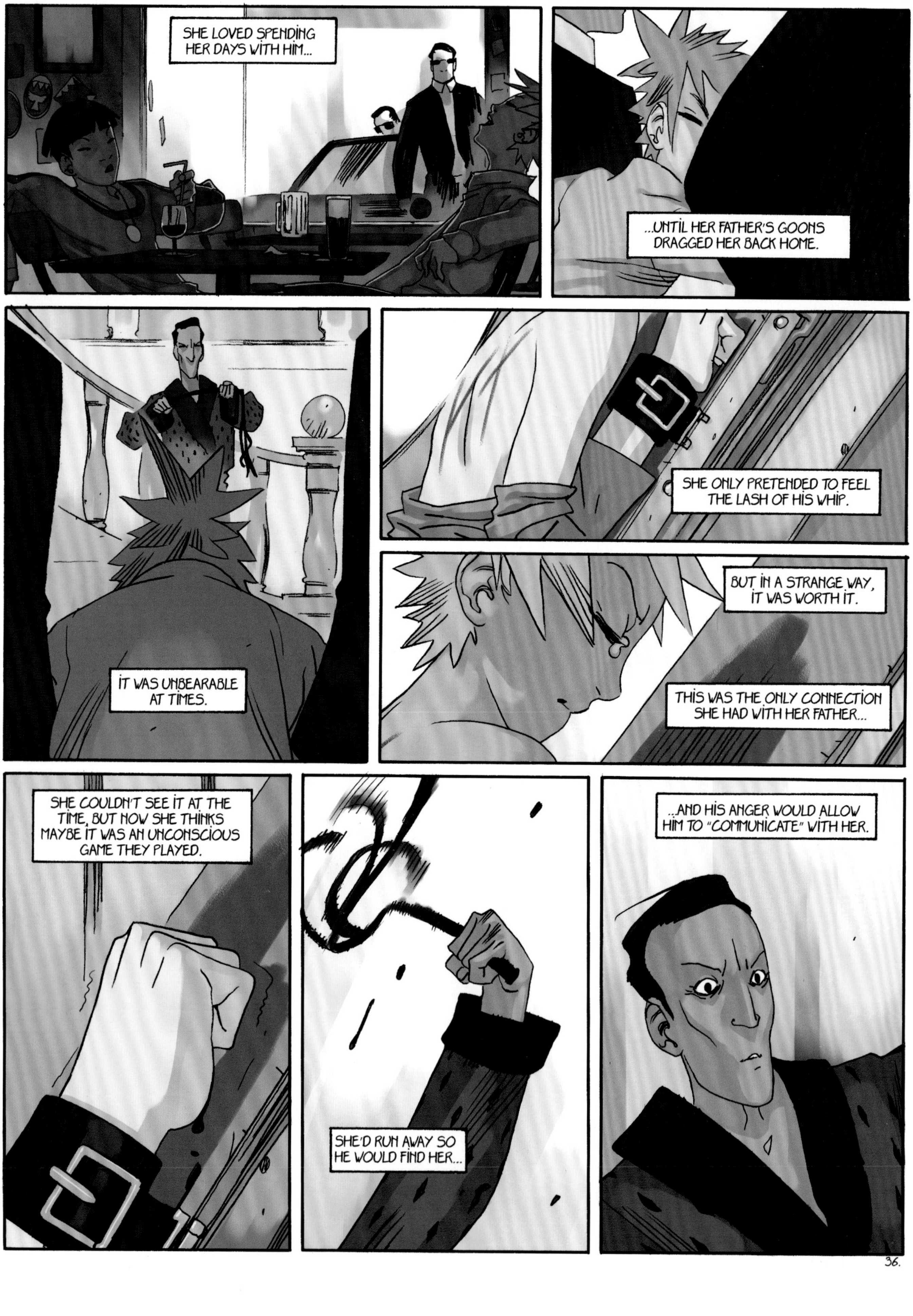
SHE LOVED SPENDING HER DAYS WITH HIM...
...UNTIL HER FATHER'S GOONS DRAGGED HER BACK HOME.
IT WAS UNBEARABLE AT TIMES.
SHE ONLY PRETENDED TO FEEL THE LASH OF HIS WHIP.
BUT IN A STRANGE WAY, IT WAS WORTH IT.
THIS WAS THE ONLY CONNECTION SHE HAD WITH HER FATHER...
SHE COULDN'T SEE IT AT THE TIME, BUT NOW SHE THINKS MAYBE IT WAS AN UNCONSCIOUS GAME THEY PLAYED.
SHE'D RUN AWAY SO HE WOULD FIND HER...
...AND HIS ANGER WOULD ALLOW HIM TO "COMMUNICATE" WITH HER.

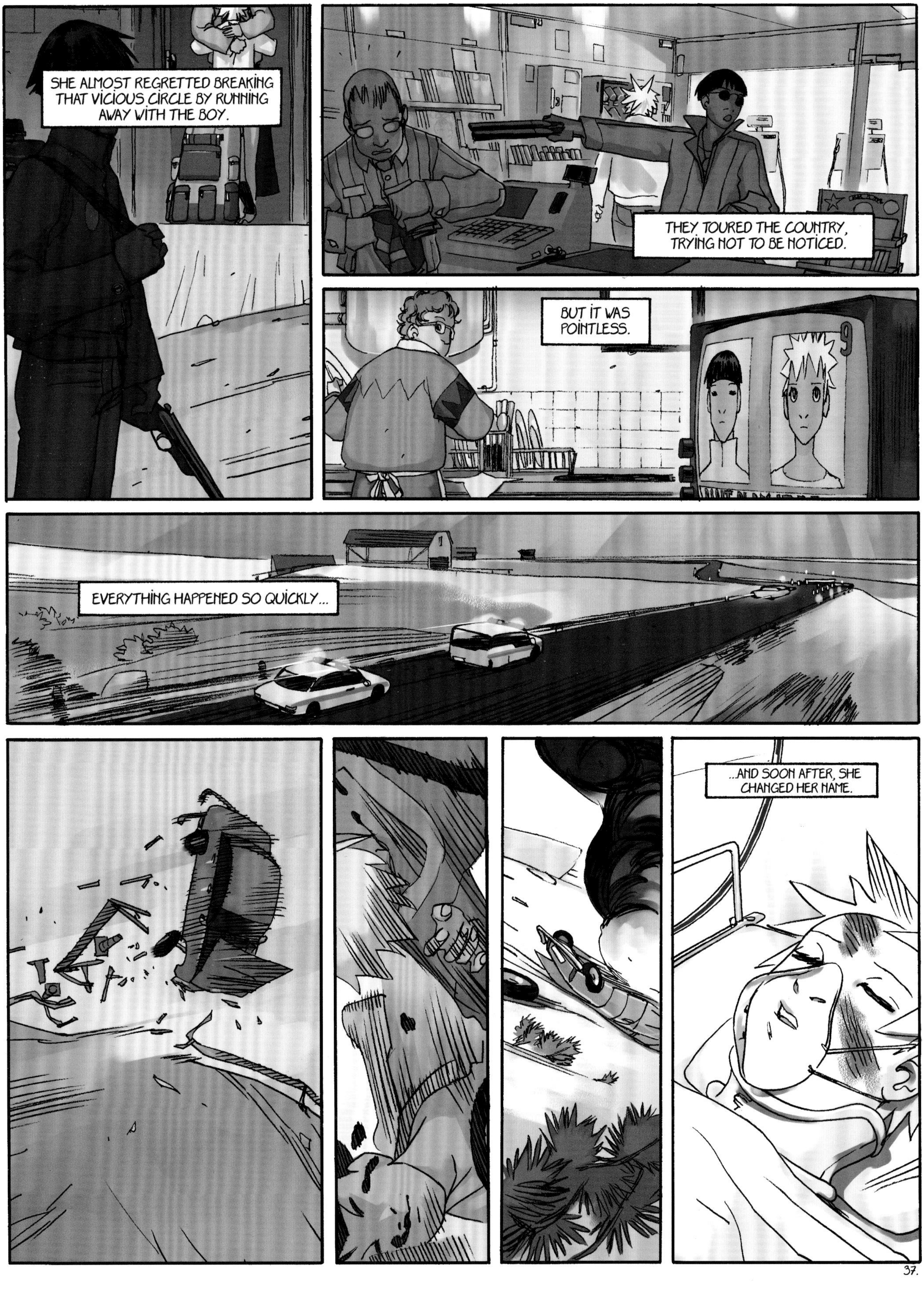
SHE ALMOST REGRETTED BREAKING THAT VICIOUS CIRCLE BY RUNNING AWAY WITH THE BOY.
THEY TOURED THE COUNTRY, TRYING NOT TO BE NOTICED.
BUT IT WAS POINTLESS.
EVERYTHING HAPPENED SO QUICKLY...
...AND SOON AFTER, SHE CHANGED HER NAME.

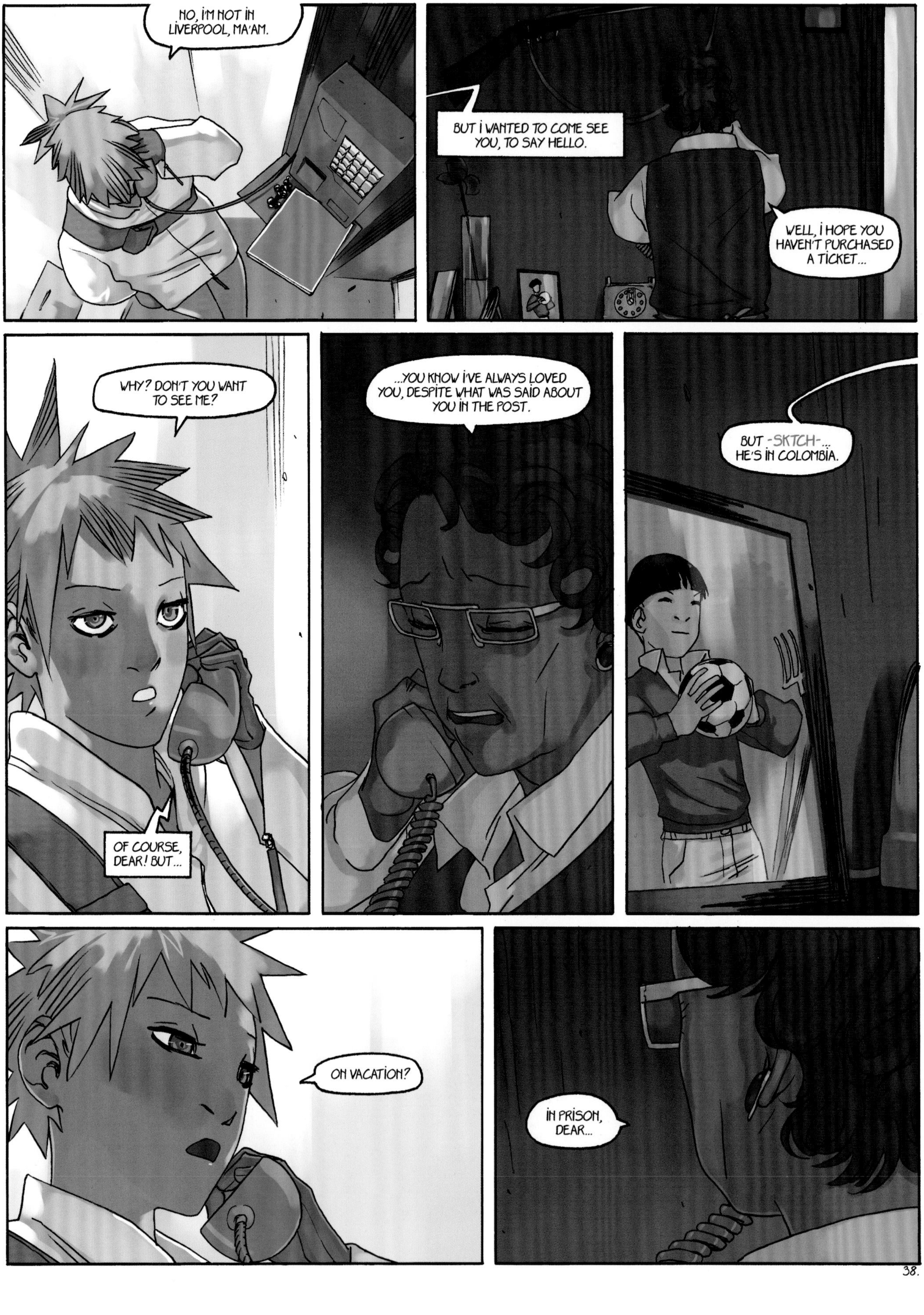

NO, I'M NOT IN LIVERPOOL, MA'AM.
BUT I WANTED TO COME SEE YOU, TO SAY HELLO.
WELL, I HOPE YOU HAVEN'T PURCHASED A TICKET...
WHY? DON'T YOU WANT TO SEE ME?
OF COURSE, DEAR! BUT...
...YOU KNOW I'VE ALWAYS LOVED YOU, DESPITE WHAT WAS SAID ABOUT YOU IN THE POST.
BUT -SKTCH-... HE'S IN COLOMBIA.
ON VACATION?
IN PRISON, DEAR...

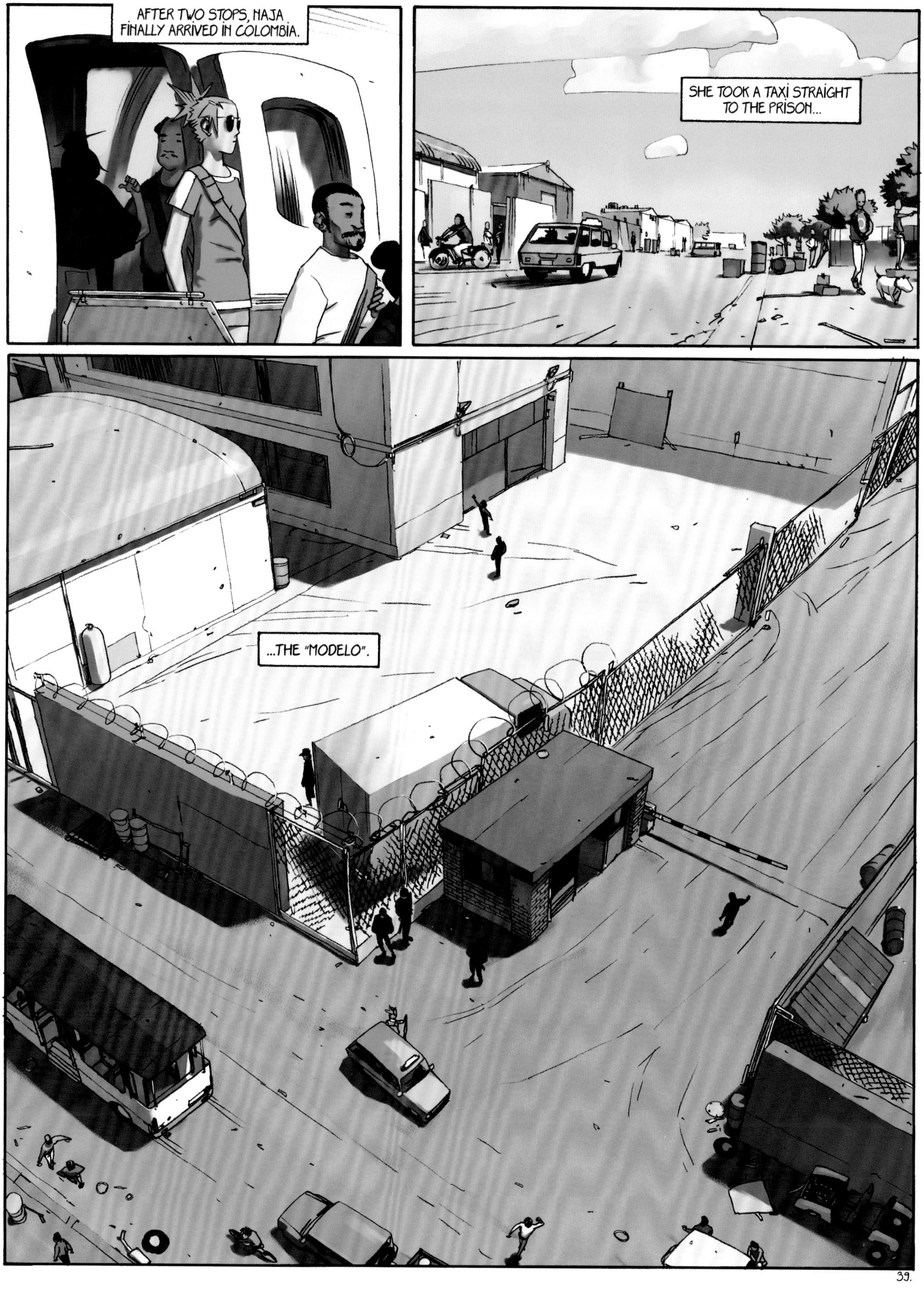
AFTER TWO STOPS, NAJA FINALLY ARRIVED IN COLOMBIA.
SHE TOOK A TAXI STRAIGHT TO THE PRISON...
...THE "MODELO".

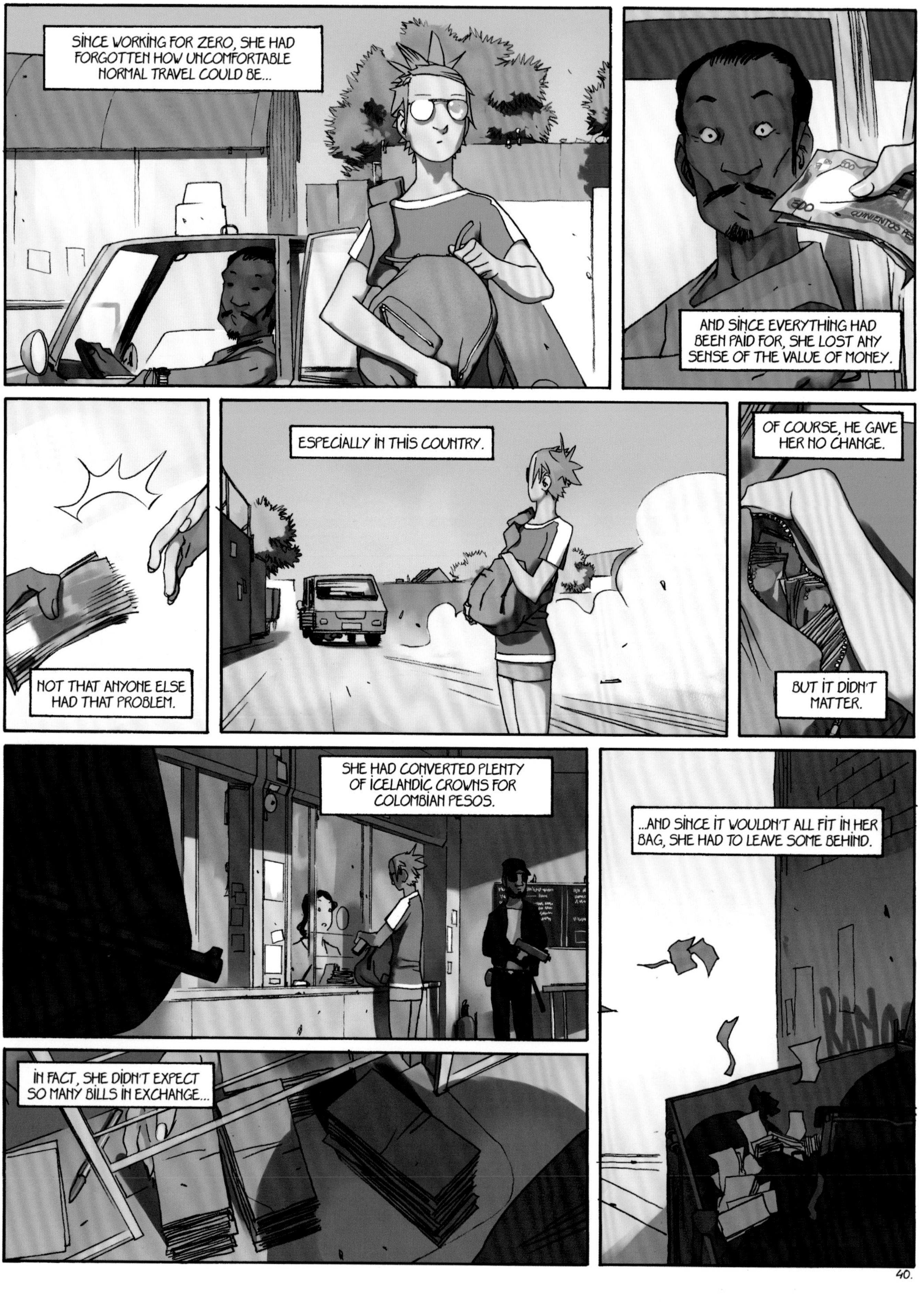
SINCE WORKING FOR ZERO, SHE HAD FORGOTTEN HOW UNCOMFORTABLE NORMAL TRAVEL COULD BE...
AND SINCE EVERYTHING HAD BEEN PAID FOR, SHE LOST ANY SENSE OF THE VALUE OF MONEY.
NOT THAT ANYONE ELSE HAD THAT PROBLEM.
ESPECIALLY IN THIS COUNTRY.
OF COURSE, HE GAVE HER NO CHANGE.
BUT IT DIDN'T MATTER.
SHE HAD CONVERTED PLENTY OF ICELANDIC CROWNS FOR COLOMBIAN PESOS.
IN FACT, SHE DIDN'T EXPECT SO MANY BILLS IN EXCHANGE...
...AND SINCE IT WOULDN'T ALL FIT IN HER BAG, SHE HAD TO LEAVE SOME BEHIND.

SURE, SHE COULD HAVE GIVEN IT AWAY. THERE ARE PLENTY OF POOR PEOPLE IN THIS COUNTRY.

BUT SHE COULDN'T THINK OF A GOOD REASON TO BOTHER...

...SINCE SHE ALSO HATES COLOMBIANS.

ALL SOUTH AMERICANS, REALLY.

TO HER, THEY FALL INTO TWO GROUPS: FILTHY PEASANTS AND DIRTY COPS.

THE FIRST COME IN TWO TYPES: THOSE WHO GROW THE COUNTRY'S MOST LUCRATIVE CROP, COCAINE, WHICH IS ESSENTIAL TO THE ECONOMY, GIVING AUTHORITIES SOMETHING TO FIGHT OVER...

...AND THOSE WHO GROW FAIR TRADE COFFEE, WHICH TASTES LIKE SHIT, BUT WE HAVE TO DRINK IT IF WE WANT TO FEEL GOOD ABOUT OURSELVES.

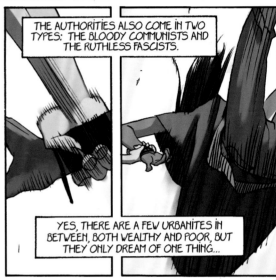

THE AUTHORITIES ALSO COME IN TWO TYPES: THE BLOODY COMMUNISTS AND THE RUTHLESS FASCISTS.

YES, THERE ARE A FEW URBANITES IN BETWEEN, BOTH WEALTHY AND POOR, BUT THEY ONLY DREAM OF ONE THING...

...BECOMING AMERICANS.

ONLY ONE THING UNITES THEM ALL: THEIR ANCESTRY.

THEIR FOREFATHERS MASSACRED SO MANY INDIANS THAT THEY HAD TO SCATTER AROUND THE WORLD IN SMALL GROUPS.

NAJA CAN NO LONGER STAND THE SOUND OF PAN FLUTES WHEN SHE WALKS DOWN THE STREET OR INTO THE SUBWAY.

YEAH, NAJA HATES INDIANS, TOO.

41.

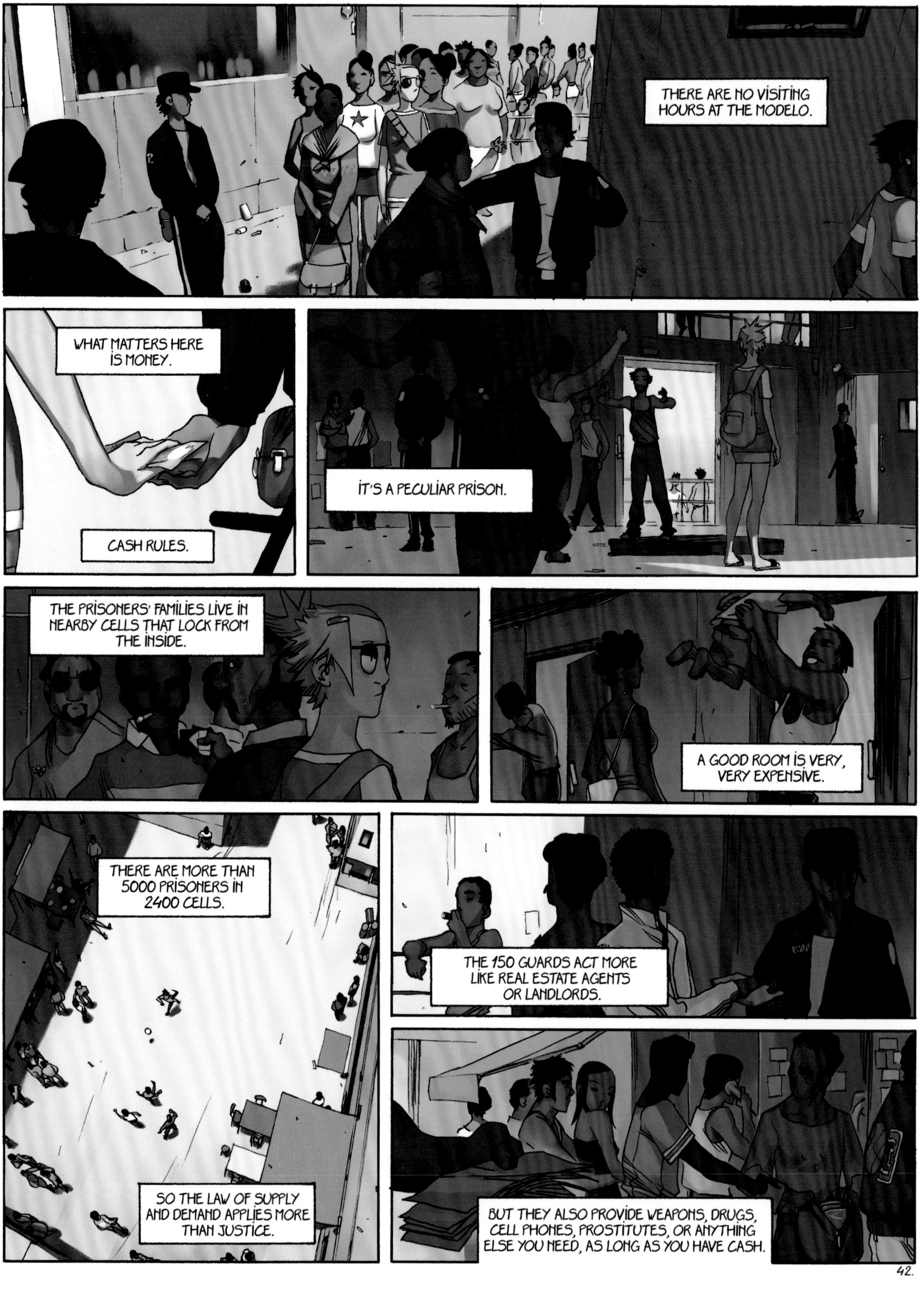
THERE ARE NO VISITING HOURS AT THE MODELO.
WHAT MATTERS HERE IS MONEY.
CASH RULES.
IT'S A PECULIAR PRISON.
THE PRISONERS' FAMILIES LIVE IN NEARBY CELLS THAT LOCK FROM THE INSIDE.
A GOOD ROOM IS VERY, VERY EXPENSIVE.
THERE ARE MORE THAN 5000 PRISONERS IN 2400 CELLS.
SO THE LAW OF SUPPLY AND DEMAND APPLIES MORE THAN JUSTICE.
THE 150 GUARDS ACT MORE LIKE REAL ESTATE AGENTS OR LANDLORDS.
BUT THEY ALSO PROVIDE WEAPONS, DRUGS, CELL PHONES, PROSTITUTES, OR ANYTHING ELSE YOU NEED, AS LONG AS YOU HAVE CASH.

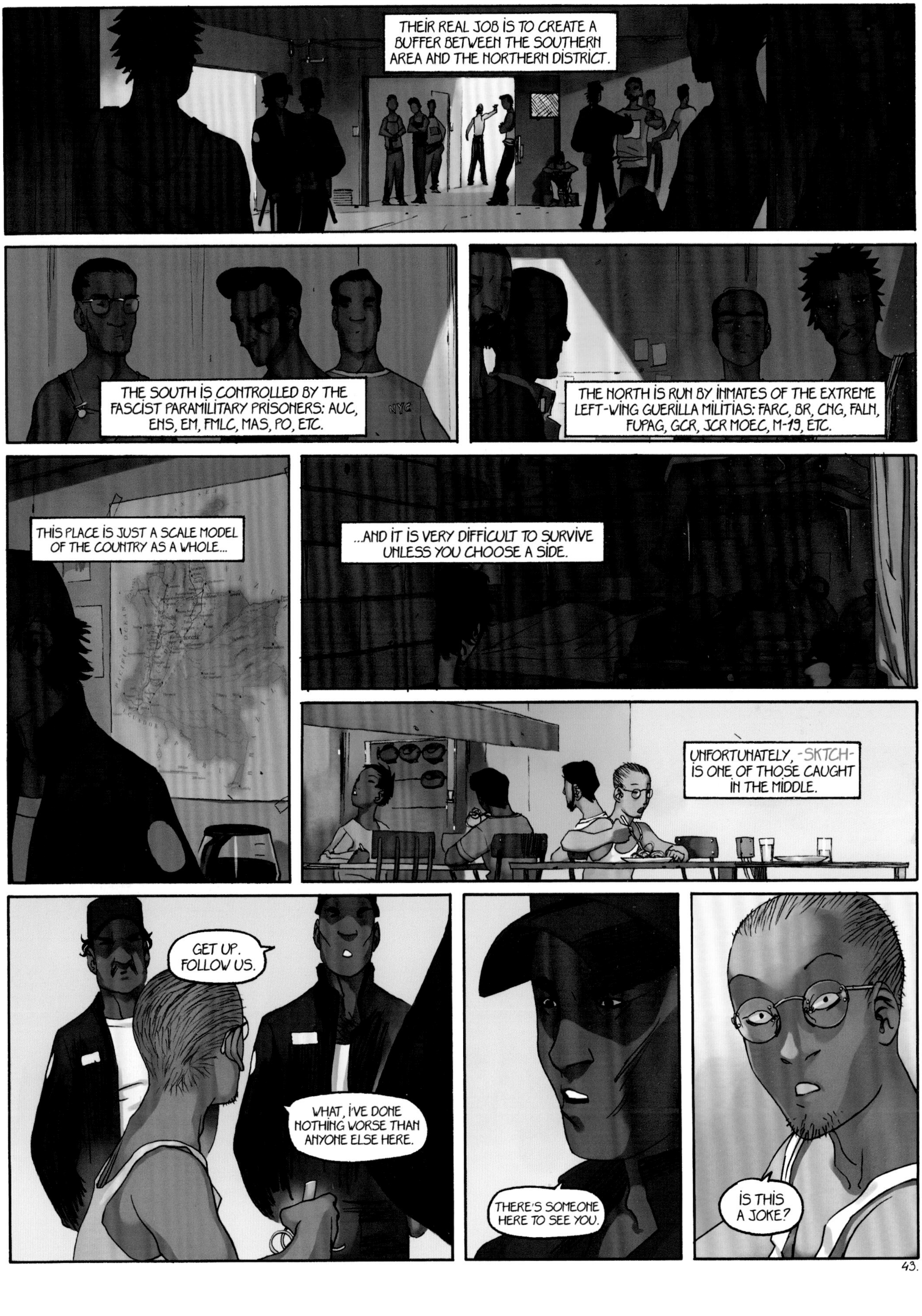
THEIR REAL JOB IS TO CREATE A BUFFER BETWEEN THE SOUTHERN AREA AND THE NORTHERN DISTRICT.
THE SOUTH IS CONTROLLED BY THE FASCIST PARAMILITARY PRISONERS: AUC, ENS, EM, FMLC, MAS, PO, ETC.
NYC
THE NORTH IS RUN BY INMATES OF THE EXTREME LEFT-WING GUERILLA MILITIAS: FARC, BR, CNG, FALN, FUPAG, GCR, JCR MOEC, M-19, ETC.
THIS PLACE IS JUST A SCALE MODEL OF THE COUNTRY AS A WHOLE...
...AND IT IS VERY DIFFICULT TO SURVIVE UNLESS YOU CHOOSE A SIDE.
UNFORTUNATELY, -SKTCH- IS ONE OF THOSE CAUGHT IN THE MIDDLE.
GET UP. FOLLOW US.
WHAT, I'VE DONE NOTHING WORSE THAN ANYONE ELSE HERE.
THERE'S SOMEONE HERE TO SEE YOU.
IS THIS A JOKE?

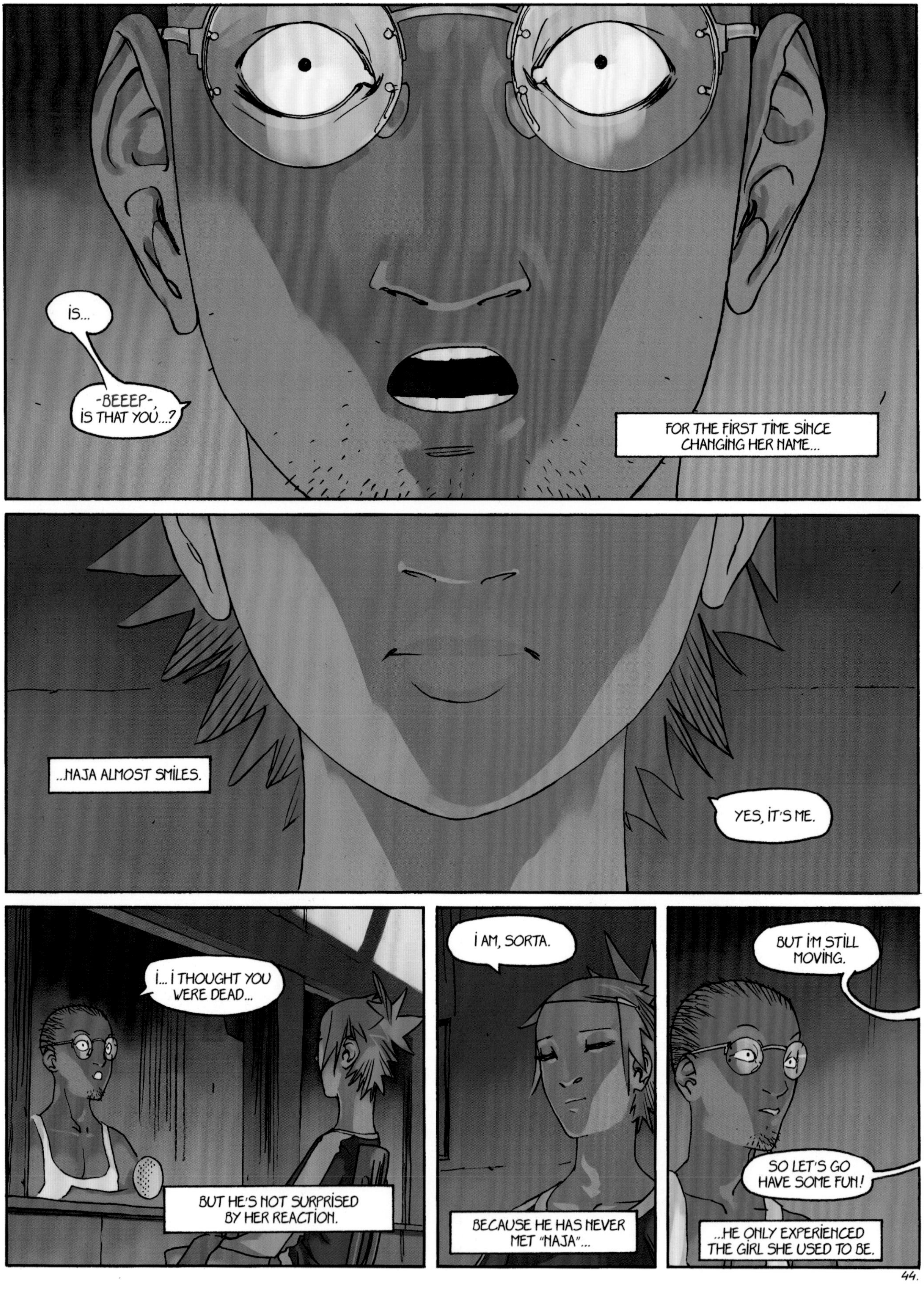
IS...
-BEEEP-, IS THAT YOU...?
FOR THE FIRST TIME SINCE CHANGING HER NAME...
...NAJA ALMOST SMILES.
YES, IT'S ME.
I... I THOUGHT YOU WERE DEAD...
BUT HE'S NOT SURPRISED BY HER REACTION.
I AM, SORTA.
BECAUSE HE HAS NEVER MET "NAJA"...
BUT I'M STILL MOVING.
SO LET'S GO HAVE SOME FUN!
...HE ONLY EXPERIENCED THE GIRL SHE USED TO BE.

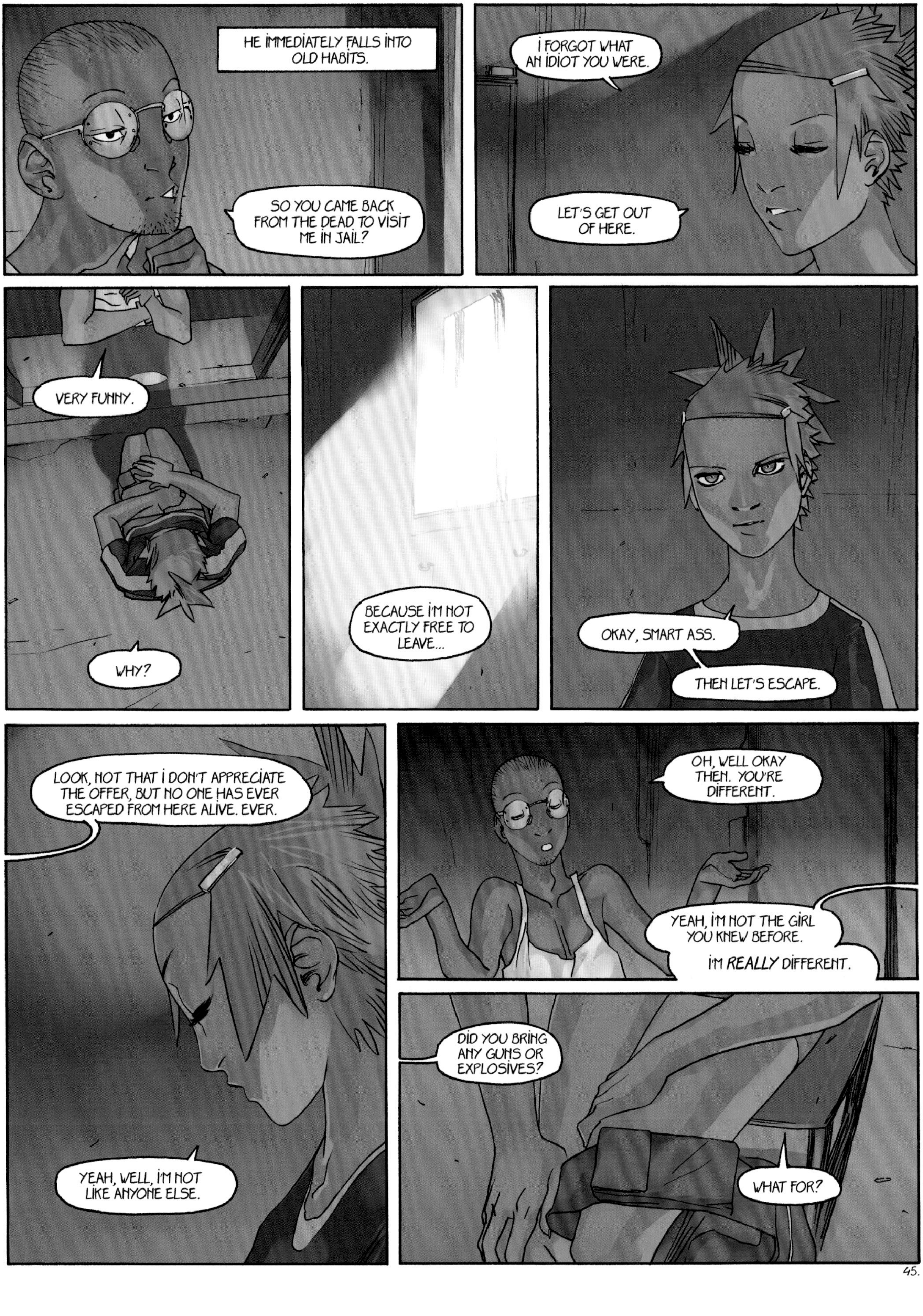
HE IMMEDIATELY FALLS INTO OLD HABITS.
SO YOU CAME BACK FROM THE DEAD TO VISIT ME IN JAIL?
I FORGOT WHAT AN IDIOT YOU WERE.
LET'S GET OUT OF HERE.
VERY FUNNY.
WHY?
BECAUSE I'M NOT EXACTLY FREE TO LEAVE...
OKAY, SMART ASS.
THEN LET'S ESCAPE.
LOOK, NOT THAT I DON'T APPRECIATE THE OFFER, BUT NO ONE HAS EVER ESCAPED FROM HERE ALIVE. EVER.
YEAH, WELL, I'M NOT LIKE ANYONE ELSE.
OH, WELL OKAY THEN. YOU'RE DIFFERENT.
YEAH, I'M NOT THE GIRL YOU KNEW BEFORE.
I'M *REALLY* DIFFERENT.
DID YOU BRING ANY GUNS OR EXPLOSIVES?
WHAT FOR?

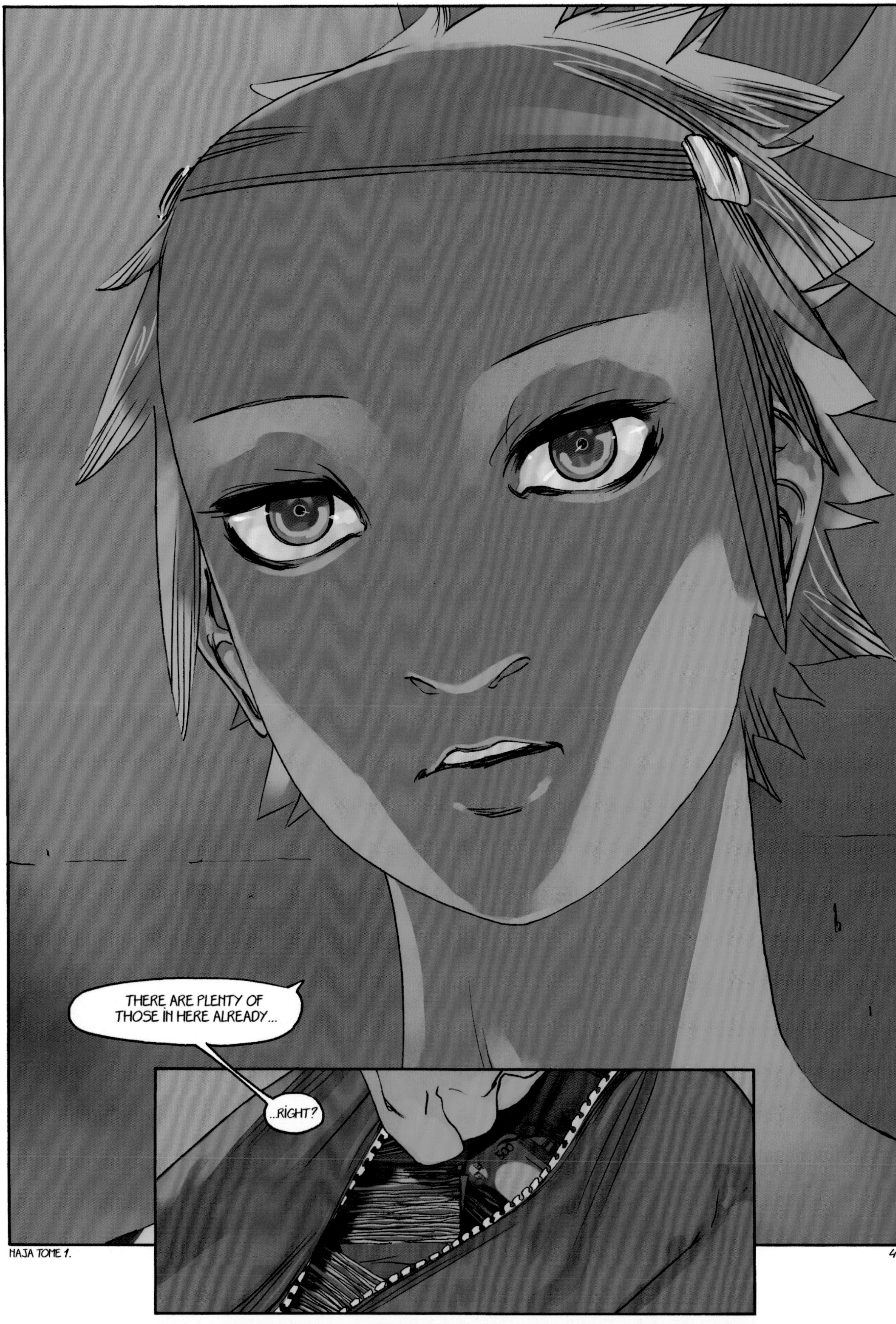
THERE ARE PLENTY OF THOSE IN HERE ALREADY...
...RIGHT?

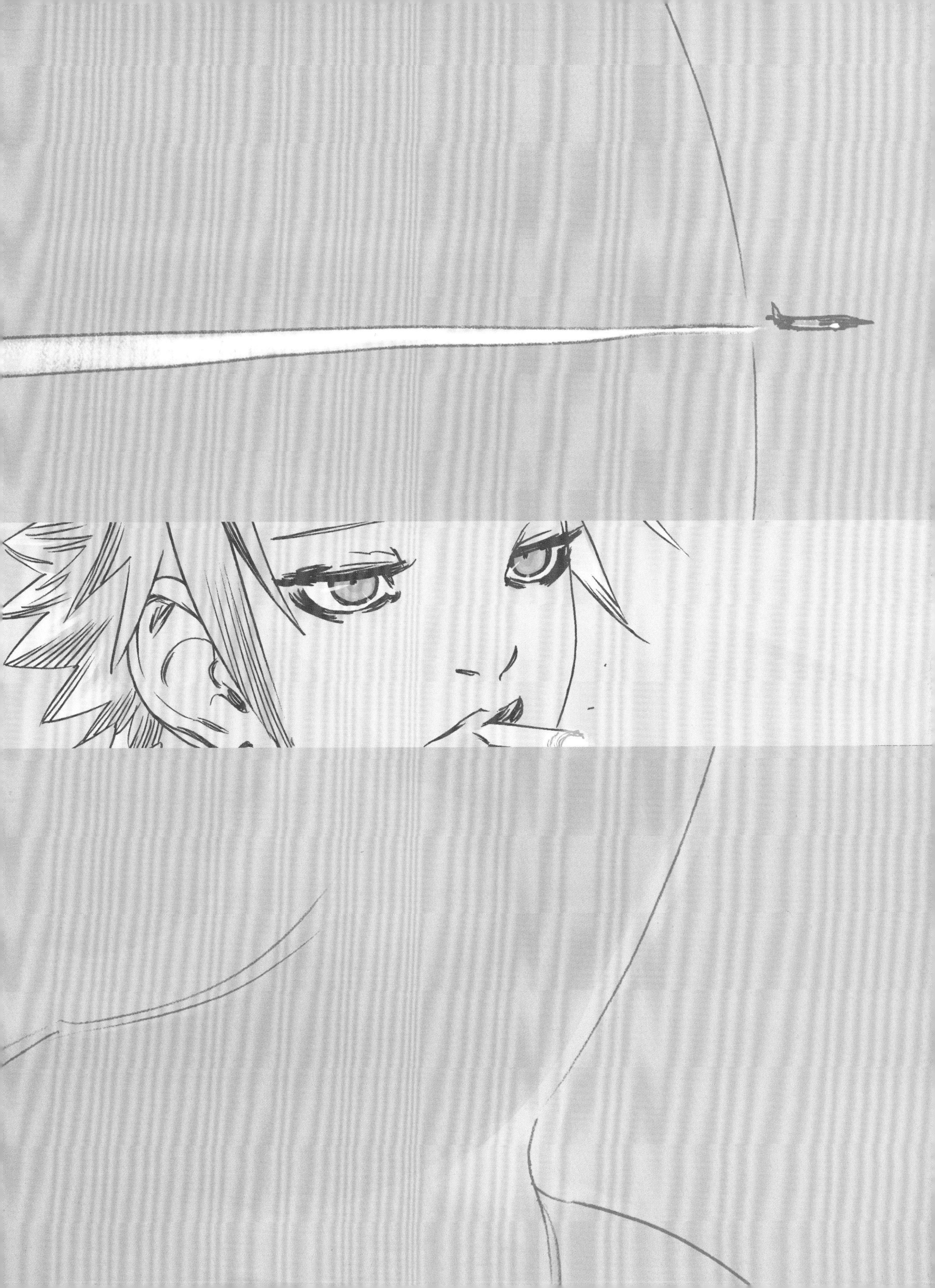

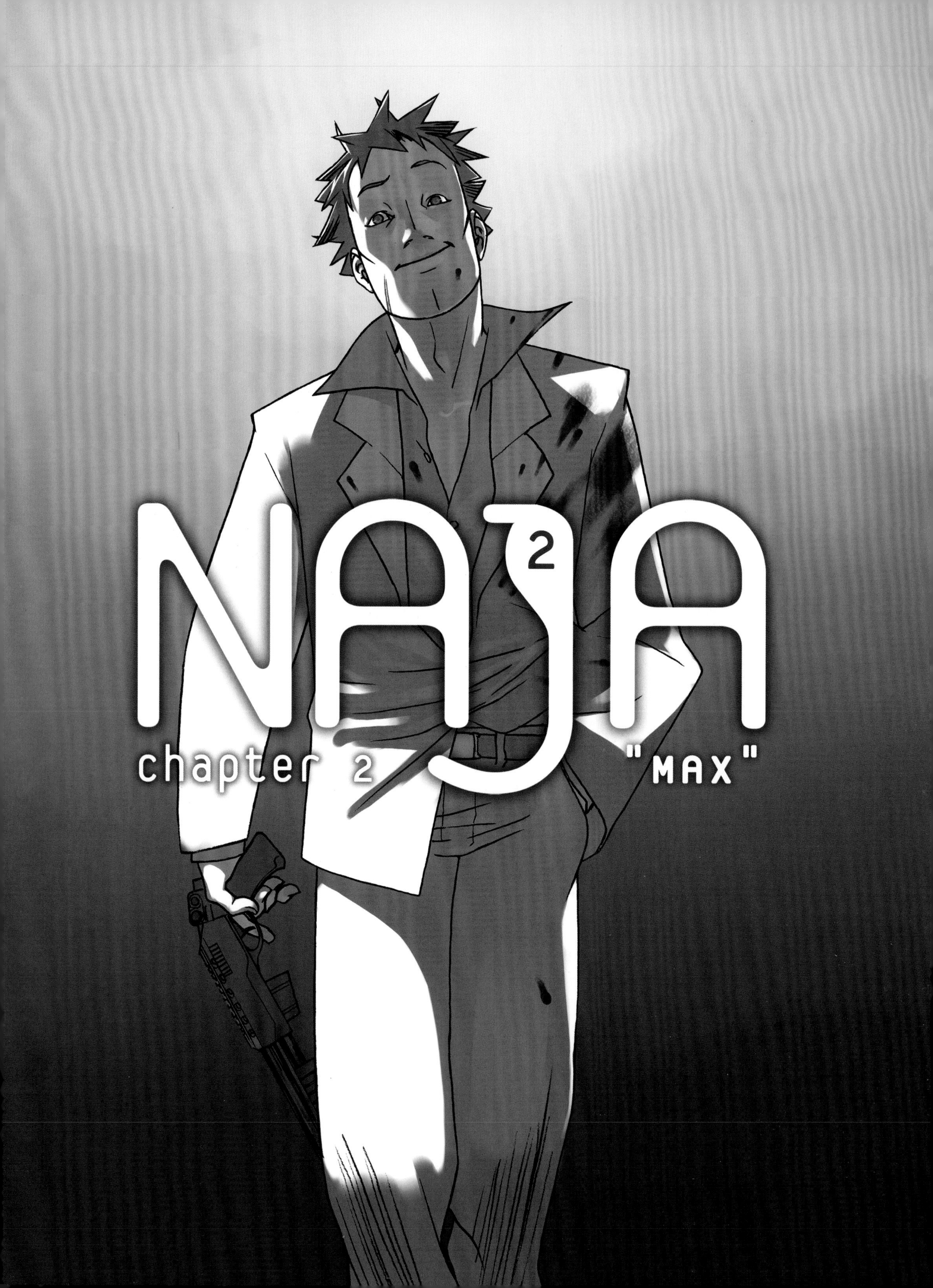
NAJA 2
chapter 2 "MAX"

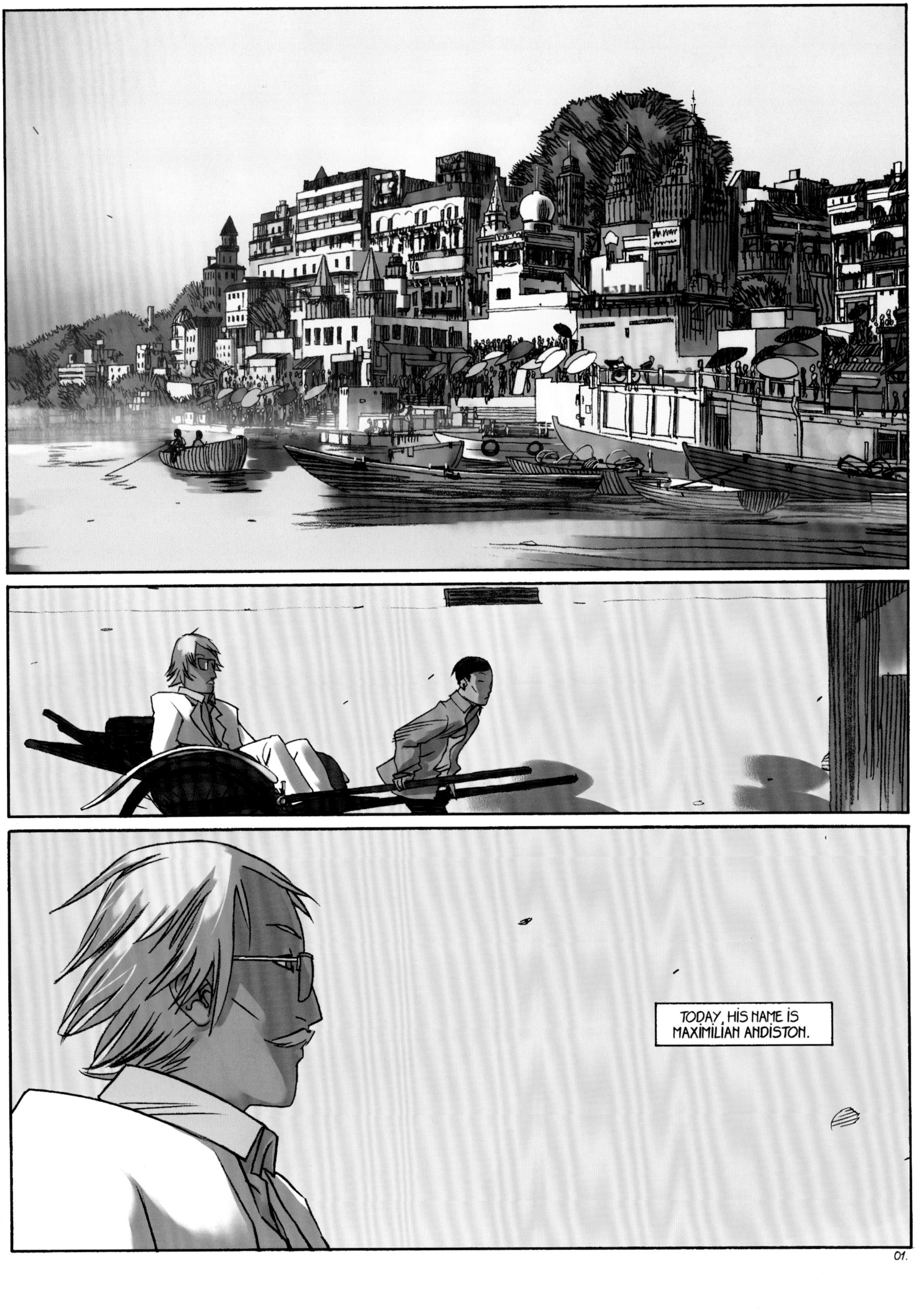
TODAY, HIS NAME IS
MAXIMILIAN ANDISTON.

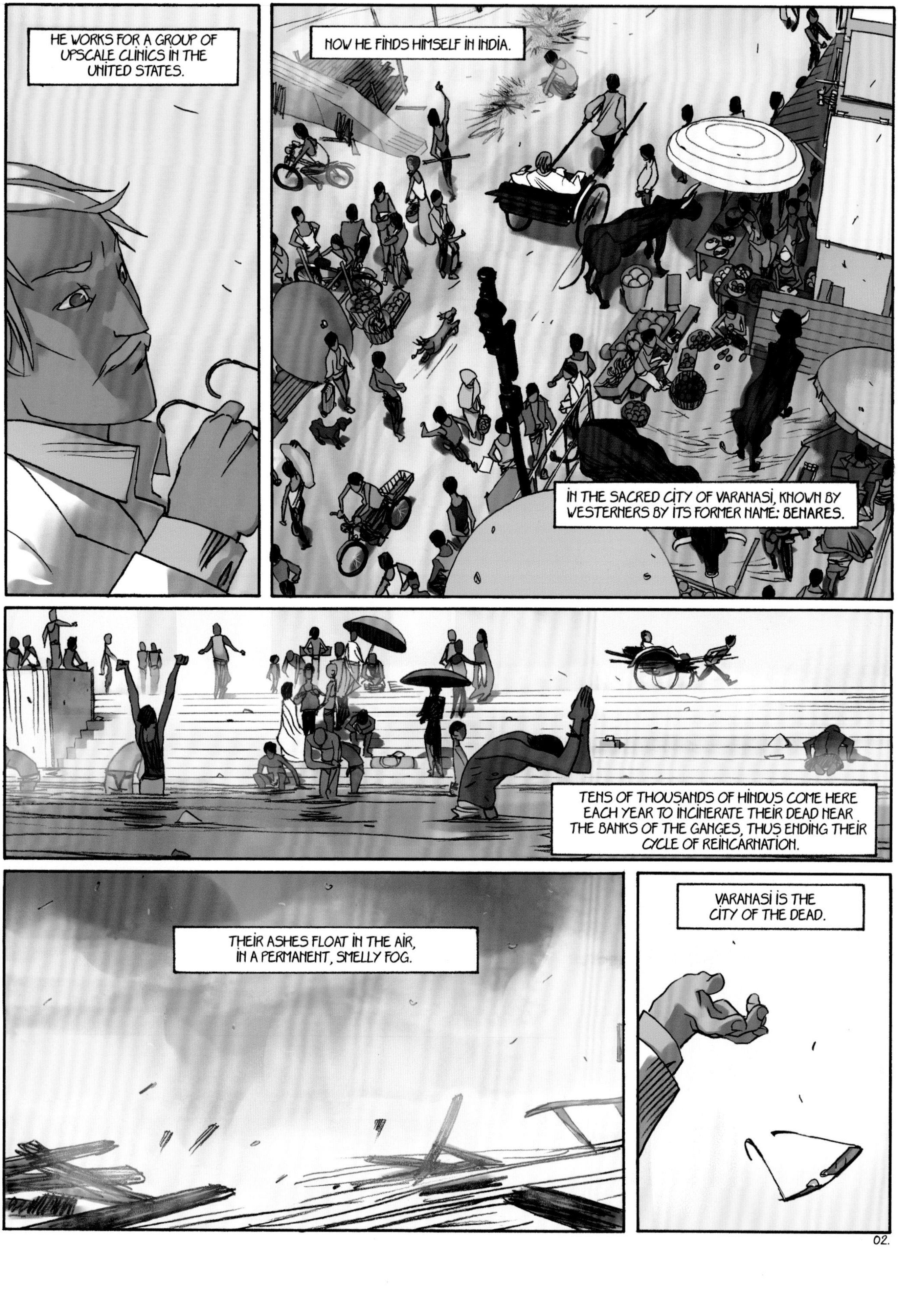
HE WORKS FOR A GROUP OF UPSCALE CLINICS IN THE UNITED STATES.
NOW HE FINDS HIMSELF IN INDIA.
IN THE SACRED CITY OF VARANASI, KNOWN BY WESTERNERS BY ITS FORMER NAME: BENARES.
TENS OF THOUSANDS OF HINDUS COME HERE EACH YEAR TO INCINERATE THEIR DEAD NEAR THE BANKS OF THE GANGES, THUS ENDING THEIR CYCLE OF REINCARNATION.
THEIR ASHES FLOAT IN THE AIR, IN A PERMANENT, SMELLY FOG.
VARANASI IS THE CITY OF THE DEAD.

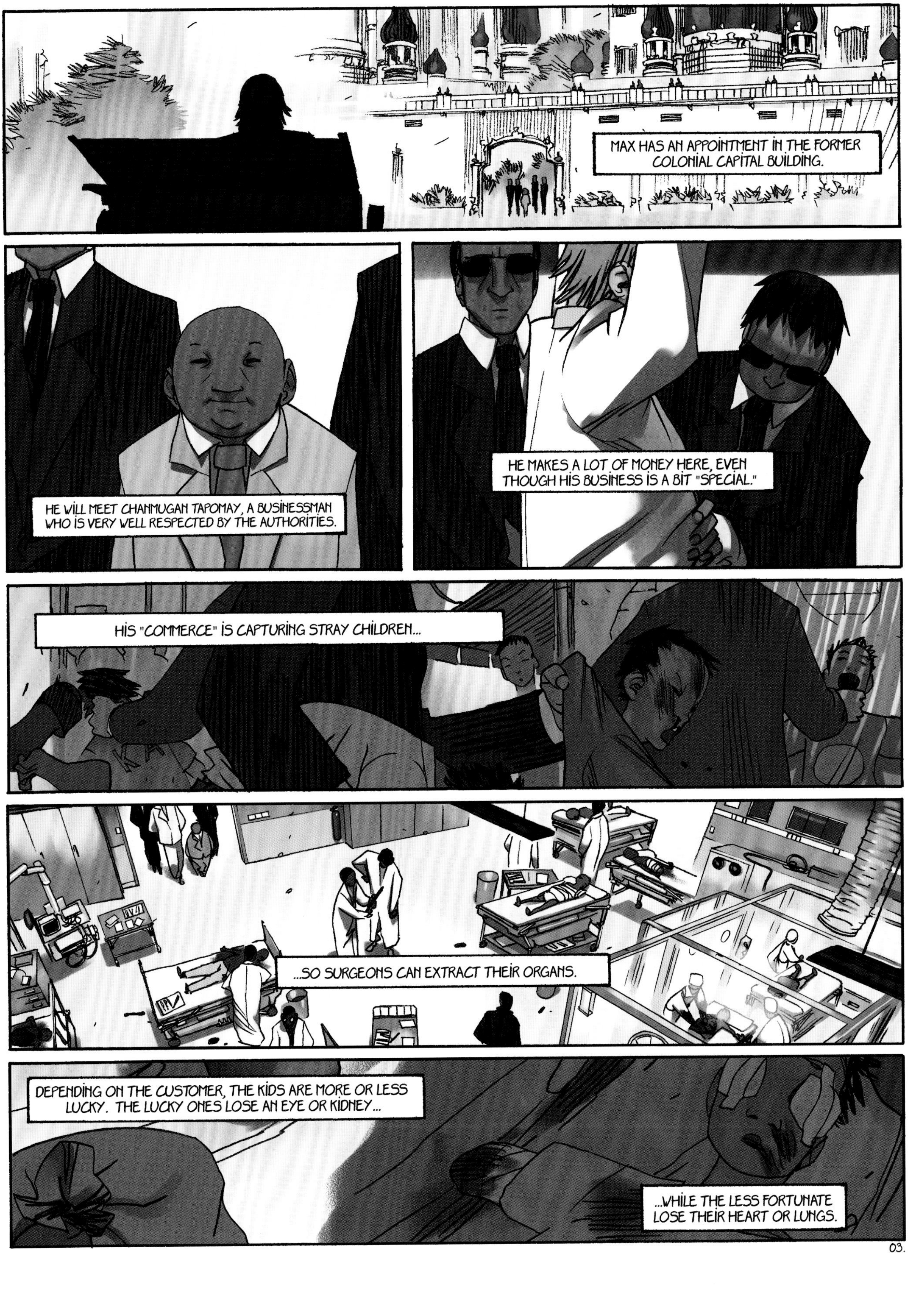

MAX HAS AN APPOINTMENT IN THE FORMER COLONIAL CAPITAL BUILDING.
HE WILL MEET CHANMUGAN TAPOMAY, A BUSINESSMAN WHO IS VERY WELL RESPECTED BY THE AUTHORITIES.
HE MAKES A LOT OF MONEY HERE, EVEN THOUGH HIS BUSINESS IS A BIT "SPECIAL."
HIS "COMMERCE" IS CAPTURING STRAY CHILDREN...
...SO SURGEONS CAN EXTRACT THEIR ORGANS.
DEPENDING ON THE CUSTOMER, THE KIDS ARE MORE OR LESS LUCKY. THE LUCKY ONES LOSE AN EYE OR KIDNEY...
...WHILE THE LESS FORTUNATE LOSE THEIR HEART OR LUNGS.

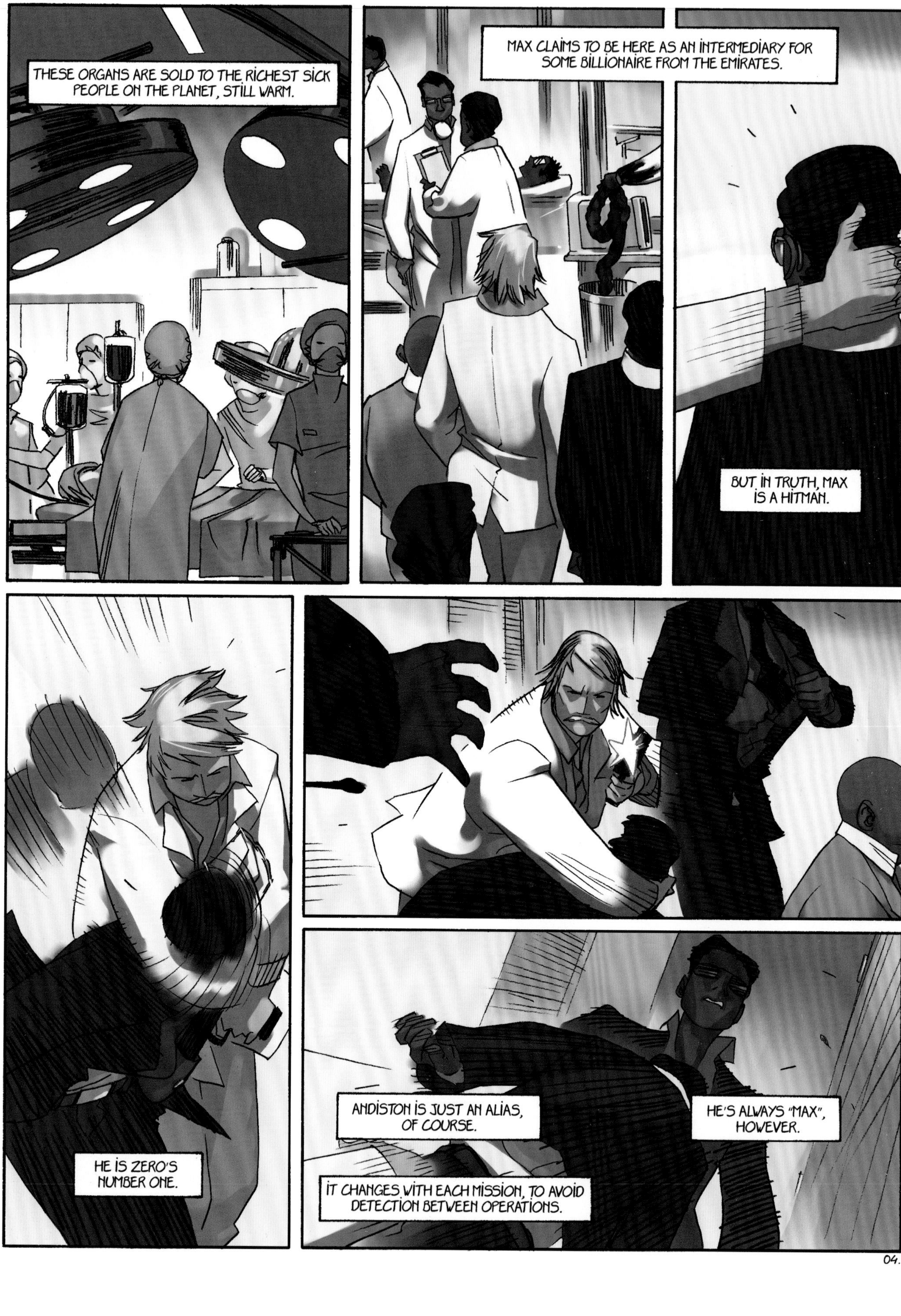
THESE ORGANS ARE SOLD TO THE RICHEST SICK PEOPLE ON THE PLANET, STILL WARM.
MAX CLAIMS TO BE HERE AS AN INTERMEDIARY FOR SOME BILLIONAIRE FROM THE EMIRATES.
BUT IN TRUTH, MAX IS A HITMAN.
HE IS ZERO'S NUMBER ONE.
ANDISTON IS JUST AN ALIAS, OF COURSE.
IT CHANGES WITH EACH MISSION, TO AVOID DETECTION BETWEEN OPERATIONS.
HE'S ALWAYS "MAX", HOWEVER.

TO BE FAIR, MAX COULD HAVE TAKEN DOWN TAPOMAY AT HOME, OR AT A RESTAURANT, OR ANYWHERE HE CHOSE.

THAT WAS ALL ZERO'S CONTRACT STIPULATED.

HE DIDN'T HAVE TO TAKE ALL THESE RISKS BY THROWING HIMSELF INTO THE LION'S DEN.

BUT ONCE YOU GET TO KNOW MAX, YOU'LL REALIZE THAT HE IS NEVER SATISFIED DOING ONLY WHAT IS ASKED.

TO BE THE BEST, HE NEEDS TO BELIEVE IN WHAT HE IS DOING.

UNLIKE NAJA, WHO DOESN'T WANT TO KNOW THE REASON FOR HER ASSIGNMENTS.

MAX IS A MAN OF CONVICTION. AND AS HIS NAME SUGGESTS, HE ALWAYS GOES THAT EXTRA MILE.

IF HE SIMPLY KILLED TAPOMAY, SOMEONE ELSE WOULD TAKE HIS PLACE.

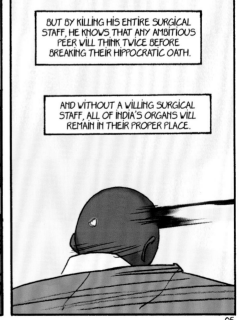

BUT BY KILLING HIS ENTIRE SURGICAL STAFF, HE KNOWS THAT ANY AMBITIOUS PEER WILL THINK TWICE BEFORE BREAKING THEIR HIPPOCRATIC OATH.

AND WITHOUT A WILLING SURGICAL STAFF, ALL OF INDIA'S ORGANS WILL REMAIN IN THEIR PROPER PLACE.

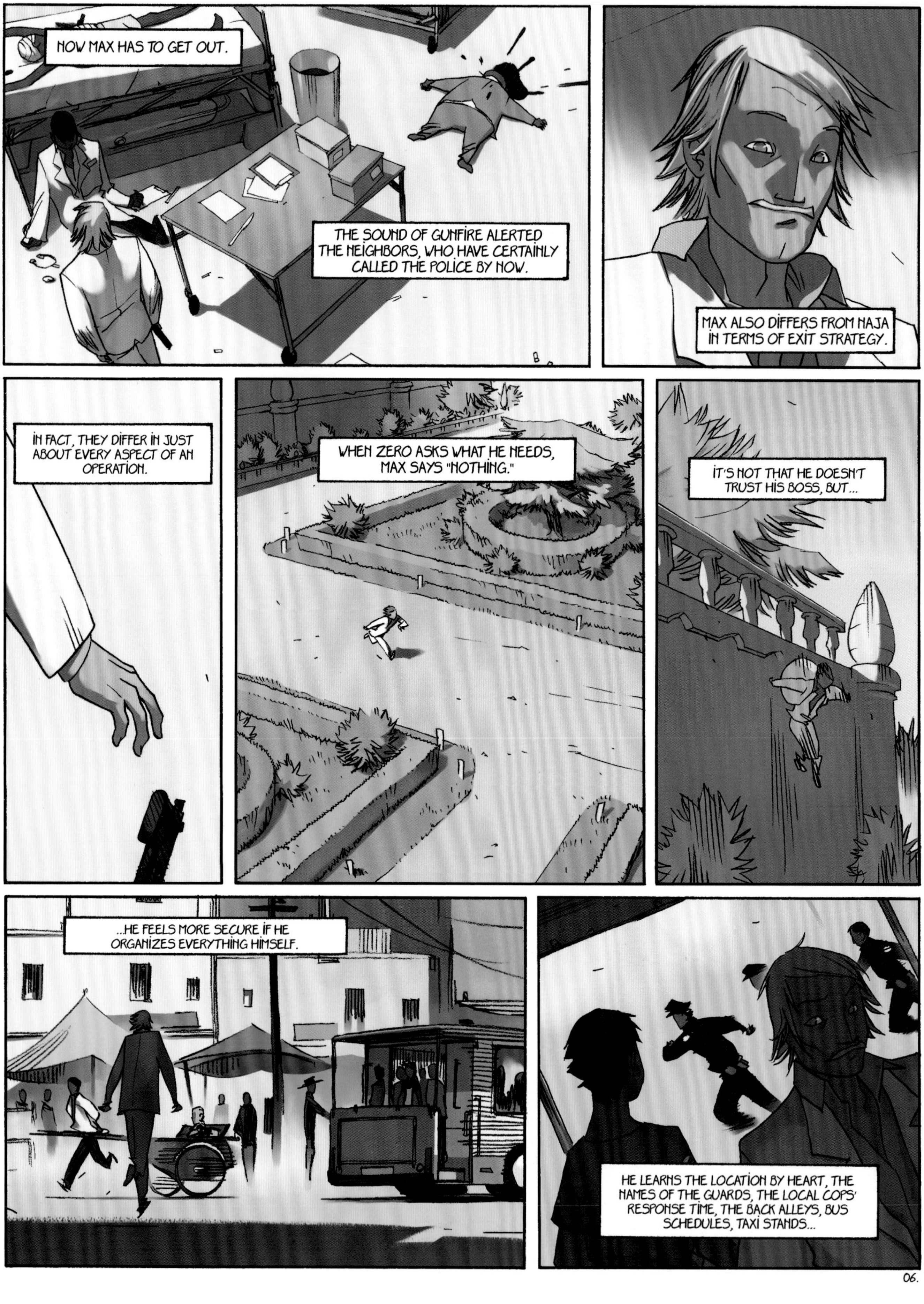
NOW MAX HAS TO GET OUT.
THE SOUND OF GUNFIRE ALERTED THE NEIGHBORS, WHO HAVE CERTAINLY CALLED THE POLICE BY NOW.
MAX ALSO DIFFERS FROM NAJA IN TERMS OF EXIT STRATEGY.
IN FACT, THEY DIFFER IN JUST ABOUT EVERY ASPECT OF AN OPERATION.
WHEN ZERO ASKS WHAT HE NEEDS, MAX SAYS "NOTHING."
IT'S NOT THAT HE DOESN'T TRUST HIS BOSS, BUT...
...HE FEELS MORE SECURE IF HE ORGANIZES EVERYTHING HIMSELF.
HE LEARNS THE LOCATION BY HEART, THE NAMES OF THE GUARDS, THE LOCAL COPS' RESPONSE TIME, THE BACK ALLEYS, BUS SCHEDULES, TAXI STANDS...

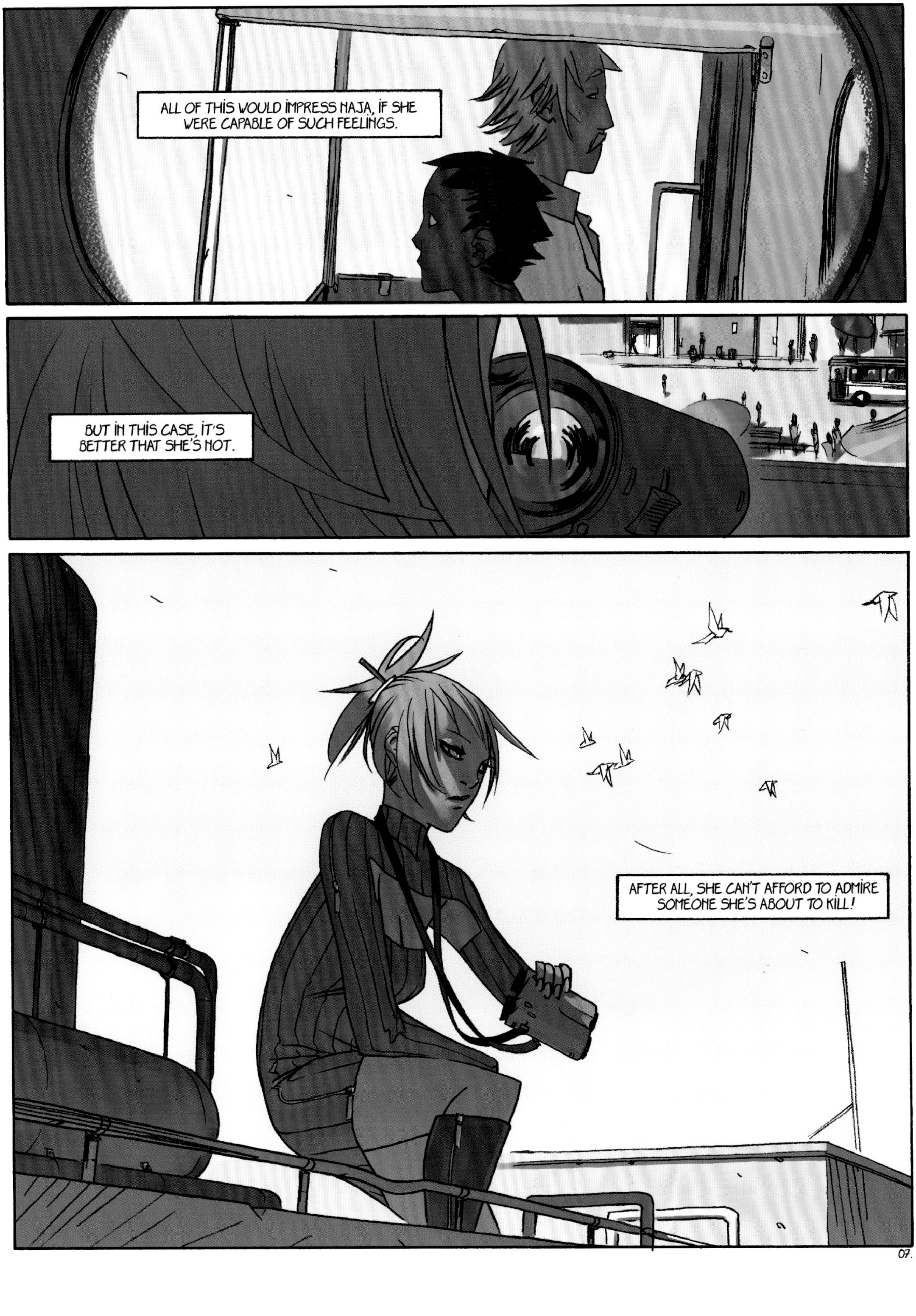
ALL OF THIS WOULD IMPRESS NAJA, IF SHE WERE CAPABLE OF SUCH FEELINGS.
BUT IN THIS CASE, IT'S BETTER THAT SHE'S NOT.
AFTER ALL, SHE CAN'T AFFORD TO ADMIRE SOMEONE SHE'S ABOUT TO KILL!

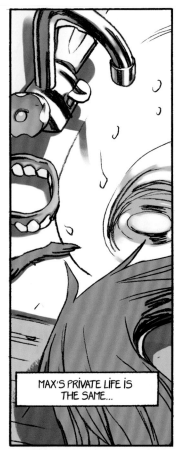

MAX'S PRIVATE LIFE IS
THE SAME...

...HE IS ALWAYS ON GUARD, POSSESSING
MANY DIFFERENT FACES AND NAMES.

EVEN WHEN HE'S NOT ON A MISSION, HE
DOESN'T MOVE WITHOUT KNOWING EVERY
INTIMATE DETAIL OF HIS SURROUNDINGS.

FOR EXAMPLE, HE HAS BEEN LIVING HERE
FOR TEN MONTHS, IN THE HEART OF
THE VAGRANT DISTRICT.

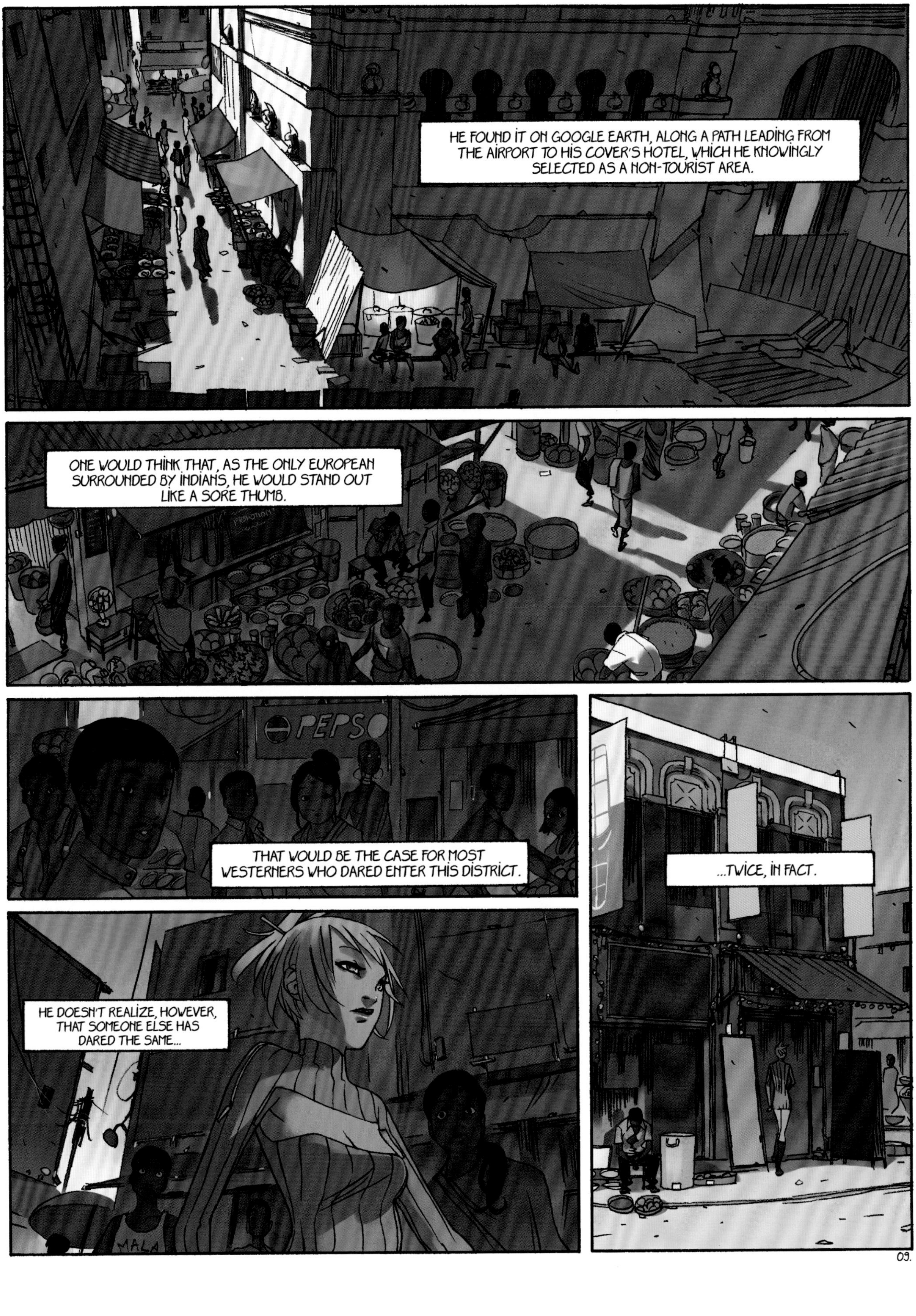
HE FOUND IT ON GOOGLE EARTH, ALONG A PATH LEADING FROM THE AIRPORT TO HIS COVER'S HOTEL, WHICH HE KNOWINGLY SELECTED AS A NON-TOURIST AREA.
ONE WOULD THINK THAT, AS THE ONLY EUROPEAN SURROUNDED BY INDIANS, HE WOULD STAND OUT LIKE A SORE THUMB.
PEPSO
THAT WOULD BE THE CASE FOR MOST WESTERNERS WHO DARED ENTER THIS DISTRICT.
HE DOESN'T REALIZE, HOWEVER, THAT SOMEONE ELSE HAS DARED THE SAME...
MALA
...TWICE, IN FACT.

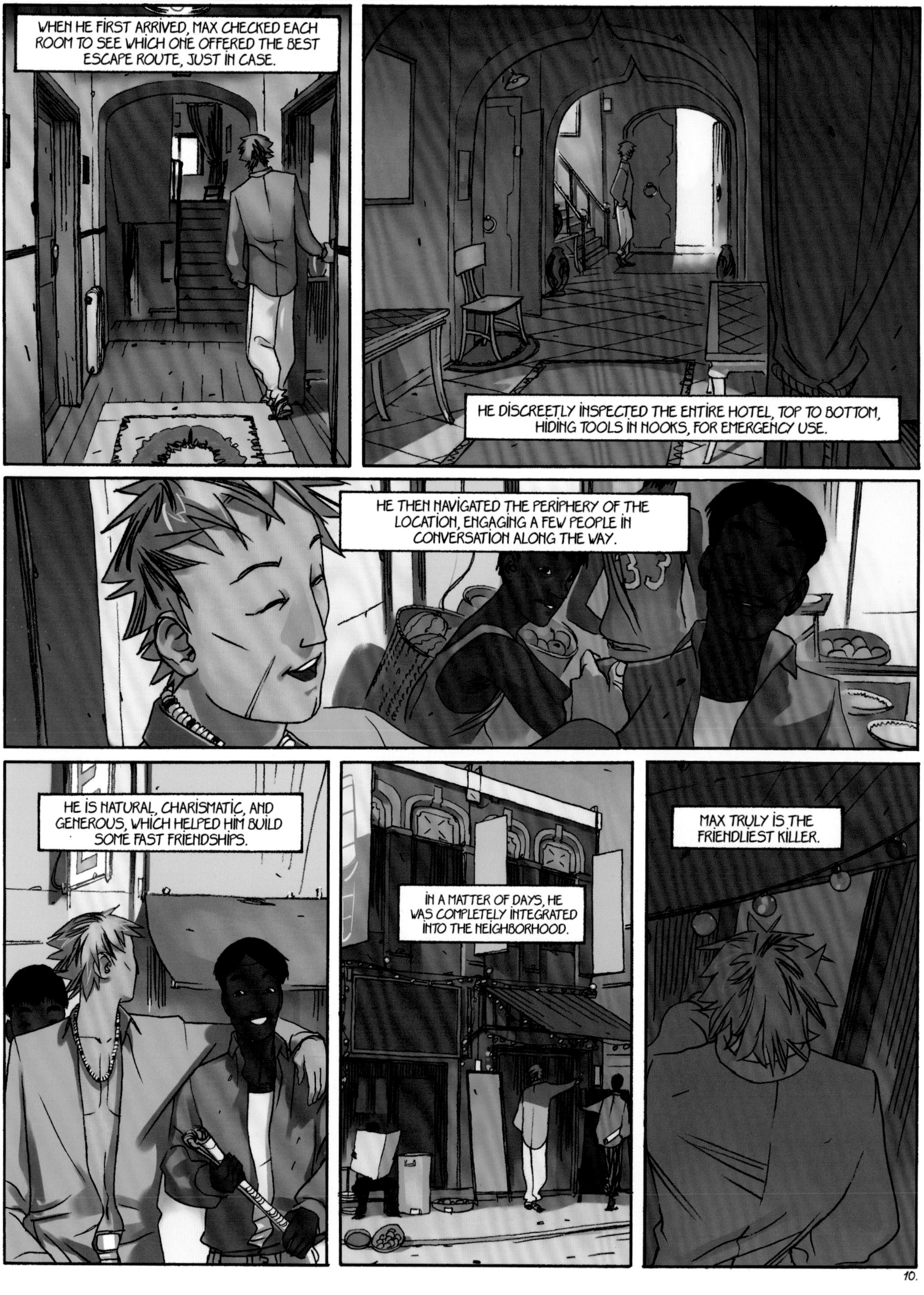
WHEN HE FIRST ARRIVED, MAX CHECKED EACH ROOM TO SEE WHICH ONE OFFERED THE BEST ESCAPE ROUTE, JUST IN CASE.
HE DISCREETLY INSPECTED THE ENTIRE HOTEL, TOP TO BOTTOM, HIDING TOOLS IN NOOKS, FOR EMERGENCY USE.
HE THEN NAVIGATED THE PERIPHERY OF THE LOCATION, ENGAGING A FEW PEOPLE IN CONVERSATION ALONG THE WAY.
33
HE IS NATURAL, CHARISMATIC, AND GENEROUS, WHICH HELPED HIM BUILD SOME FAST FRIENDSHIPS.
IN A MATTER OF DAYS, HE WAS COMPLETELY INTEGRATED INTO THE NEIGHBORHOOD.
MAX TRULY IS THE FRIENDLIEST KILLER.

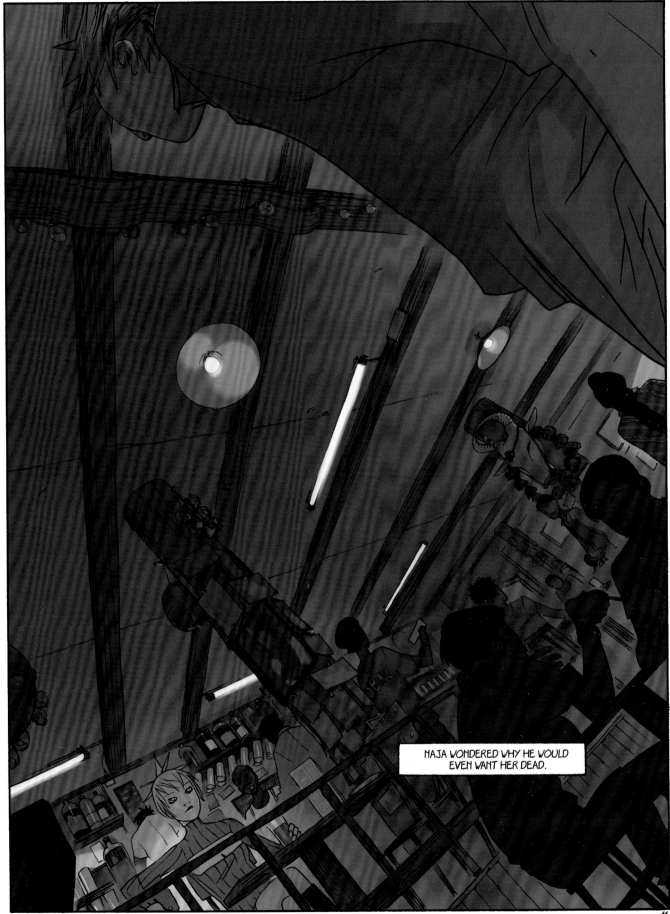

NAJA WONDERED WHY HE WOULD EVEN WANT HER DEAD.

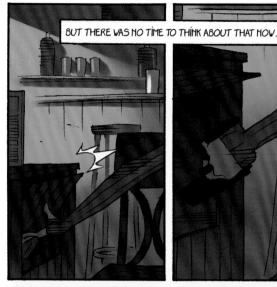
BUT THERE WAS NO TIME TO THINK ABOUT THAT NOW.

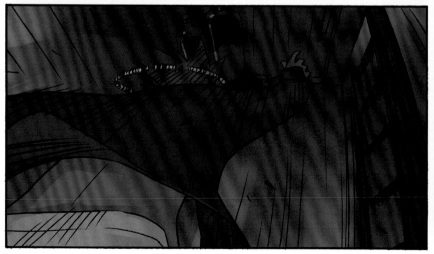
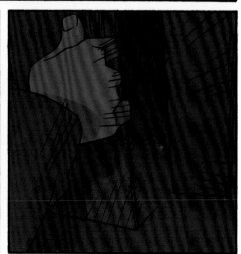

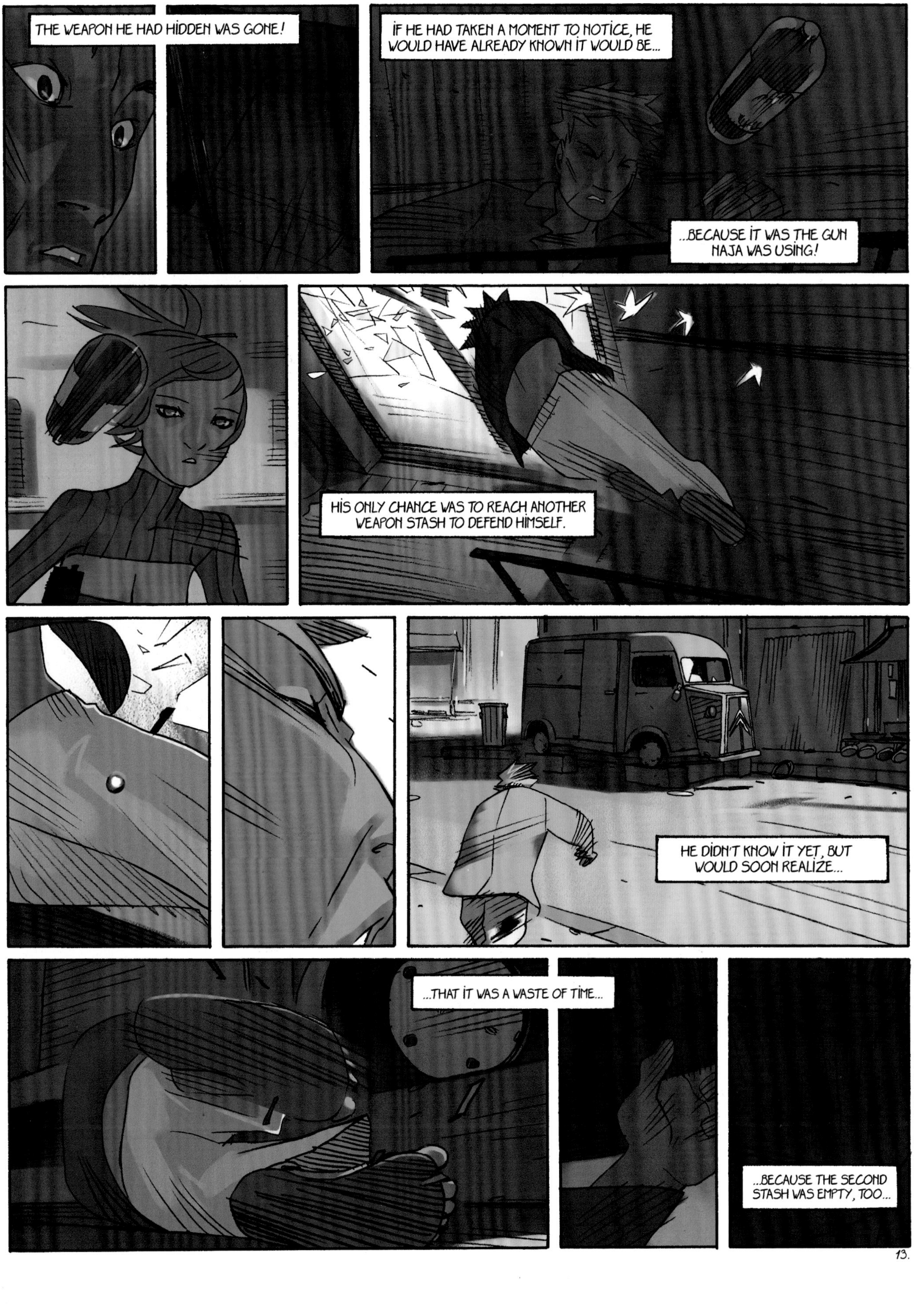
THE WEAPON HE HAD HIDDEN WAS GONE!
IF HE HAD TAKEN A MOMENT TO NOTICE, HE WOULD HAVE ALREADY KNOWN IT WOULD BE...
...BECAUSE IT WAS THE GUN NAJA WAS USING!
HIS ONLY CHANCE WAS TO REACH ANOTHER WEAPON STASH TO DEFEND HIMSELF.
HE DIDN'T KNOW IT YET, BUT WOULD SOON REALIZE...
...THAT IT WAS A WASTE OF TIME...
...BECAUSE THE SECOND STASH WAS EMPTY, TOO...

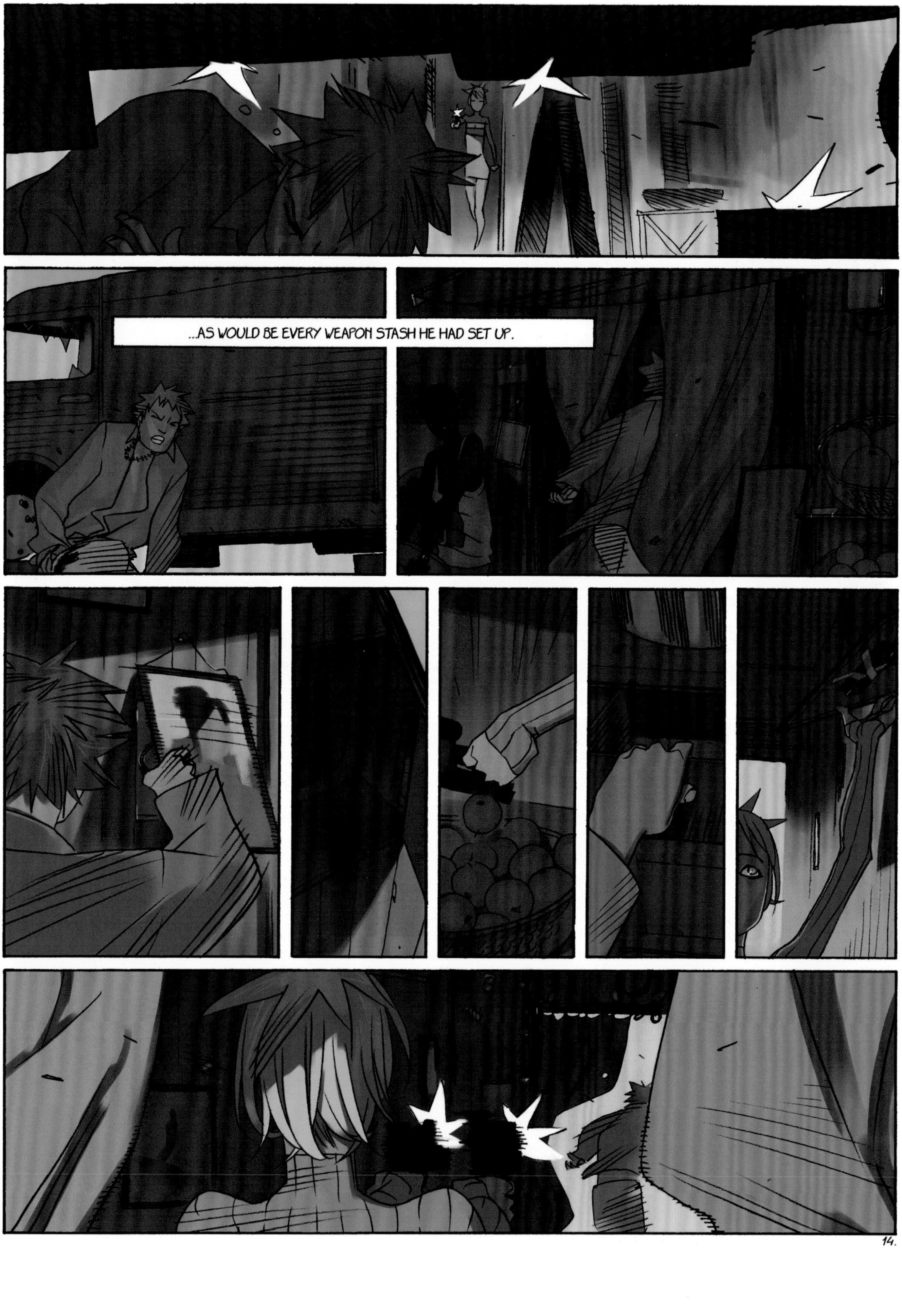
...AS WOULD BE EVERY WEAPON STASH HE HAD SET UP.

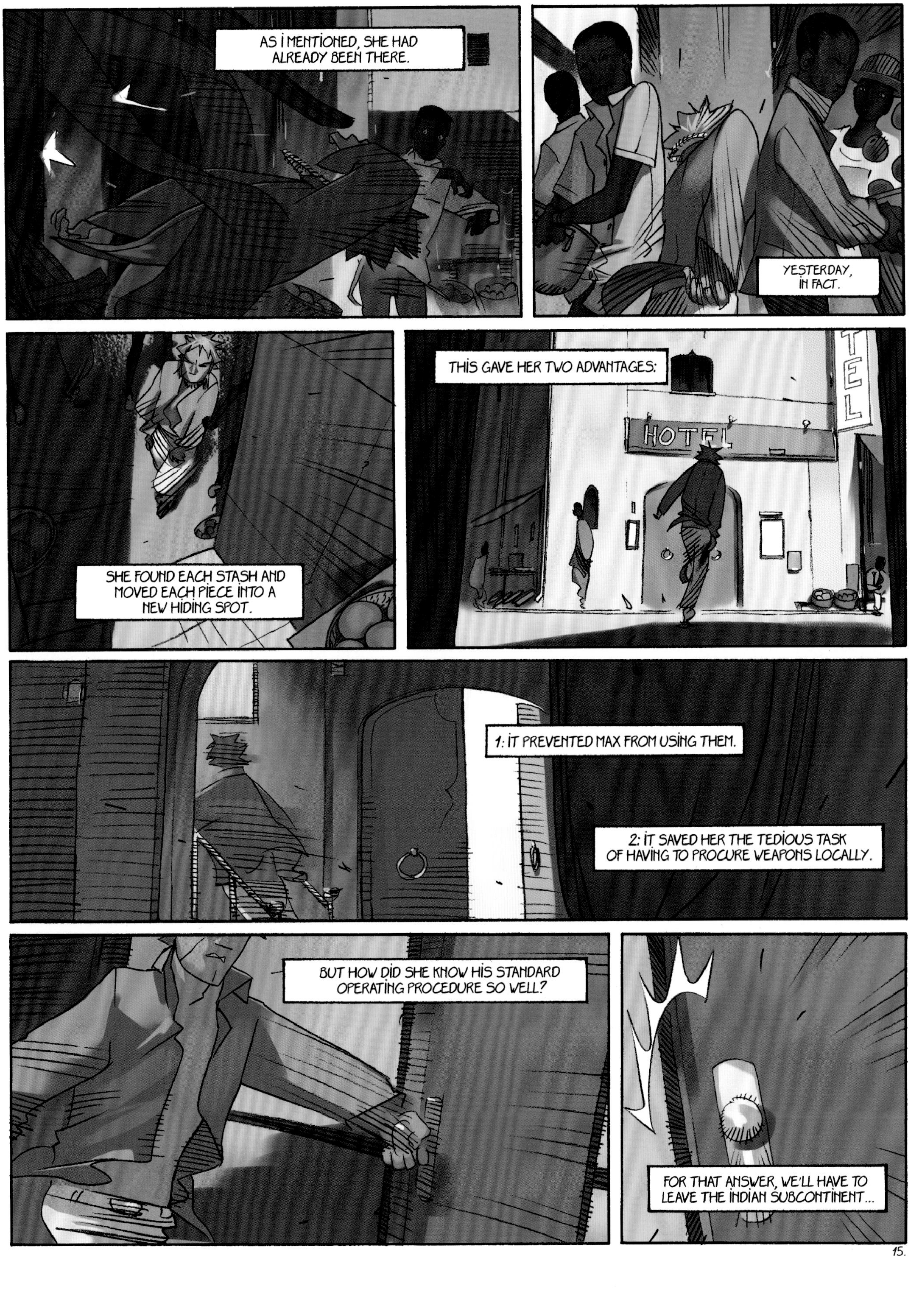

AS I MENTIONED, SHE HAD ALREADY BEEN THERE.
YESTERDAY, IN FACT.
SHE FOUND EACH STASH AND MOVED EACH PIECE INTO A NEW HIDING SPOT.
THIS GAVE HER TWO ADVANTAGES:
HOTEL
1: IT PREVENTED MAX FROM USING THEM.
2: IT SAVED HER THE TEDIOUS TASK OF HAVING TO PROCURE WEAPONS LOCALLY.
BUT HOW DID SHE KNOW HIS STANDARD OPERATING PROCEDURE SO WELL?
FOR THAT ANSWER, WE'LL HAVE TO LEAVE THE INDIAN SUBCONTINENT...

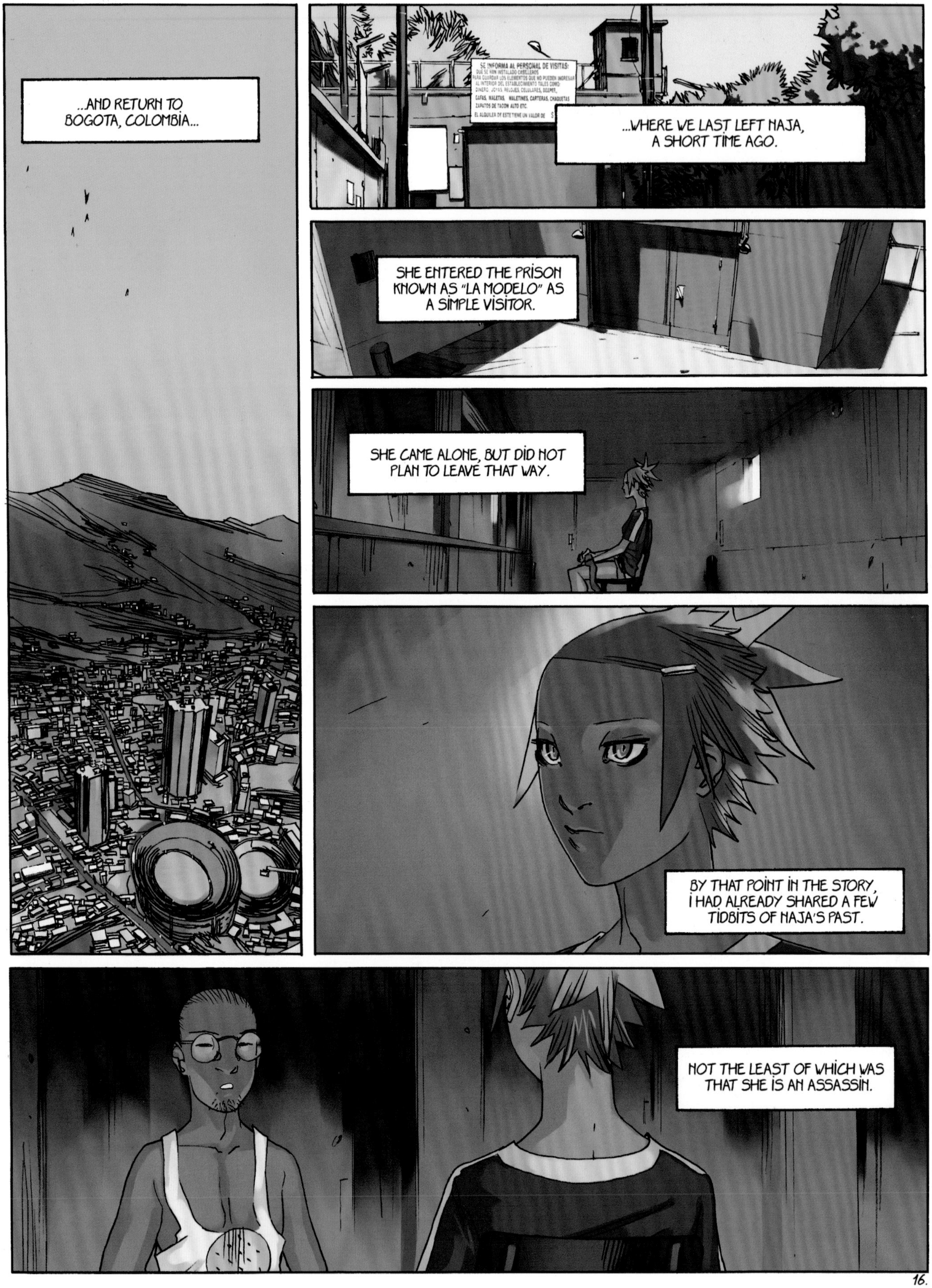
...AND RETURN TO BOGOTA, COLOMBIA...
SE INFORMA AL PERSONAL DE VISITAS:
QUE SE HAN INSTALADO CASILLEROS
PARA GUARDAR LOS ELEMENTOS QUE NO PUEDEN INGRESAR
AL INTERIOR DEL ESTABLECIMIENTO TALES COMO:
DINERO, JOYAS, RELOJES, CELULARES, BEEPER,
GAFAS, MALETAS, MALETINES, CARTERAS, CHAQUETAS
ZAPATOS DE TACON ALTO ETC.
EL ALQUILER DE ESTE TIENE UN VALOR DE $
...WHERE WE LAST LEFT NAJA, A SHORT TIME AGO.
SHE ENTERED THE PRISON KNOWN AS "LA MODELO" AS A SIMPLE VISITOR.
SHE CAME ALONE, BUT DID NOT PLAN TO LEAVE THAT WAY.
BY THAT POINT IN THE STORY, I HAD ALREADY SHARED A FEW TIDBITS OF NAJA'S PAST.
NOT THE LEAST OF WHICH WAS THAT SHE IS AN ASSASSIN.

WHAT MAKES HER DIFFERENT FROM OTHER KILLERS, HOWEVER, IS THAT SHE FEELS NO PAIN.

WHICH MAKES HER A TENACIOUS HUNTER, EVEN AT THE RISK OF DYING.

SHE IS EMPLOYED BY THE SAME ORGANIZATION AS MAX, WITH UNLIMITED CREDIT AT THEIR DISPOSAL.

NOBODY HERE REALIZES THAT SHE IS THE NUMBER THREE KILLER FOR A MAN KNOWN AS ZERO.

SHE HAS NEVER MET THE MAN, WHICH IS FORTUNATE.

BECAUSE NAJA HATES EVERYONE.

AND IT WOULD BE FATAL TO HATE SUCH A POWERFUL CRIMELORD.

NO ONE IN THE WORLD HAS EVER FOUND GRACE IN HER EYES...

...EXCEPT FOR TWO.

DON'T GET CONFUSED, I DON'T MEAN ZERO'S NUMBER TWO KILLER.

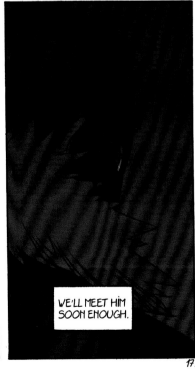

WE'LL MEET HIM SOON ENOUGH.

 NO, I MEAN *TWO DIFFERENT INDIVIDUALS.*

I CAN'T TELL YOU THEIR NAMES, BUT REALLY, WHAT DIFFERENCE WOULD THAT MAKE?

 SHE ENCOUNTERED THE FIRST ONE TWO DAYS AGO.

WE'LL CALL HIM "HE."

 "HE" BROKE INTO HER HOUSE IN ICELAND, AFTER SHE RETURNED FROM A MISSION IN PARIS.

 "HE" RUDELY AWAKENED HER, AND TOLD HER THAT ZERO'S NUMBER ONE KILLER WANTED TO GET RID OF NUMBER THREE - HERSELF.

 "HE" THEN VANISHED, WITHOUT SAYING ANOTHER WORD.

BUT HE LEFT QUITE AN IMPRESSION, IN MORE WAYS THAN ONE.

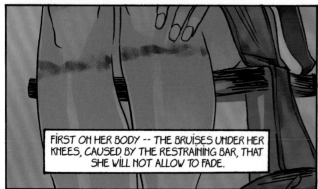 FIRST ON HER BODY -- THE BRUISES UNDER HER KNEES, CAUSED BY THE RESTRAINING BAR, THAT SHE WILL NOT ALLOW TO FADE.

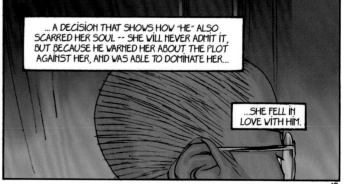 ... A DECISION THAT SHOWS HOW "HE" ALSO SCARRED HER SOUL -- SHE WILL NEVER ADMIT IT, BUT BECAUSE HE WARNED HER ABOUT THE PLOT AGAINST HER, AND WAS ABLE TO DOMINATE HER...

...SHE FELL IN LOVE WITH HIM.

18.

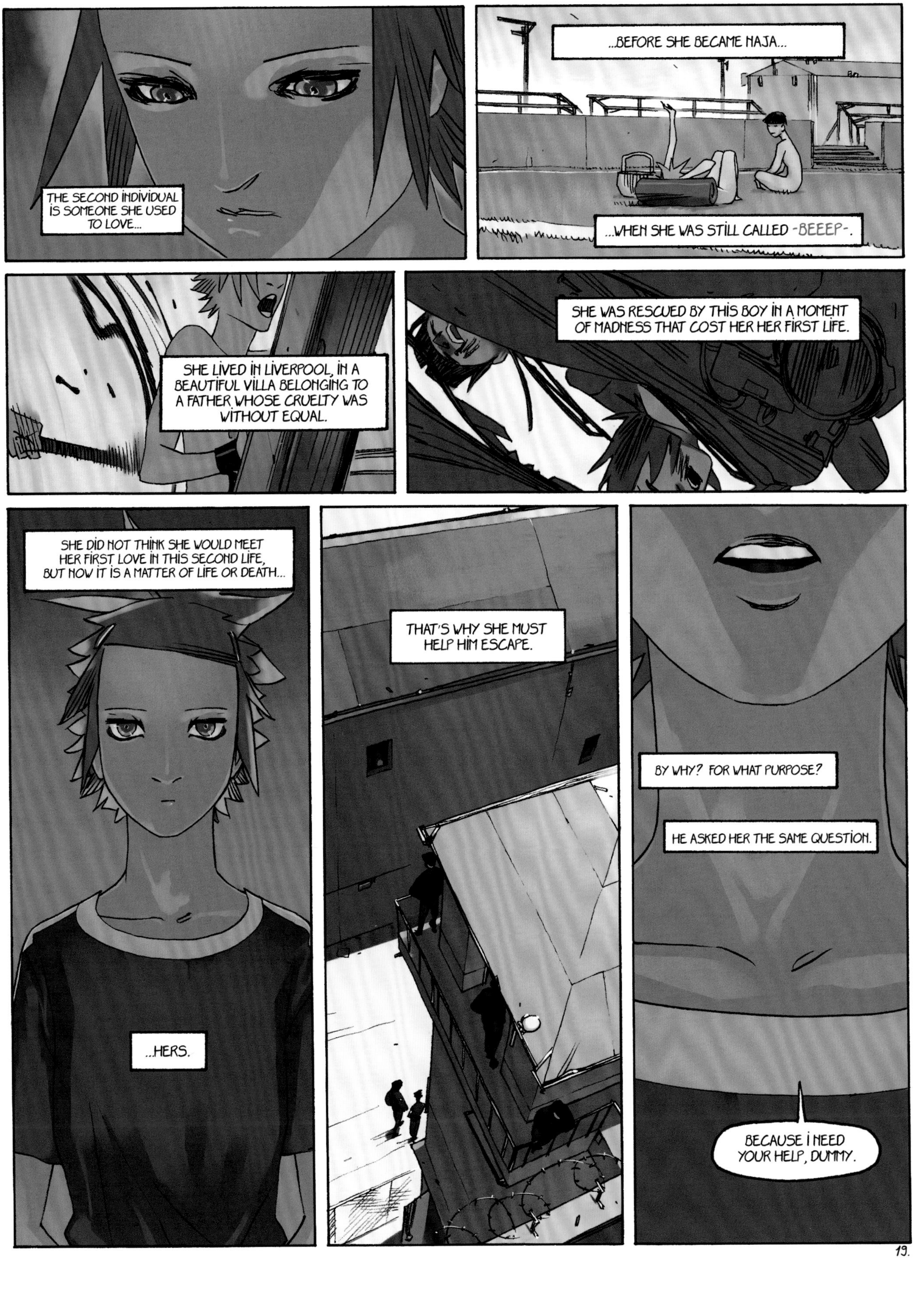
THE SECOND INDIVIDUAL IS SOMEONE SHE USED TO LOVE...
...BEFORE SHE BECAME NAJA...
...WHEN SHE WAS STILL CALLED -BEEEP-.
SHE LIVED IN LIVERPOOL, IN A BEAUTIFUL VILLA BELONGING TO A FATHER WHOSE CRUELTY WAS WITHOUT EQUAL.
SHE WAS RESCUED BY THIS BOY IN A MOMENT OF MADNESS THAT COST HER HER FIRST LIFE.
SHE DID NOT THINK SHE WOULD MEET HER FIRST LOVE IN THIS SECOND LIFE, BUT NOW IT IS A MATTER OF LIFE OR DEATH...
...HERS.
THAT'S WHY SHE MUST HELP HIM ESCAPE.
BY WHY? FOR WHAT PURPOSE?
HE ASKED HER THE SAME QUESTION.
BECAUSE I NEED YOUR HELP, DUMMY.

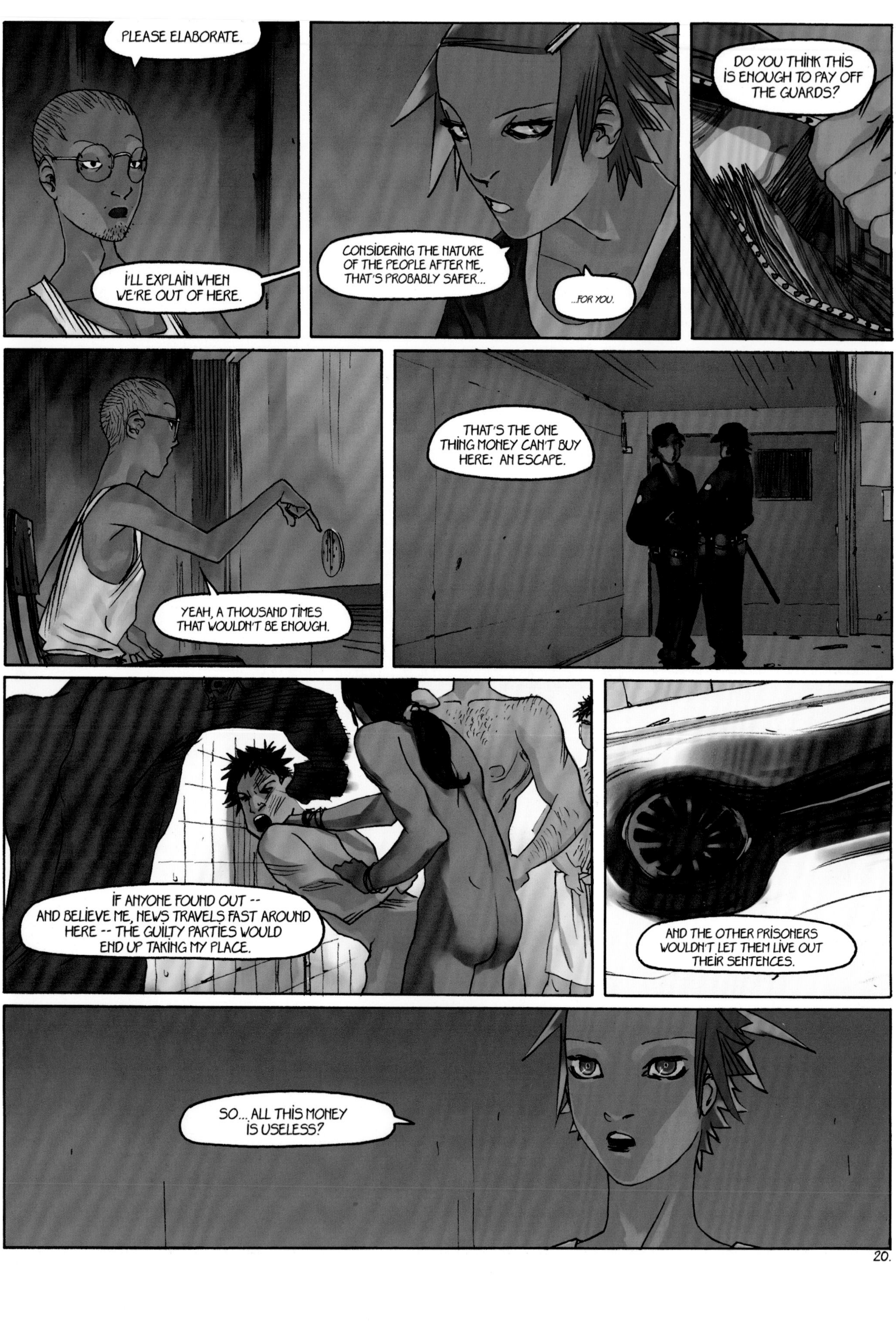

PLEASE ELABORATE.
I'LL EXPLAIN WHEN WE'RE OUT OF HERE.
CONSIDERING THE NATURE OF THE PEOPLE AFTER ME, THAT'S PROBABLY SAFER...
...FOR YOU.
DO YOU THINK THIS IS ENOUGH TO PAY OFF THE GUARDS?
YEAH, A THOUSAND TIMES THAT WOULDN'T BE ENOUGH.
THAT'S THE ONE THING MONEY CAN'T BUY HERE: AN ESCAPE.
IF ANYONE FOUND OUT -- AND BELIEVE ME, NEWS TRAVELS FAST AROUND HERE -- THE GUILTY PARTIES WOULD END UP TAKING MY PLACE.
AND THE OTHER PRISONERS WOULDN'T LET THEM LIVE OUT THEIR SENTENCES.
SO... ALL THIS MONEY IS USELESS?

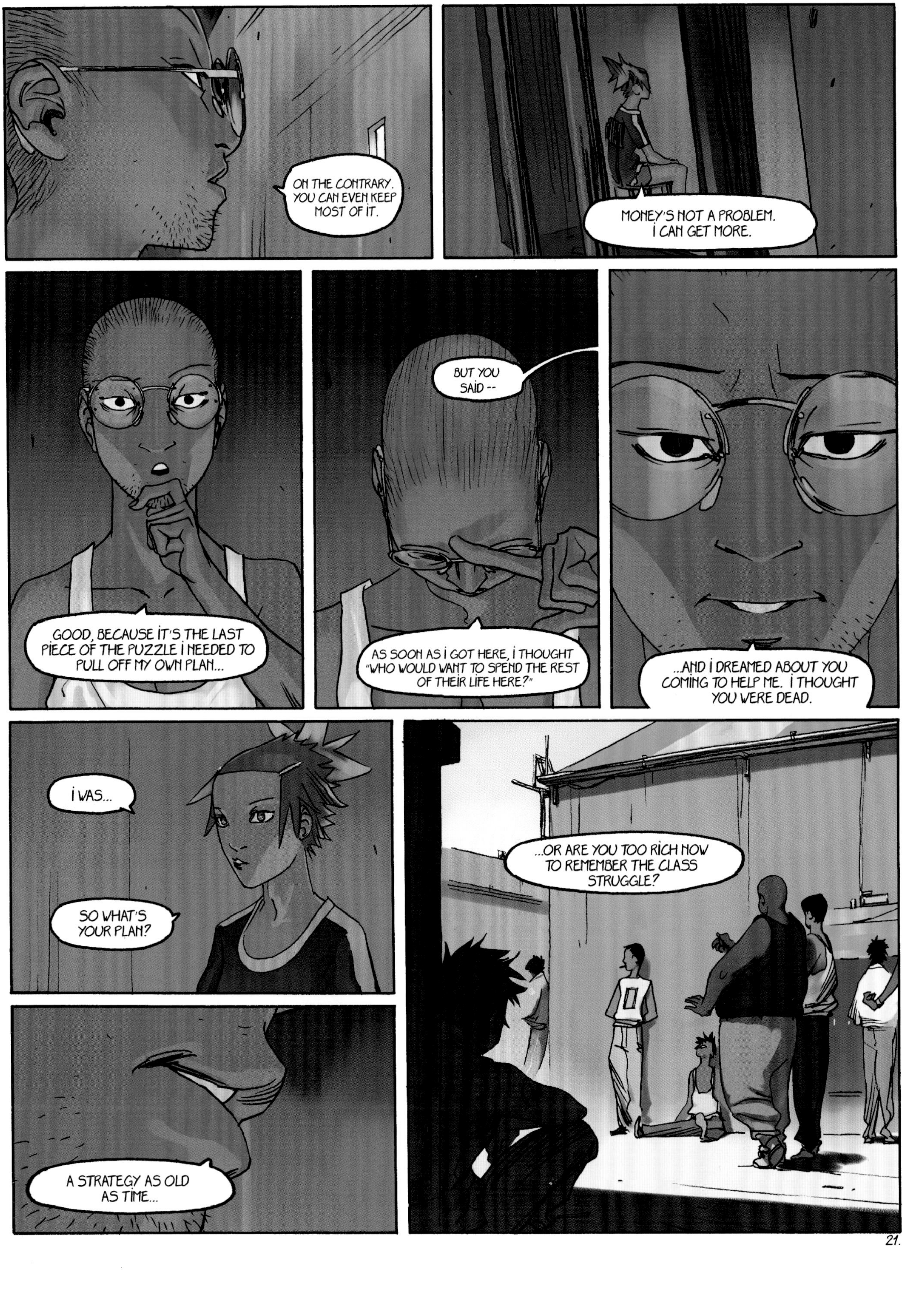
ON THE CONTRARY. YOU CAN EVEN KEEP MOST OF IT.
MONEY'S NOT A PROBLEM. I CAN GET MORE.
GOOD, BECAUSE IT'S THE LAST PIECE OF THE PUZZLE I NEEDED TO PULL OFF MY OWN PLAN...
BUT YOU SAID --
AS SOON AS I GOT HERE, I THOUGHT "WHO WOULD WANT TO SPEND THE REST OF THEIR LIFE HERE?"
...AND I DREAMED ABOUT YOU COMING TO HELP ME. I THOUGHT YOU WERE DEAD.
I WAS...
SO WHAT'S YOUR PLAN?
A STRATEGY AS OLD AS TIME...
...OR ARE YOU TOO RICH NOW TO REMEMBER THE CLASS STRUGGLE?

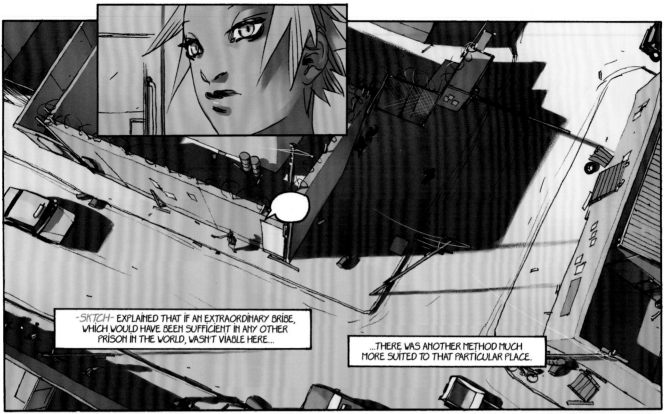

-SKTCH- EXPLAINED THAT IF AN EXTRAORDINARY BRIBE, WHICH WOULD HAVE BEEN SUFFICIENT IN ANY OTHER PRISON IN THE WORLD, WASN'T VIABLE HERE...
...THERE WAS ANOTHER METHOD MUCH MORE SUITED TO THAT PARTICULAR PLACE.
HE TOLD HER THAT THE RIGHT-WING PARAMILITARY -- THE AUC (UNITED DEFENSE FORCES OF COLOMBIA)...
AUTODEFENSAS UNIDAS DE COLOMBIA
...AND THE LEFT-WING FARC (REVOLUTIONARY ARMED FORCES) HAD SEPARATE TURF WITHIN THE PRISON GROUNDS.
FARC-EP
THEY ARE BOTH SUPPORTED FINANCIALLY BY THEIR RESPECTIVE ORGANIZATIONS' WORK OUTSIDE THE PRISON WALLS...
...DRUGS...
...KIDNAPPING...
...LOOTING VILLAGES...
...THE LIST GOES ON AND ON.

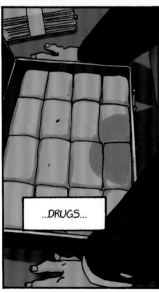

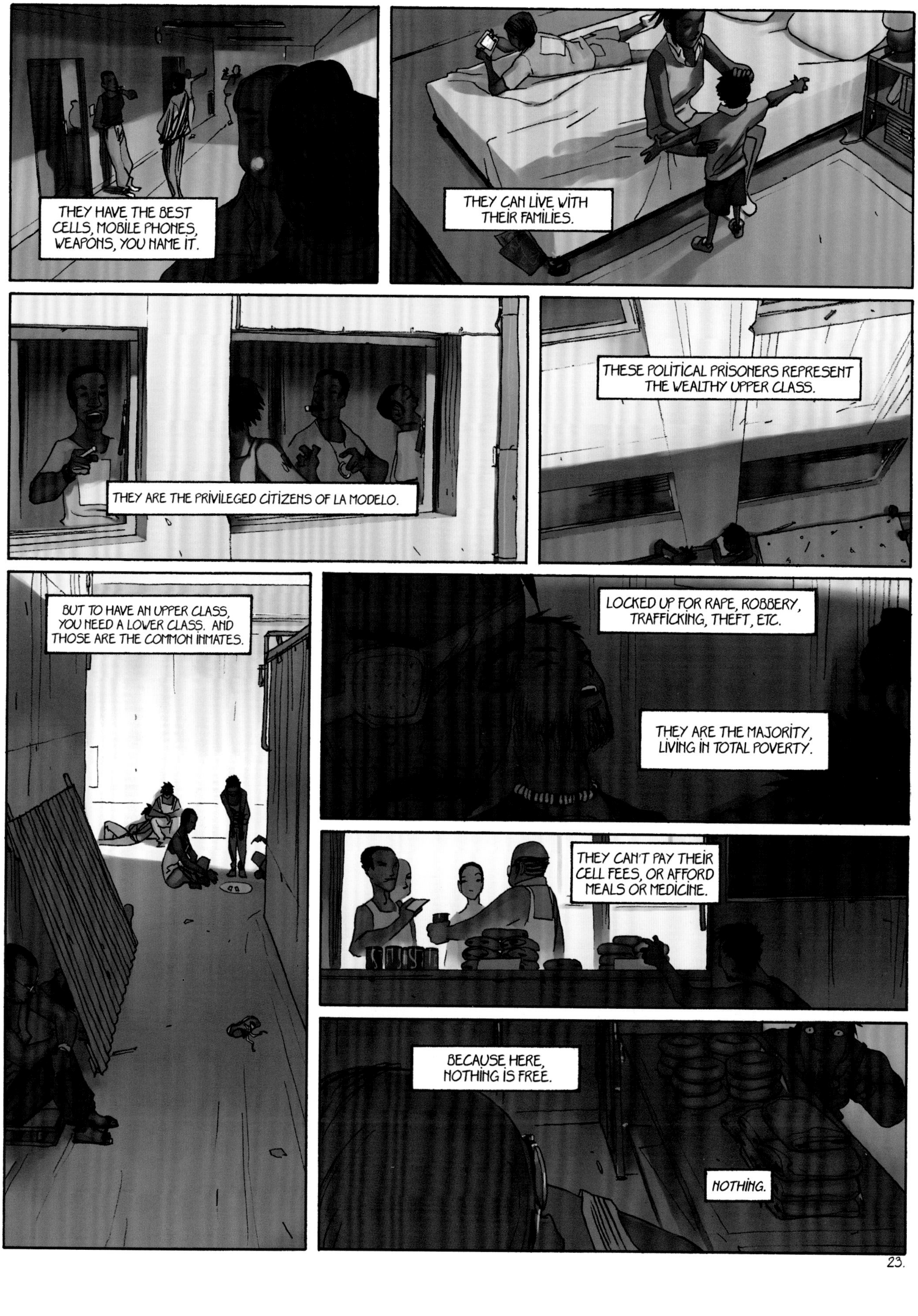
THEY HAVE THE BEST CELLS, MOBILE PHONES, WEAPONS, YOU NAME IT.
THEY CAN LIVE WITH THEIR FAMILIES.
THEY ARE THE PRIVILEGED CITIZENS OF LA MODELO.
THESE POLITICAL PRISONERS REPRESENT THE WEALTHY UPPER CLASS.
BUT TO HAVE AN UPPER CLASS, YOU NEED A LOWER CLASS. AND THOSE ARE THE COMMON INMATES.
LOCKED UP FOR RAPE, ROBBERY, TRAFFICKING, THEFT, ETC.
THEY ARE THE MAJORITY, LIVING IN TOTAL POVERTY.
THEY CAN'T PAY THEIR CELL FEES, OR AFFORD MEALS OR MEDICINE.
BECAUSE HERE, NOTHING IS FREE.
NOTHING.

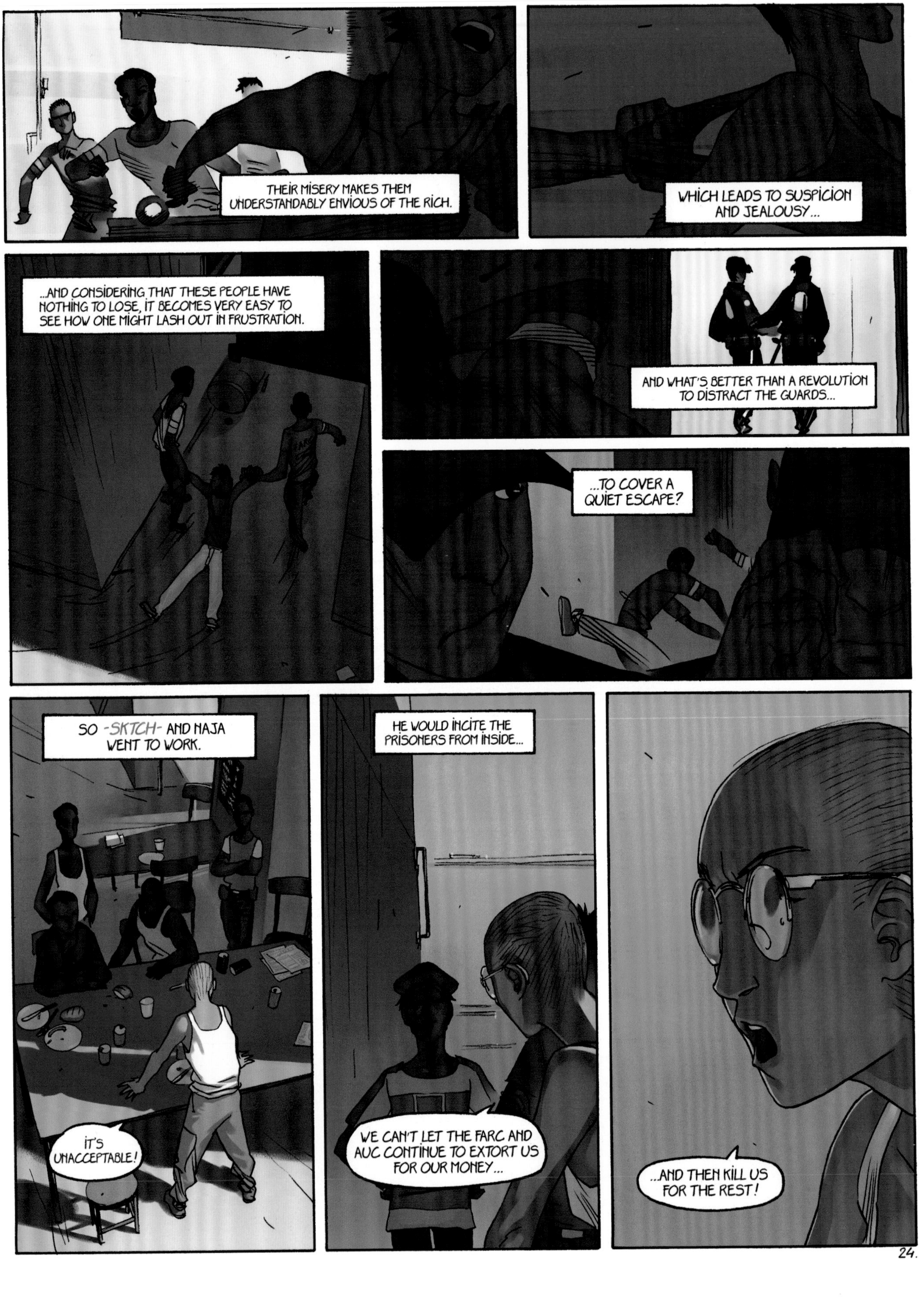
THEIR MISERY MAKES THEM UNDERSTANDABLY ENVIOUS OF THE RICH.
WHICH LEADS TO SUSPICION AND JEALOUSY...
...AND CONSIDERING THAT THESE PEOPLE HAVE NOTHING TO LOSE, IT BECOMES VERY EASY TO SEE HOW ONE MIGHT LASH OUT IN FRUSTRATION.
AND WHAT'S BETTER THAN A REVOLUTION TO DISTRACT THE GUARDS...
...TO COVER A QUIET ESCAPE?
SO -SKTCH- AND NAJA WENT TO WORK.
IT'S UNACCEPTABLE!
HE WOULD INCITE THE PRISONERS FROM INSIDE...
WE CAN'T LET THE FARC AND AUC CONTINUE TO EXTORT US FOR OUR MONEY...
...AND THEN KILL US FOR THE REST!

NAJA WOULD TAKE CARE OF THE MATERIALS ON THE OUTSIDE.

SHE FOUND A MARKET FOR WHAT SHE NEEDED, SOMETHING NEUTRAL.

SO THAT NEITHER FACTION WOULD KNOW WHAT SHE WAS UP TO.

IT WASN'T HARD, SINCE AROUND THERE IT WAS A JOB USUALLY DONE BY MEN.

MANY OF THEM WOULD TRY TO SCREW HER, BOTH LITERALLY AND FIGURATIVELY.

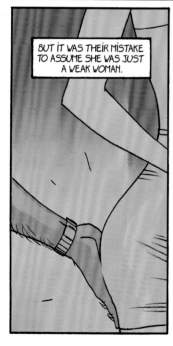

BUT IT WAS THEIR MISTAKE TO ASSUME SHE WAS JUST A WEAK WOMAN.

NAJA HATES MACHO MEN BECAUSE THEY CAN'T BELIEVE A WOMAN CAN BE STRONGER THAN THEM.

UNTIL SHE PROVES THEM WRONG.

I'M NOT LOOKING FOR A MAN, BUT SOME-THING THAT PUTS BIG HOLES IN THEM...

WHERE CAN A GIRL BUY A GUN AROUND HERE?

25.

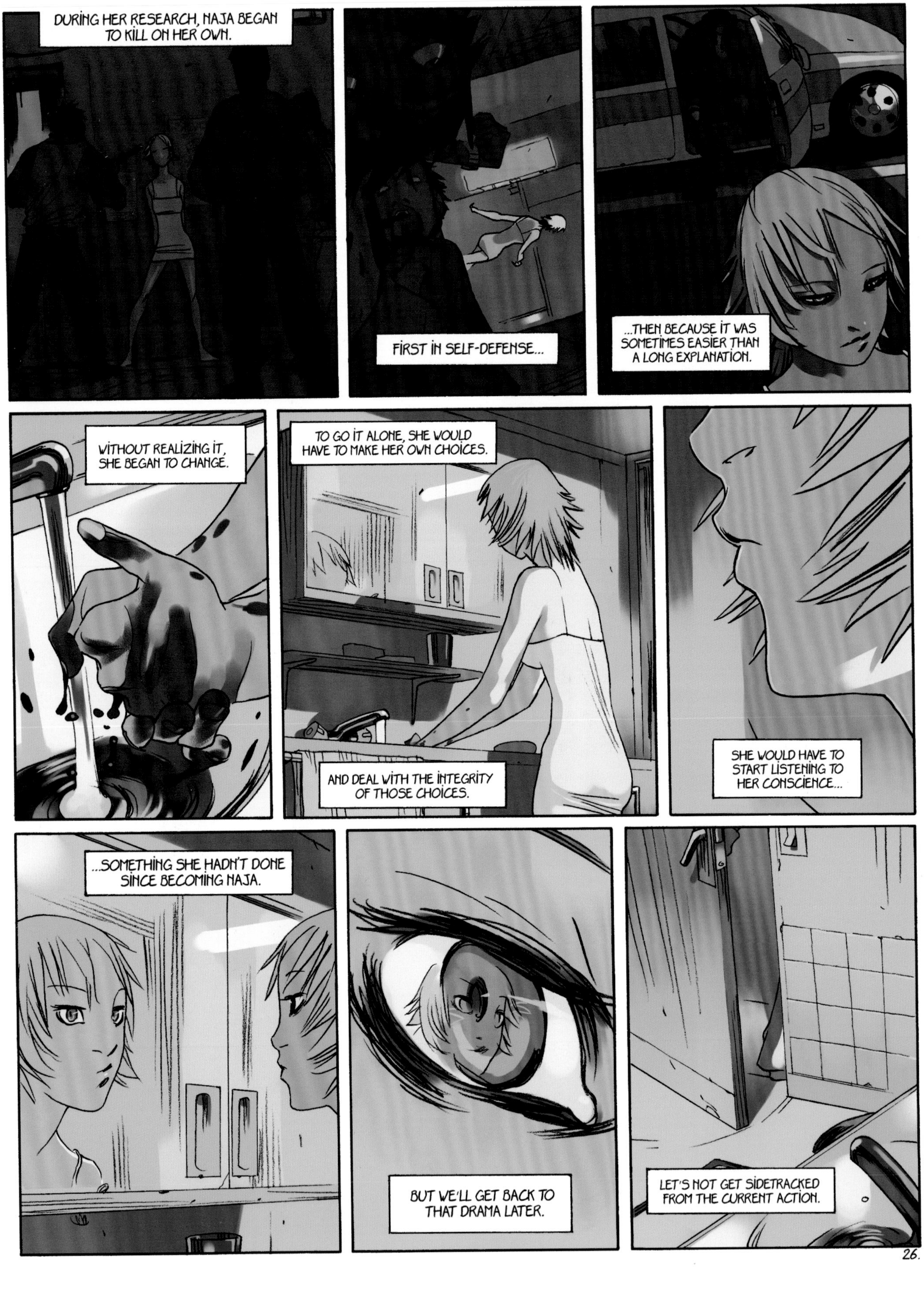
DURING HER RESEARCH, NAJA BEGAN TO KILL ON HER OWN.
FIRST IN SELF-DEFENSE...
...THEN BECAUSE IT WAS SOMETIMES EASIER THAN A LONG EXPLANATION.
WITHOUT REALIZING IT, SHE BEGAN TO CHANGE.
TO GO IT ALONE, SHE WOULD HAVE TO MAKE HER OWN CHOICES.
AND DEAL WITH THE INTEGRITY OF THOSE CHOICES.
SHE WOULD HAVE TO START LISTENING TO HER CONSCIENCE...
...SOMETHING SHE HADN'T DONE SINCE BECOMING NAJA.
BUT WE'LL GET BACK TO THAT DRAMA LATER.
LET'S NOT GET SIDETRACKED FROM THE CURRENT ACTION.

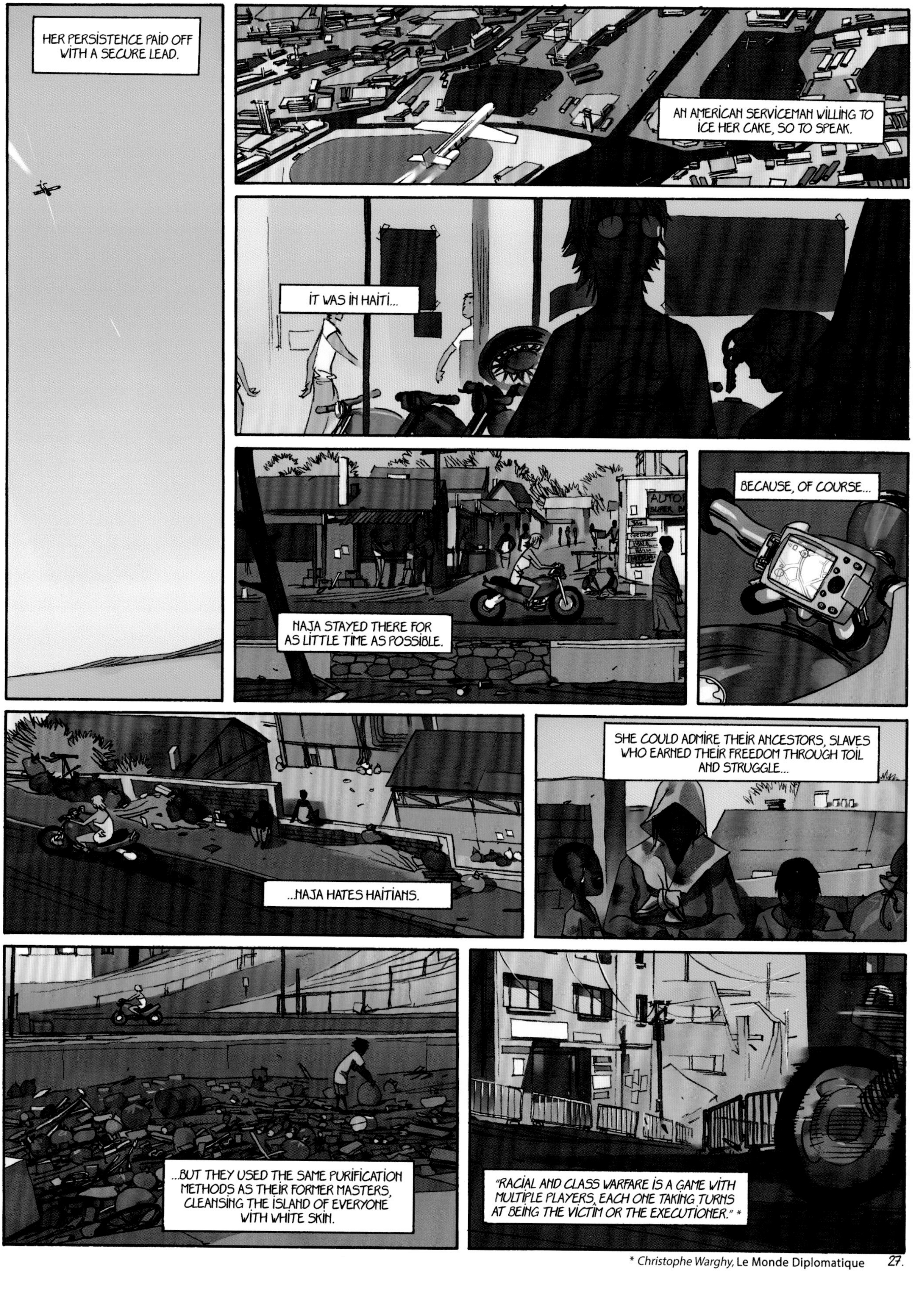
HER PERSISTENCE PAID OFF WITH A SECURE LEAD.
AN AMERICAN SERVICEMAN WILLING TO ICE HER CAKE, SO TO SPEAK.
IT WAS IN HAITI...
NAJA STAYED THERE FOR AS LITTLE TIME AS POSSIBLE.
BECAUSE, OF COURSE...
..NAJA HATES HAITIANS.
SHE COULD ADMIRE THEIR ANCESTORS, SLAVES WHO EARNED THEIR FREEDOM THROUGH TOIL AND STRUGGLE...
...BUT THEY USED THE SAME PURIFICATION METHODS AS THEIR FORMER MASTERS, CLEANSING THE ISLAND OF EVERYONE WITH WHITE SKIN.
"RACIAL AND CLASS WARFARE IS A GAME WITH MULTIPLE PLAYERS, EACH ONE TAKING TURNS AT BEING THE VICTIM OR THE EXECUTIONER." *

* *Christophe Warghy,* Le Monde Diplomatique

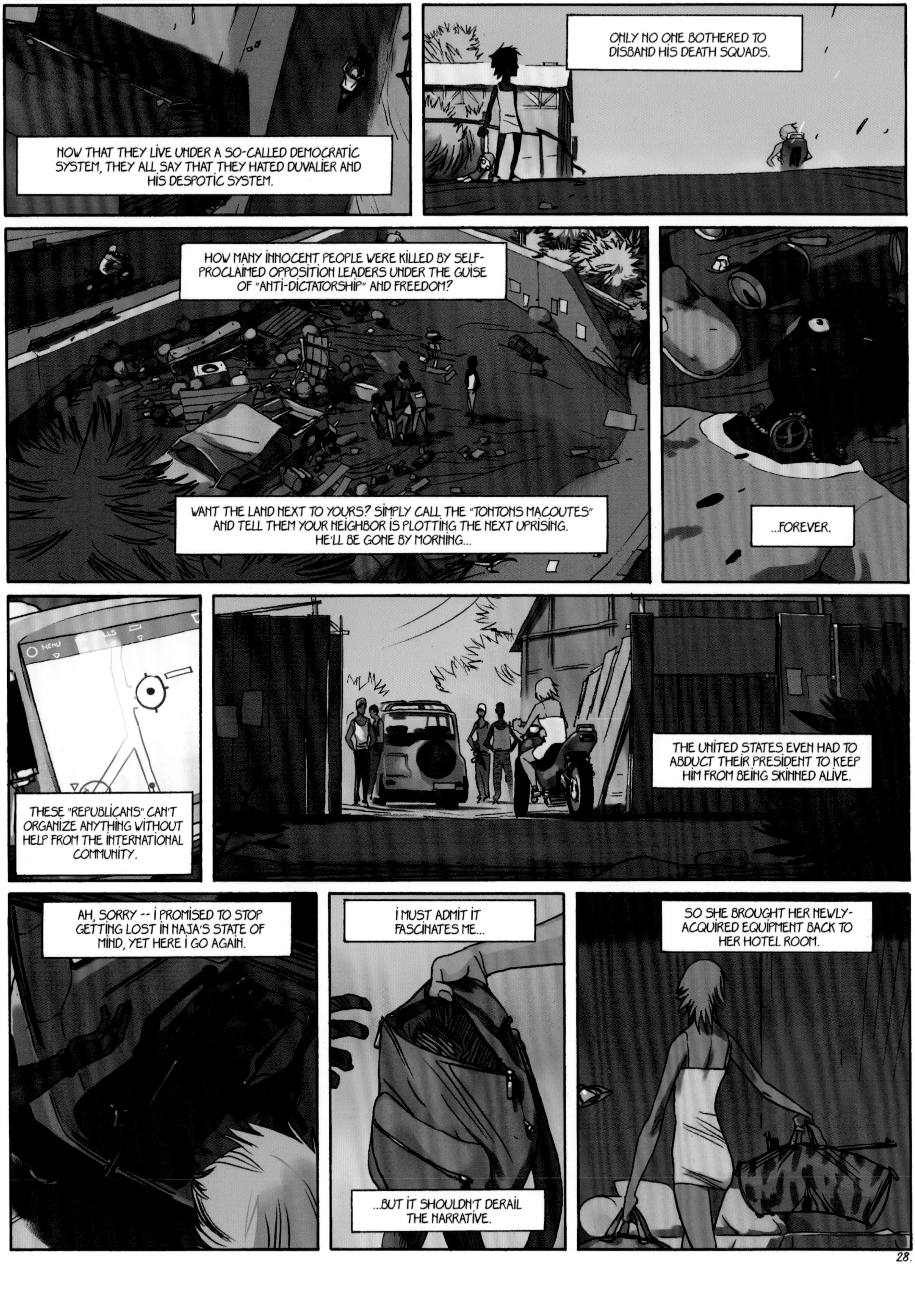

NOW THAT THEY LIVE UNDER A SO-CALLED DEMOCRATIC SYSTEM, THEY ALL SAY THAT THEY HATED DUVALIER AND HIS DESPOTIC SYSTEM.
ONLY NO ONE BOTHERED TO DISBAND HIS DEATH SQUADS.
HOW MANY INNOCENT PEOPLE WERE KILLED BY SELF-PROCLAIMED OPPOSITION LEADERS UNDER THE GUISE OF "ANTI-DICTATORSHIP" AND FREEDOM?
WANT THE LAND NEXT TO YOURS? SIMPLY CALL THE "TONTONS MACOUTES" AND TELL THEM YOUR NEIGHBOR IS PLOTTING THE NEXT UPRISING. HE'LL BE GONE BY MORNING...
...FOREVER.
MENU
THESE "REPUBLICANS" CAN'T ORGANIZE ANYTHING WITHOUT HELP FROM THE INTERNATIONAL COMMUNITY.
THE UNITED STATES EVEN HAD TO ABDUCT THEIR PRESIDENT TO KEEP HIM FROM BEING SKINNED ALIVE.
AH, SORRY -- I PROMISED TO STOP GETTING LOST IN NAJA'S STATE OF MIND, YET HERE I GO AGAIN.
I MUST ADMIT IT FASCINATES ME...
...BUT IT SHOULDN'T DERAIL THE NARRATIVE.
SO SHE BROUGHT HER NEWLY-ACQUIRED EQUIPMENT BACK TO HER HOTEL ROOM.

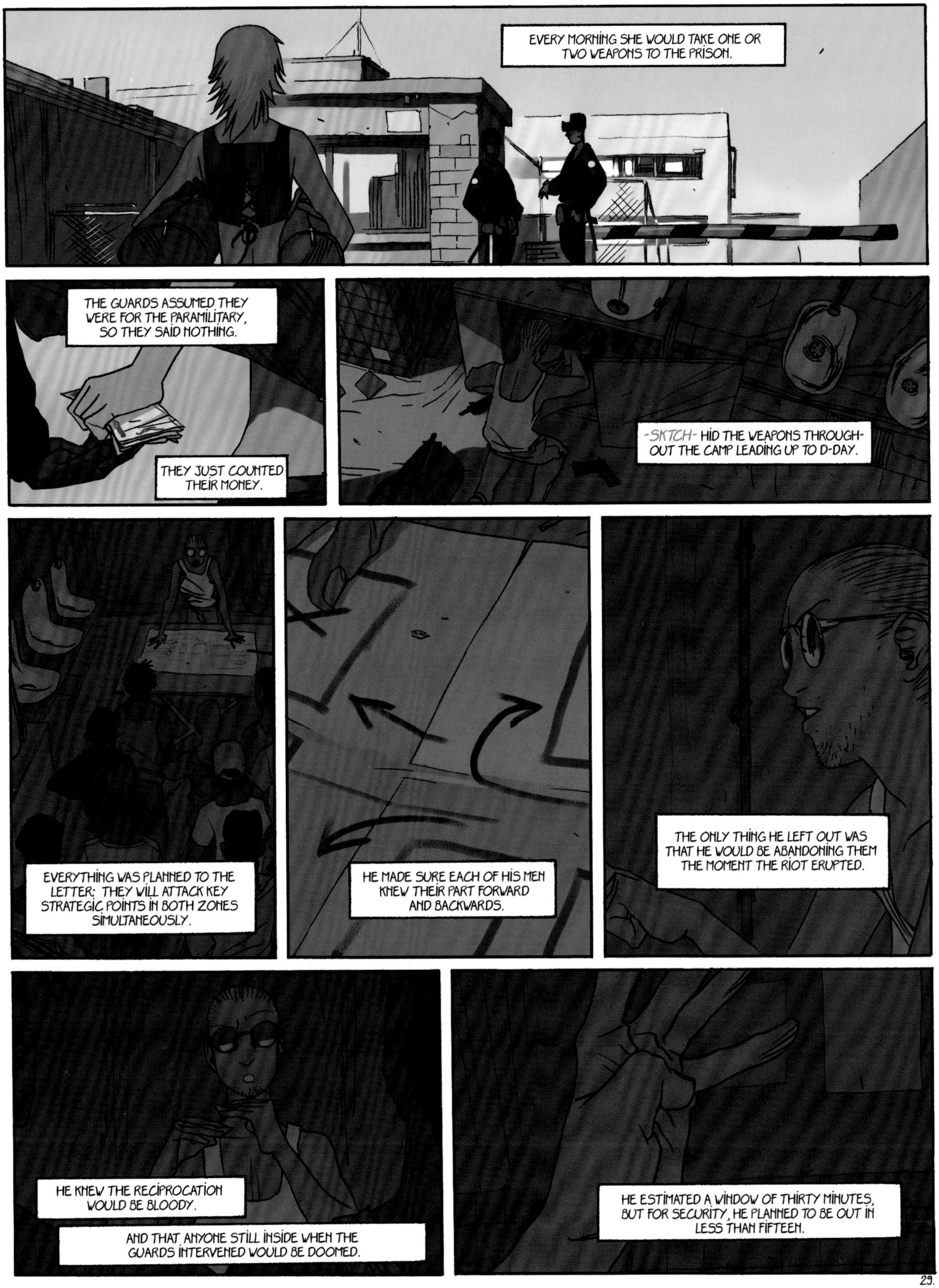

EVERY MORNING SHE WOULD TAKE ONE OR TWO WEAPONS TO THE PRISON.
THE GUARDS ASSUMED THEY WERE FOR THE PARAMILITARY, SO THEY SAID NOTHING.
THEY JUST COUNTED THEIR MONEY.
-SKTCH- HID THE WEAPONS THROUGH-OUT THE CAMP LEADING UP TO D-DAY.
EVERYTHING WAS PLANNED TO THE LETTER: THEY WILL ATTACK KEY STRATEGIC POINTS IN BOTH ZONES SIMULTANEOUSLY.
HE MADE SURE EACH OF HIS MEN KNEW THEIR PART FORWARD AND BACKWARDS.
THE ONLY THING HE LEFT OUT WAS THAT HE WOULD BE ABANDONING THEM THE MOMENT THE RIOT ERUPTED.
HE KNEW THE RECIPROCATION WOULD BE BLOODY.
AND THAT ANYONE STILL INSIDE WHEN THE GUARDS INTERVENED WOULD BE DOOMED.
HE ESTIMATED A WINDOW OF THIRTY MINUTES, BUT FOR SECURITY, HE PLANNED TO BE OUT IN LESS THAN FIFTEEN.

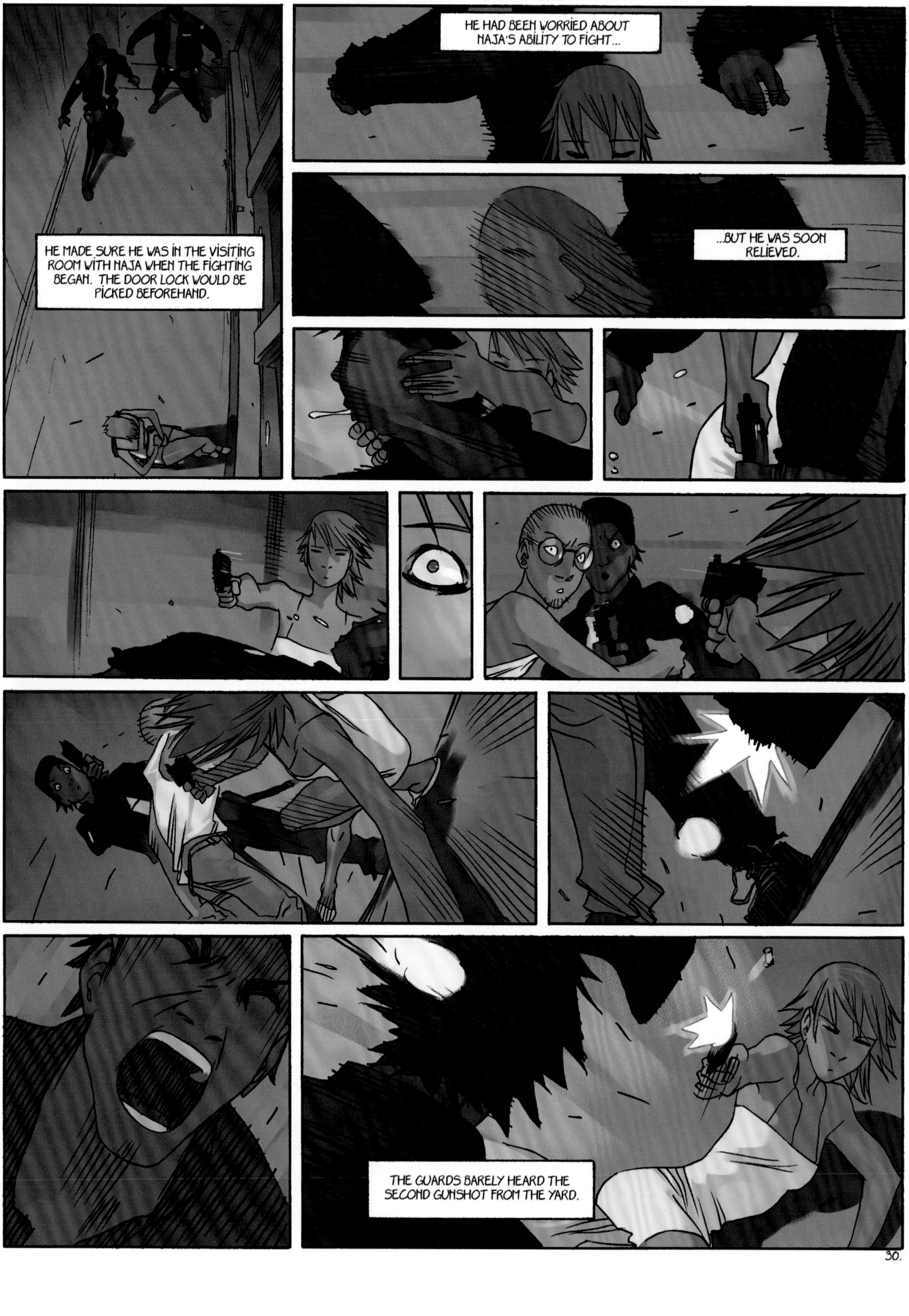
HE MADE SURE HE WAS IN THE VISITING ROOM WITH NAJA WHEN THE FIGHTING BEGAN. THE DOOR LOCK WOULD BE PICKED BEFOREHAND.
HE HAD BEEN WORRIED ABOUT NAJA'S ABILITY TO FIGHT...
...BUT HE WAS SOON RELIEVED.
THE GUARDS BARELY HEARD THE SECOND GUNSHOT FROM THE YARD.

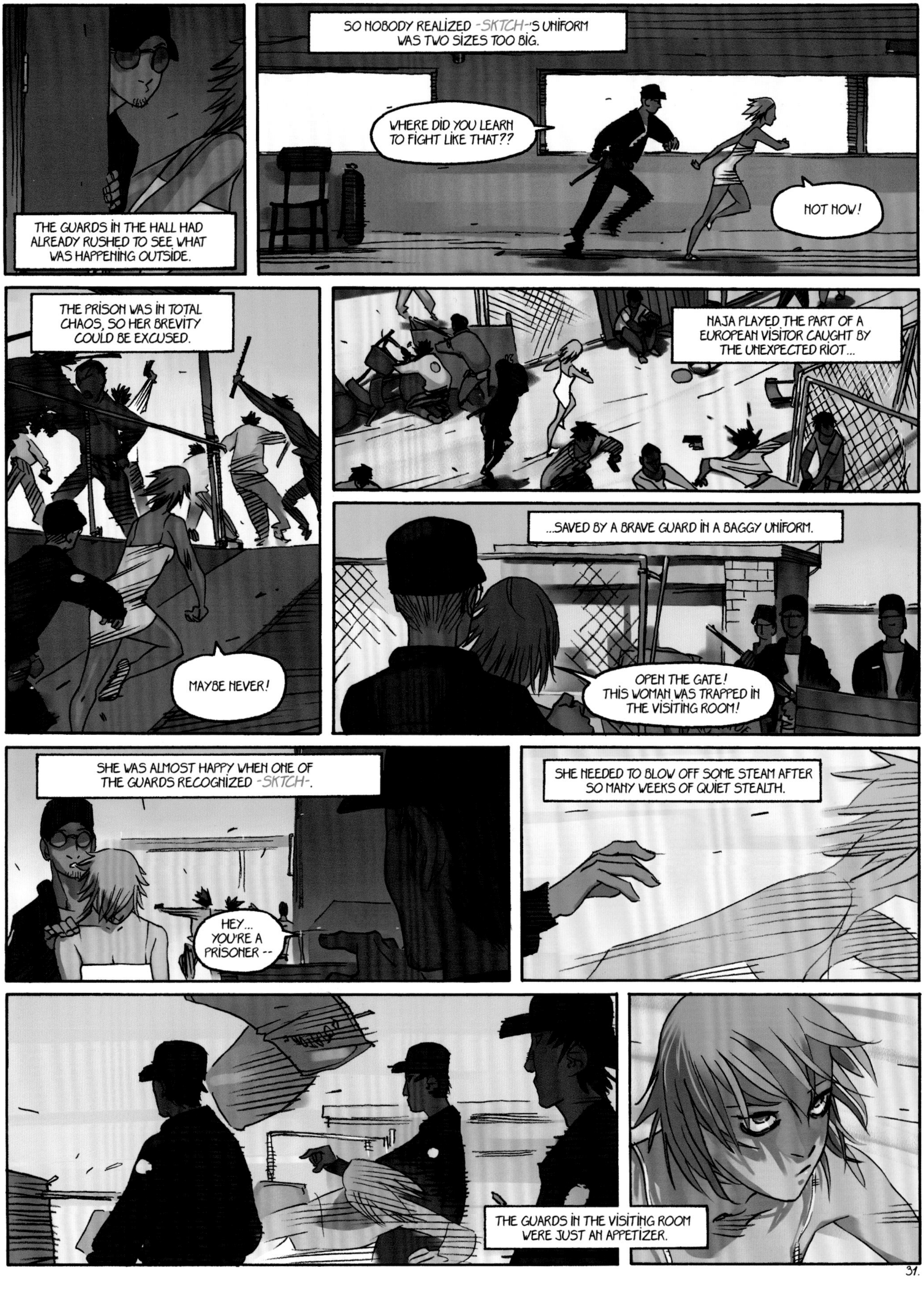

THE GUARDS IN THE HALL HAD ALREADY RUSHED TO SEE WHAT WAS HAPPENING OUTSIDE.
SO NOBODY REALIZED -SKTCH-'S UNIFORM WAS TWO SIZES TOO BIG.
WHERE DID YOU LEARN TO FIGHT LIKE THAT??
NOT NOW!
THE PRISON WAS IN TOTAL CHAOS, SO HER BREVITY COULD BE EXCUSED.
MAYBE NEVER!
NAJA PLAYED THE PART OF A EUROPEAN VISITOR CAUGHT BY THE UNEXPECTED RIOT...
...SAVED BY A BRAVE GUARD IN A BAGGY UNIFORM.
OPEN THE GATE! THIS WOMAN WAS TRAPPED IN THE VISITING ROOM!
SHE WAS ALMOST HAPPY WHEN ONE OF THE GUARDS RECOGNIZED -SKTCH-.
HEY... YOU'RE A PRISONER --
SHE NEEDED TO BLOW OFF SOME STEAM AFTER SO MANY WEEKS OF QUIET STEALTH.
THE GUARDS IN THE VISITING ROOM WERE JUST AN APPETIZER.

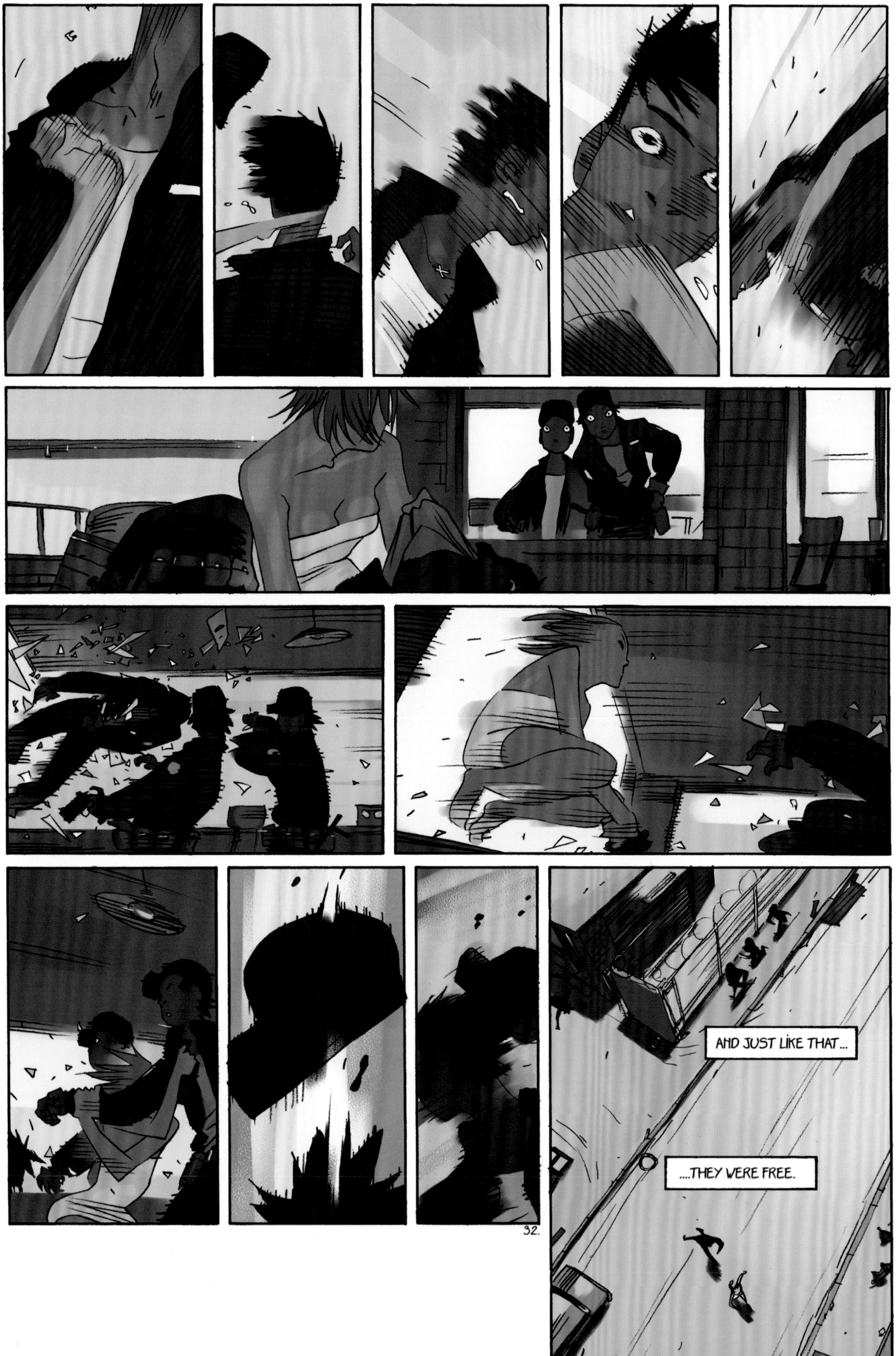
AND JUST LIKE THAT...
....THEY WERE FREE.

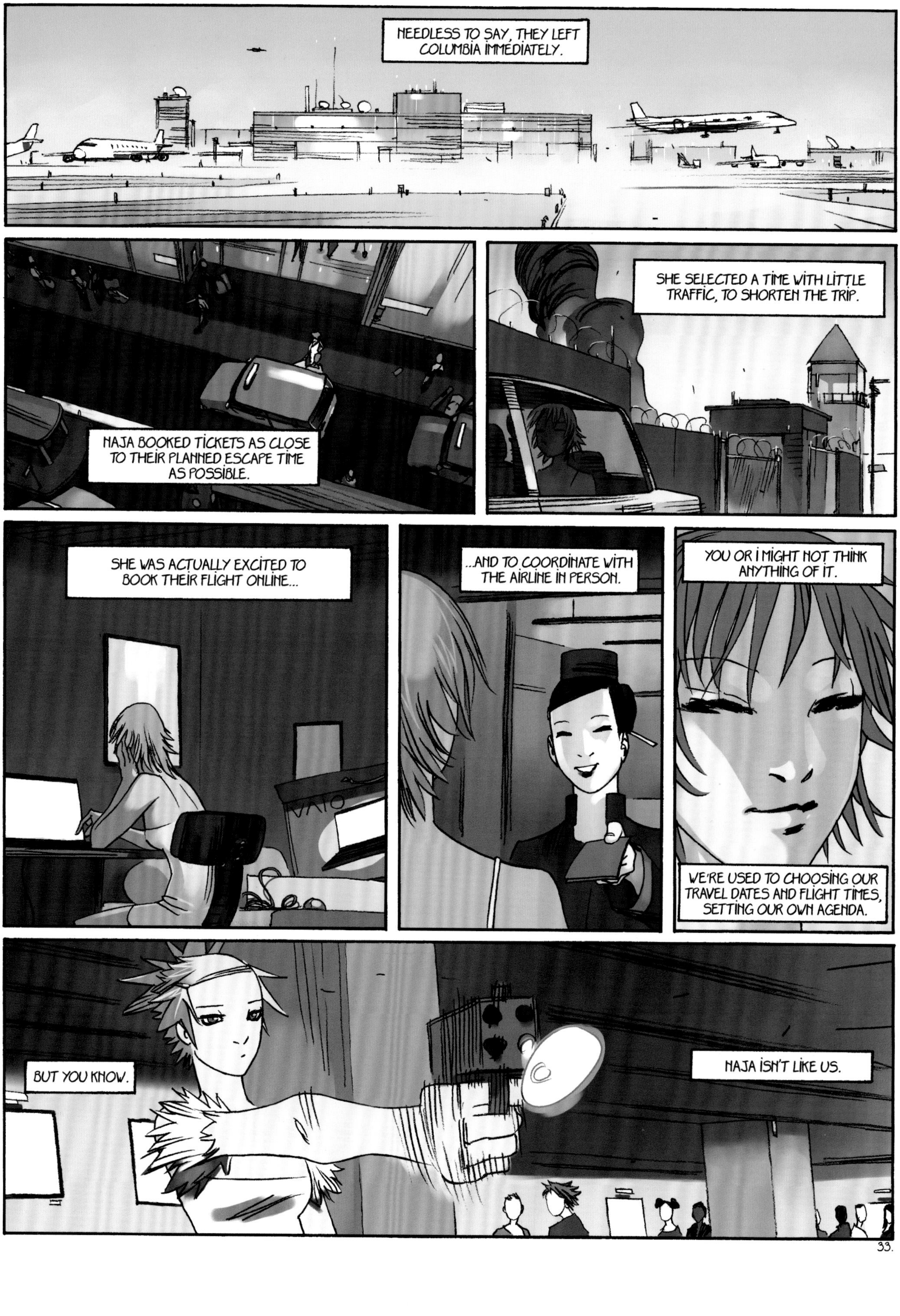
NEEDLESS TO SAY, THEY LEFT COLUMBIA IMMEDIATELY.
NAJA BOOKED TICKETS AS CLOSE TO THEIR PLANNED ESCAPE TIME AS POSSIBLE.
SHE SELECTED A TIME WITH LITTLE TRAFFIC, TO SHORTEN THE TRIP.
SHE WAS ACTUALLY EXCITED TO BOOK THEIR FLIGHT ONLINE...
VAIO
...AND TO COORDINATE WITH THE AIRLINE IN PERSON.
YOU OR I MIGHT NOT THINK ANYTHING OF IT.
WE'RE USED TO CHOOSING OUR TRAVEL DATES AND FLIGHT TIMES, SETTING OUR OWN AGENDA.
BUT YOU KNOW.
NAJA ISN'T LIKE US.

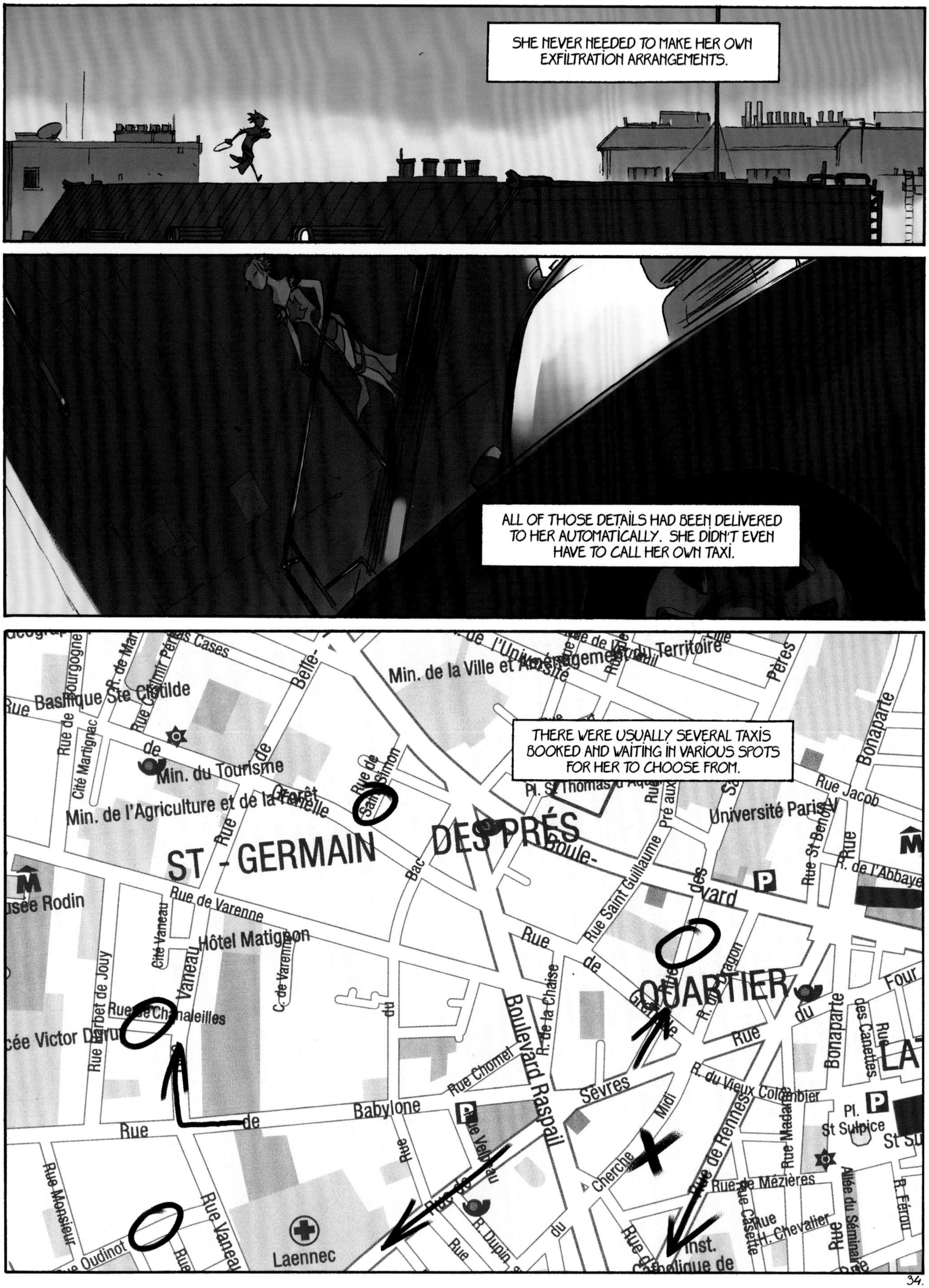
SHE NEVER NEEDED TO MAKE HER OWN EXFILTRATION ARRANGEMENTS.
ALL OF THOSE DETAILS HAD BEEN DELIVERED TO HER AUTOMATICALLY. SHE DIDN'T EVEN HAVE TO CALL HER OWN TAXI.
THERE WERE USUALLY SEVERAL TAXIS BOOKED AND WAITING IN VARIOUS SPOTS FOR HER TO CHOOSE FROM.
ST - GERMAIN
DES PRÉS
QUARTIER
Min. de la Ville et
Min. du Tourisme
Min. de l'Agriculture et de la
Rue Basilique Ste Clotilde
Hôtel Matignon
Rue de Varenne
Boulevard Raspail
Rue de Rennes
Babylone
Sèvres
Université Paris V
Rue Jacob
R. de l'Abbaye
Rue Saint Guillaume
Rue Chomel
R. du Vieux Colombier
Pl. St Sulpice
Rue de Mézières
Laennec
Rue Vaneau
Rue Oudinot
Rue Monsieur
Cité Martignac
Cité Vaneau
Rue Barbet de Jouy
Boulevard
Rue du Four
Bonaparte
R. de la Chaise
Rue St Benoît
Rue Madame
R. Dupin
Rue des Canettes
Rue Cassette
Allée du Séminaire
R. Férou
Inst.

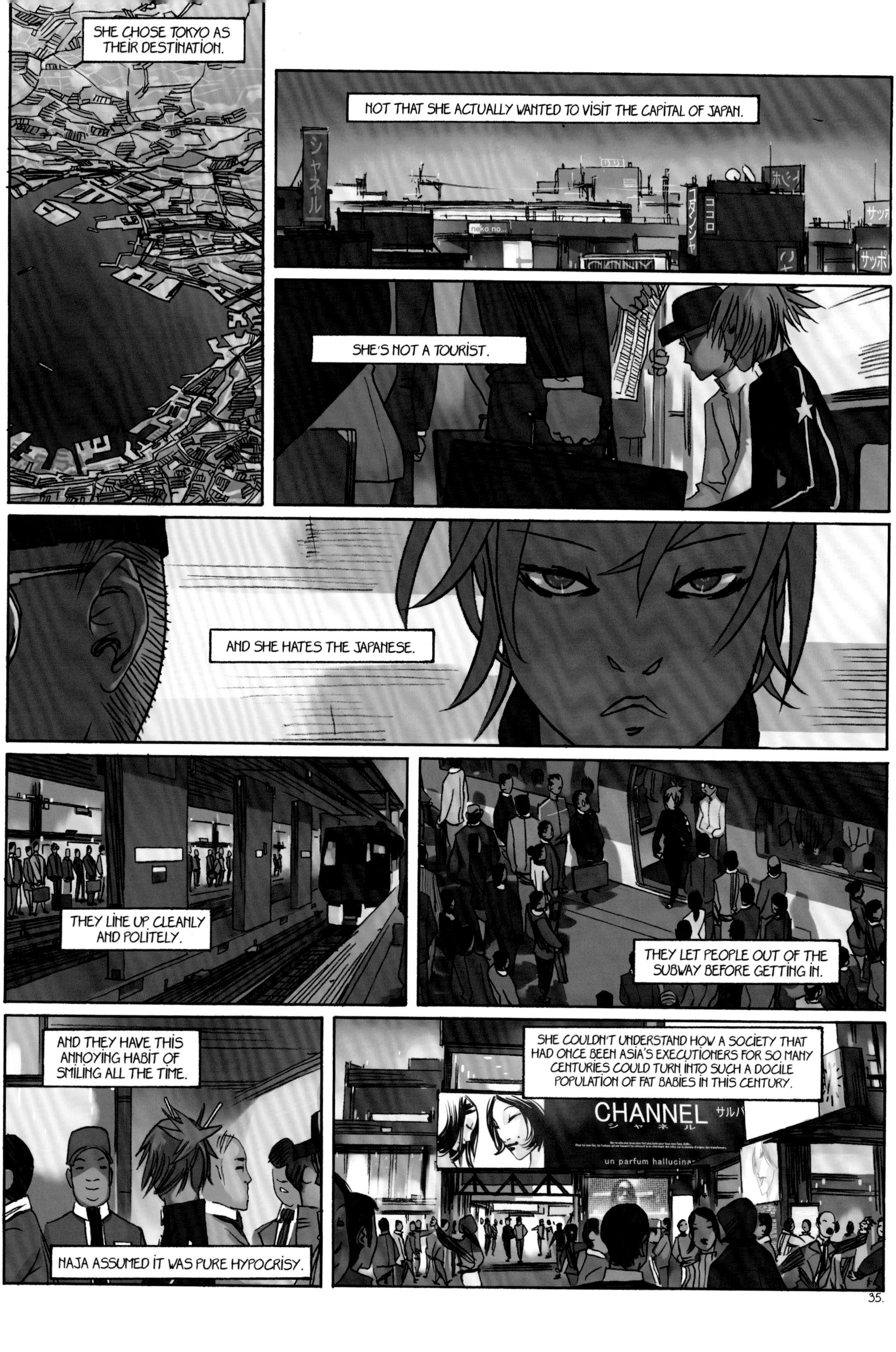
SHE CHOSE TOKYO AS THEIR DESTINATION.
NOT THAT SHE ACTUALLY WANTED TO VISIT THE CAPITAL OF JAPAN.
シャネル
ココロ
SHE'S NOT A TOURIST.
AND SHE HATES THE JAPANESE.
THEY LINE UP CLEANLY AND POLITELY.
THEY LET PEOPLE OUT OF THE SUBWAY BEFORE GETTING IN.
AND THEY HAVE THIS ANNOYING HABIT OF SMILING ALL THE TIME.
NAJA ASSUMED IT WAS PURE HYPOCRISY.
SHE COULDN'T UNDERSTAND HOW A SOCIETY THAT HAD ONCE BEEN ASIA'S EXECUTIONERS FOR SO MANY CENTURIES COULD TURN INTO SUCH A DOCILE POPULATION OF FAT BABIES IN THIS CENTURY.
CHANNEL
シャネル

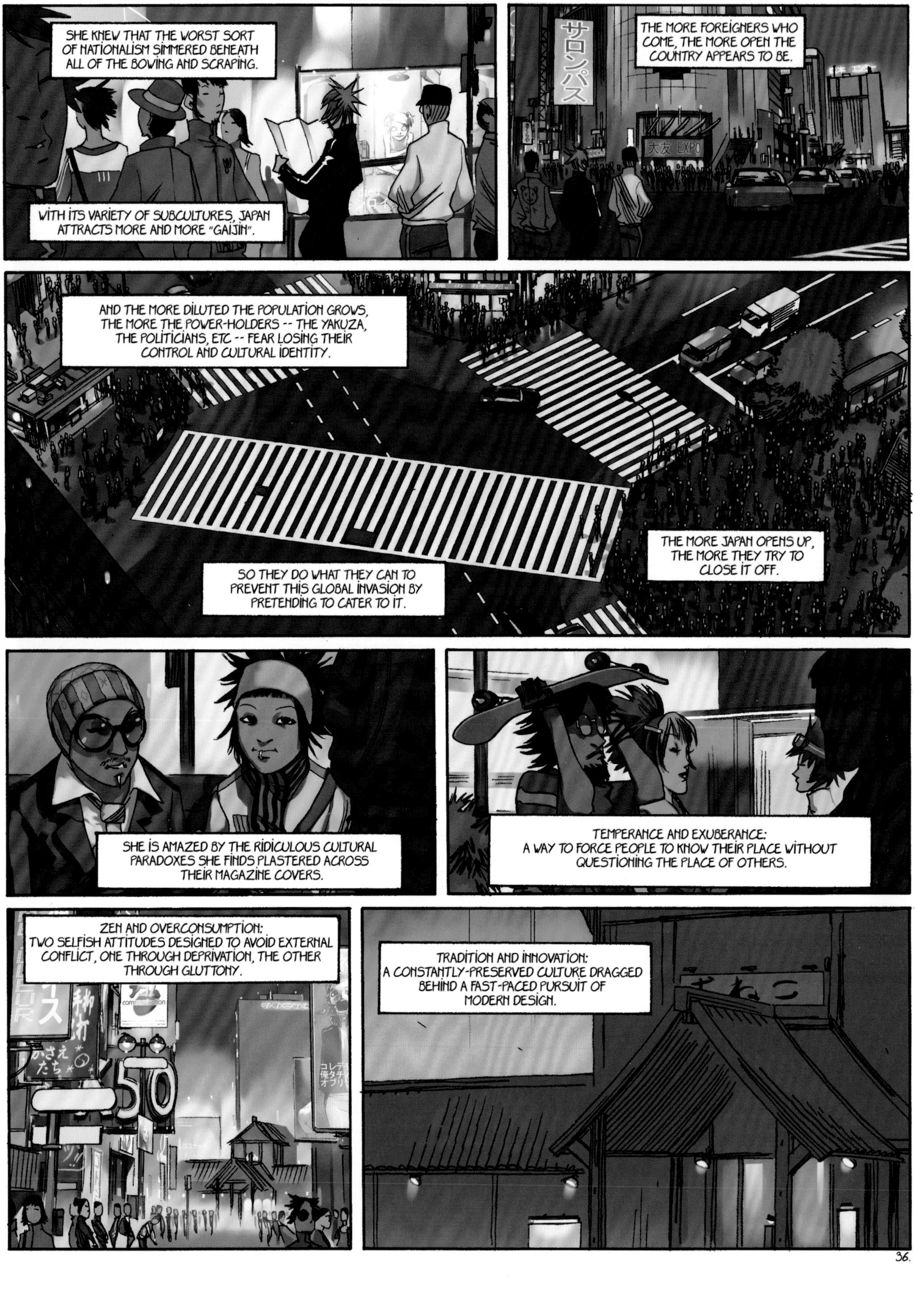
SHE KNEW THAT THE WORST SORT OF NATIONALISM SIMMERED BENEATH ALL OF THE BOWING AND SCRAPING.
WITH ITS VARIETY OF SUBCULTURES, JAPAN ATTRACTS MORE AND MORE "GAIJIN".
THE MORE FOREIGNERS WHO COME, THE MORE OPEN THE COUNTRY APPEARS TO BE.
AND THE MORE DILUTED THE POPULATION GROWS, THE MORE THE POWER-HOLDERS -- THE YAKUZA, THE POLITICIANS, ETC -- FEAR LOSING THEIR CONTROL AND CULTURAL IDENTITY.
SO THEY DO WHAT THEY CAN TO PREVENT THIS GLOBAL INVASION BY PRETENDING TO CATER TO IT.
THE MORE JAPAN OPENS UP, THE MORE THEY TRY TO CLOSE IT OFF.
SHE IS AMAZED BY THE RIDICULOUS CULTURAL PARADOXES SHE FINDS PLASTERED ACROSS THEIR MAGAZINE COVERS.
TEMPERANCE AND EXUBERANCE: A WAY TO FORCE PEOPLE TO KNOW THEIR PLACE WITHOUT QUESTIONING THE PLACE OF OTHERS.
ZEN AND OVERCONSUMPTION: TWO SELFISH ATTITUDES DESIGNED TO AVOID EXTERNAL CONFLICT, ONE THROUGH DEPRIVATION, THE OTHER THROUGH GLUTTONY.
TRADITION AND INNOVATION: A CONSTANTLY-PRESERVED CULTURE DRAGGED BEHIND A FAST-PACED PURSUIT OF MODERN DESIGN.

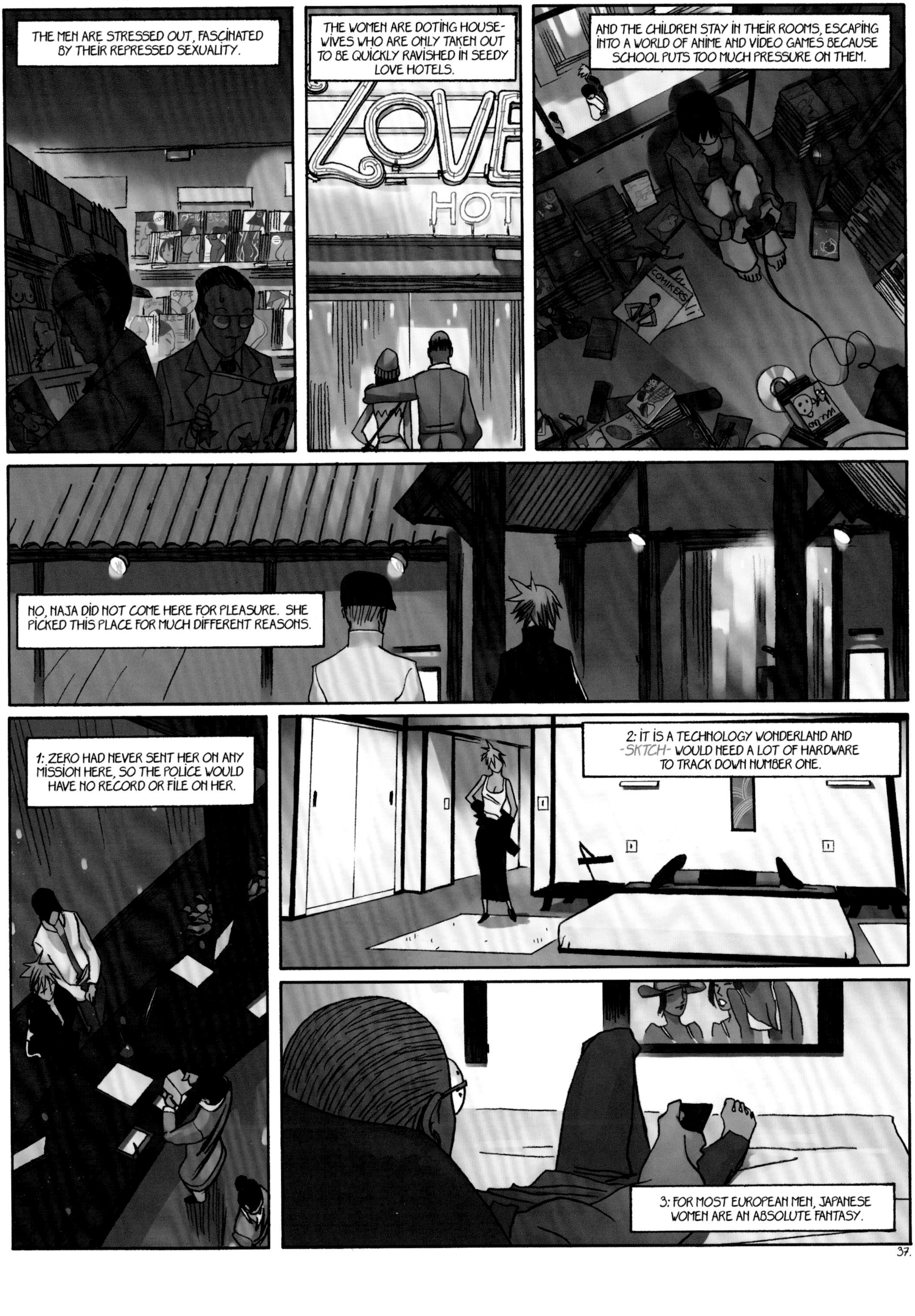
THE MEN ARE STRESSED OUT, FASCINATED BY THEIR REPRESSED SEXUALITY.
THE WOMEN ARE DOTING HOUSE-WIVES WHO ARE ONLY TAKEN OUT TO BE QUICKLY RAVISHED IN SEEDY LOVE HOTELS.
LOVE
HOT
AND THE CHILDREN STAY IN THEIR ROOMS, ESCAPING INTO A WORLD OF ANIME AND VIDEO GAMES BECAUSE SCHOOL PUTS TOO MUCH PRESSURE ON THEM.
COMIKERS
NO, NAJA DID NOT COME HERE FOR PLEASURE. SHE PICKED THIS PLACE FOR MUCH DIFFERENT REASONS.
1: ZERO HAD NEVER SENT HER ON ANY MISSION HERE, SO THE POLICE WOULD HAVE NO RECORD OR FILE ON HER.
2: IT IS A TECHNOLOGY WONDERLAND AND -SKTCH- WOULD NEED A LOT OF HARDWARE TO TRACK DOWN NUMBER ONE.
3: FOR MOST EUROPEAN MEN, JAPANESE WOMEN ARE AN ABSOLUTE FANTASY.

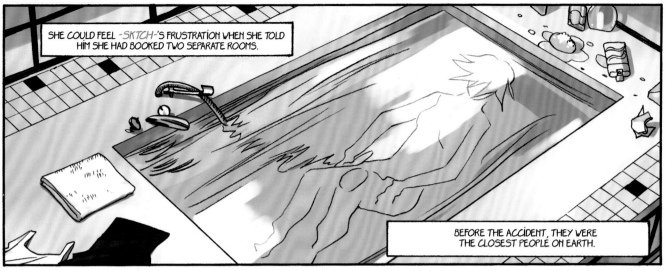

SHE COULD FEEL -*SKTCH*-'S FRUSTRATION WHEN SHE TOLD HIM SHE HAD BOOKED TWO SEPARATE ROOMS.

BEFORE THE ACCIDENT, THEY WERE THE CLOSEST PEOPLE ON EARTH.

BUT THE FACT THAT SHE HAD BEEN DECLARED DEAD LEFT HER WITH THE BELIEF THAT SHE COULD NEVER FEEL ANYTHING FOR ANYONE AGAIN.

AS IF SHE HAD BEEN EMPTIED, IN THE BLINK OF AN EYE, OF ANY ABILITY TO PRODUCE FEELINGS.

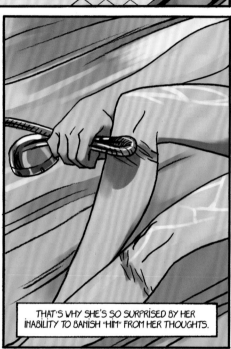

THAT'S WHY SHE'S SO SURPRISED BY HER INABILITY TO BANISH "HIM" FROM HER THOUGHTS.

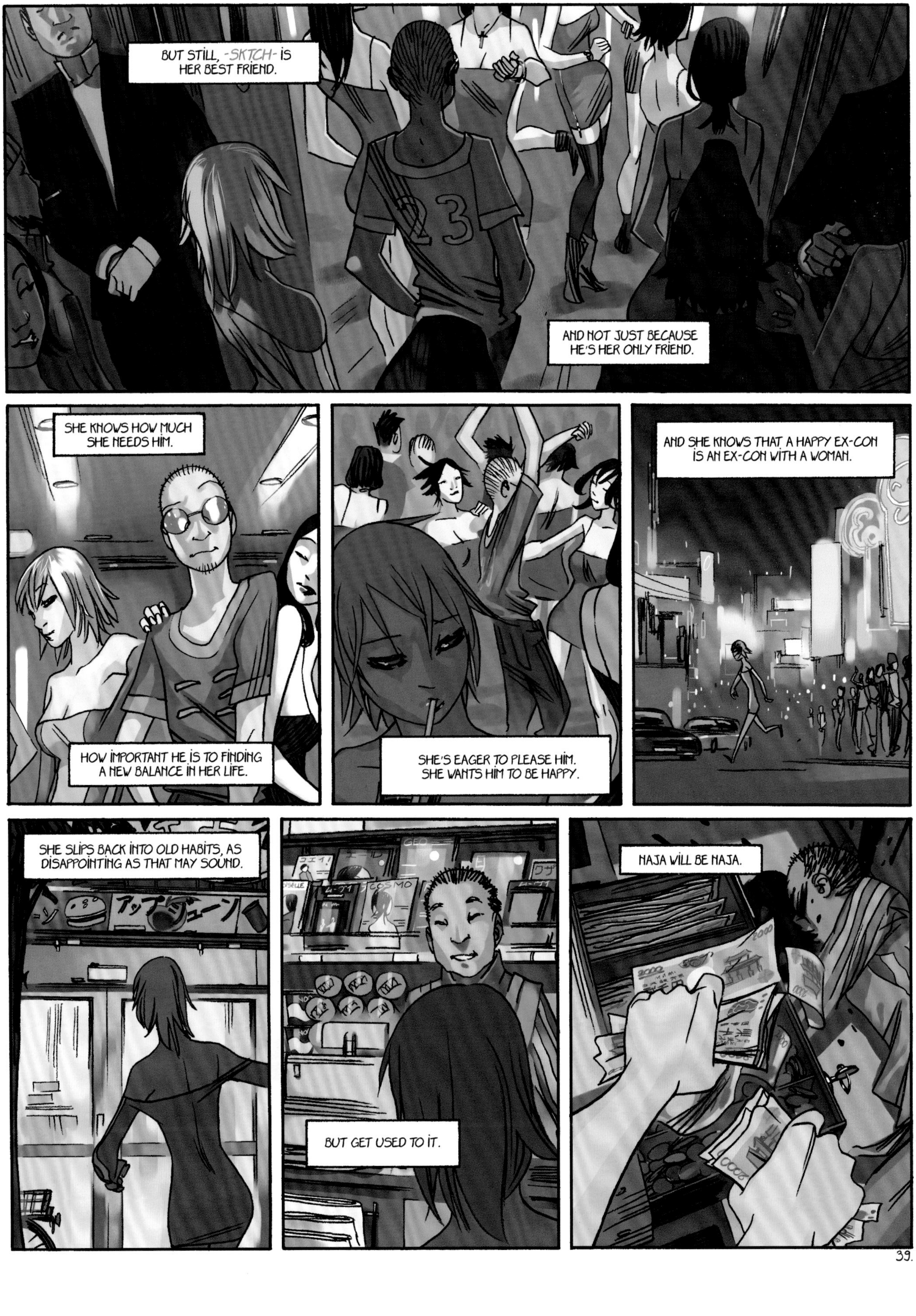
BUT STILL, -SKTCH- IS HER BEST FRIEND.
AND NOT JUST BECAUSE HE'S HER ONLY FRIEND.
SHE KNOWS HOW MUCH SHE NEEDS HIM.
HOW IMPORTANT HE IS TO FINDING A NEW BALANCE IN HER LIFE.
SHE'S EAGER TO PLEASE HIM. SHE WANTS HIM TO BE HAPPY.
AND SHE KNOWS THAT A HAPPY EX-CON IS AN EX-CON WITH A WOMAN.
SHE SLIPS BACK INTO OLD HABITS, AS DISAPPOINTING AS THAT MAY SOUND.
BUT GET USED TO IT.
NAJA WILL BE NAJA.

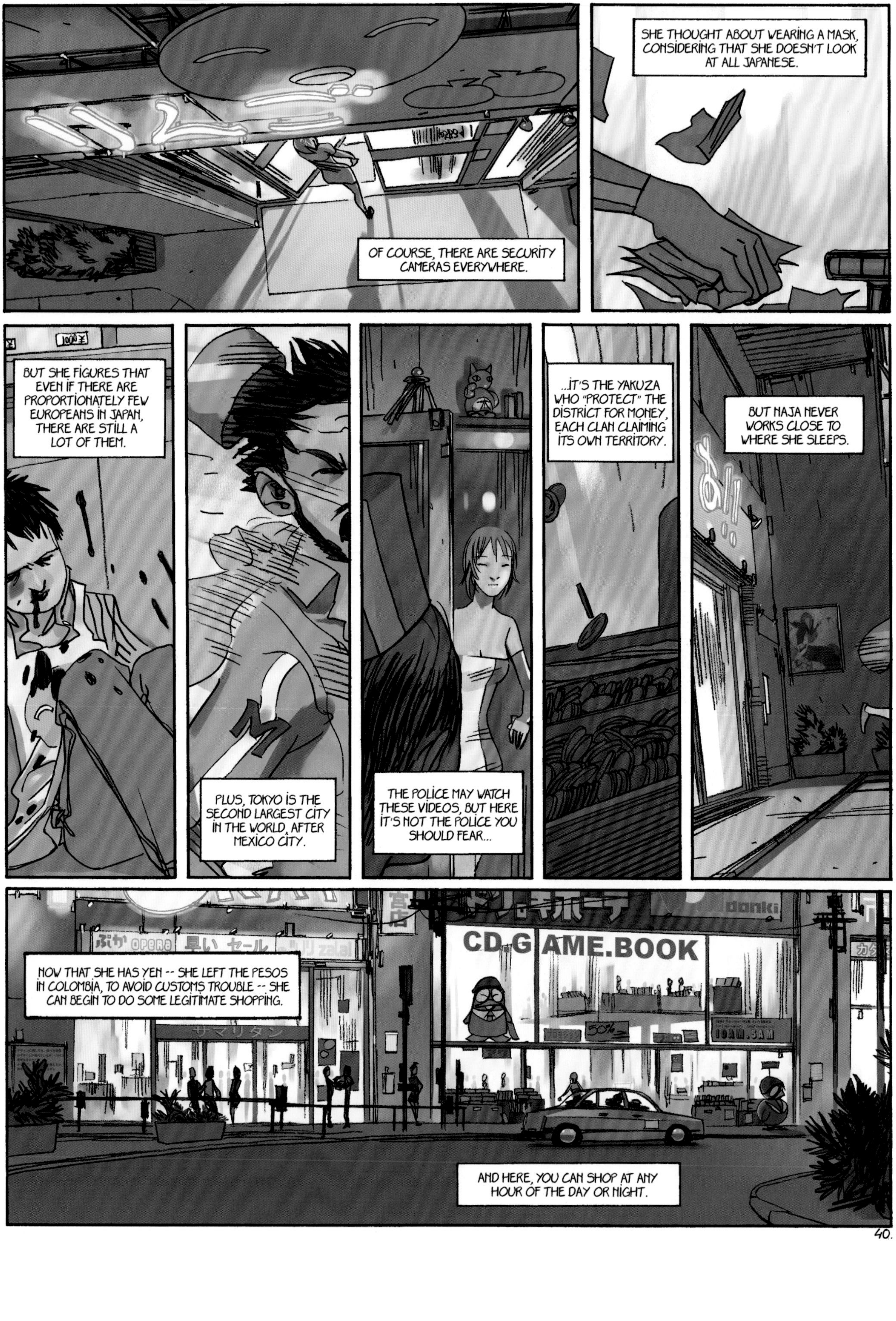
OF COURSE, THERE ARE SECURITY CAMERAS EVERYWHERE.
SHE THOUGHT ABOUT WEARING A MASK, CONSIDERING THAT SHE DOESN'T LOOK AT ALL JAPANESE.
BUT SHE FIGURES THAT EVEN IF THERE ARE PROPORTIONATELY FEW EUROPEANS IN JAPAN, THERE ARE STILL A LOT OF THEM.
PLUS, TOKYO IS THE SECOND LARGEST CITY IN THE WORLD, AFTER MEXICO CITY.
THE POLICE MAY WATCH THESE VIDEOS, BUT HERE IT'S NOT THE POLICE YOU SHOULD FEAR...
...IT'S THE YAKUZA WHO "PROTECT" THE DISTRICT FOR MONEY, EACH CLAN CLAIMING ITS OWN TERRITORY.
BUT NAJA NEVER WORKS CLOSE TO WHERE SHE SLEEPS.
CD.GAME.BOOK
NOW THAT SHE HAS YEN -- SHE LEFT THE PESOS IN COLOMBIA, TO AVOID CUSTOMS TROUBLE -- SHE CAN BEGIN TO DO SOME LEGITIMATE SHOPPING.
AND HERE, YOU CAN SHOP AT ANY HOUR OF THE DAY OR NIGHT.

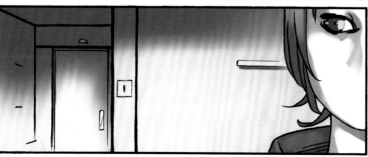

WHERE THE HELL HAVE YOU BEEN??
I LOOKED EVERYWHERE FOR YOU!
I WAS WORRIED SICK!!

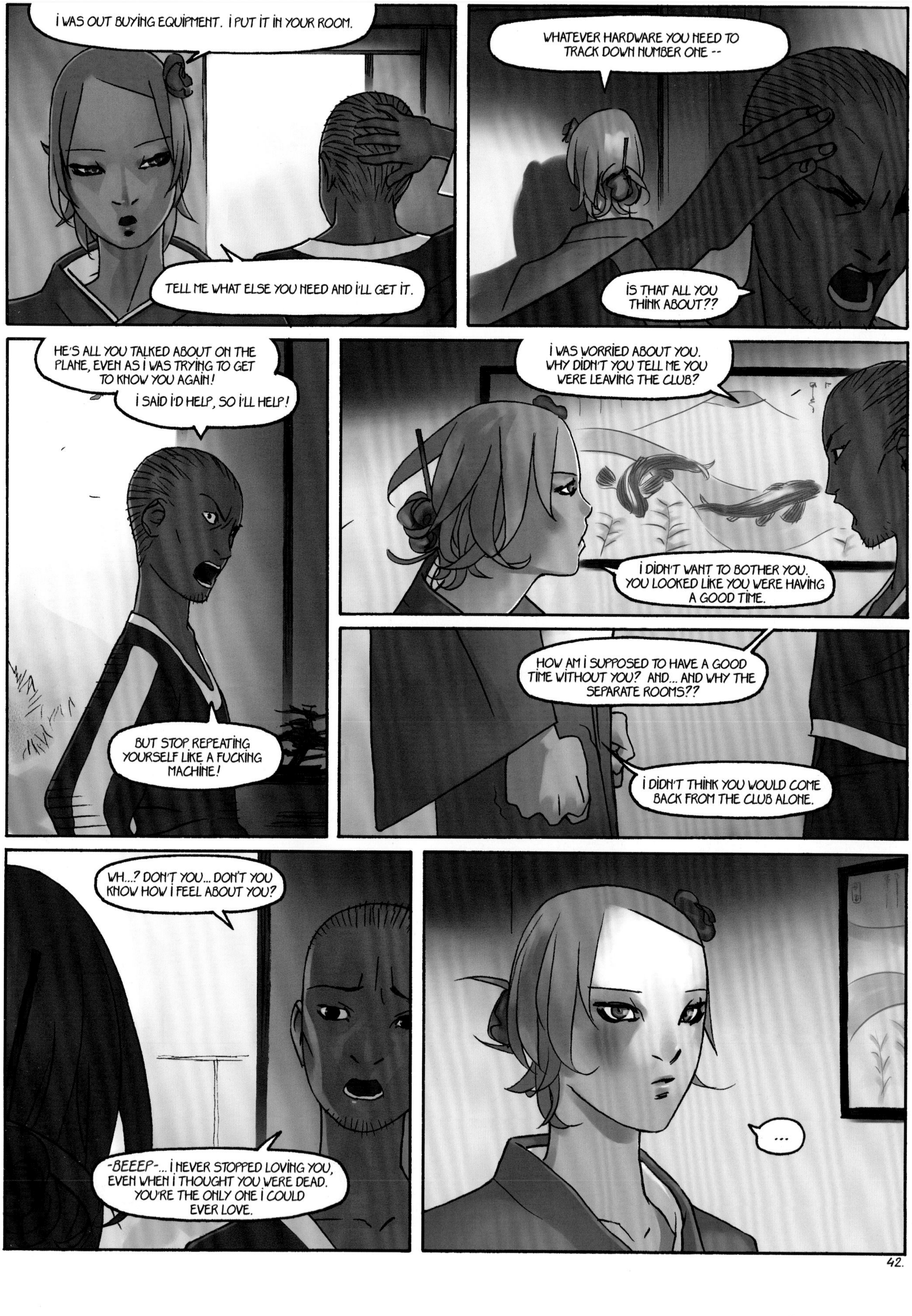
I WAS OUT BUYING EQUIPMENT. I PUT IT IN YOUR ROOM.
TELL ME WHAT ELSE YOU NEED AND I'LL GET IT.
WHATEVER HARDWARE YOU NEED TO TRACK DOWN NUMBER ONE --
IS THAT ALL YOU THINK ABOUT??
HE'S ALL YOU TALKED ABOUT ON THE PLANE, EVEN AS I WAS TRYING TO GET TO KNOW YOU AGAIN!
I SAID I'D HELP, SO I'LL HELP!
BUT STOP REPEATING YOURSELF LIKE A FUCKING MACHINE!
I WAS WORRIED ABOUT YOU. WHY DIDN'T YOU TELL ME YOU WERE LEAVING THE CLUB?
I DIDN'T WANT TO BOTHER YOU. YOU LOOKED LIKE YOU WERE HAVING A GOOD TIME.
HOW AM I SUPPOSED TO HAVE A GOOD TIME WITHOUT YOU? AND... AND WHY THE SEPARATE ROOMS??
I DIDN'T THINK YOU WOULD COME BACK FROM THE CLUB ALONE.
WH...? DON'T YOU... DON'T YOU KNOW HOW I FEEL ABOUT YOU?
-BEEEP-... I NEVER STOPPED LOVING YOU, EVEN WHEN I THOUGHT YOU WERE DEAD. YOU'RE THE ONLY ONE I COULD EVER LOVE.
...

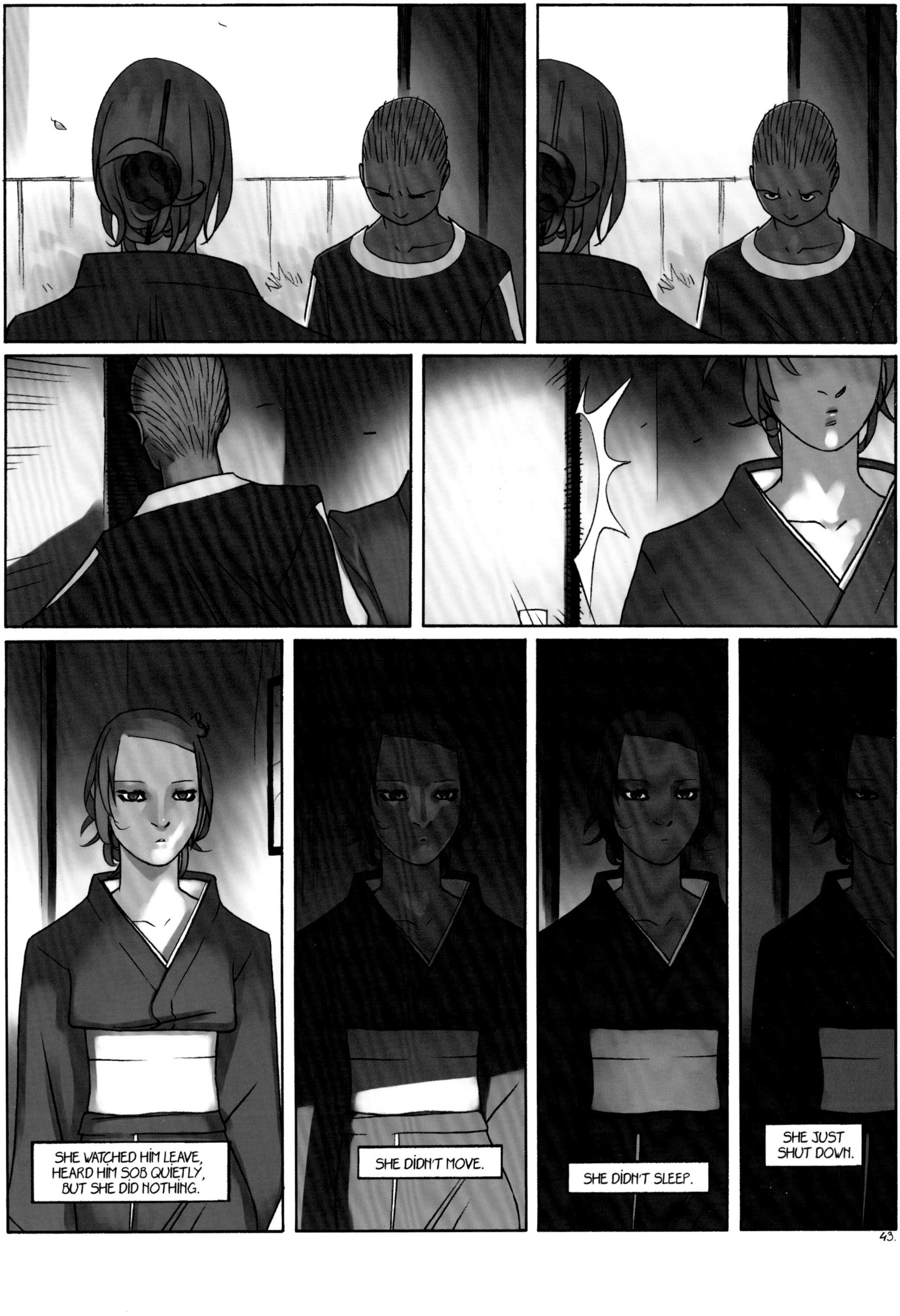
SHE WATCHED HIM LEAVE, HEARD HIM SOB QUIETLY, BUT SHE DID NOTHING.
SHE DIDN'T MOVE.
SHE DIDN'T SLEEP.
SHE JUST SHUT DOWN.

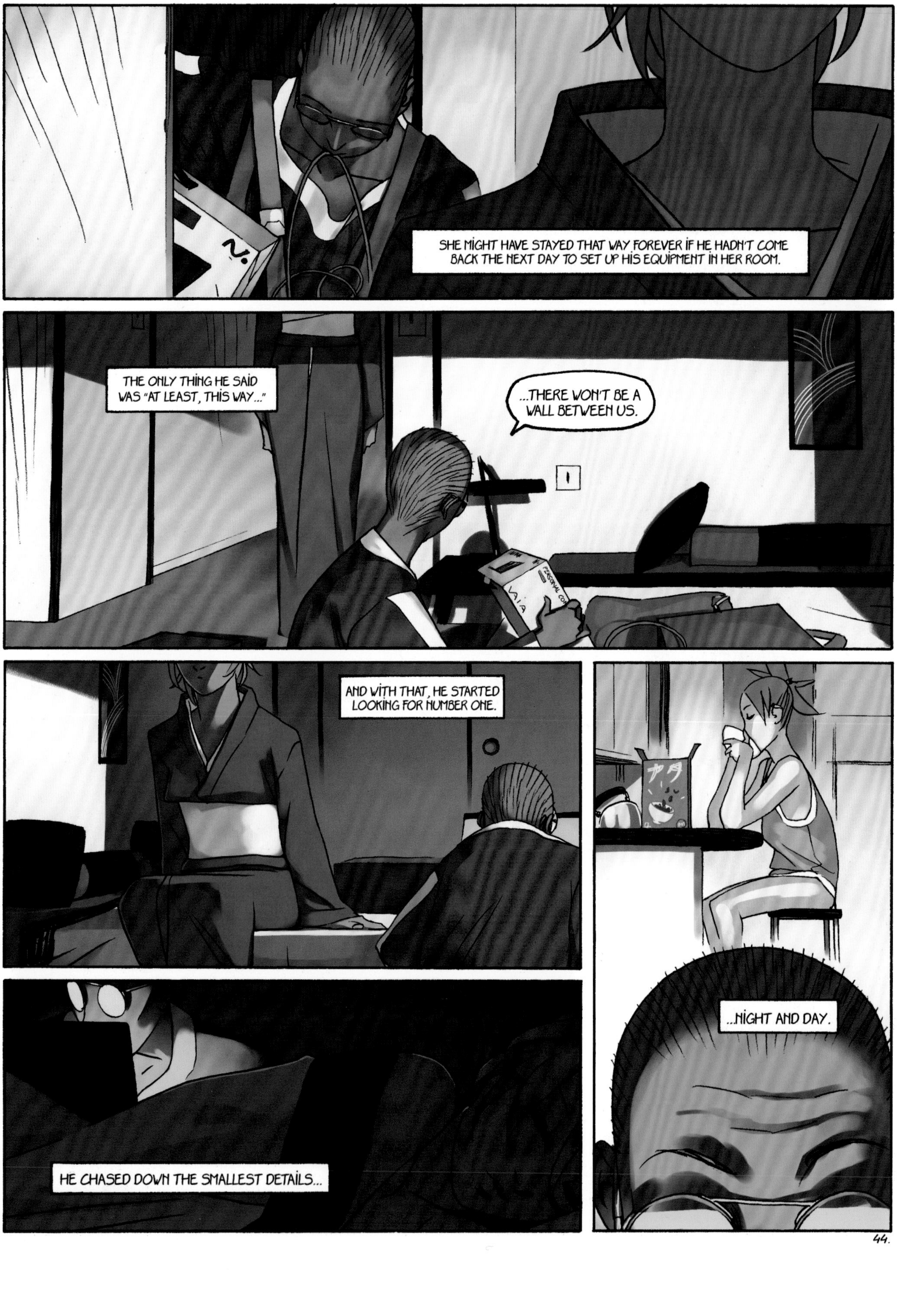
SHE MIGHT HAVE STAYED THAT WAY FOREVER IF HE HADN'T COME BACK THE NEXT DAY TO SET UP HIS EQUIPMENT IN HER ROOM.
THE ONLY THING HE SAID WAS "AT LEAST, THIS WAY..."
...THERE WON'T BE A WALL BETWEEN US.
AND WITH THAT, HE STARTED LOOKING FOR NUMBER ONE.
HE CHASED DOWN THE SMALLEST DETAILS...
...NIGHT AND DAY.

WHO...

WHAT...

HOW...

WHEN...

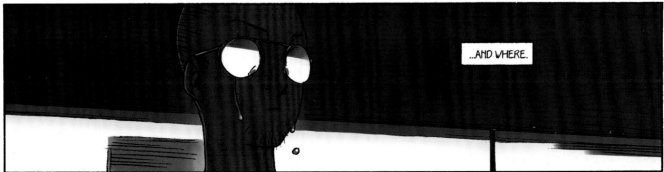

...AND WHERE.

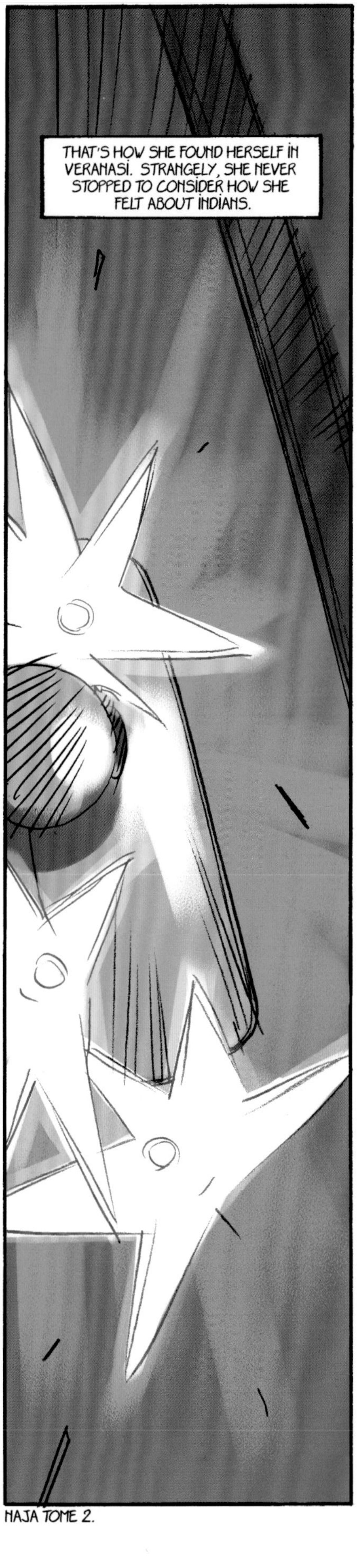
THAT'S HOW SHE FOUND HERSELF IN VERANASI. STRANGELY, SHE NEVER STOPPED TO CONSIDER HOW SHE FELT ABOUT INDIANS.

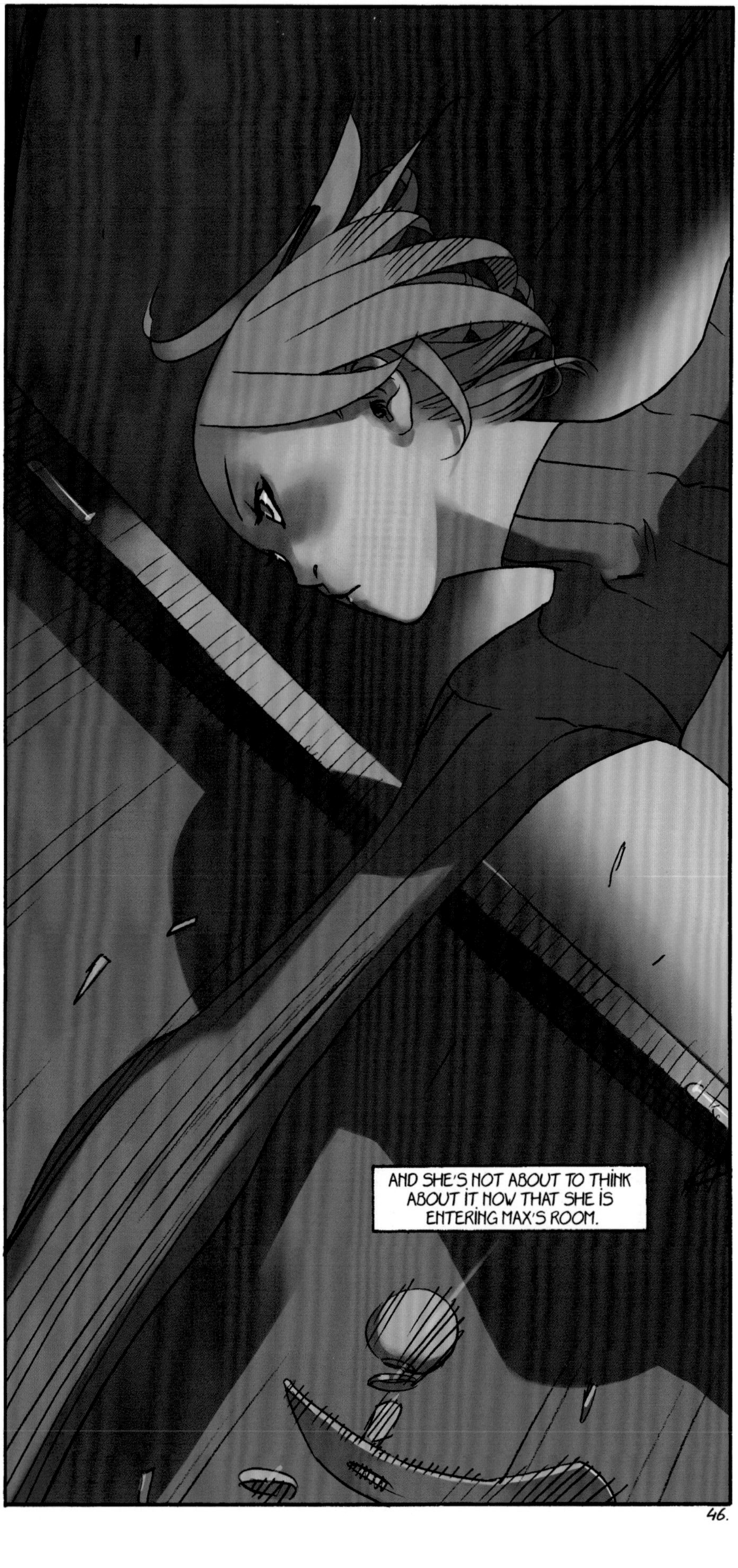
AND SHE'S NOT ABOUT TO THINK ABOUT IT NOW THAT SHE IS ENTERING MAX'S ROOM.

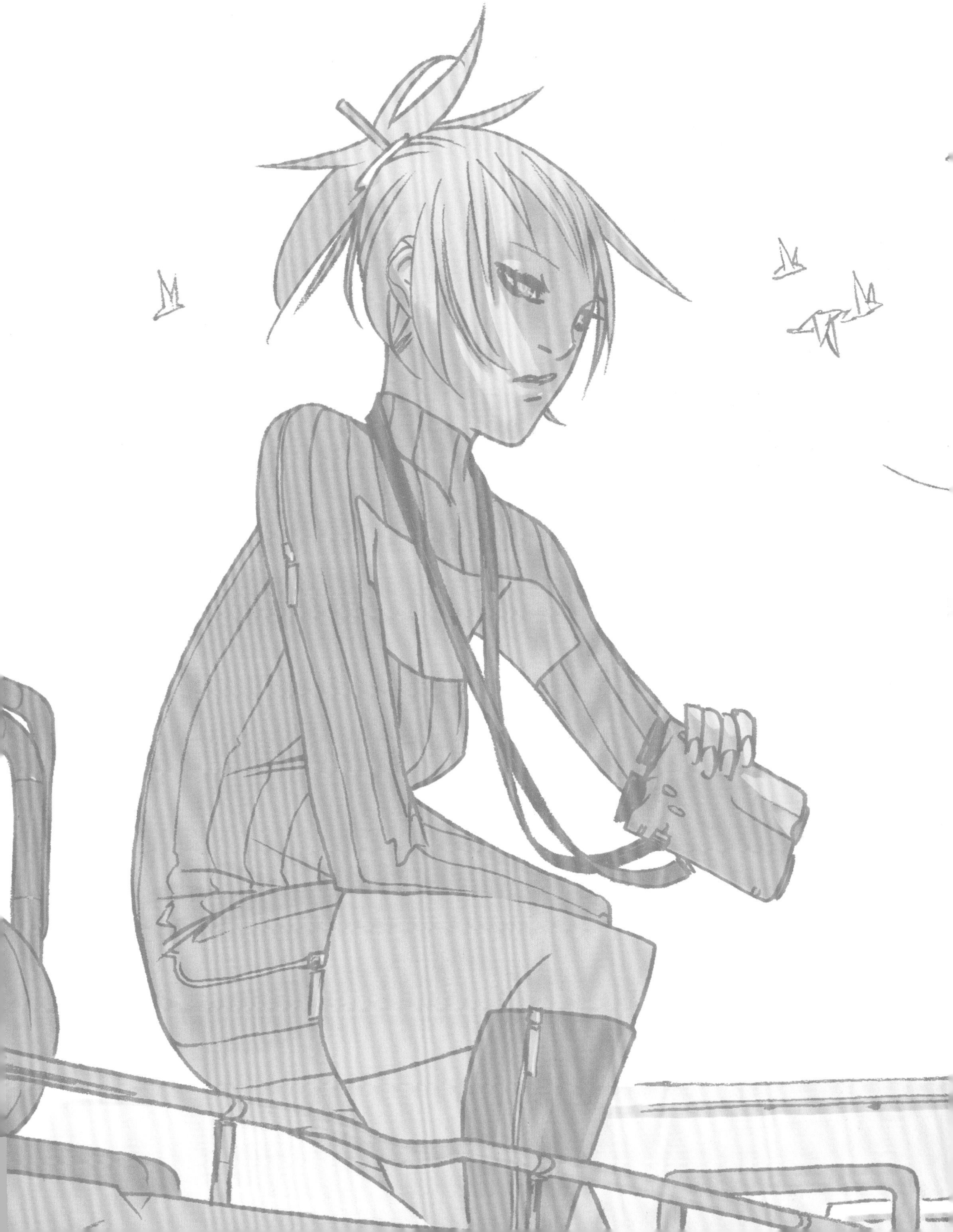

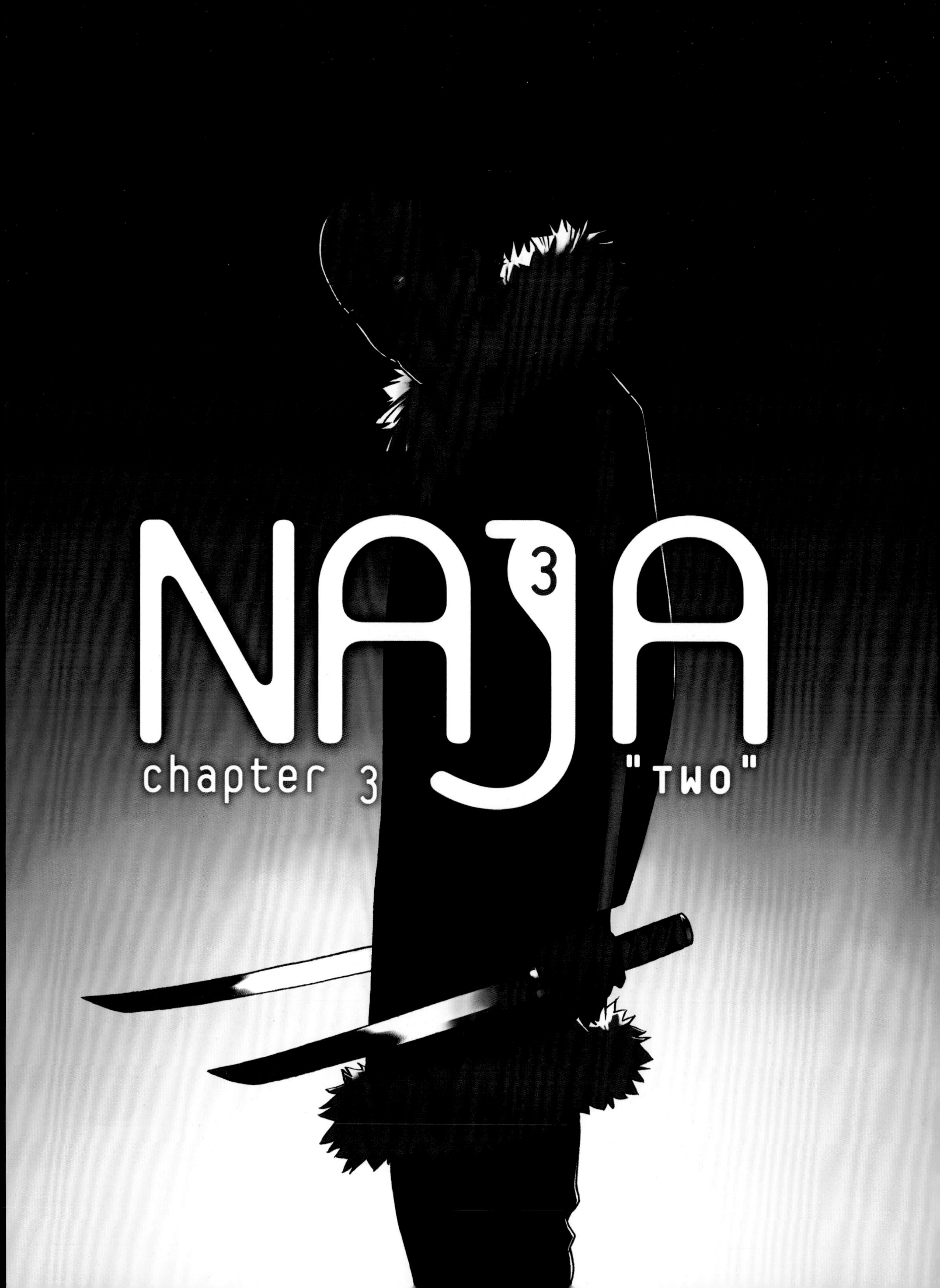
NAJA 3
chapter 3
"TWO"

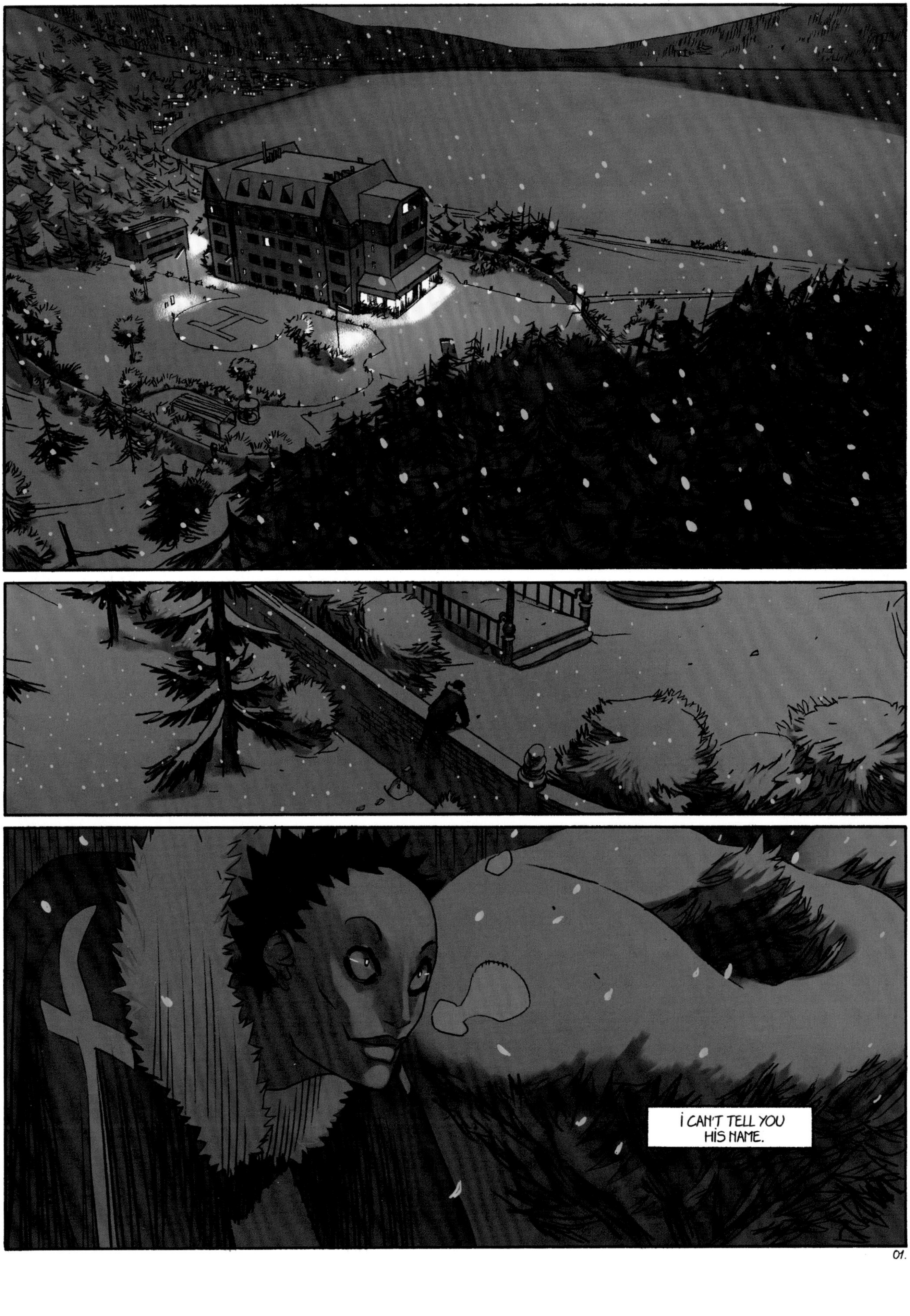
I CAN'T TELL YOU
HIS NAME.

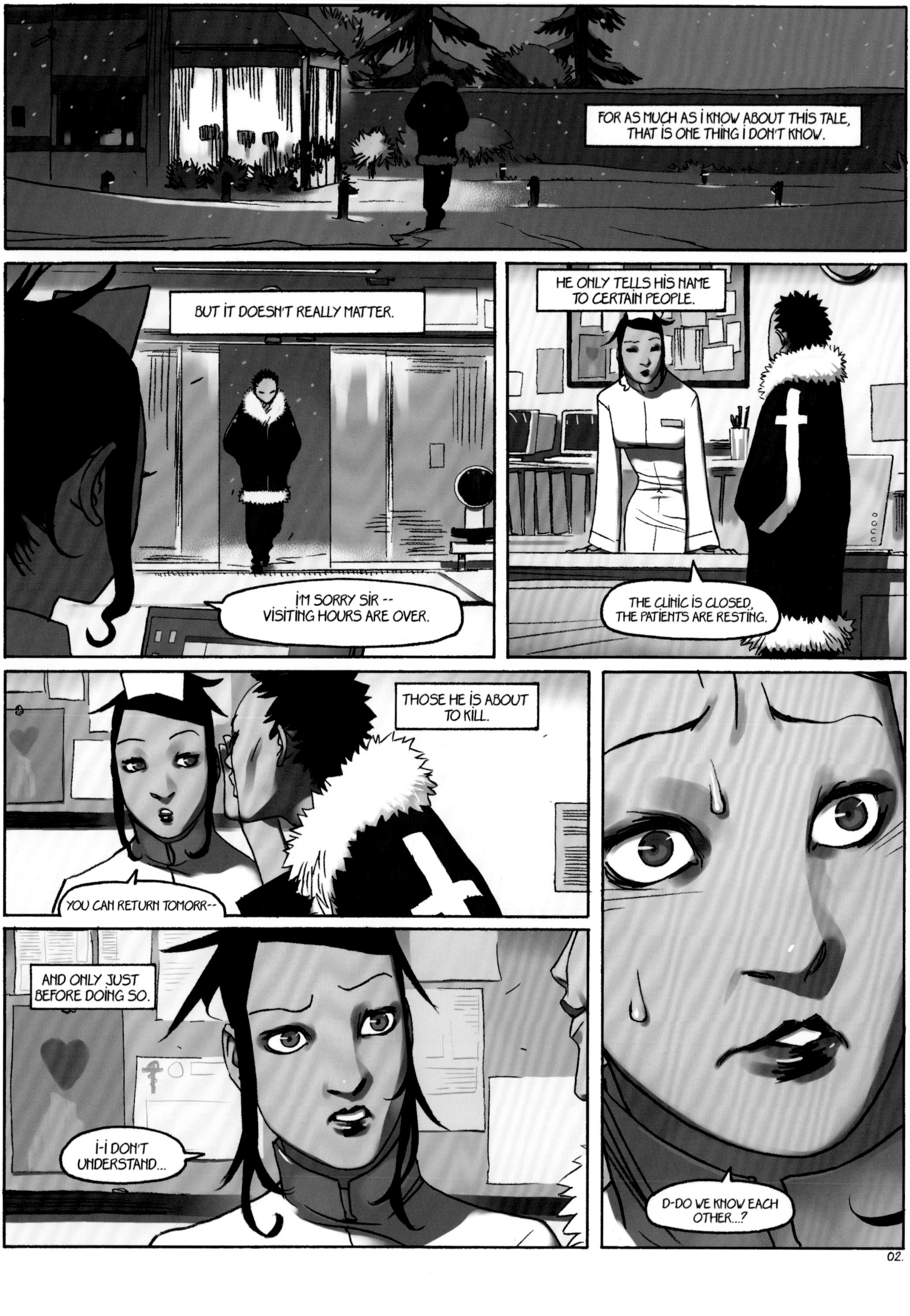
FOR AS MUCH AS I KNOW ABOUT THIS TALE, THAT IS ONE THING I DON'T KNOW.
BUT IT DOESN'T REALLY MATTER.
I'M SORRY SIR -- VISITING HOURS ARE OVER.
HE ONLY TELLS HIS NAME TO CERTAIN PEOPLE.
THE CLINIC IS CLOSED, THE PATIENTS ARE RESTING.
THOSE HE IS ABOUT TO KILL.
YOU CAN RETURN TOMORR--
AND ONLY JUST BEFORE DOING SO.
I-I DON'T UNDERSTAND...
D-DO WE KNOW EACH OTHER...?

SO FOR YOUR OWN SAFETY...

...WE'LL JUST CALL HIM:

TWO.

r215 Michel Renau
r216 Andrew Tene
r207 Michael Jacks
r208 Abraham San
r203 Maxence Dézi
r204 Ma   Clansw
r211 P   ne Leg
r212   que Jea
r21   Smith
r2
        donna
        divine Cox

5 Johnny
   Harold
   kagu

BECAUSE HE IS ZERO'S NUMBER TWO KILLER.

03.

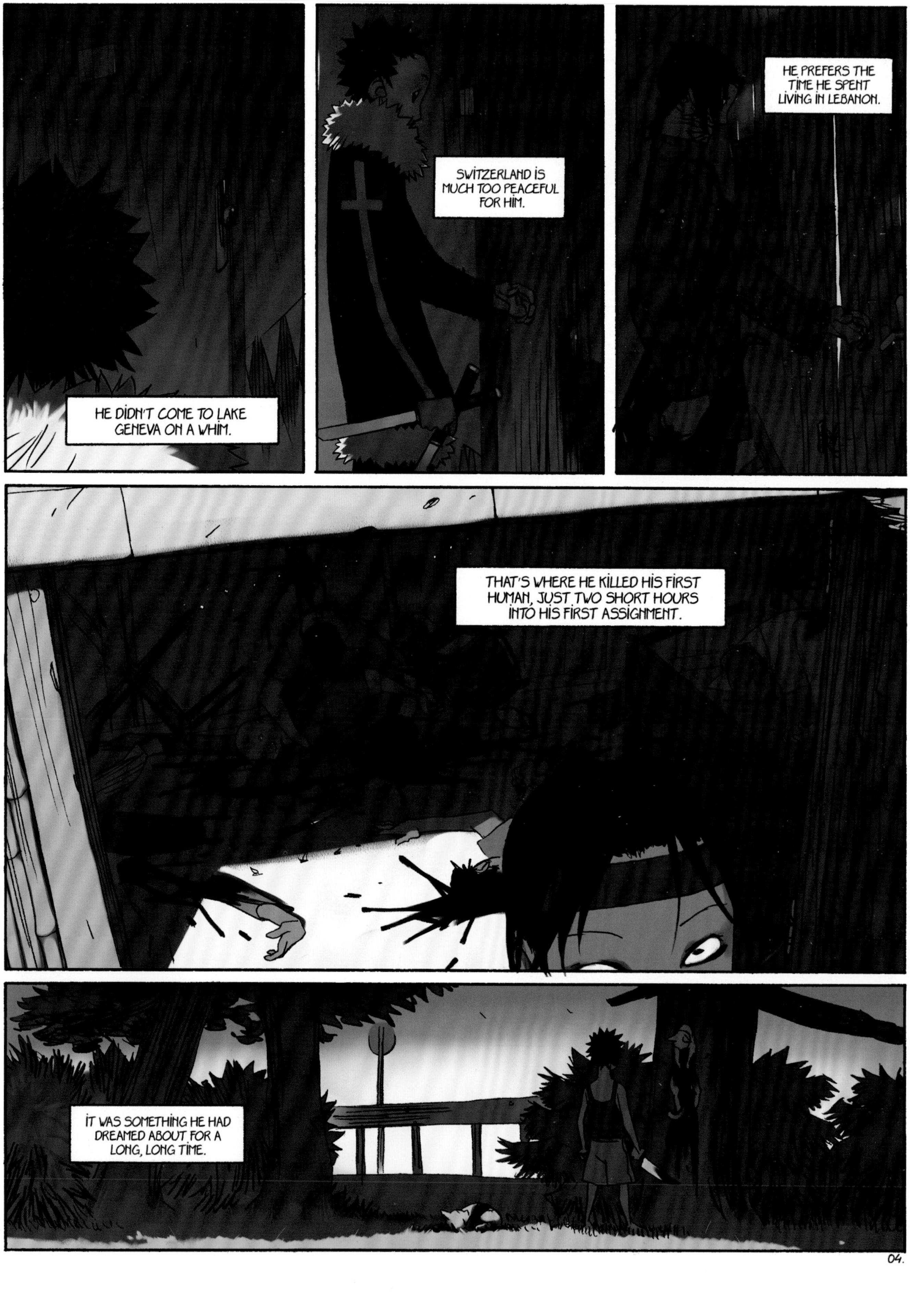
HE DIDN'T COME TO LAKE GENEVA ON A WHIM.
SWITZERLAND IS MUCH TOO PEACEFUL FOR HIM.
HE PREFERS THE TIME HE SPENT LIVING IN LEBANON.
THAT'S WHERE HE KILLED HIS FIRST HUMAN, JUST TWO SHORT HOURS INTO HIS FIRST ASSIGNMENT.
IT WAS SOMETHING HE HAD DREAMED ABOUT FOR A LONG, LONG TIME.

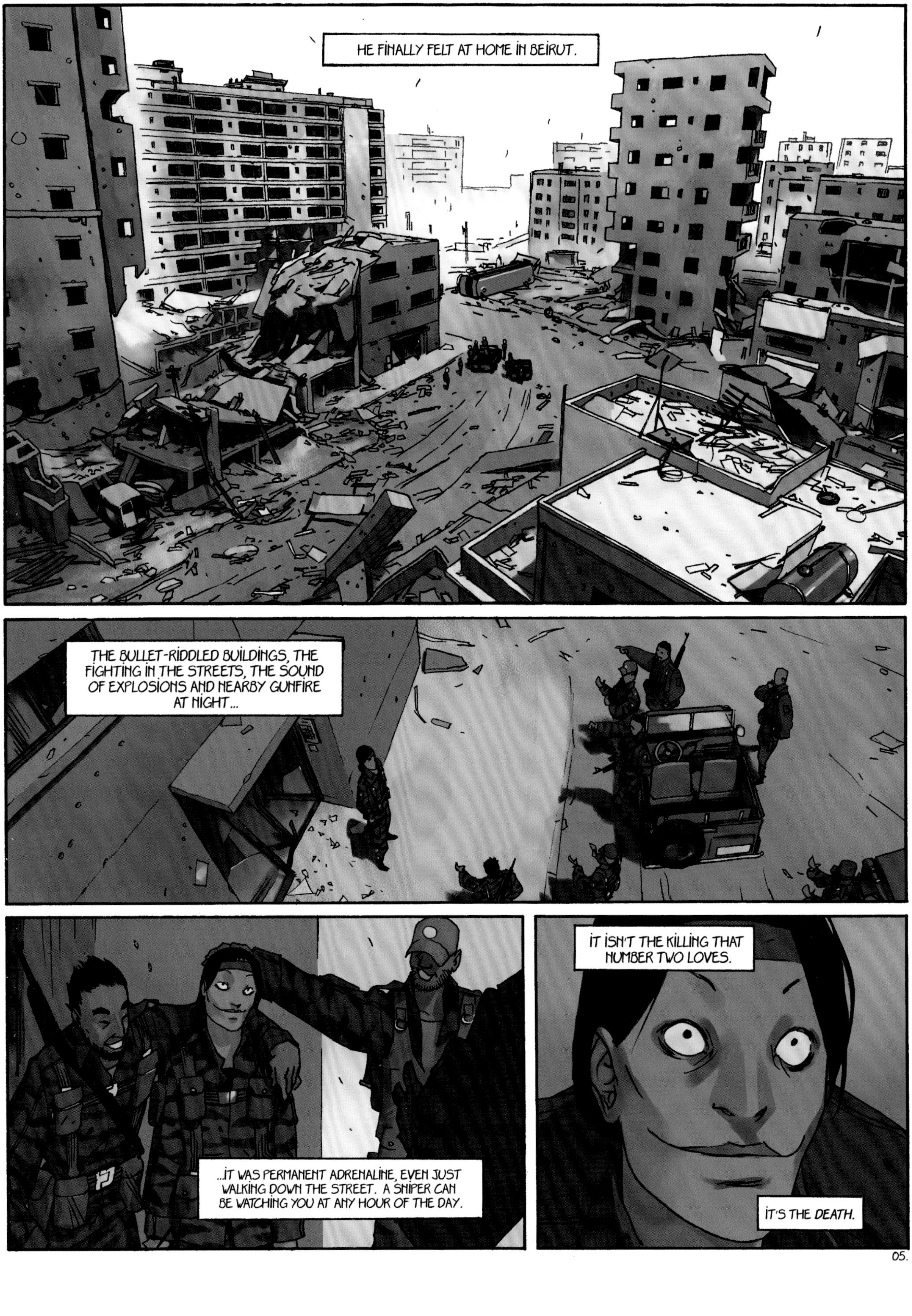
HE FINALLY FELT AT HOME IN BEIRUT.
THE BULLET-RIDDLED BUILDINGS, THE FIGHTING IN THE STREETS, THE SOUND OF EXPLOSIONS AND NEARBY GUNFIRE AT NIGHT...
...IT WAS PERMANENT ADRENALINE, EVEN JUST WALKING DOWN THE STREET. A SNIPER CAN BE WATCHING YOU AT ANY HOUR OF THE DAY.
IT ISN'T THE KILLING THAT NUMBER TWO LOVES.
IT'S THE *DEATH*.

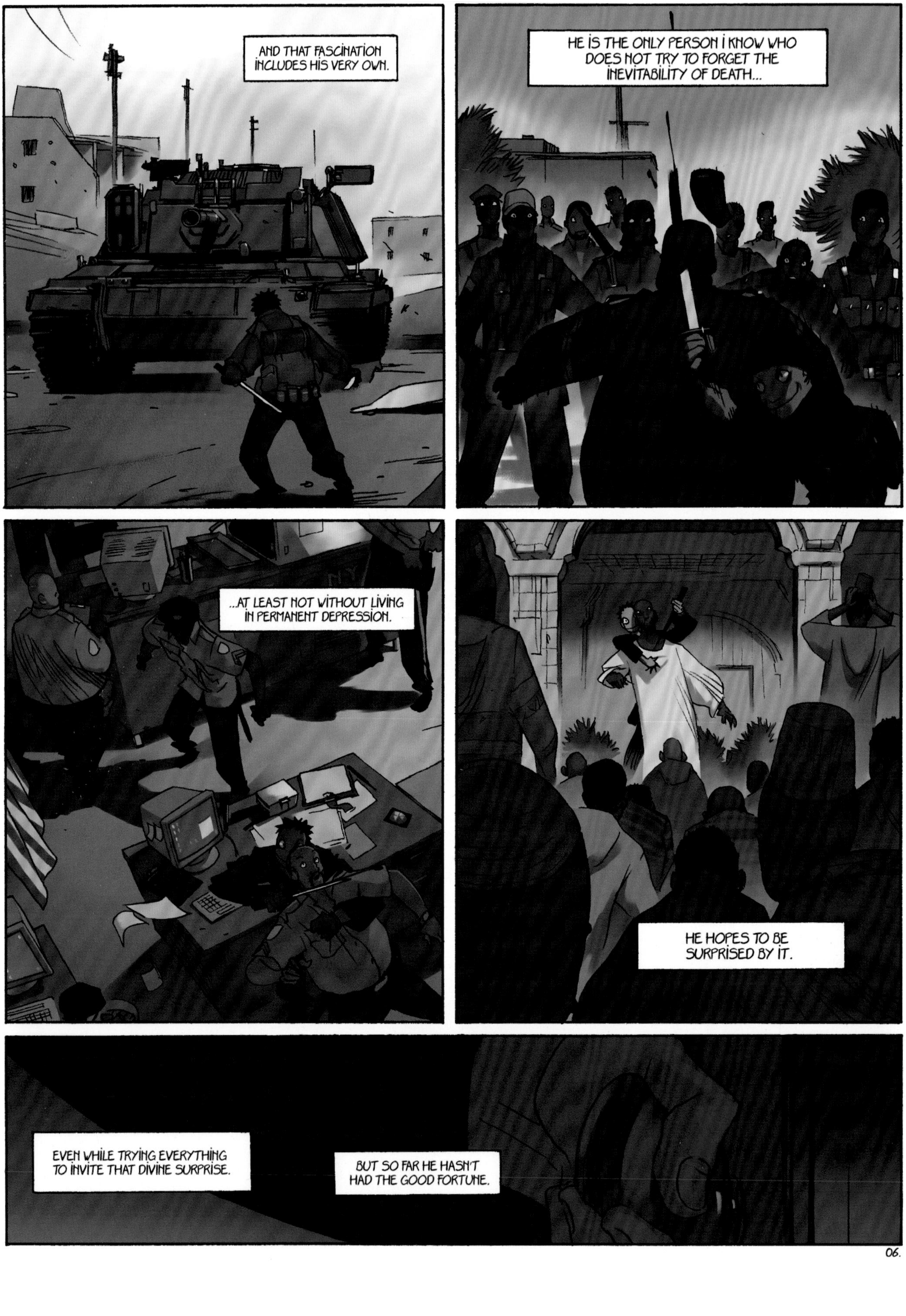
AND THAT FASCINATION INCLUDES HIS VERY OWN.
HE IS THE ONLY PERSON I KNOW WHO DOES NOT TRY TO FORGET THE INEVITABILITY OF DEATH...
...AT LEAST NOT WITHOUT LIVING IN PERMANENT DEPRESSION.
HE HOPES TO BE SURPRISED BY IT.
EVEN WHILE TRYING EVERYTHING TO INVITE THAT DIVINE SURPRISE.
BUT SO FAR HE HASN'T HAD THE GOOD FORTUNE.

SURE, THERE ARE MANY WHO WOULD LOVE TO GRANT HIM HIS WISH.

BUT NO ONE HAS BEEN CAPABLE SO FAR...

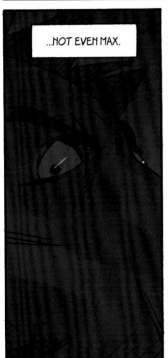

...NOT EVEN MAX.

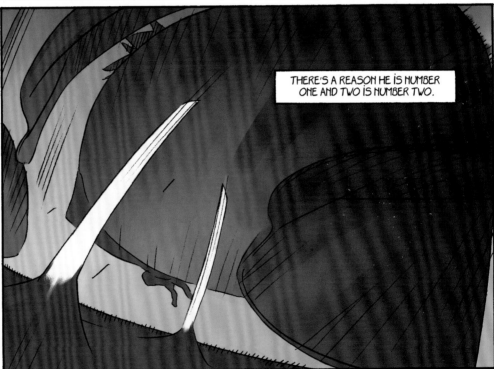

THERE'S A REASON HE IS NUMBER ONE AND TWO IS NUMBER TWO.

EVEN THOUGH THEIR STRENGTHS DIFFER, THEY AREN'T THAT FAR FROM EQUAL.

AND IT WOULD HAVE BEEN A BEAUTIFUL DUEL IF MAX HADN'T STARTED OUT WITH A SMALL HANDICAP...

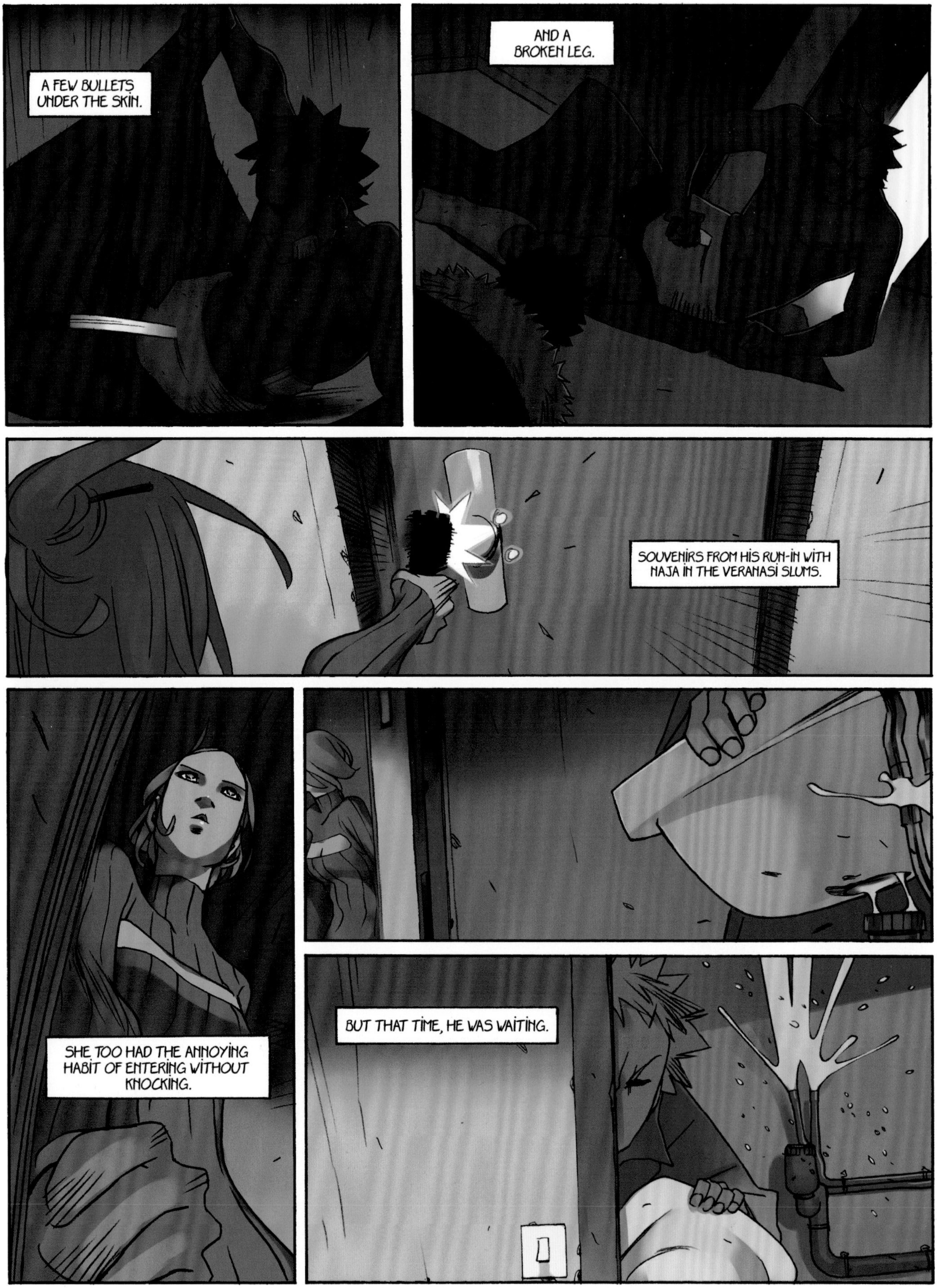
A FEW BULLETS UNDER THE SKIN.
AND A BROKEN LEG.
SOUVENIRS FROM HIS RUN-IN WITH NAJA IN THE VERANASI SLUMS.
SHE TOO HAD THE ANNOYING HABIT OF ENTERING WITHOUT KNOCKING.
BUT THAT TIME, HE WAS WAITING.

NAJA IS UNDENIABLY A PROFESSIONAL.

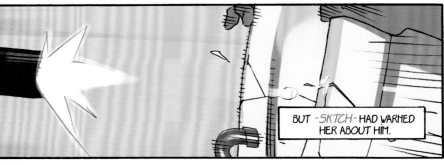

BUT -SKTCH- HAD WARNED HER ABOUT HIM.

SHE KNEW SHE WASN'T AS EXPERIENCED.

SHE WAS CAREFUL NOT TO UNDERESTIMATE HIS TALENT.

... THAT WASN'T ENOUGH.

SHE PUT THE ODDS ON HIS SIDE.

BUT IN THE END...

MAX THOUGHT HE HAD HURT HER.

THE PAIN WOULD HAVE CAUSED A NORMAL PERSON TO PASS OUT. SO HE FELT MOMENTARILY SAFE.

NAJA ALSO KNEW THAT IF SHE WERE NORMAL, SHE WOULD BE IN AGONY.

PART OF HER WAS DISAPPOINTED SHE COULDN'T FEEL HER CRACKED RIBS...

BUT SHE ALSO KNEW THAT IF SHE WERE NORMAL, SHE WOULD HAVE FAINTED, AND MAX WOULD THEN FINISH HER OFF.

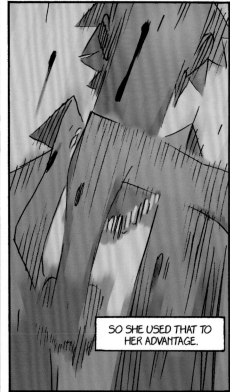

SO SHE USED THAT TO HER ADVANTAGE.

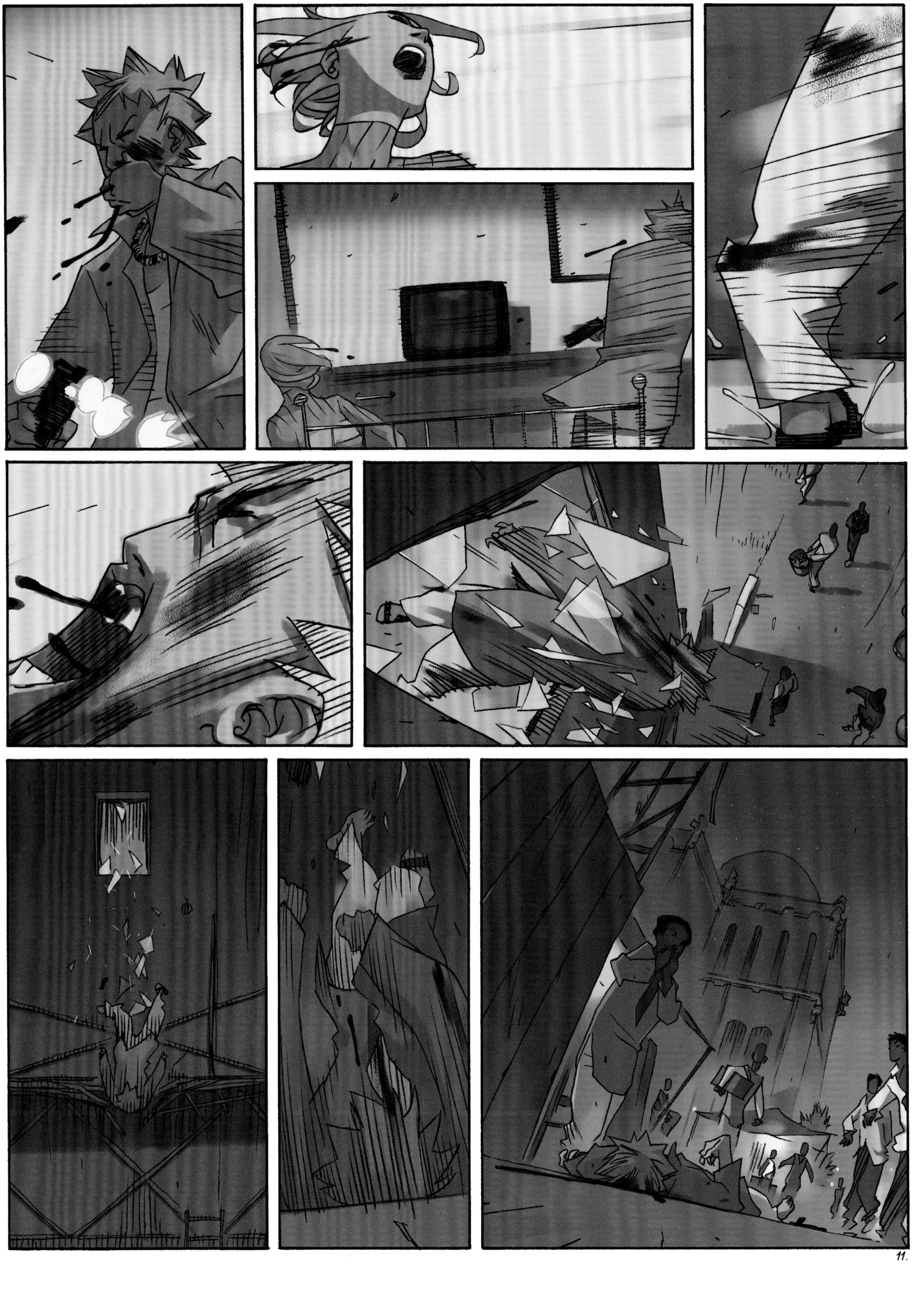

MAX'S LOCAL FRIENDS TOOK CARE OF HIM UNTIL HE REGAINED CONSCIOUSNESS.

THEY EVEN CHIPPED IN TO PAY FOR A TICKET BACK TO SWITZERLAND.

(THE GIFTS HE SENT THEM ONCE HE RETURNED MADE THEM RICH FOR LIFE.)

THERE, HE WAS TREATED IN ONE OF THE MOST HIGH-TECH CLINICS IN THE WORLD.

HE DIDN'T EXPECT TO HAVE TO FIGHT FOR HIS LIFE AGAIN SO QUICKLY...

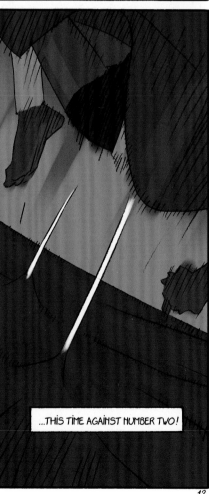

...THIS TIME AGAINST NUMBER TWO!

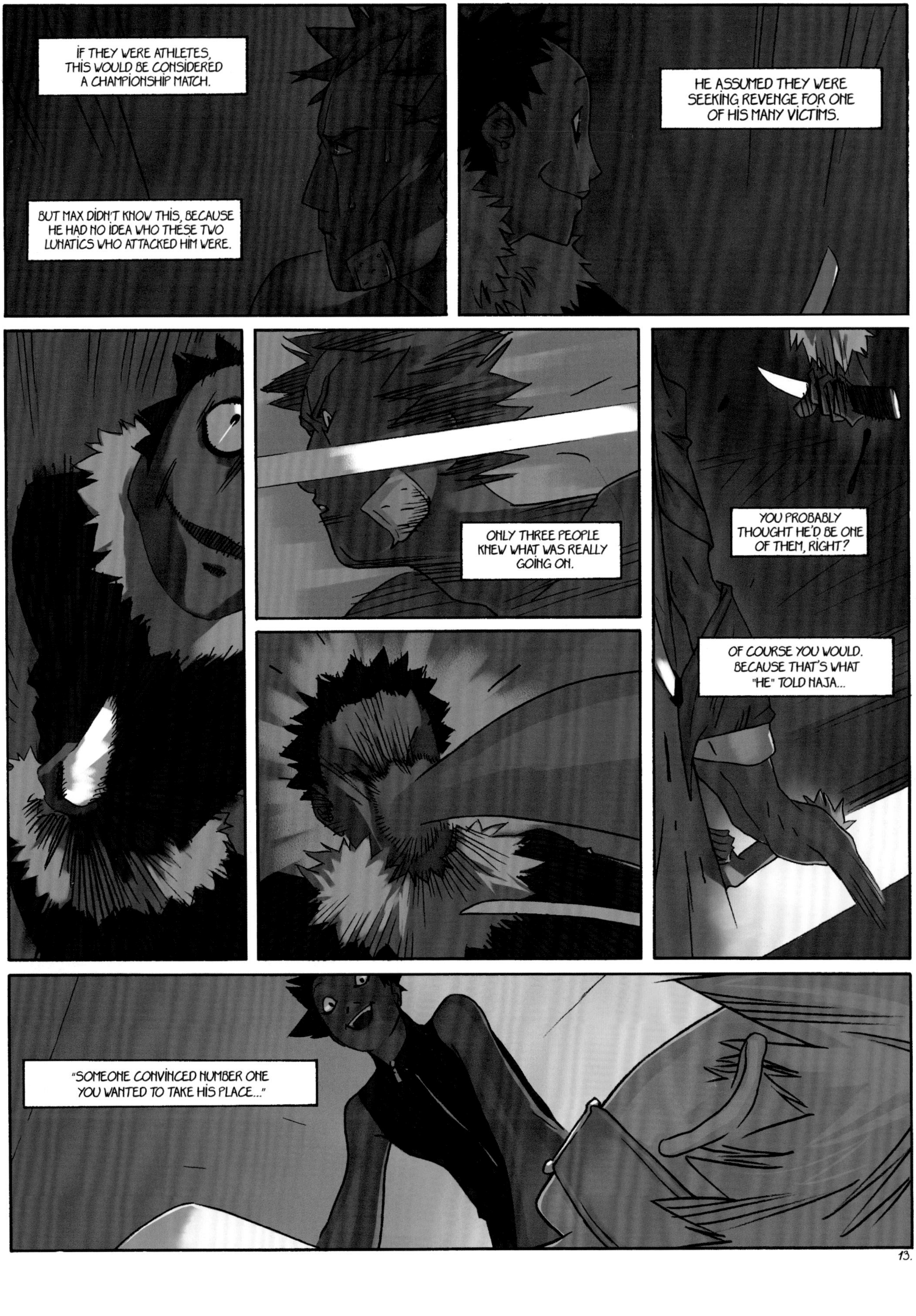

IF THEY WERE ATHLETES, THIS WOULD BE CONSIDERED A CHAMPIONSHIP MATCH.
BUT MAX DIDN'T KNOW THIS, BECAUSE HE HAD NO IDEA WHO THESE TWO LUNATICS WHO ATTACKED HIM WERE.
HE ASSUMED THEY WERE SEEKING REVENGE FOR ONE OF HIS MANY VICTIMS.
ONLY THREE PEOPLE KNEW WHAT WAS REALLY GOING ON.
YOU PROBABLY THOUGHT HE'D BE ONE OF THEM, RIGHT?
OF COURSE YOU WOULD. BECAUSE THAT'S WHAT "HE" TOLD NAJA...
"SOMEONE CONVINCED NUMBER ONE YOU WANTED TO TAKE HIS PLACE..."

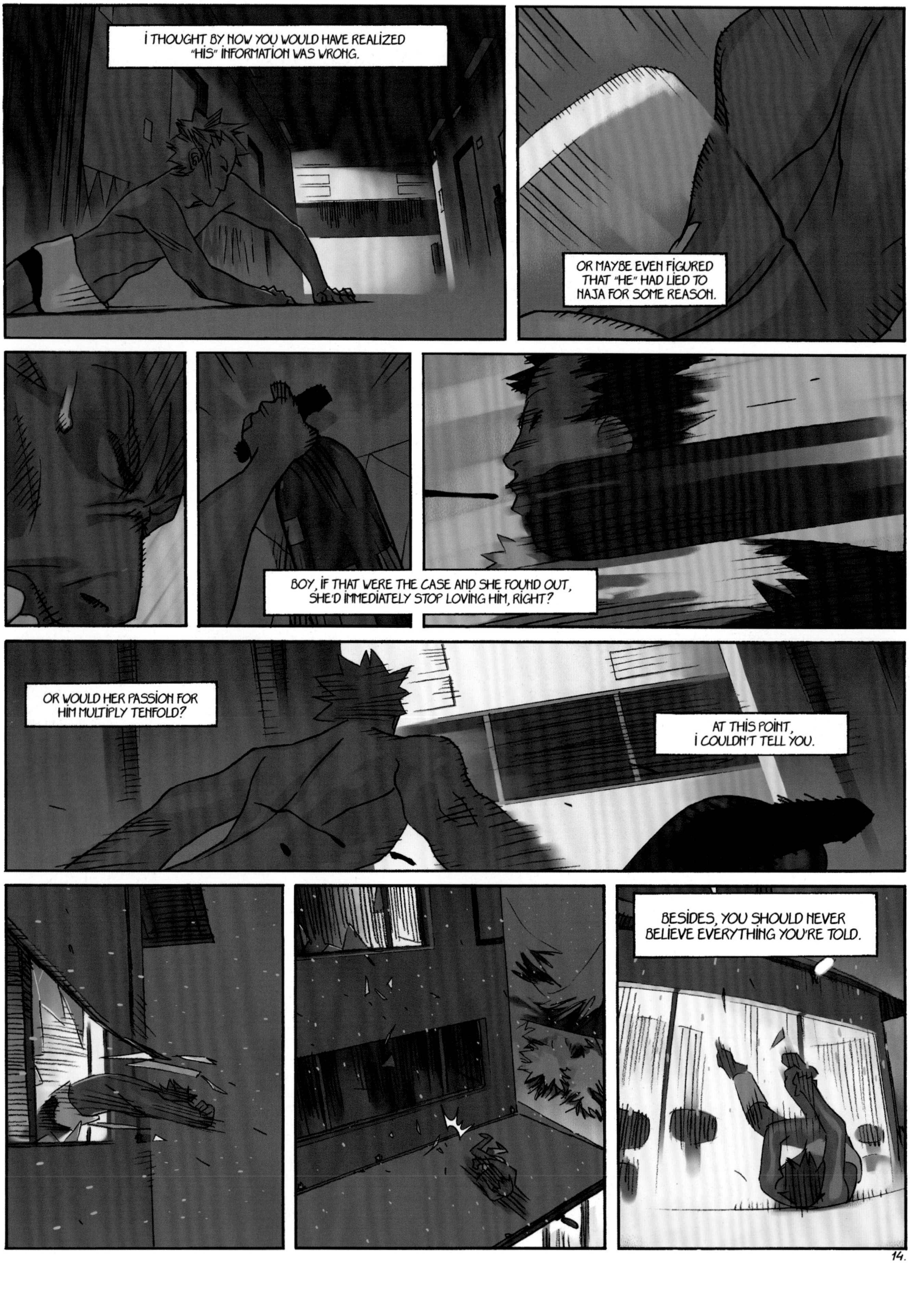
I THOUGHT BY NOW YOU WOULD HAVE REALIZED "HIS" INFORMATION WAS WRONG.
OR MAYBE EVEN FIGURED THAT "HE" HAD LIED TO NAJA FOR SOME REASON.
BOY, IF THAT WERE THE CASE AND SHE FOUND OUT, SHE'D IMMEDIATELY STOP LOVING HIM, RIGHT?
OR WOULD HER PASSION FOR HIM MULTIPLY TENFOLD?
AT THIS POINT, I COULDN'T TELL YOU.
BESIDES, YOU SHOULD NEVER BELIEVE EVERYTHING YOU'RE TOLD.

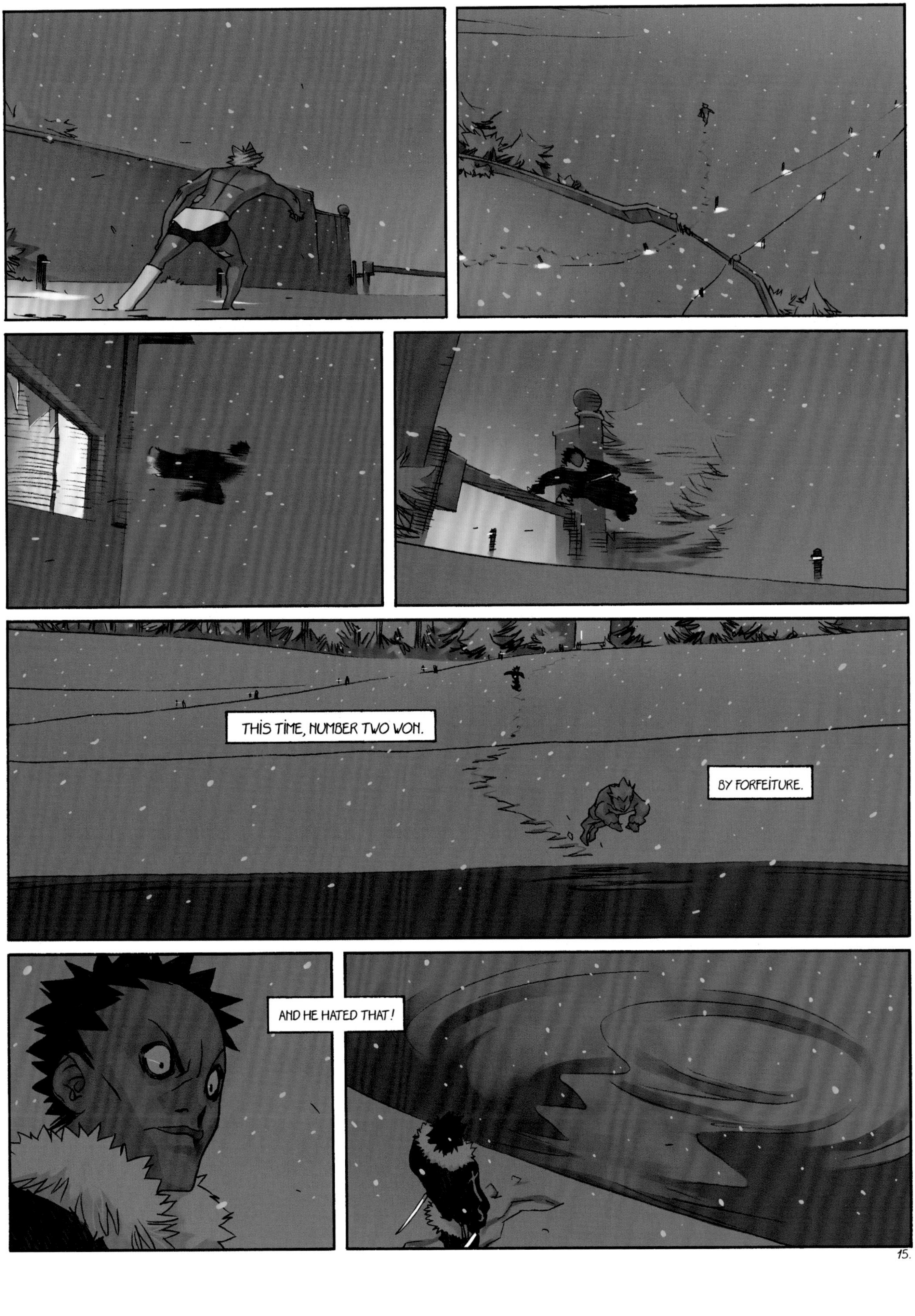
THIS TIME, NUMBER TWO WON.
BY FORFEITURE.
AND HE HATED THAT!

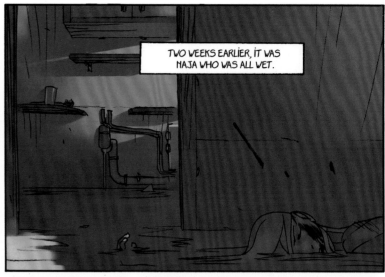

TWO WEEKS EARLIER, IT WAS NAJA WHO WAS ALL WET.

AND SHE REFUSED TO STAGNATE IN THE WARM INDIAN SEWAGE.

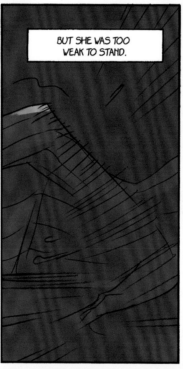

BUT SHE WAS TOO WEAK TO STAND.

SHE WAS GOING TO DROWN THERE...

...IN TEN CENTIMETERS OF LIQUID FILTH.

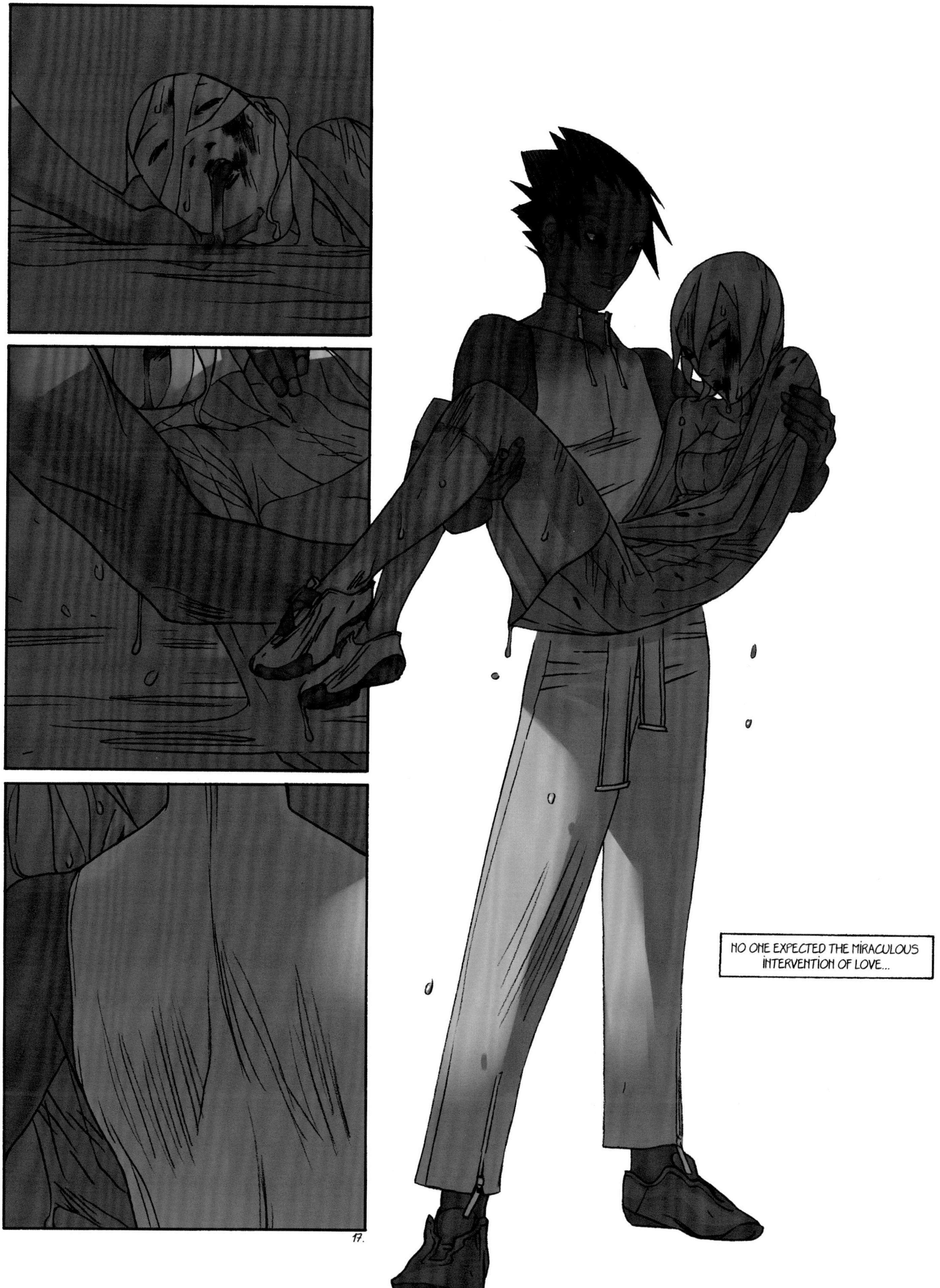
NO ONE EXPECTED THE MIRACULOUS INTERVENTION OF LOVE...

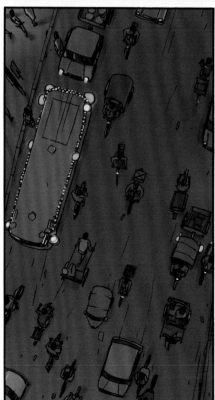

18.

NAJA WAS A MESS.

SHE NEEDED IMMEDIATE TREATMENT.

BUT "HE" KNEW THAT HE COULDN'T TAKE HER TO A HOSPITAL. IF THEY CALLED THE COPS...

...THEY'D BOTH BE ARRESTED.

HE HAD NO CHOICE BUT TO CARE FOR HER HIMSELF.

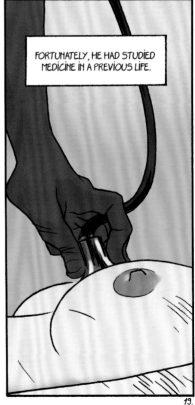

FORTUNATELY, HE HAD STUDIED MEDICINE IN A PREVIOUS LIFE.

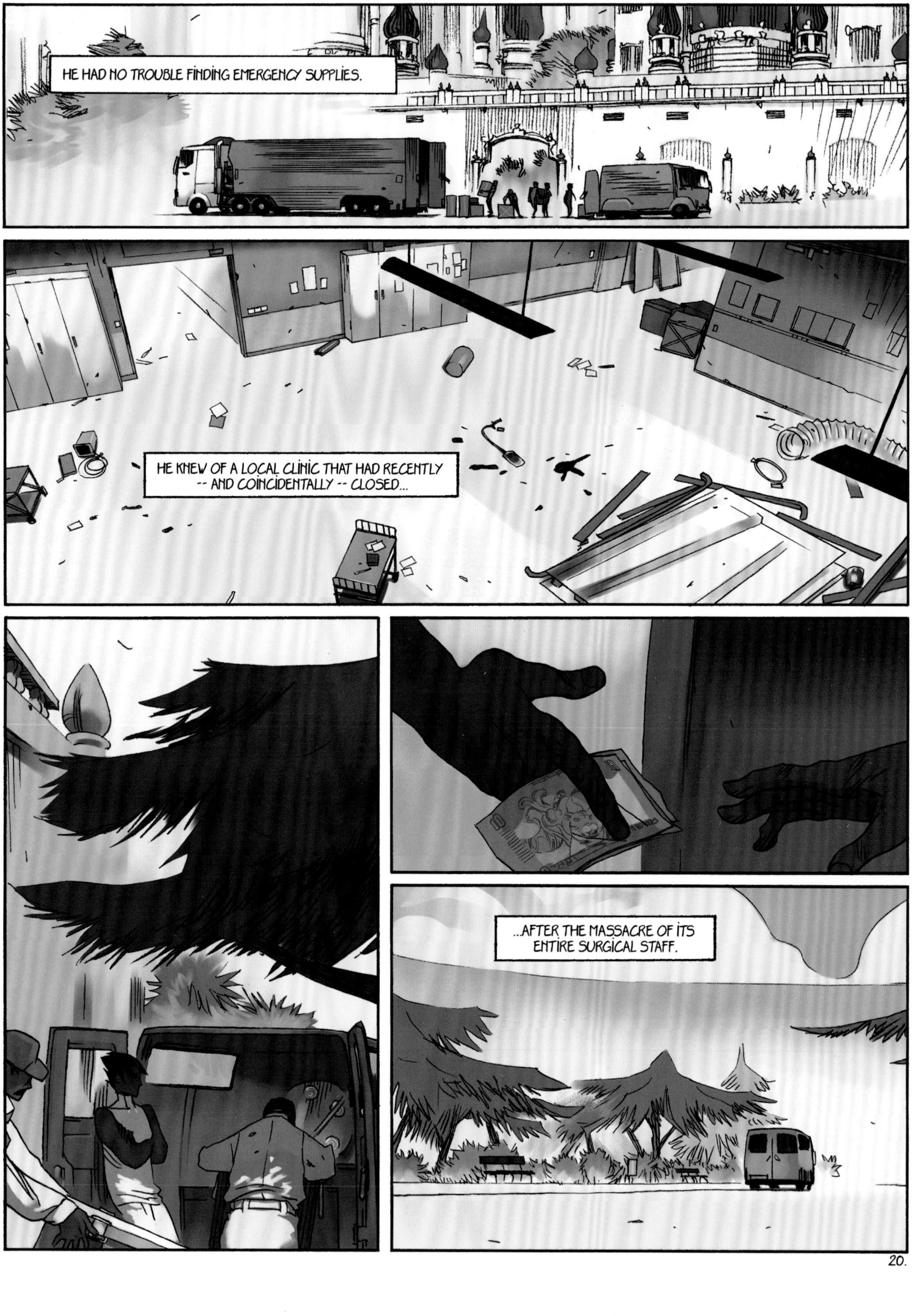
HE HAD NO TROUBLE FINDING EMERGENCY SUPPLIES.
HE KNEW OF A LOCAL CLINIC THAT HAD RECENTLY -- AND COINCIDENTALLY -- CLOSED...
...AFTER THE MASSACRE OF ITS ENTIRE SURGICAL STAFF.

HE TRANSFORMED HIS HOTEL ROOM INTO AN OPERATING CHAMBER AND BEGAN WORK.

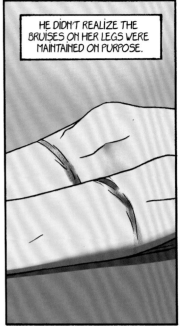

HE DIDN'T REALIZE THE BRUISES ON HER LEGS WERE MAINTAINED ON PURPOSE.

IT'S HARD TO SAY WHETHER IT WAS INTENTIONAL, BUT SHE REQUIRED VERY LITTLE ANESTHESIA.

IT WAS IRRELEVANT, HOWEVER, BECAUSE HE KNOWS -- AS WE DO -- THAT SHE FEELS NO PAIN.

SHE FLOATED IN A STATE OF HALF-CONSCIOUSNESS, SO SHE COULD WATCH "HIM" TAKE CARE OF HER.

21.

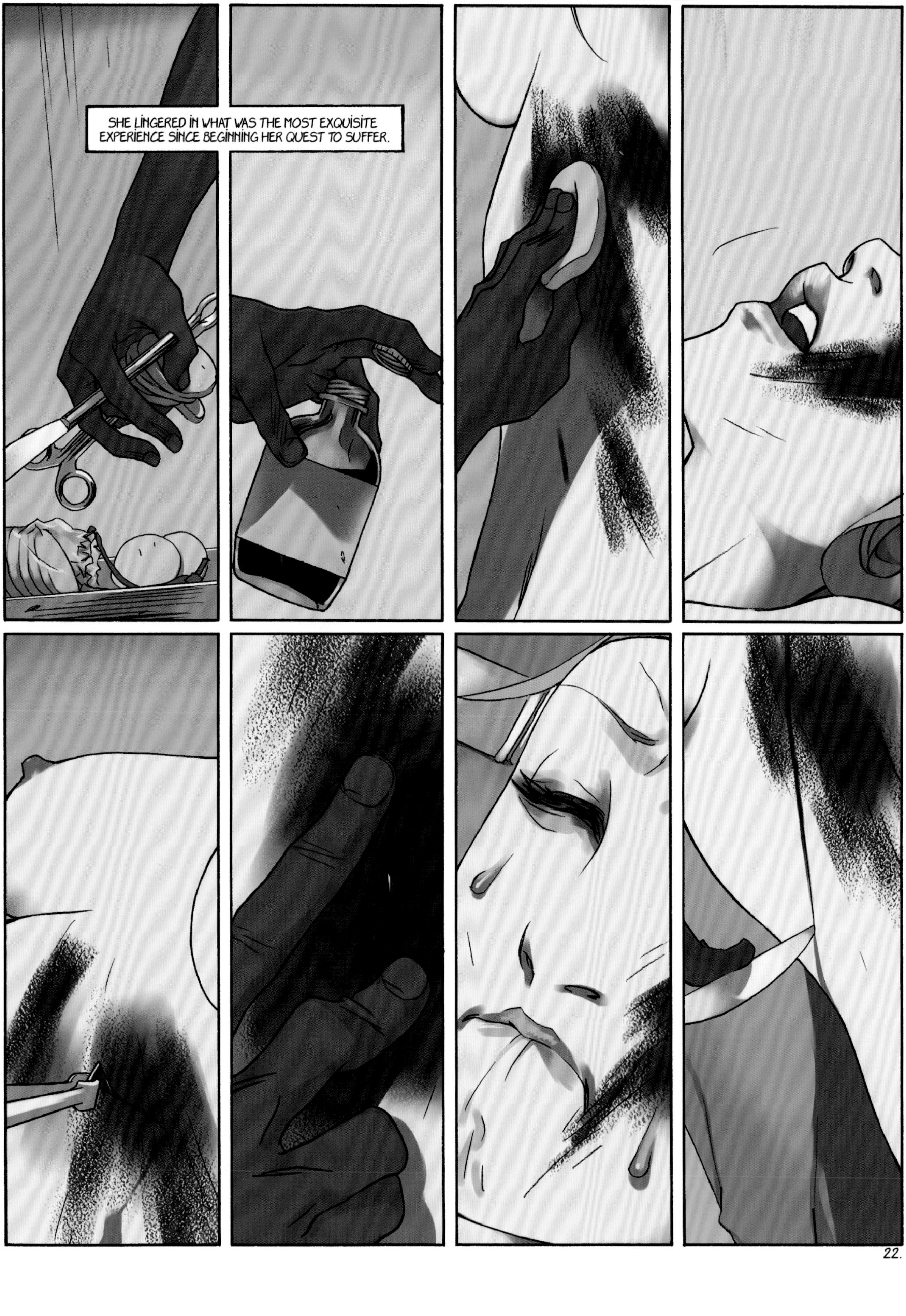
SHE LINGERED IN WHAT WAS THE MOST EXQUISITE EXPERIENCE SINCE BEGINNING HER QUEST TO SUFFER.

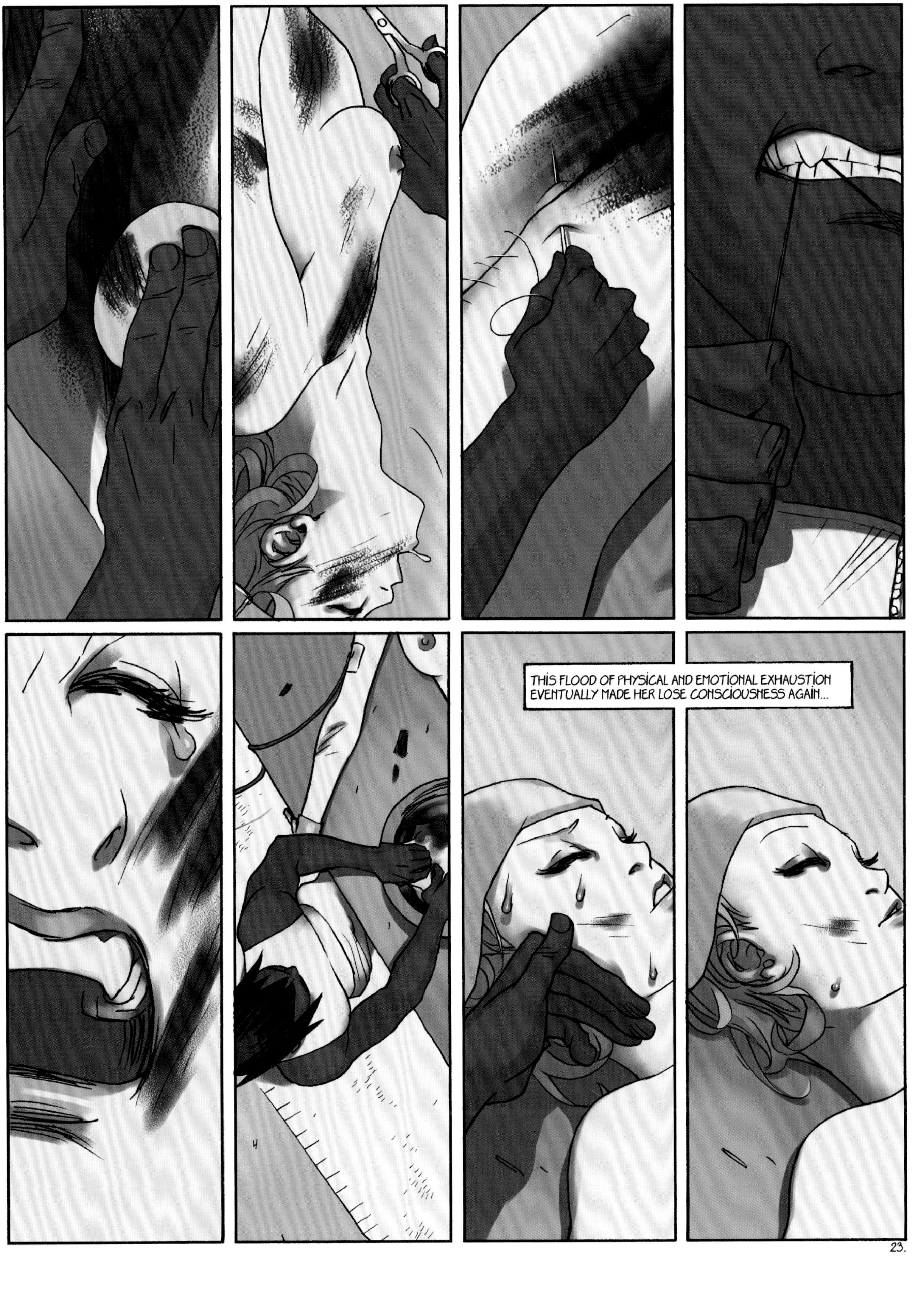
THIS FLOOD OF PHYSICAL AND EMOTIONAL EXHAUSTION EVENTUALLY MADE HER LOSE CONSCIOUSNESS AGAIN...

I SUSPECT SHE EXPERIENCED SEVERAL ORGASMS DURING THE OPERATION.

MAYBE FOUR.

SHE POSSIBLY MISINTERPRETED THAT PLEASURE FOR SPASMS OF TRUE PAIN.

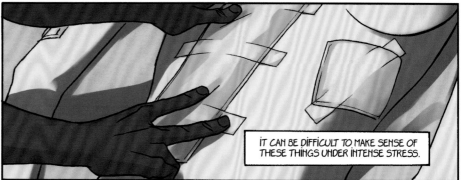

IT CAN BE DIFFICULT TO MAKE SENSE OF THESE THINGS UNDER INTENSE STRESS.

EVERYONE INTERPRETS SUCH INTIMATE SENSATIONS DIFFERENTLY.

BUT HOWEVER SHE CLASSIFIED THOSE FEELINGS, ONE THING IS FOR SURE...

...ONLY "HE" WAS ABLE TO GIVE THEM TO HER.

24.

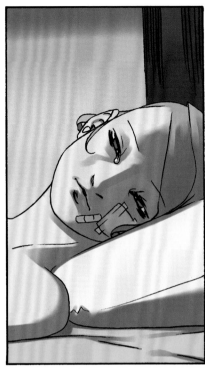

AND BECAUSE OF THAT, HER CRUSH MATURED INTO GENUINE ADORATION.

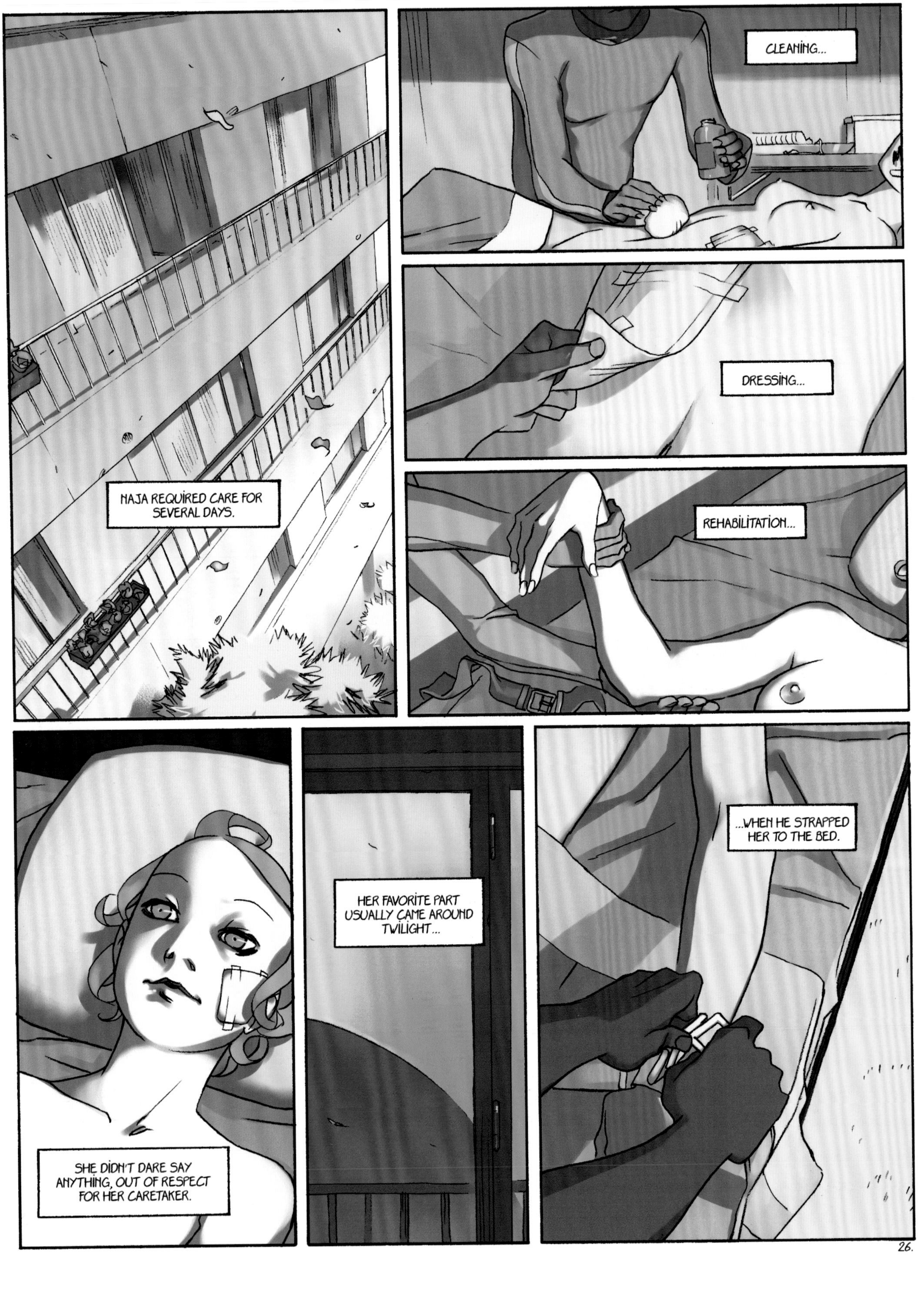
NAJA REQUIRED CARE FOR SEVERAL DAYS.
CLEANING...
DRESSING...
REHABILITATION...
SHE DIDN'T DARE SAY ANYTHING, OUT OF RESPECT FOR HER CARETAKER.
HER FAVORITE PART USUALLY CAME AROUND TWILIGHT...
...WHEN HE STRAPPED HER TO THE BED.

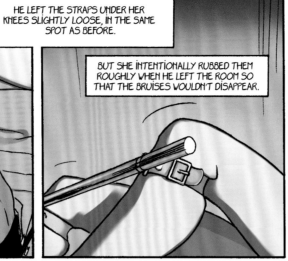

HE LEFT THE STRAPS UNDER HER KNEES SLIGHTLY LOOSE, IN THE SAME SPOT AS BEFORE.

BUT SHE INTENTIONALLY RUBBED THEM ROUGHLY WHEN HE LEFT THE ROOM SO THAT THE BRUISES WOULDN'T DISAPPEAR.

IT BECAME A BEDTIME RITUAL.

UNTIL ONE MORNING, WHEN SHE AWOKE WITH A STRANGE SENSE OF FREEDOM.

"HE" HAD UNSTRAPPED HER...

...BEFORE DISAPPEARING.

27.

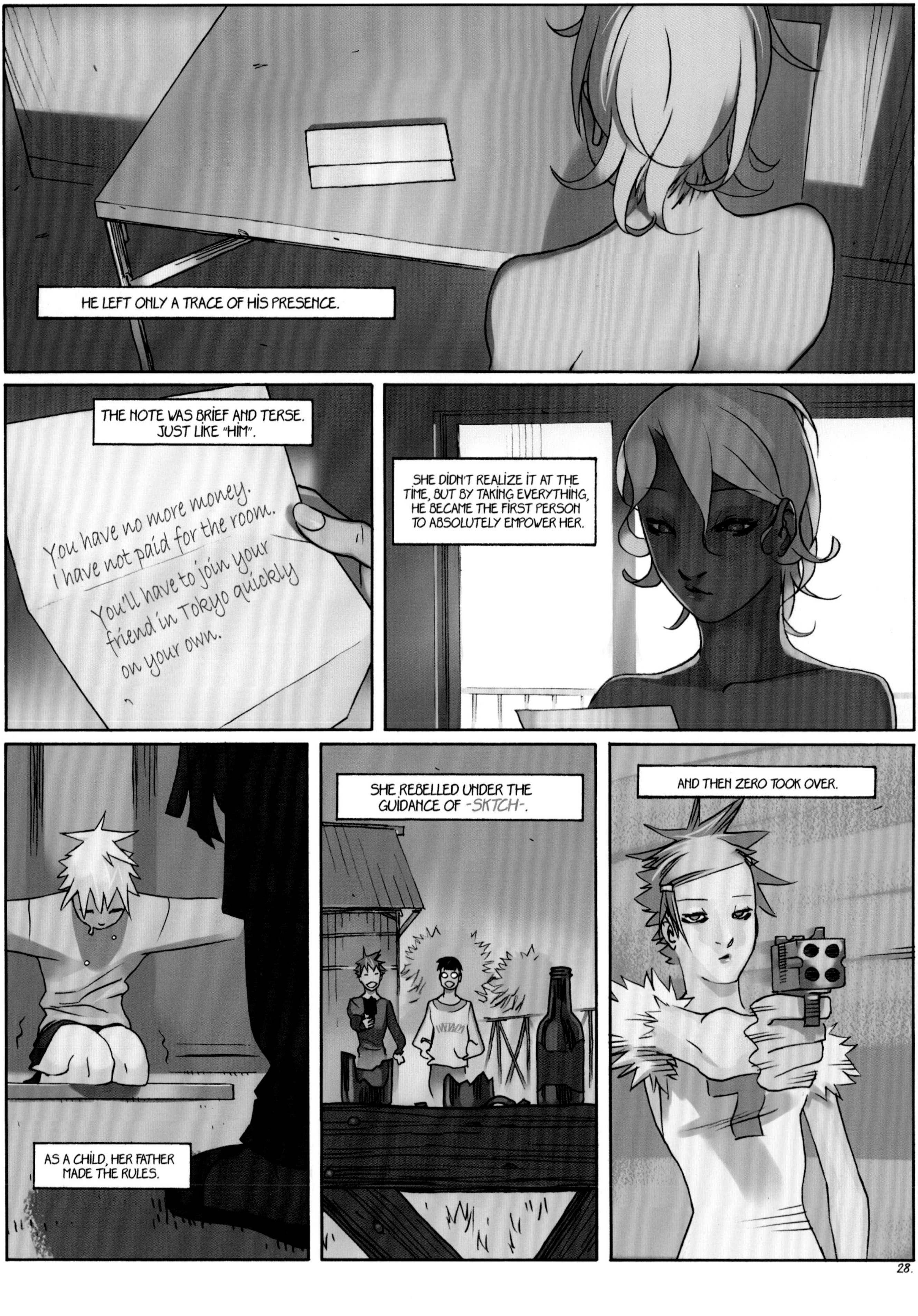
HE LEFT ONLY A TRACE OF HIS PRESENCE.
THE NOTE WAS BRIEF AND TERSE. JUST LIKE "HIM".
You have no more money. I have not paid for the room.
You'll have to join your friend in Tokyo quickly on your own.
SHE DIDN'T REALIZE IT AT THE TIME, BUT BY TAKING EVERYTHING, HE BECAME THE FIRST PERSON TO ABSOLUTELY EMPOWER HER.
AS A CHILD, HER FATHER MADE THE RULES.
SHE REBELLED UNDER THE GUIDANCE OF -SKTCH-.
AND THEN ZERO TOOK OVER.

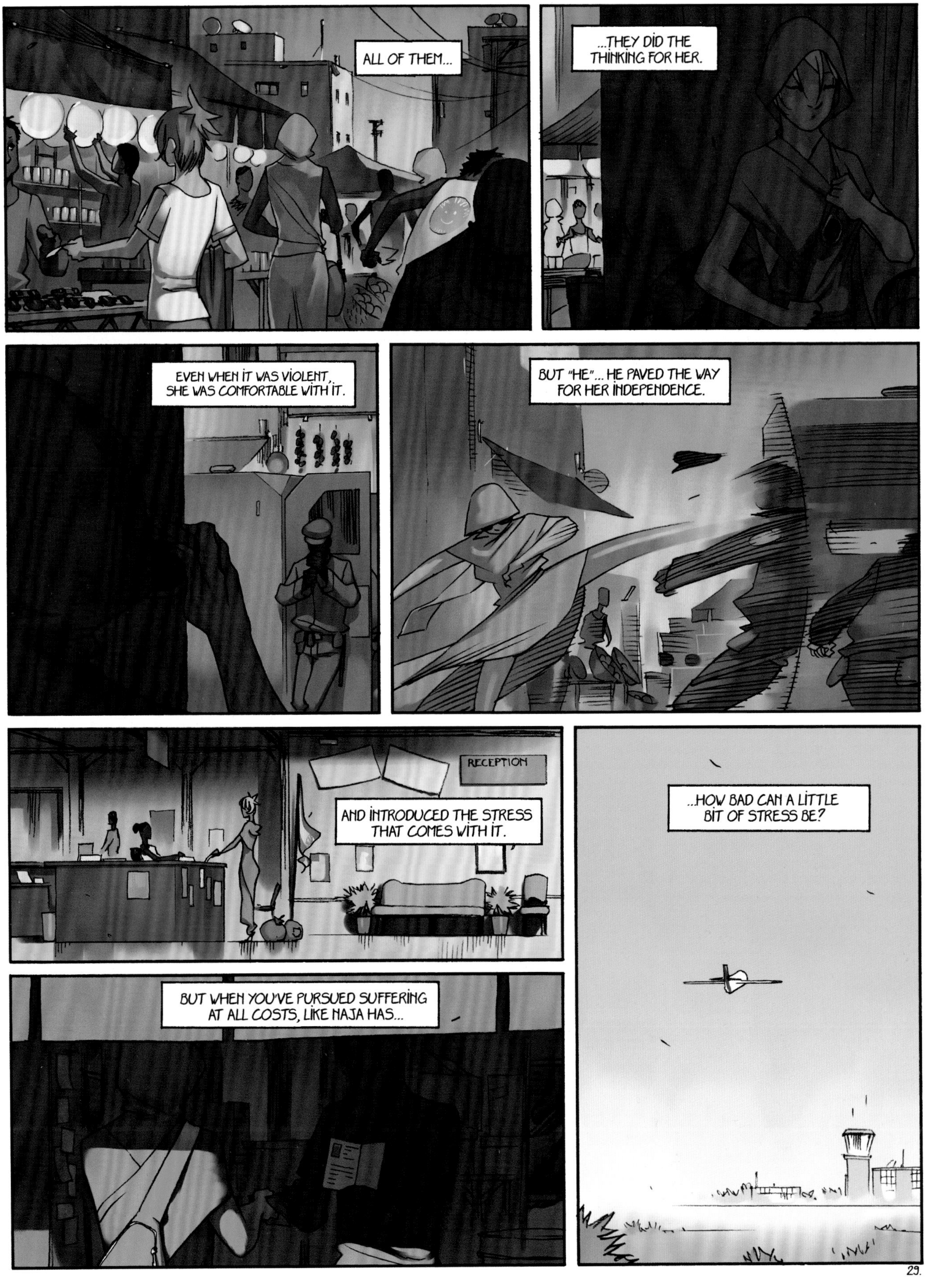
ALL OF THEM...
...THEY DID THE THINKING FOR HER.
EVEN WHEN IT WAS VIOLENT, SHE WAS COMFORTABLE WITH IT.
BUT "HE"... HE PAVED THE WAY FOR HER INDEPENDENCE.
RECEPTION
AND INTRODUCED THE STRESS THAT COMES WITH IT.
BUT WHEN YOU'VE PURSUED SUFFERING AT ALL COSTS, LIKE NAJA HAS...
...HOW BAD CAN A LITTLE BIT OF STRESS BE?

RIGHT NOW, NAJA'S STRESS LEVEL WAS SKYROCKETING.

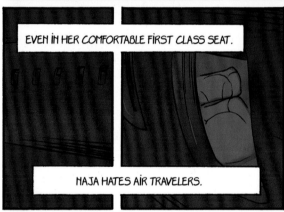

EVEN IN HER COMFORTABLE FIRST CLASS SEAT.

NAJA HATES AIR TRAVELERS.

THOSE IN ECONOMY ARE MOSTLY TOURISTS WHO TALK INCESSANTLY ABOUT THEIR VACATION PLANS, REPEATING EVERY STUPID LITTLE DETAIL THEY READ IN SOME EVIL LITTLE TRAVEL GUIDE.

OR, IF THEY'RE RETURNING, THEY COMPLAIN ABOUT THE STATE OF THE MONUMENTS, THE COMPLEXITY OF THE LOCAL TRANSIT SYSTEM, OR THE STUPIDITY OF THE NATIVES.

EITHER WAY, THEY'RE ALL ELBOWS, LAUGHING TOO LOUD, SNORING, DRIPPING, FARTING, AND COMPLAINING, WITH THEIR SMELLY FEET AND MUSIC TUNED TOO LOUD FOR THEIR HEADSETS.

IN A WORD, THEY LIVE.

AND THAT'S TOO MUCH FOR NAJA.

30.

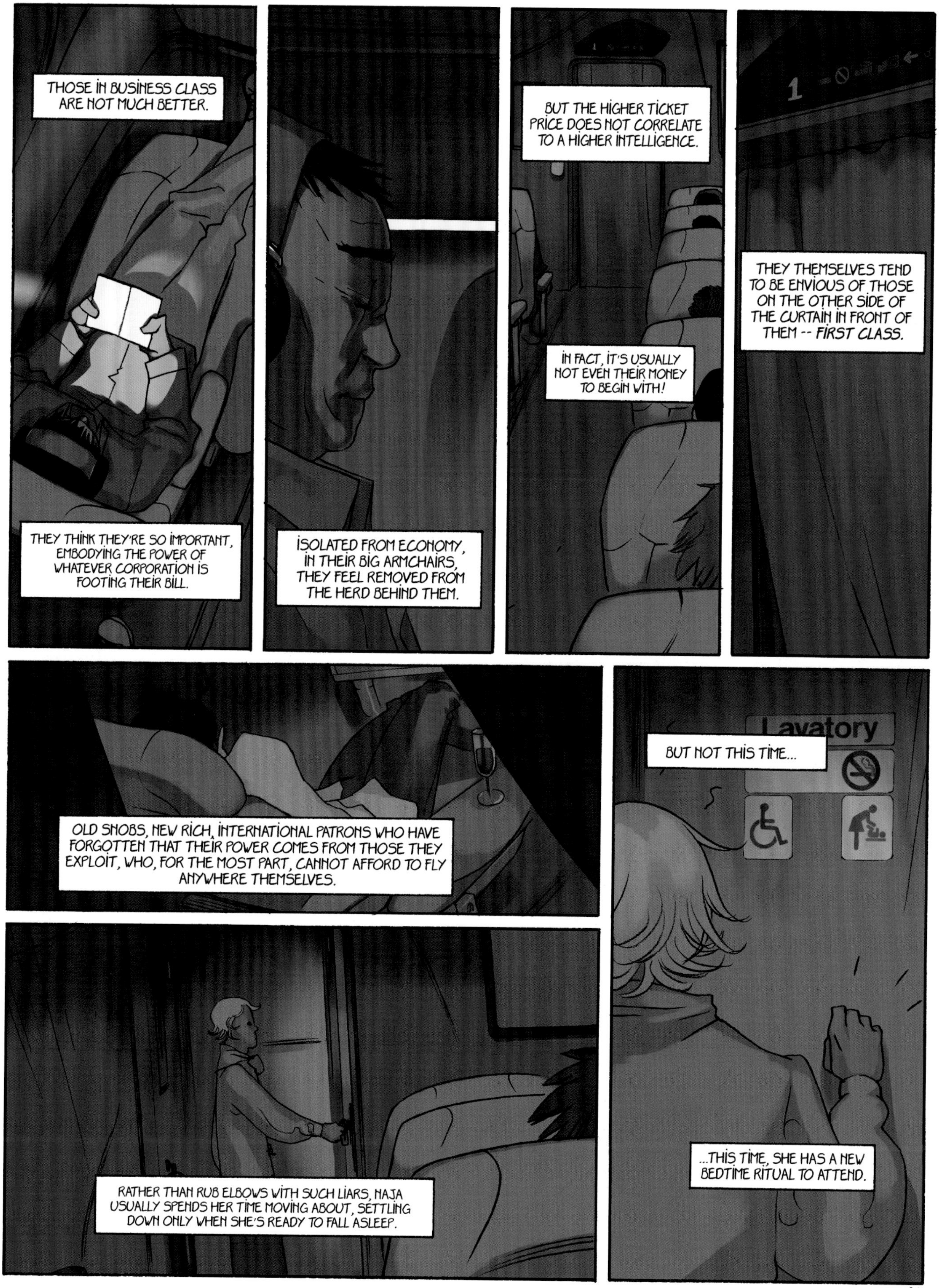
THOSE IN BUSINESS CLASS ARE NOT MUCH BETTER.
THEY THINK THEY'RE SO IMPORTANT, EMBODYING THE POWER OF WHATEVER CORPORATION IS FOOTING THEIR BILL.
ISOLATED FROM ECONOMY, IN THEIR BIG ARMCHAIRS, THEY FEEL REMOVED FROM THE HERD BEHIND THEM.
BUT THE HIGHER TICKET PRICE DOES NOT CORRELATE TO A HIGHER INTELLIGENCE.
IN FACT, IT'S USUALLY NOT EVEN THEIR MONEY TO BEGIN WITH!
THEY THEMSELVES TEND TO BE ENVIOUS OF THOSE ON THE OTHER SIDE OF THE CURTAIN IN FRONT OF THEM -- *FIRST CLASS.*
OLD SNOBS, NEW RICH, INTERNATIONAL PATRONS WHO HAVE FORGOTTEN THAT THEIR POWER COMES FROM THOSE THEY EXPLOIT, WHO, FOR THE MOST PART, CANNOT AFFORD TO FLY ANYWHERE THEMSELVES.
RATHER THAN RUB ELBOWS WITH SUCH LIARS, NAJA USUALLY SPENDS HER TIME MOVING ABOUT, SETTLING DOWN ONLY WHEN SHE'S READY TO FALL ASLEEP.
Lavatory
BUT NOT THIS TIME...
...THIS TIME, SHE HAS A NEW BEDTIME RITUAL TO ATTEND.

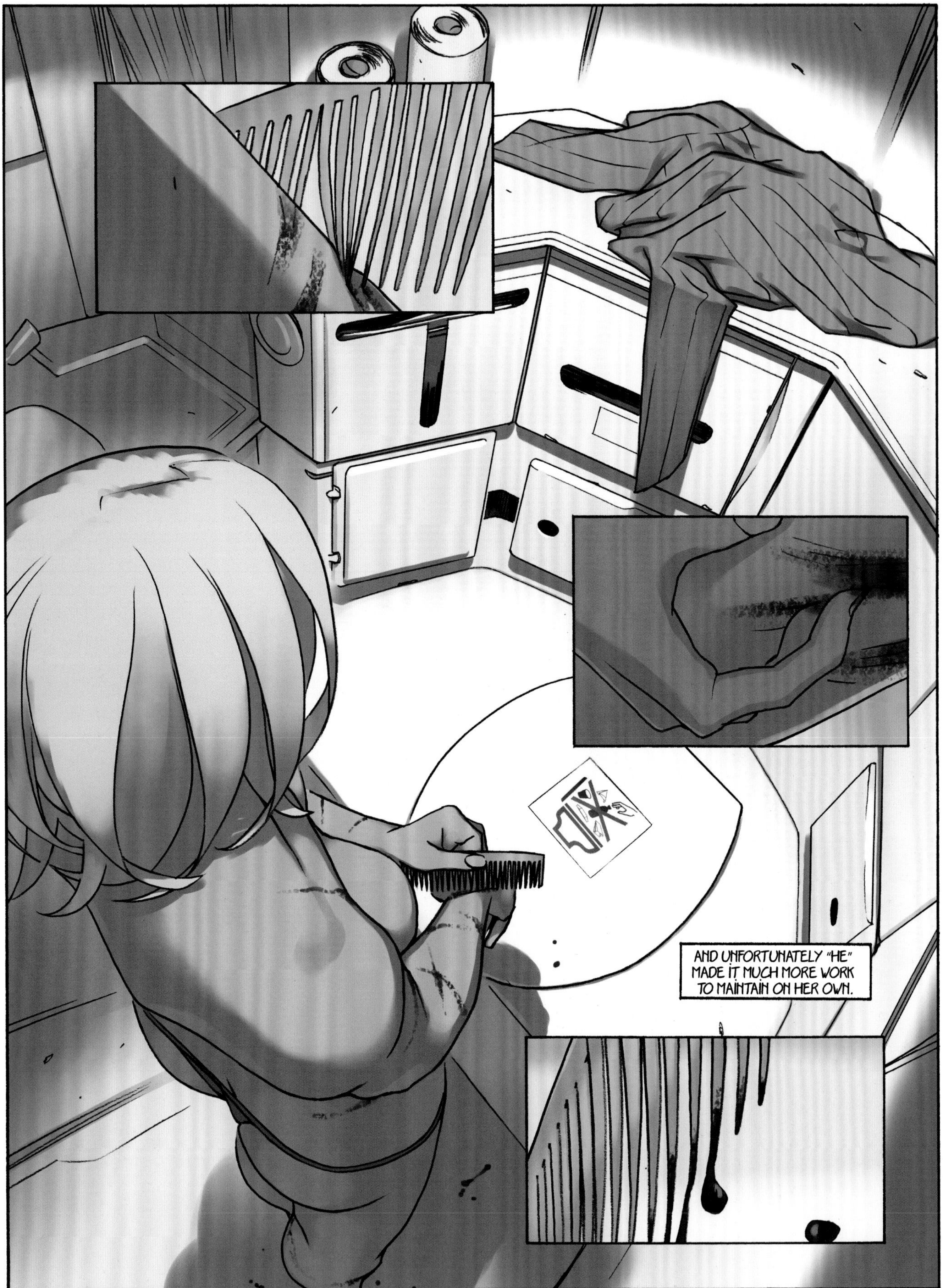
AND UNFORTUNATELY "HE" MADE IT MUCH MORE WORK TO MAINTAIN ON HER OWN.

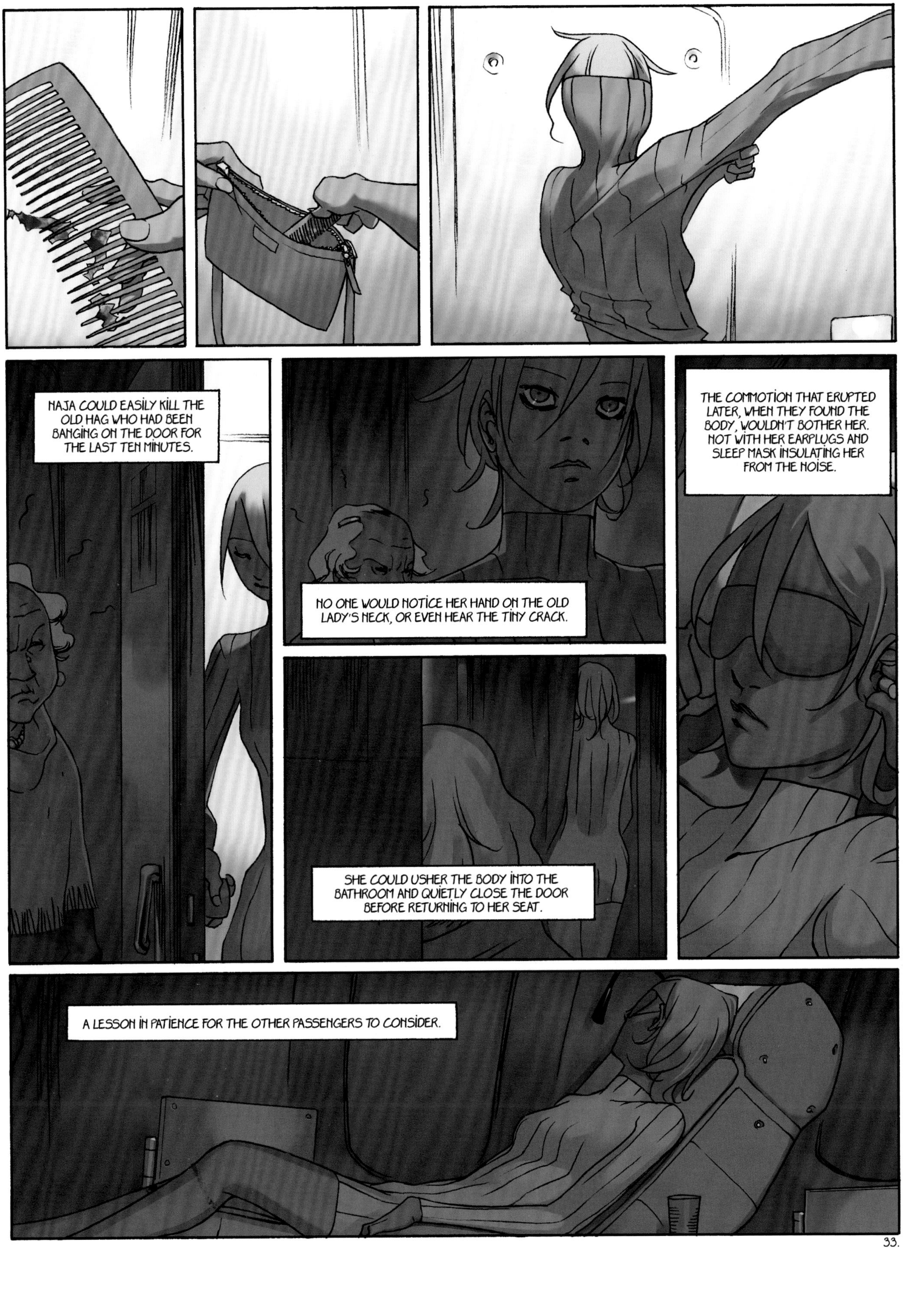
NAJA COULD EASILY KILL THE OLD HAG WHO HAD BEEN BANGING ON THE DOOR FOR THE LAST TEN MINUTES.
NO ONE WOULD NOTICE HER HAND ON THE OLD LADY'S NECK, OR EVEN HEAR THE TINY CRACK.
SHE COULD USHER THE BODY INTO THE BATHROOM AND QUIETLY CLOSE THE DOOR BEFORE RETURNING TO HER SEAT.
THE COMMOTION THAT ERUPTED LATER, WHEN THEY FOUND THE BODY, WOULDN'T BOTHER HER. NOT WITH HER EARPLUGS AND SLEEP MASK INSULATING HER FROM THE NOISE.
A LESSON IN PATIENCE FOR THE OTHER PASSENGERS TO CONSIDER.

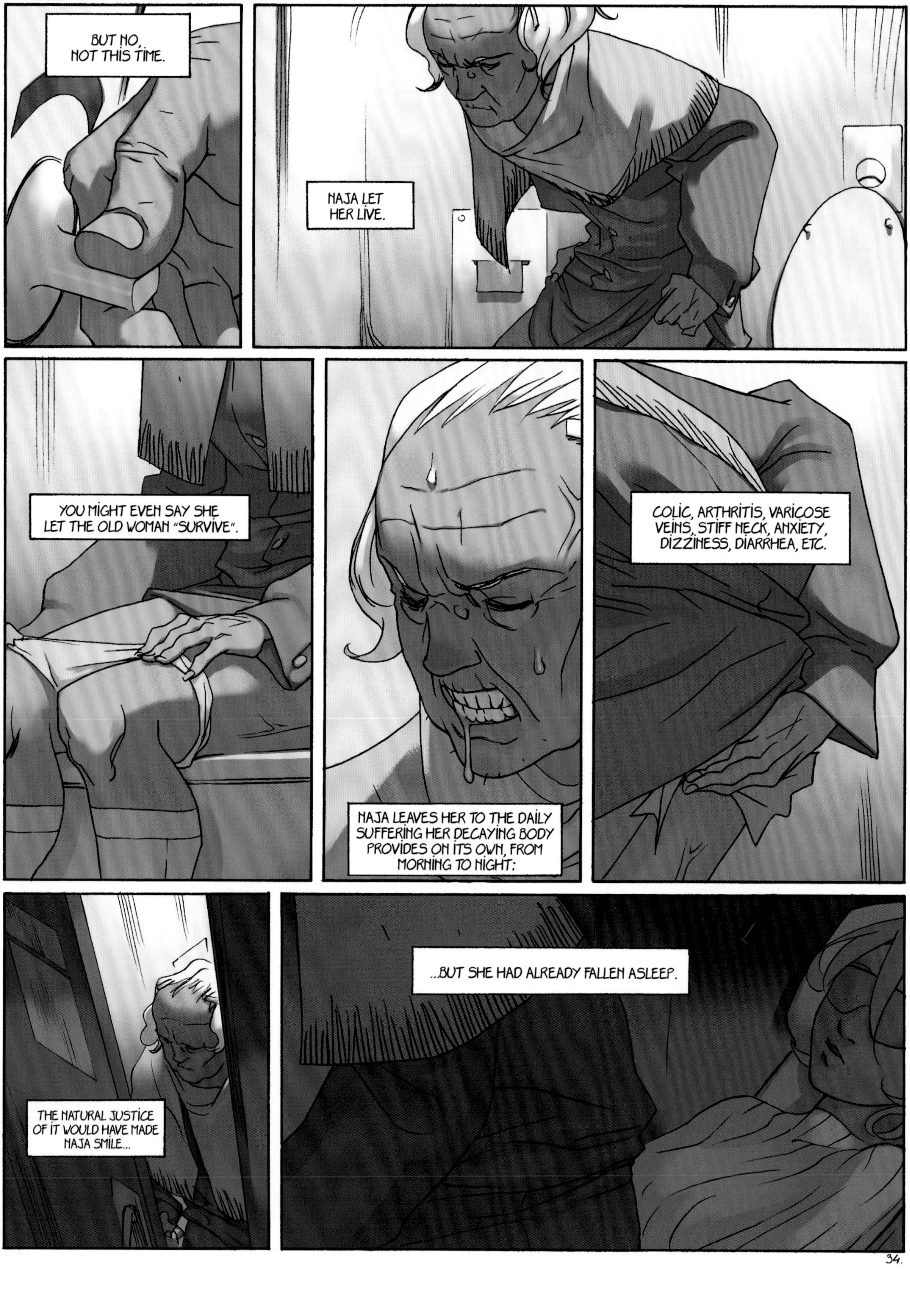
BUT NO, NOT THIS TIME.
NAJA LET HER LIVE.
YOU MIGHT EVEN SAY SHE LET THE OLD WOMAN "SURVIVE".
NAJA LEAVES HER TO THE DAILY SUFFERING HER DECAYING BODY PROVIDES ON ITS OWN, FROM MORNING TO NIGHT:
COLIC, ARTHRITIS, VARICOSE VEINS, STIFF NECK, ANXIETY, DIZZINESS, DIARRHEA, ETC.
THE NATURAL JUSTICE OF IT WOULD HAVE MADE NAJA SMILE...
...BUT SHE HAD ALREADY FALLEN ASLEEP.

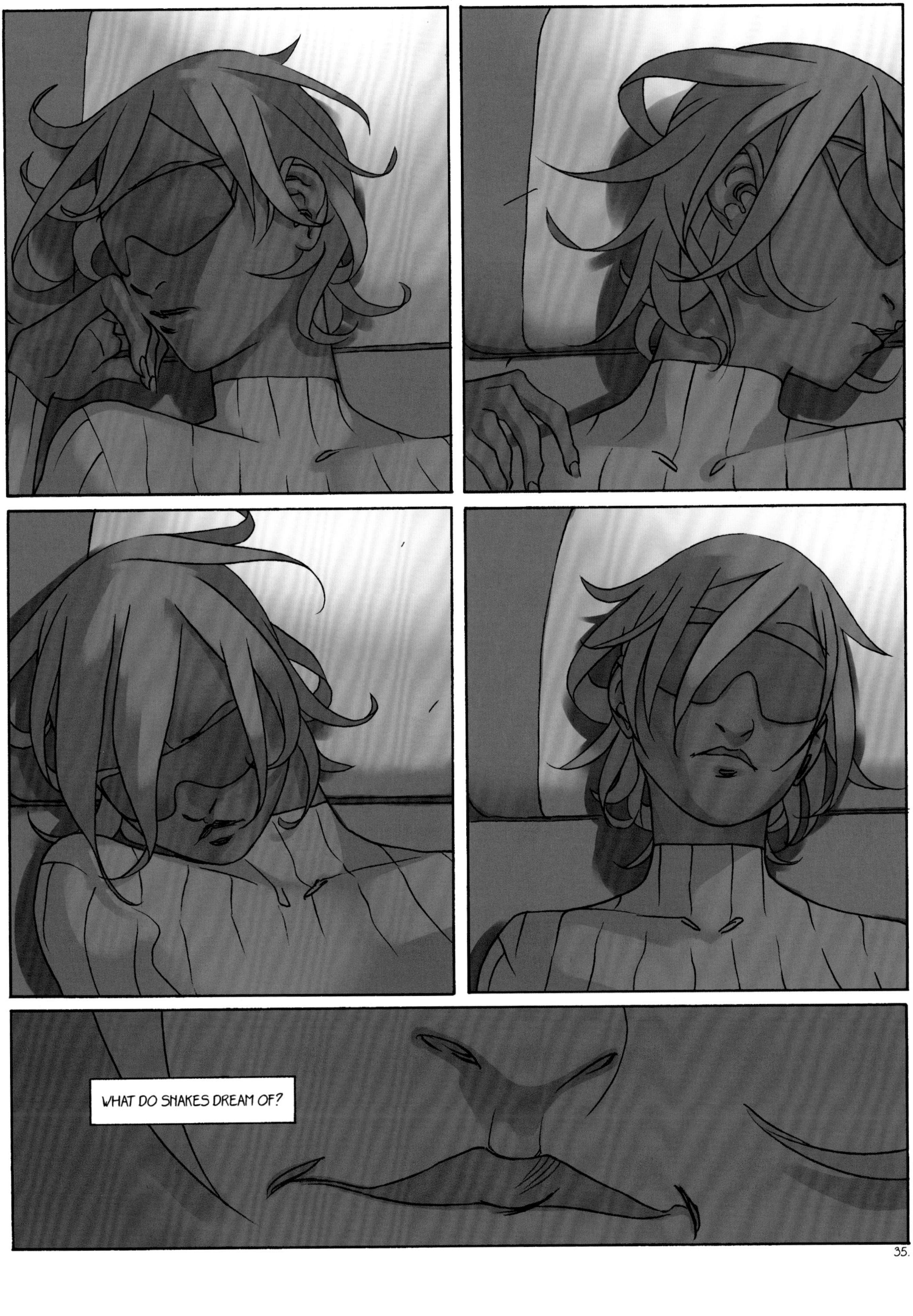
WHAT DO SNAKES DREAM OF?

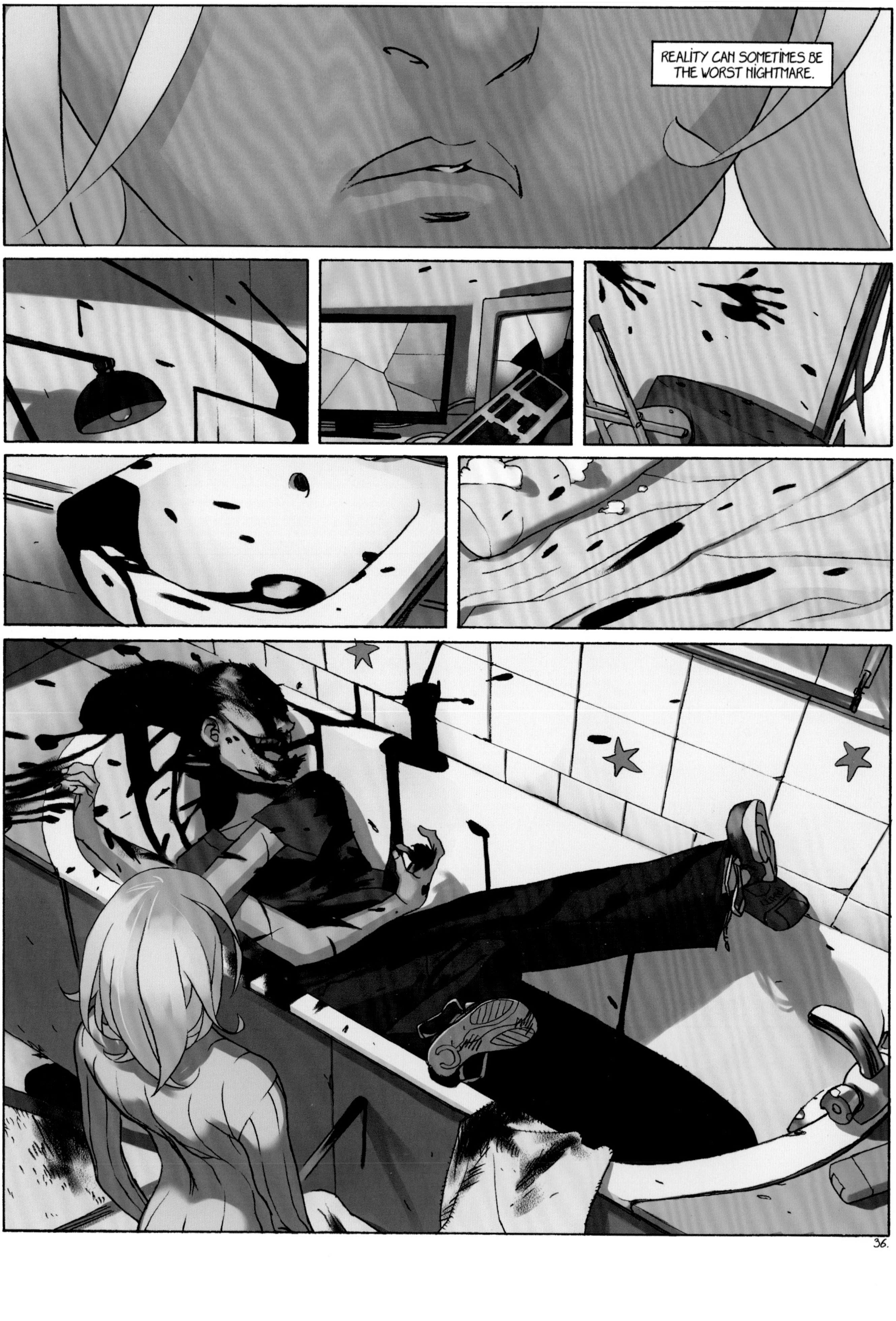
REALITY CAN SOMETIMES BE THE WORST NIGHTMARE.

TO SEE YOUR BEST FRIEND BUTCHERED SO HORRIBLY WOULD HAVE SENT ANYONE ELSE BURSTING INTO TEARS AND SCREAMS OF RAGE.

BUT NOT NAJA.

BECAUSE NAJA...

(...WELL, YOU KNOW....)

...NAJA WOULDN'T KNOW WHAT SUCH EMOTIONAL PAIN FEELS LIKE.

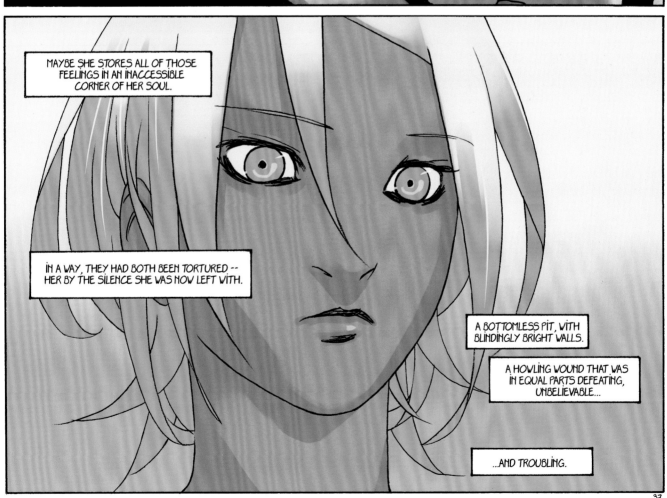

MAYBE SHE STORES ALL OF THOSE FEELINGS IN AN INACCESSIBLE CORNER OF HER SOUL.

IN A WAY, THEY HAD BOTH BEEN TORTURED -- HER BY THE SILENCE SHE WAS NOW LEFT WITH.

A BOTTOMLESS PIT, WITH BLINDINGLY BRIGHT WALLS.

A HOWLING WOUND THAT WAS IN EQUAL PARTS DEFEATING, UNBELIEVABLE...

...AND TROUBLING.

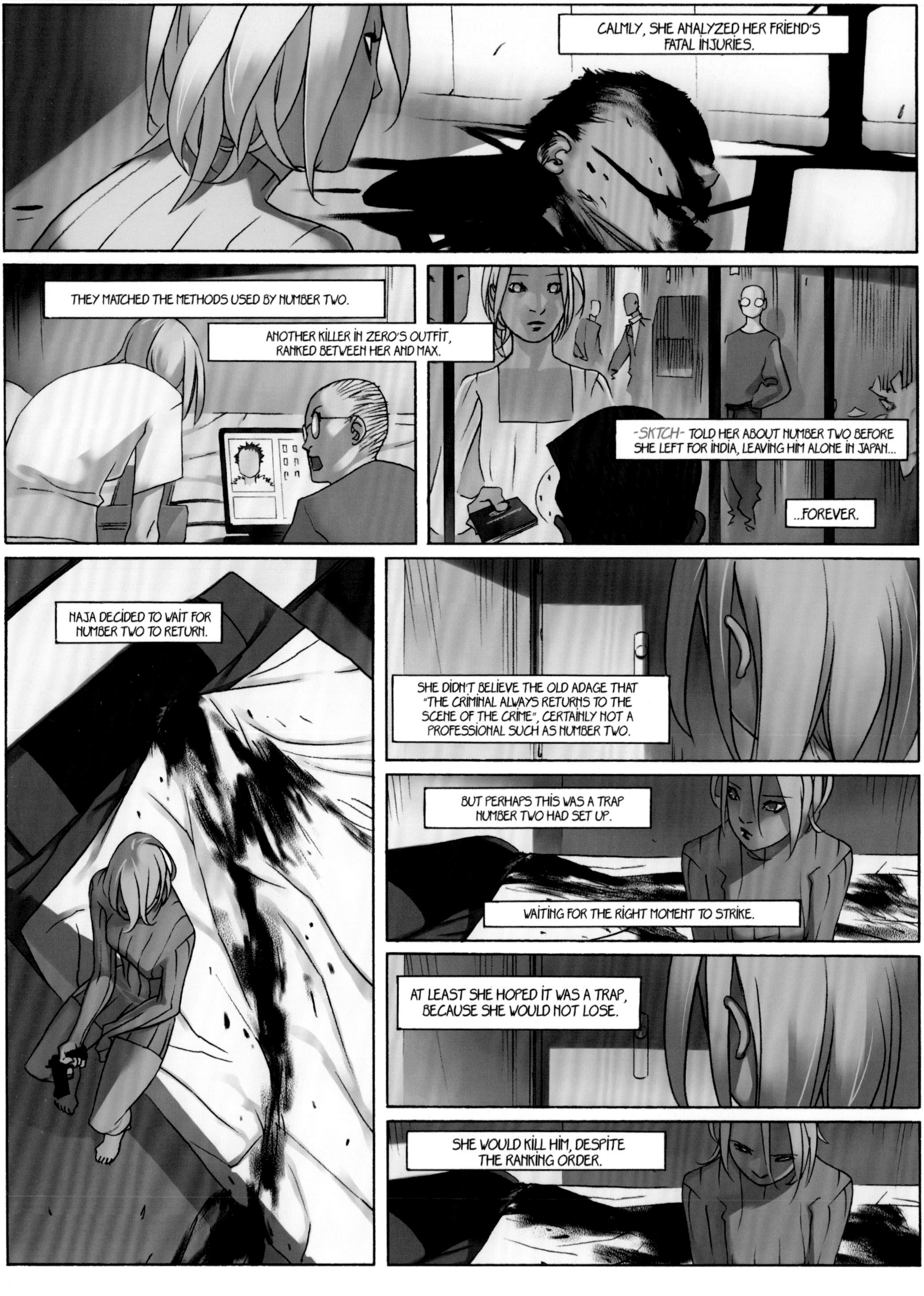
CALMLY, SHE ANALYZED HER FRIEND'S FATAL INJURIES.
THEY MATCHED THE METHODS USED BY NUMBER TWO.
ANOTHER KILLER IN ZERO'S OUTFIT, RANKED BETWEEN HER AND MAX.
-SKTCH- TOLD HER ABOUT NUMBER TWO BEFORE SHE LEFT FOR INDIA, LEAVING HIM ALONE IN JAPAN...
...FOREVER.
NAJA DECIDED TO WAIT FOR NUMBER TWO TO RETURN.
SHE DIDN'T BELIEVE THE OLD ADAGE THAT "THE CRIMINAL ALWAYS RETURNS TO THE SCENE OF THE CRIME", CERTAINLY NOT A PROFESSIONAL SUCH AS NUMBER TWO.
BUT PERHAPS THIS WAS A TRAP NUMBER TWO HAD SET UP.
WAITING FOR THE RIGHT MOMENT TO STRIKE.
AT LEAST SHE HOPED IT WAS A TRAP, BECAUSE SHE WOULD NOT LOSE.
SHE WOULD KILL HIM, DESPITE THE RANKING ORDER.

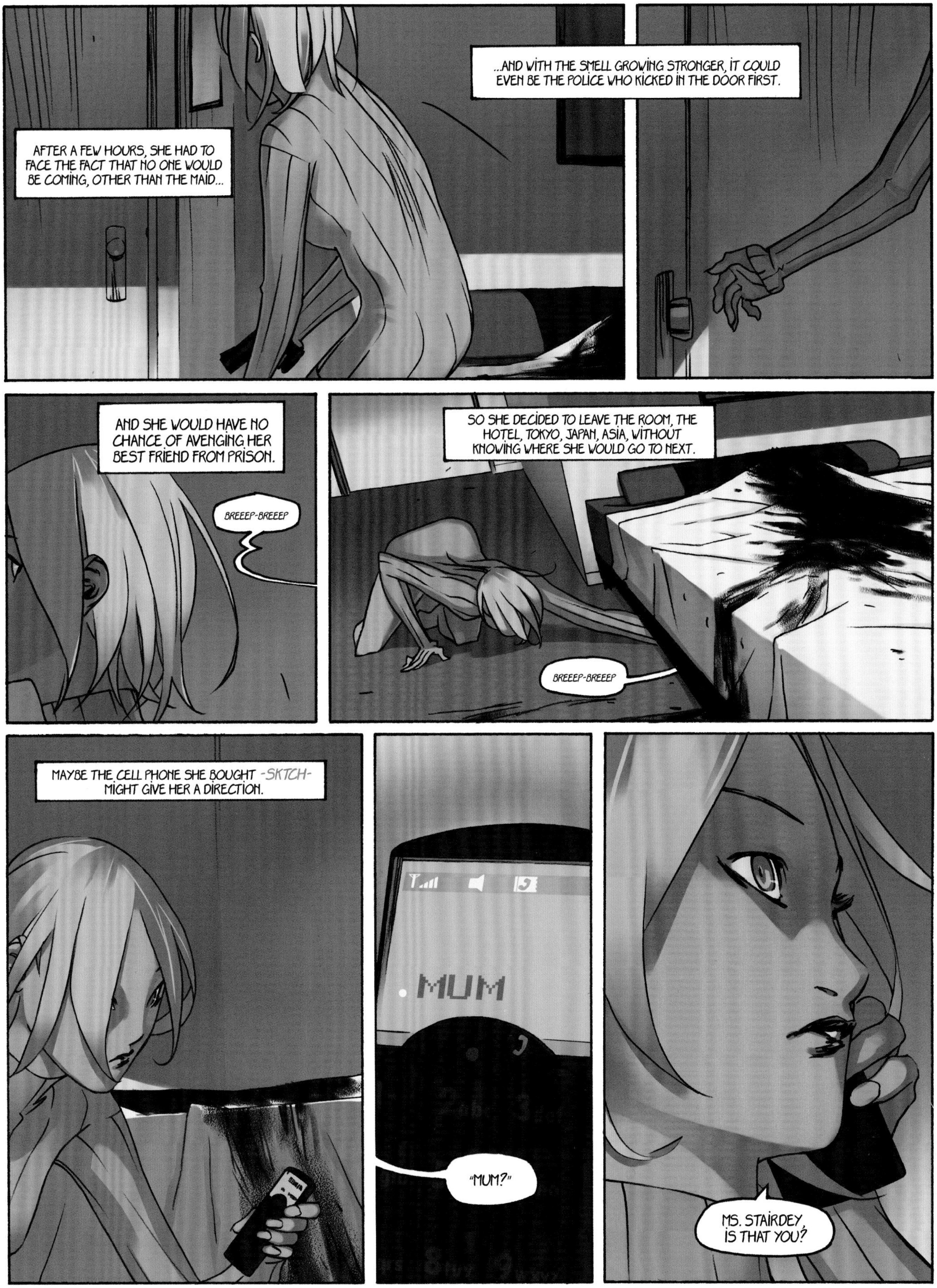
AFTER A FEW HOURS, SHE HAD TO FACE THE FACT THAT NO ONE WOULD BE COMING, OTHER THAN THE MAID...
...AND WITH THE SMELL GROWING STRONGER, IT COULD EVEN BE THE POLICE WHO KICKED IN THE DOOR FIRST.
AND SHE WOULD HAVE NO CHANCE OF AVENGING HER BEST FRIEND FROM PRISON.
BREEEP-BREEEP
SO SHE DECIDED TO LEAVE THE ROOM, THE HOTEL, TOKYO, JAPAN, ASIA, WITHOUT KNOWING WHERE SHE WOULD GO TO NEXT.
BREEEP-BREEEP
MAYBE THE CELL PHONE SHE BOUGHT -SKTCH- MIGHT GIVE HER A DIRECTION.
MUM
"MUM?"
MS. STAIRDEY, IS THAT YOU?

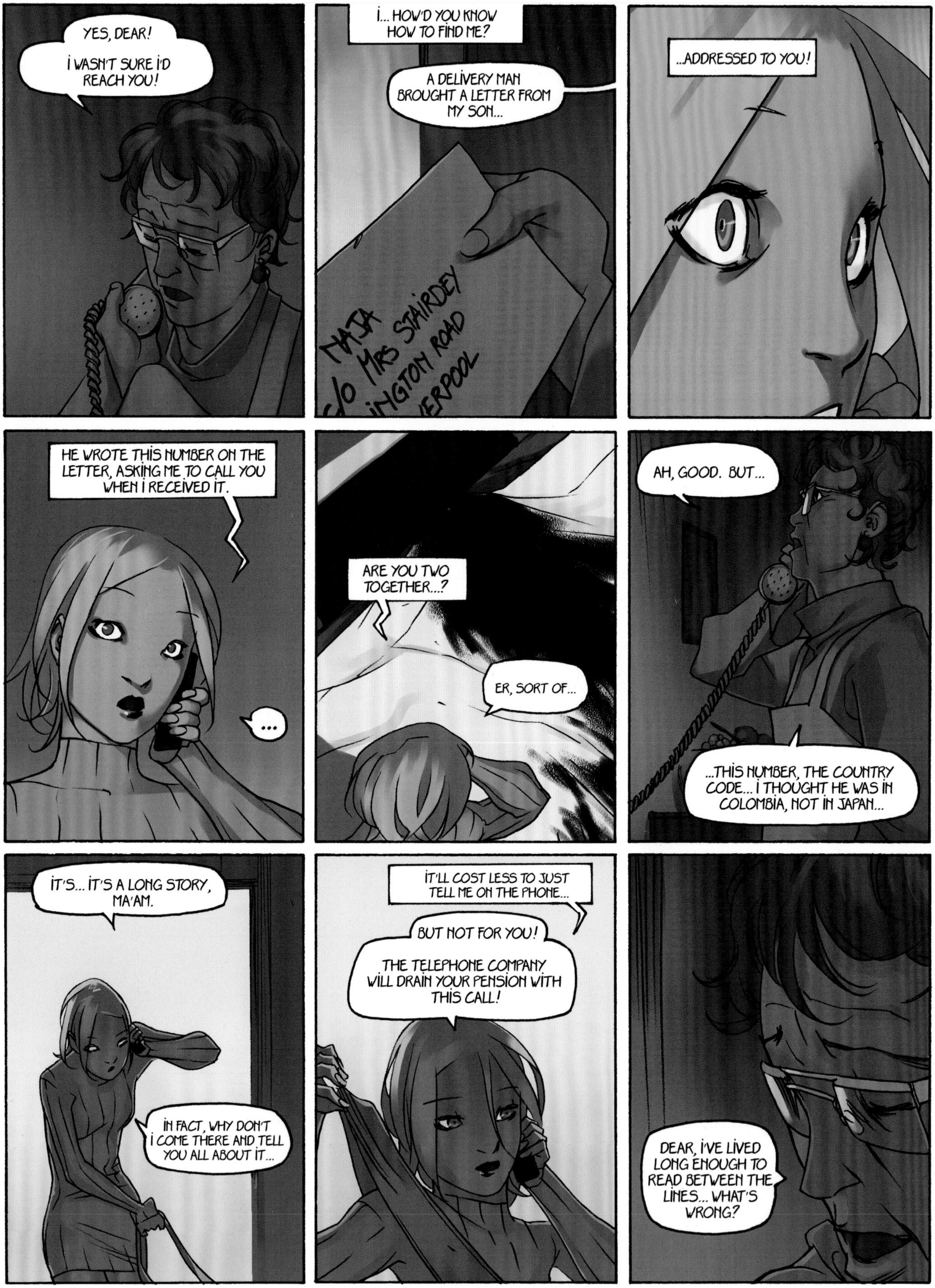
YES, DEAR!
I WASN'T SURE I'D REACH YOU!
I... HOW'D YOU KNOW HOW TO FIND ME?
A DELIVERY MAN BROUGHT A LETTER FROM MY SON...
MAJA
C/O MRS STAIRDEY
...INGTON ROAD
...ERPOOL
...ADDRESSED TO YOU!
HE WROTE THIS NUMBER ON THE LETTER, ASKING ME TO CALL YOU WHEN I RECEIVED IT.
...
ARE YOU TWO TOGETHER...?
ER, SORT OF...
AH, GOOD. BUT...
...THIS NUMBER, THE COUNTRY CODE... I THOUGHT HE WAS IN COLOMBIA, NOT IN JAPAN...
IT'S... IT'S A LONG STORY, MA'AM.
IN FACT, WHY DON'T I COME THERE AND TELL YOU ALL ABOUT IT...
IT'LL COST LESS TO JUST TELL ME ON THE PHONE...
BUT NOT FOR YOU!
THE TELEPHONE COMPANY WILL DRAIN YOUR PENSION WITH THIS CALL!
DEAR, I'VE LIVED LONG ENOUGH TO READ BETWEEN THE LINES... WHAT'S WRONG?

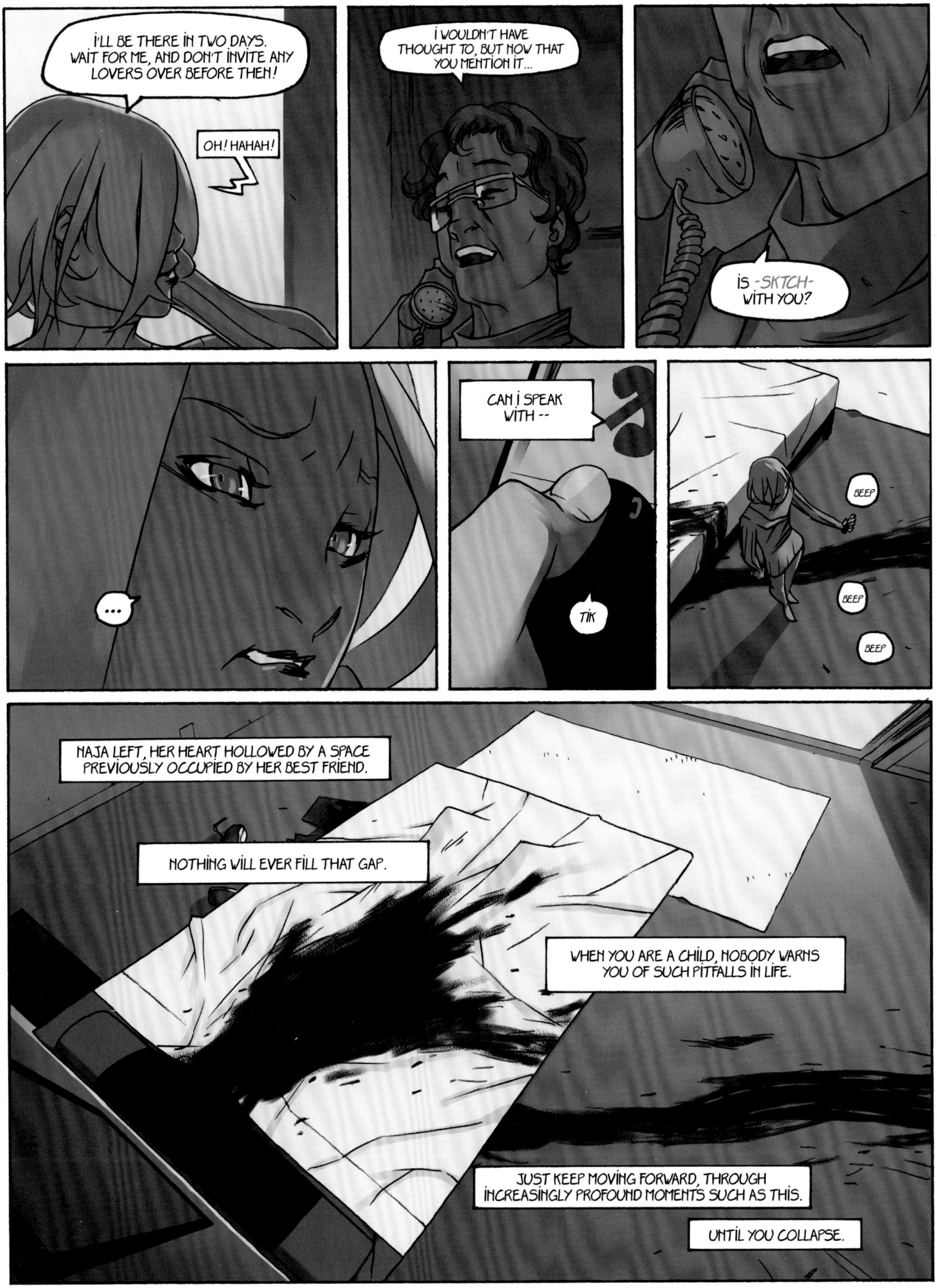

I'LL BE THERE IN TWO DAYS. WAIT FOR ME, AND DON'T INVITE ANY LOVERS OVER BEFORE THEN!
OH! HAHAH!
I WOULDN'T HAVE THOUGHT TO, BUT NOW THAT YOU MENTION IT...
IS -SKTCH- WITH YOU?
...
CAN I SPEAK WITH --
TIK
BEEP
BEEP
BEEP
NAJA LEFT, HER HEART HOLLOWED BY A SPACE PREVIOUSLY OCCUPIED BY HER BEST FRIEND.
NOTHING WILL EVER FILL THAT GAP.
WHEN YOU ARE A CHILD, NOBODY WARNS YOU OF SUCH PITFALLS IN LIFE.
JUST KEEP MOVING FORWARD, THROUGH INCREASINGLY PROFOUND MOMENTS SUCH AS THIS.
UNTIL YOU COLLAPSE.

NAJA WAS AIRBORNE WHEN THE HOTEL FIRE WAS FINALLY EXTINGUISHED.

SHE TOOK OFF AS THEY DISCOVERED IN WHICH ROOM THE FIRE STARTED.

AS THE FLAMES SPREAD ACROSS THE FLOOR, SHE WAS ALREADY IN A TAXI.

THE PORTER COLLECTED HER BAGS AS A GROOM SPOTTED THE FIRST SMOKE.

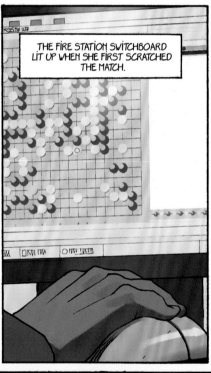

THE FIRE STATION SWITCHBOARD LIT UP WHEN SHE FIRST SCRATCHED THE MATCH.

AND WHEN SHE RETURNED TO THE ROOM FOR THE LAST TIME...

...NAJA TOLD HERSELF HER FRIEND HAD ALREADY BEEN DEAD FOR TOO LONG.

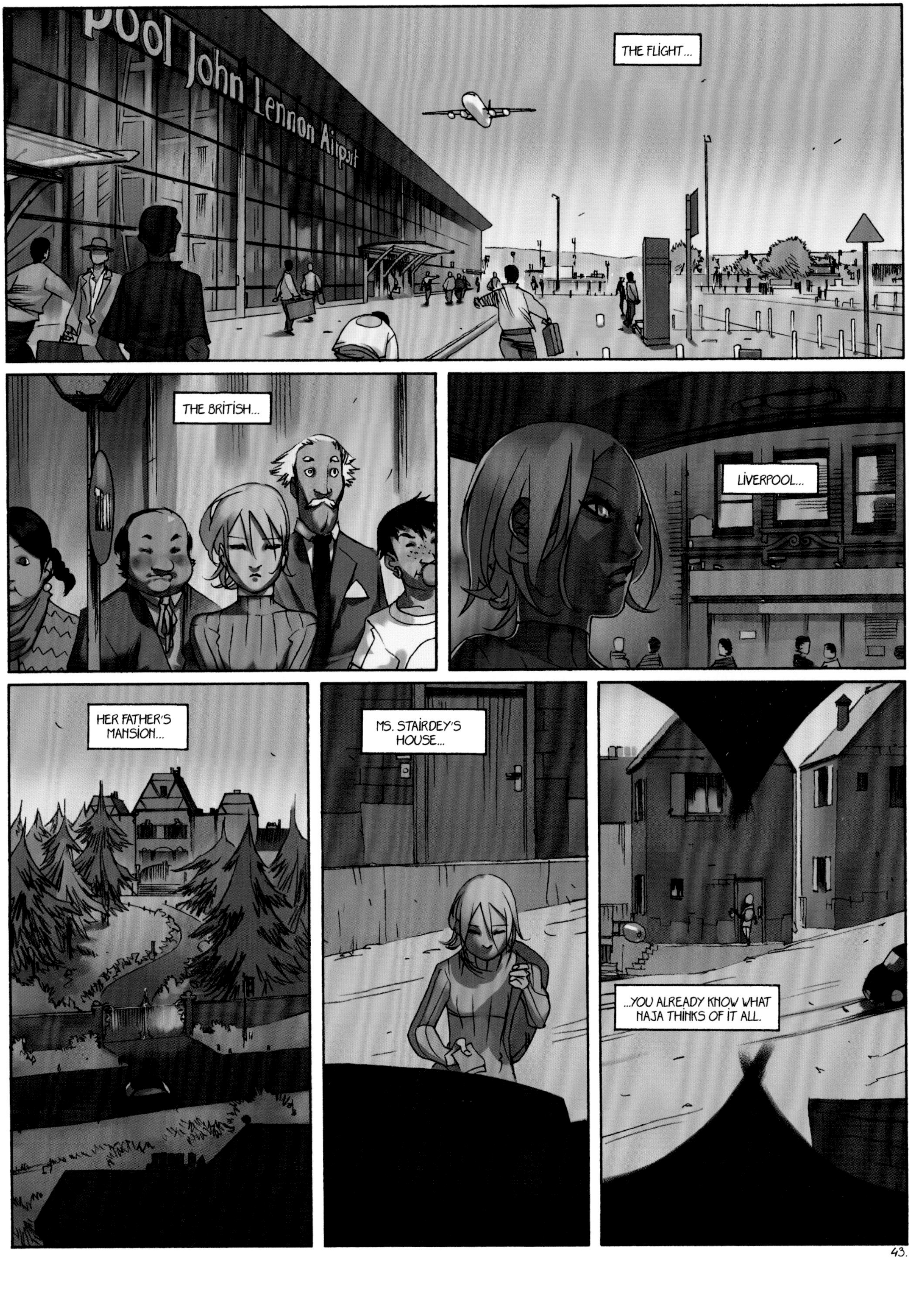
pool John Lennon Airport
THE FLIGHT...
THE BRITISH...
LIVERPOOL...
HER FATHER'S MANSION...
MS. STAIRDEY'S HOUSE...
...YOU ALREADY KNOW WHAT NAJA THINKS OF IT ALL.

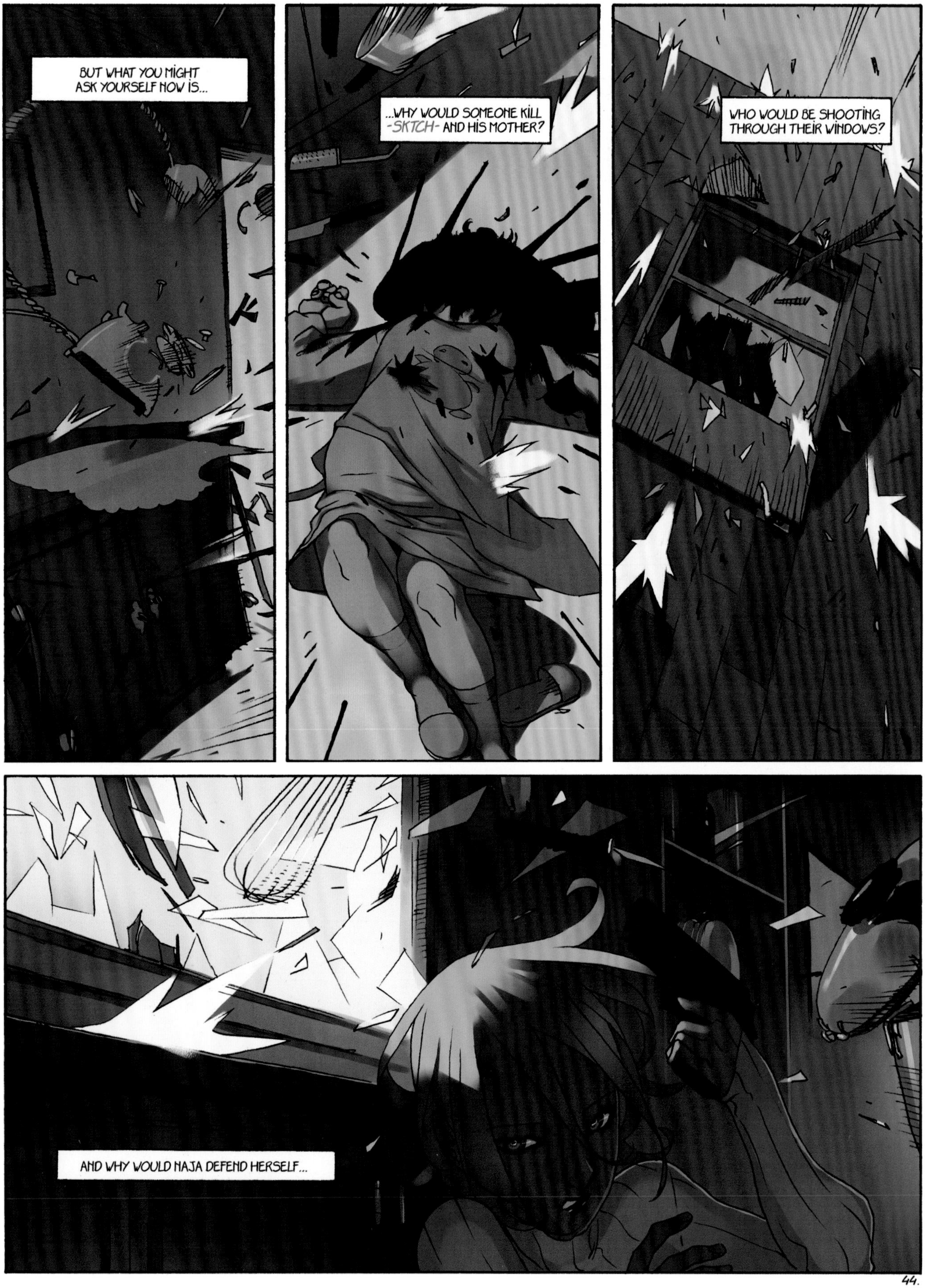

BUT WHAT YOU MIGHT ASK YOURSELF NOW IS...
...WHY WOULD SOMEONE KILL -SKTCH- AND HIS MOTHER?
WHO WOULD BE SHOOTING THROUGH THEIR WINDOWS?
AND WHY WOULD NAJA DEFEND HERSELF...

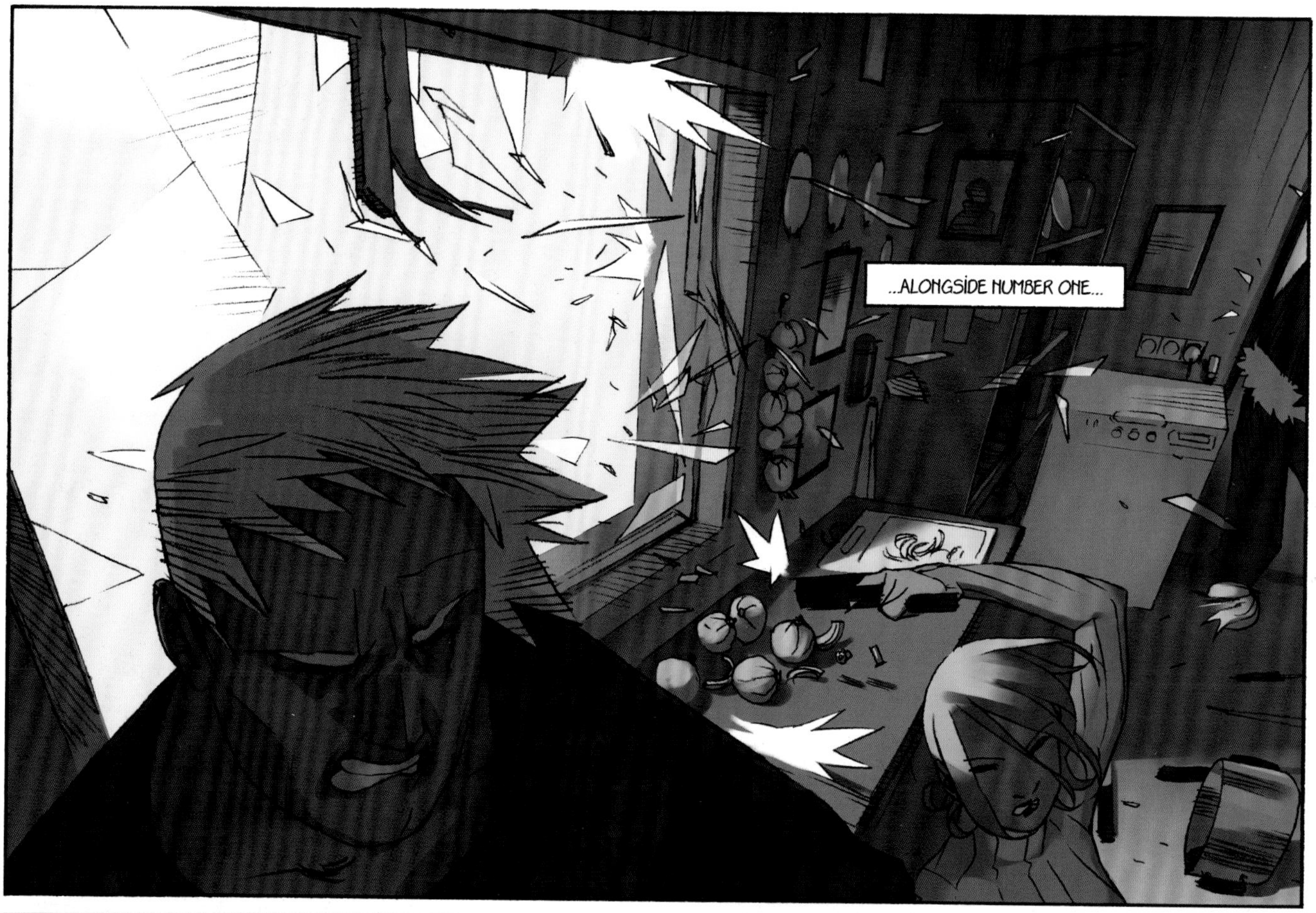
...ALONGSIDE NUMBER ONE...

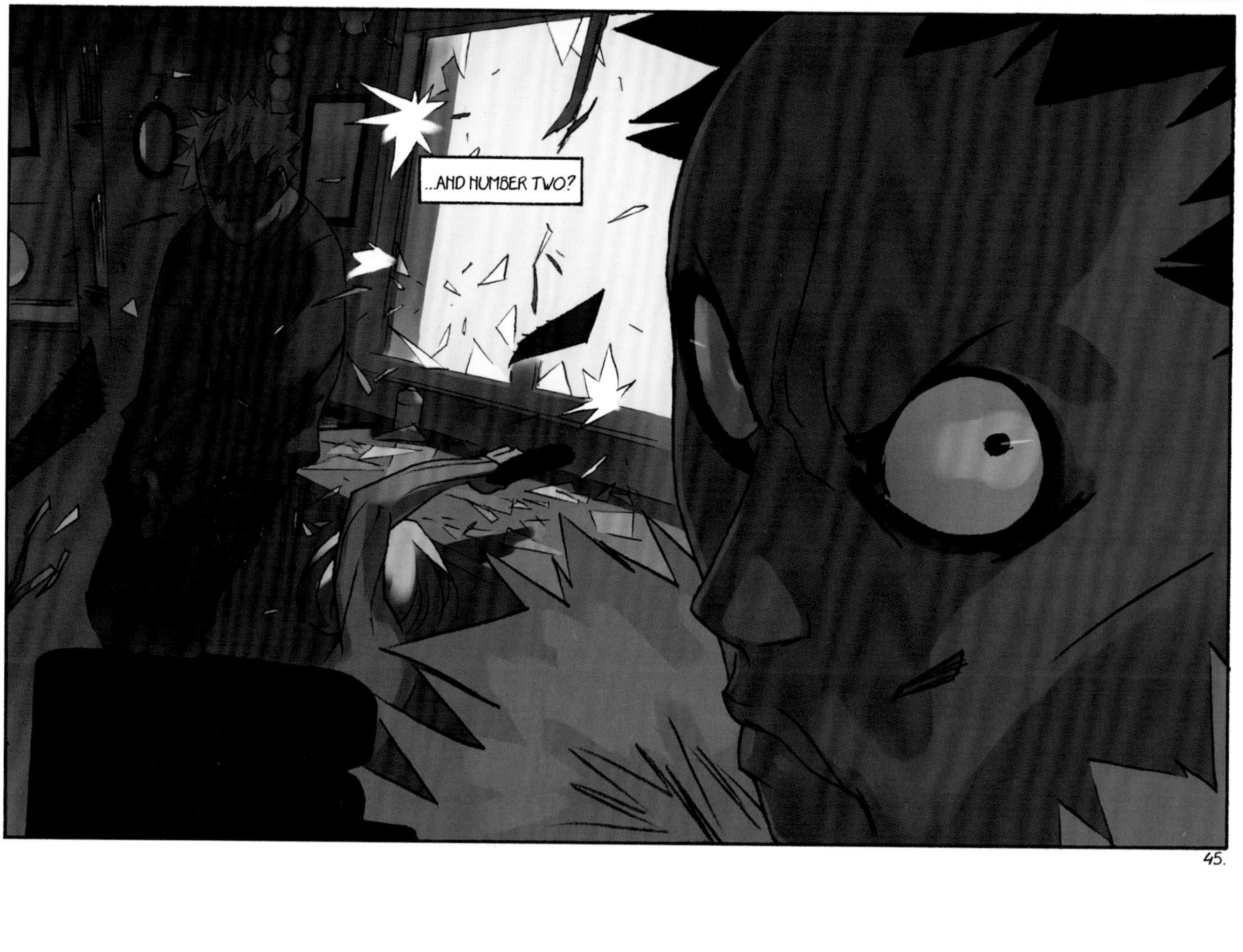
...AND NUMBER TWO?

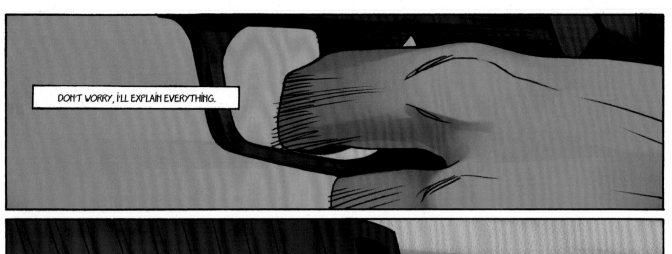

DON'T WORRY, I'LL EXPLAIN EVERYTHING.

IT WILL ALL MAKE SENSE SHORTLY.

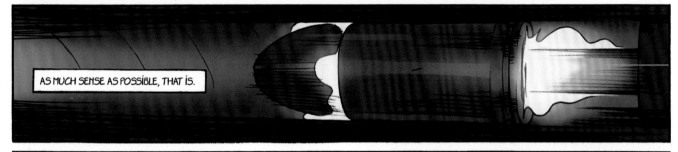

AS MUCH SENSE AS POSSIBLE, THAT IS.

YOU SEE, I HOLD ALL THE CARDS...

...AND I INTEND TO TAKE FULL ADVANTAGE OF THAT FACT!

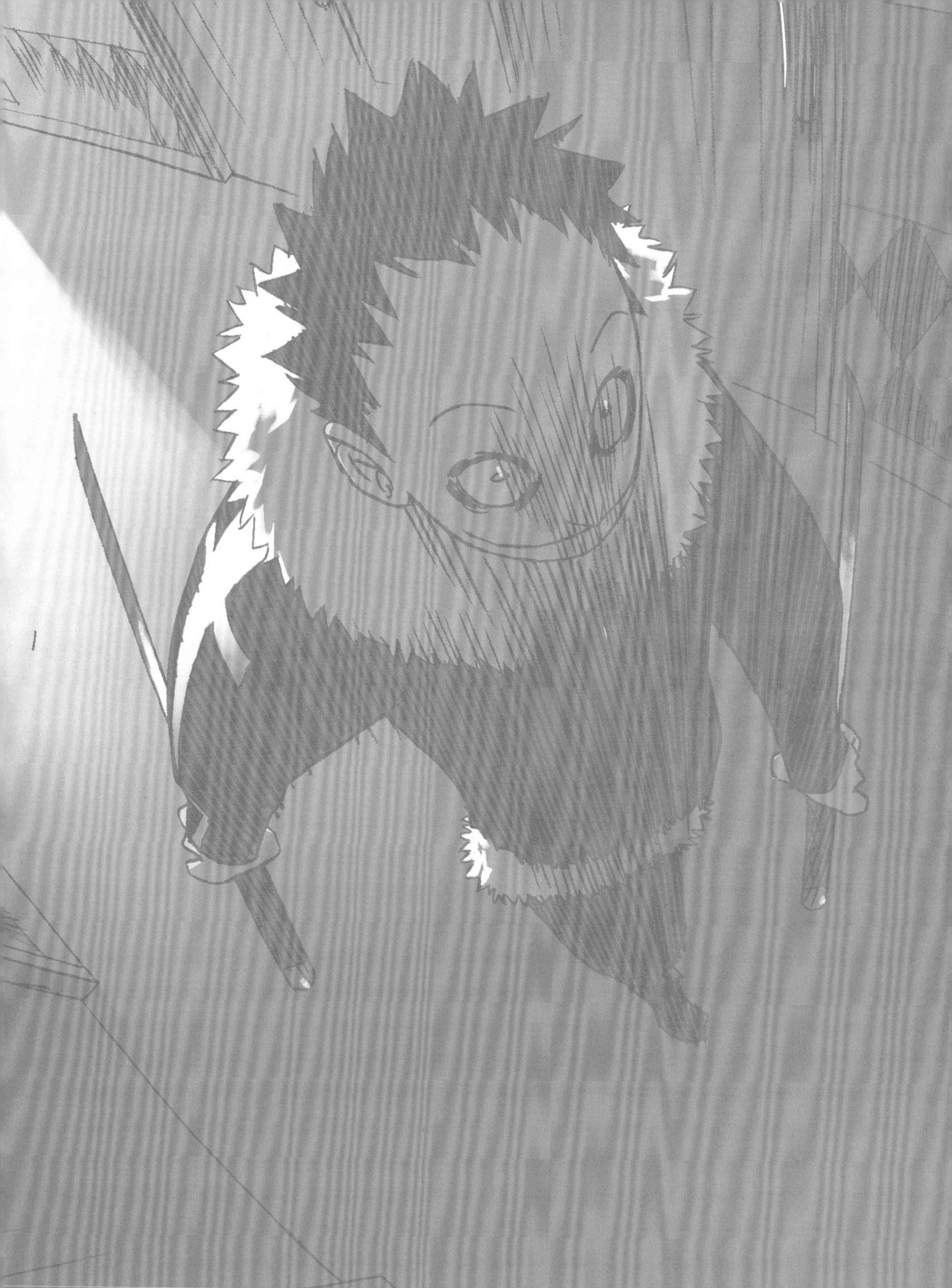

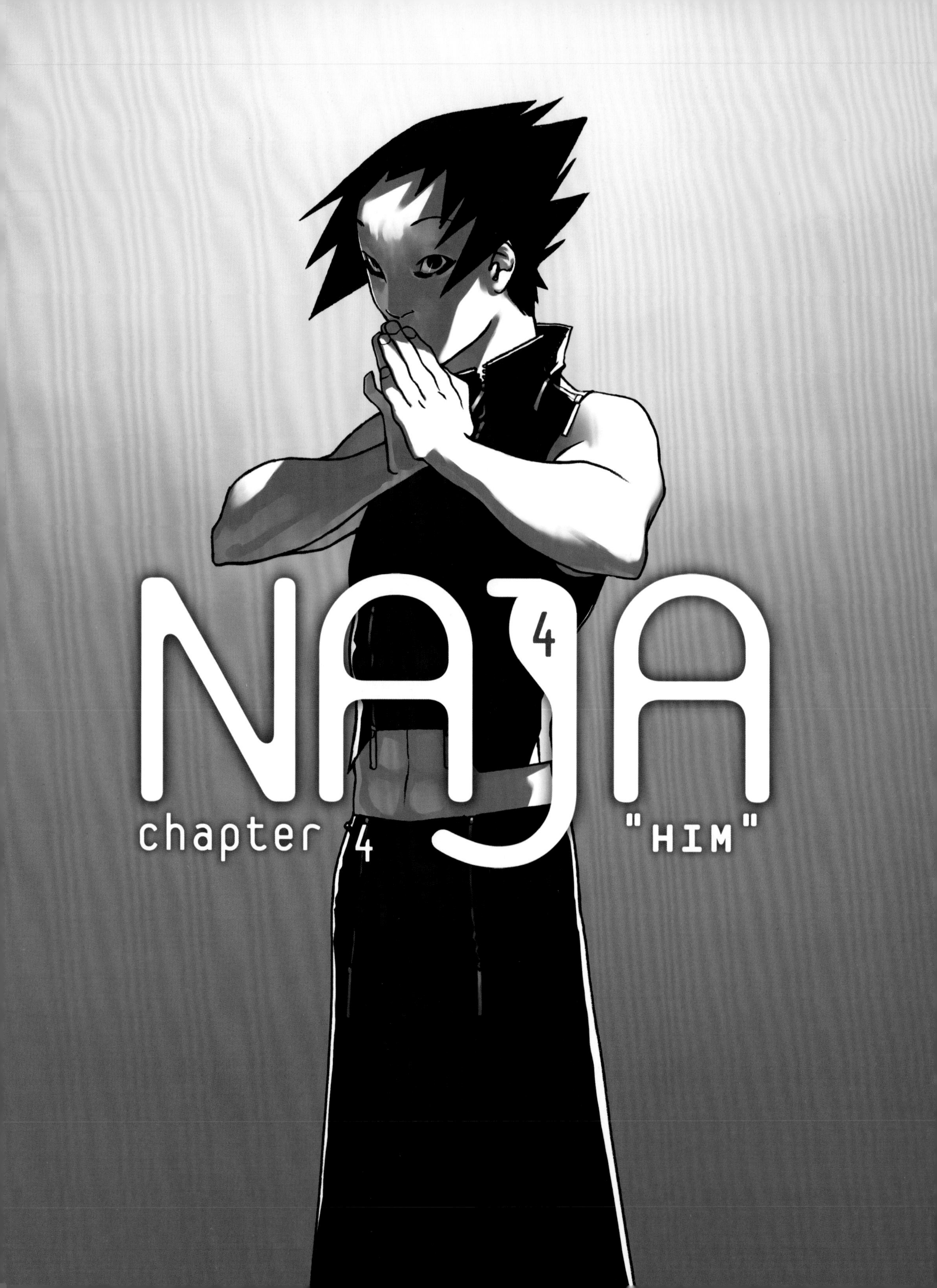
NAJA 4
chapter 4
"HIM"

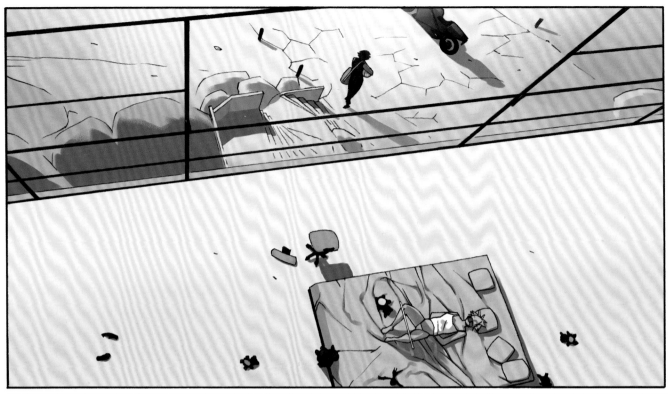

NAJA CALLS HIM "HE."

01.

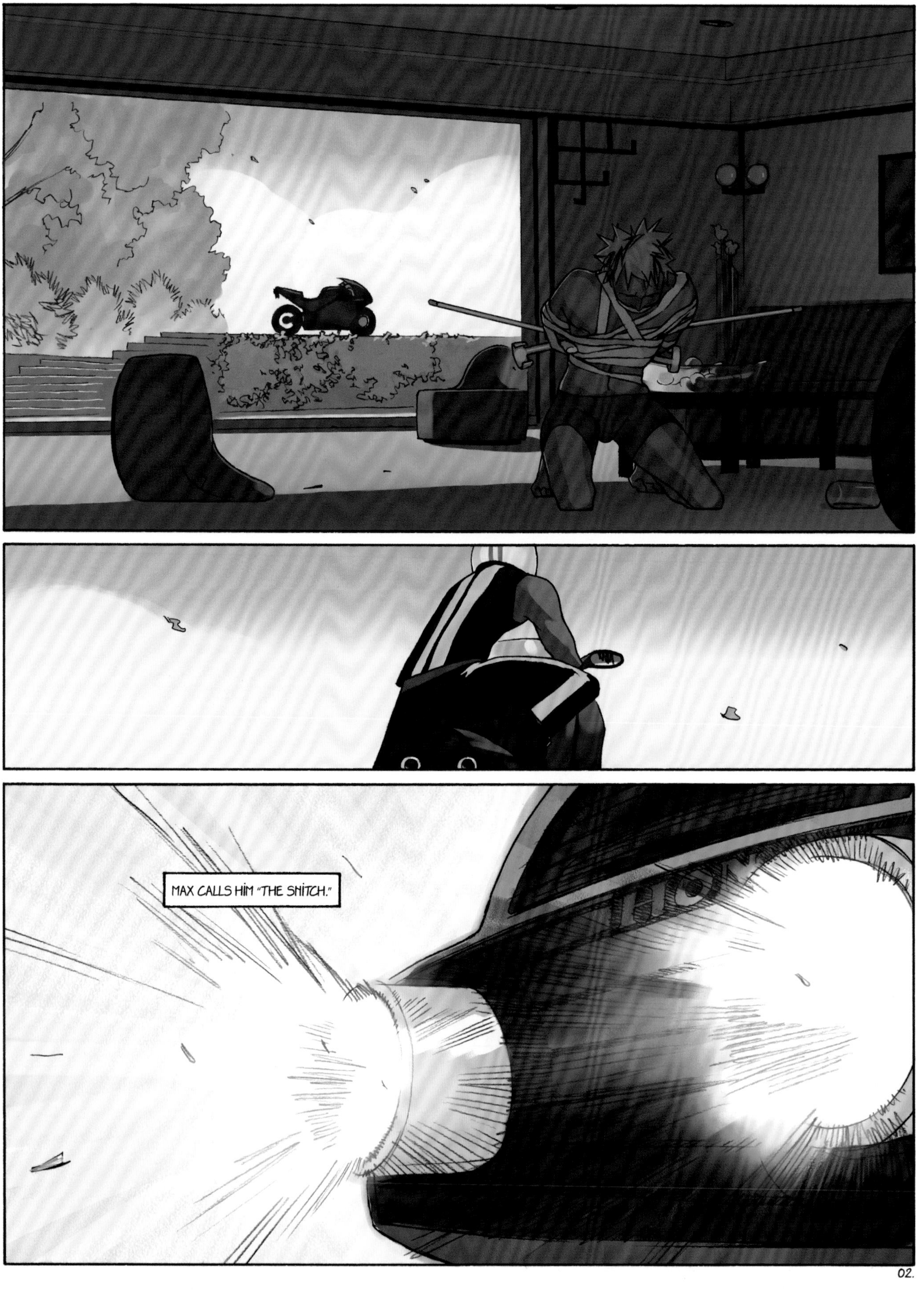
MAX CALLS HIM "THE SNITCH."

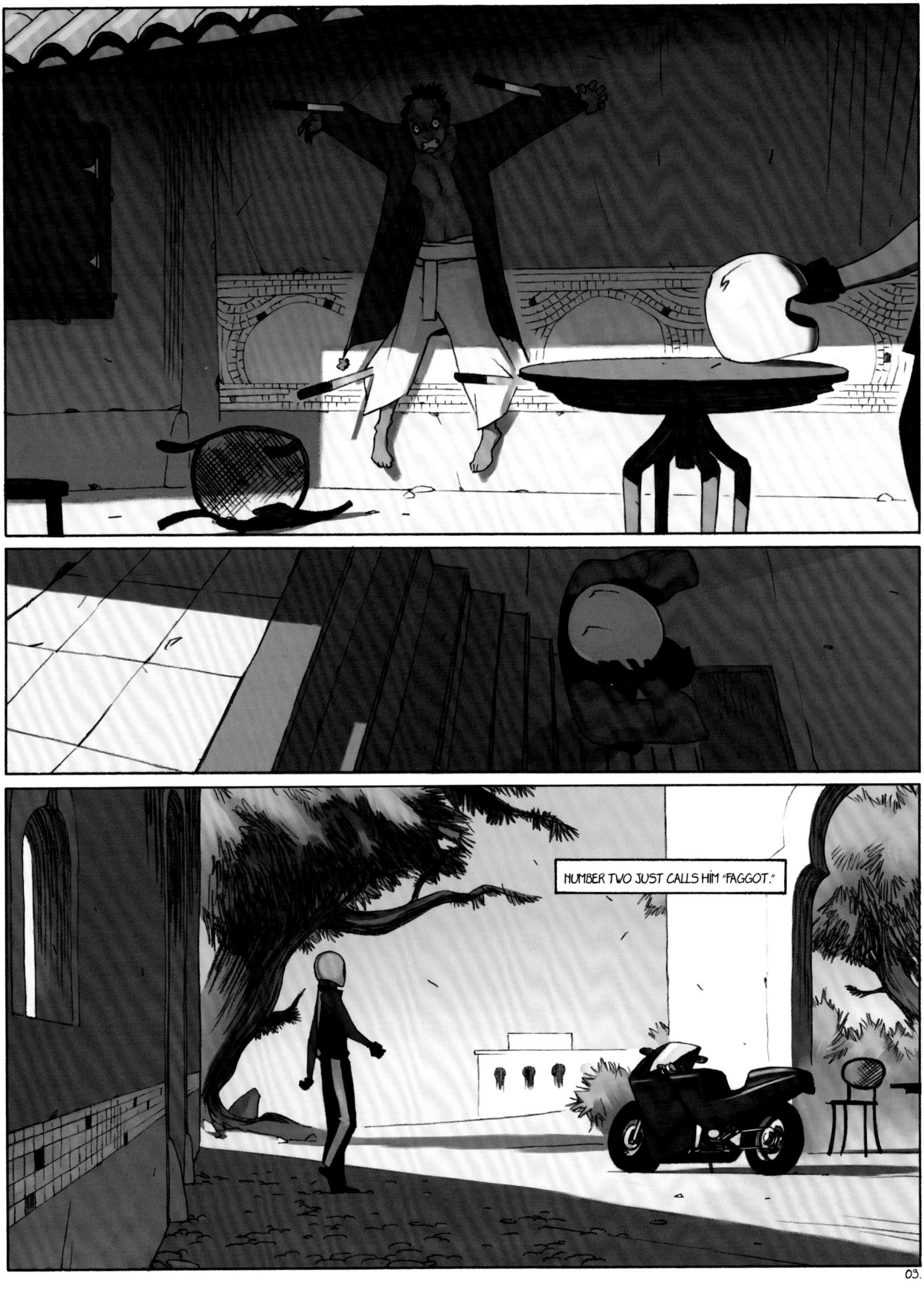
NUMBER TWO JUST CALLS HIM "FAGGOT."

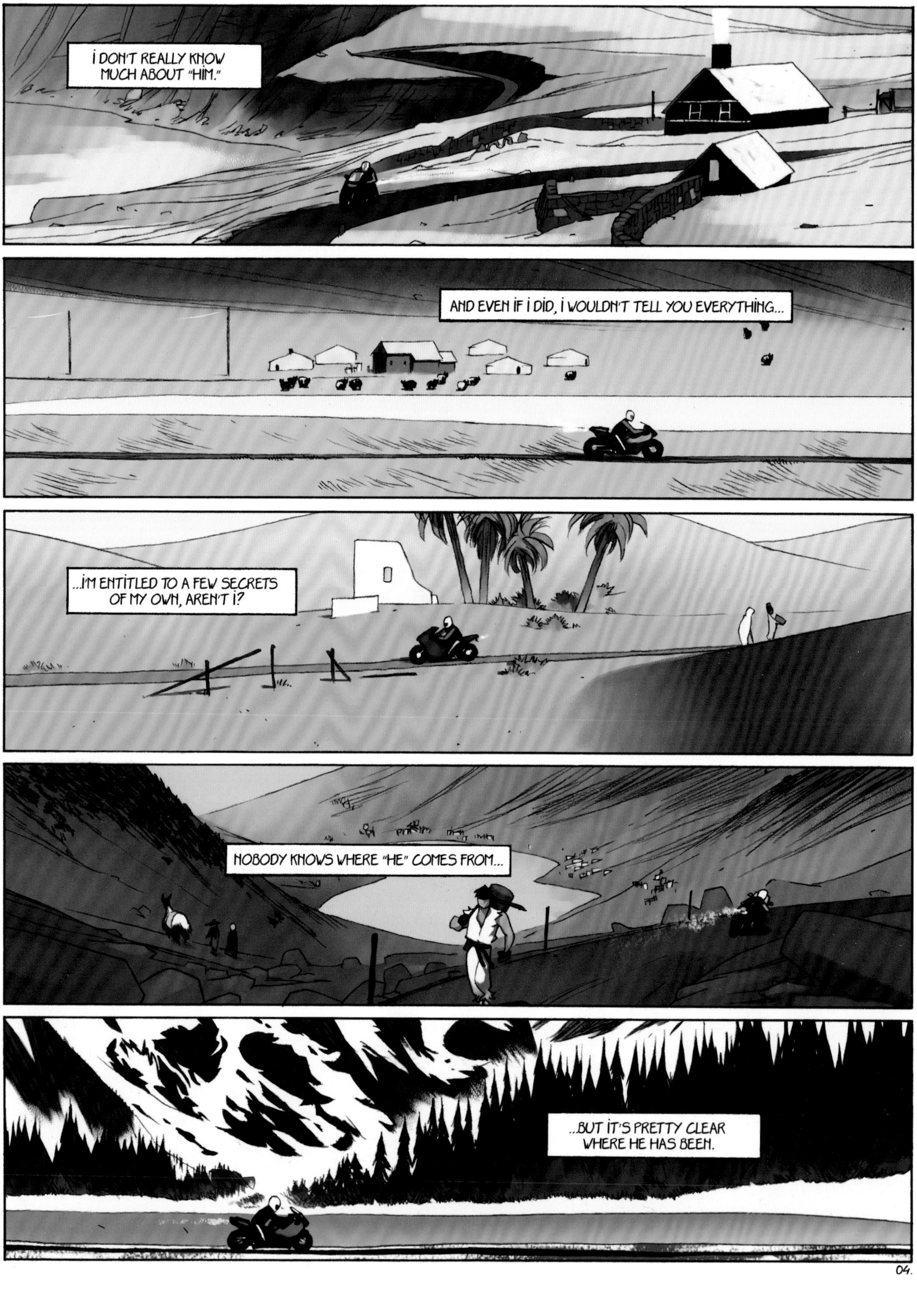
I DON'T REALLY KNOW MUCH ABOUT "HIM."
AND EVEN IF I DID, I WOULDN'T TELL YOU EVERYTHING...
...I'M ENTITLED TO A FEW SECRETS OF MY OWN, AREN'T I?
NOBODY KNOWS WHERE "HE" COMES FROM...
...BUT IT'S PRETTY CLEAR WHERE HE HAS BEEN.

EACH OF OUR FAVORITE KILLERS HAVE HAD, AT DIFFERENT TIMES, THE PLEASURE OF A STEALTHY VISIT.

HE DEFEATED ALL THREE.

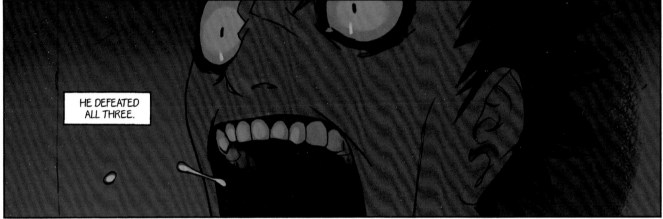

ZERO'S TOP ASSASSINS, BENT TO HIS WILL. HE COULD HAVE EASILY KILLED THEM ALL...

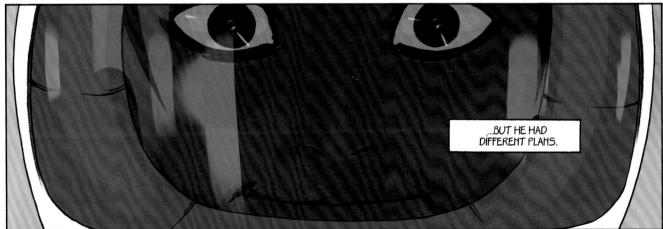

...BUT HE HAD DIFFERENT PLANS.

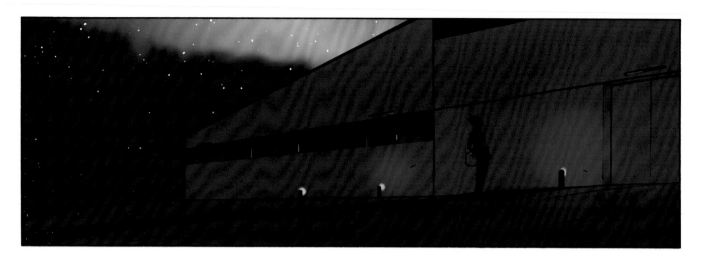

"HE" WAS IN ICELAND WITH NAJA.
YOU REMEMBER THE THINGS HE TOLD HER.

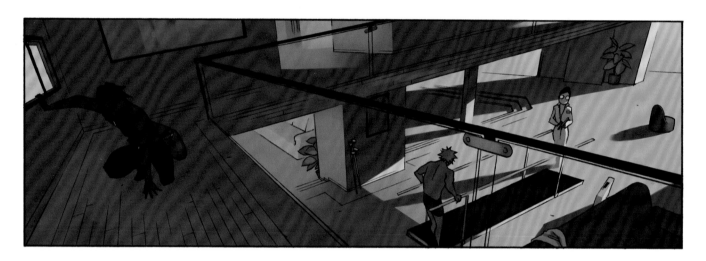

"THE SNITCH" ALSO VISITED MAX IN LA.
THE REVELATION HE SHARED WITH MAX LEFT HIM ON HIS KNEES.

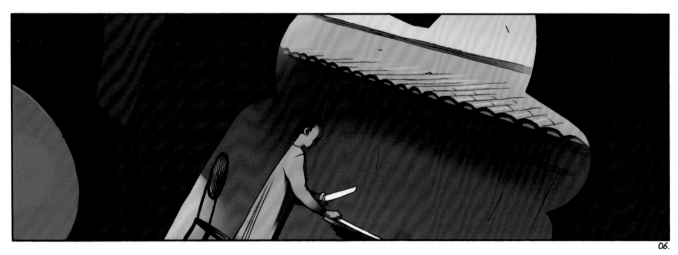

"THE FAGGOT" THEN VISITED NUMBER TWO IN BAGHDAD.
WHAT HE SAID LEFT TWO NAILED TO THE WALL.

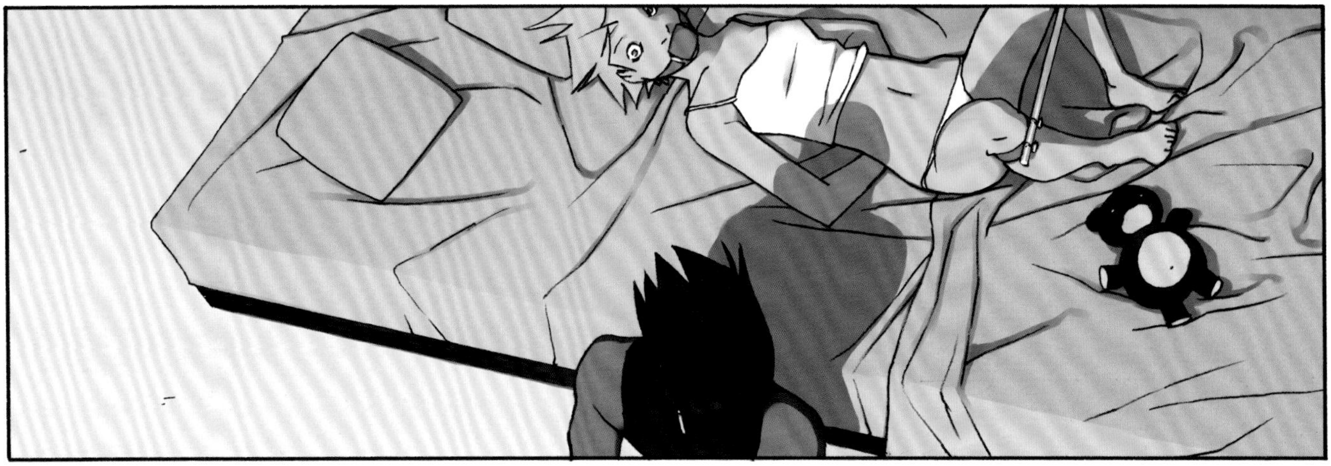

"NUMBER ONE WANTS TO ELIMINATE YOU.
SOMEONE HAS CONVINCED HIM YOU WANT TO TAKE HIS PLACE."

"WE BOTH KNOW THAT IS NOT TRUE. THAT YOU HAVE NO TASTE FOR COMPETITION."

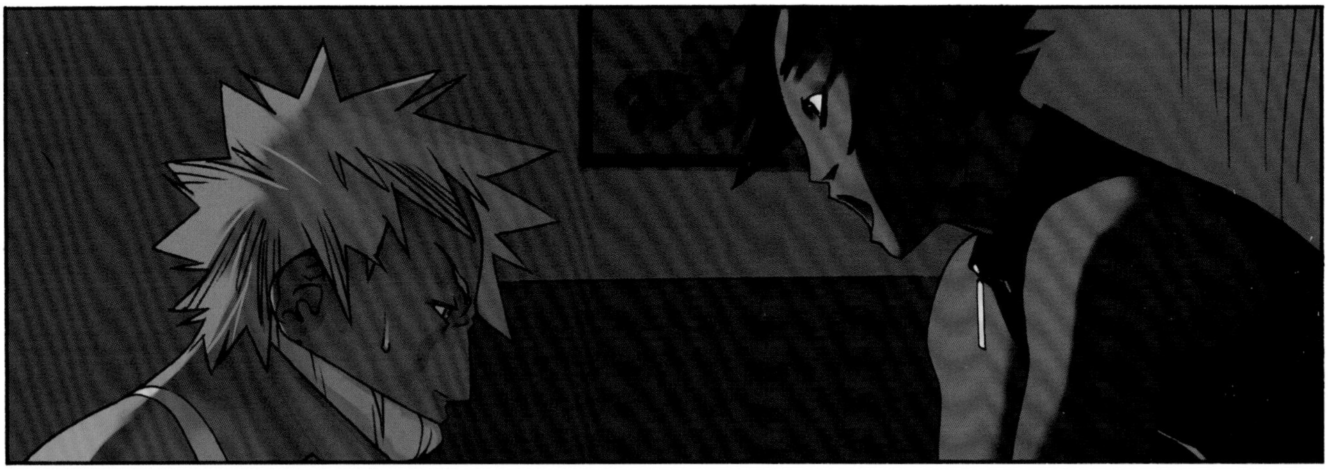

"IT WAS NUMBER THREE WHO ATTACKED YOU IN VARANASI.

AND NUMBER TWO WHO WANTED TO KILL YOU IN SWITZERLAND."

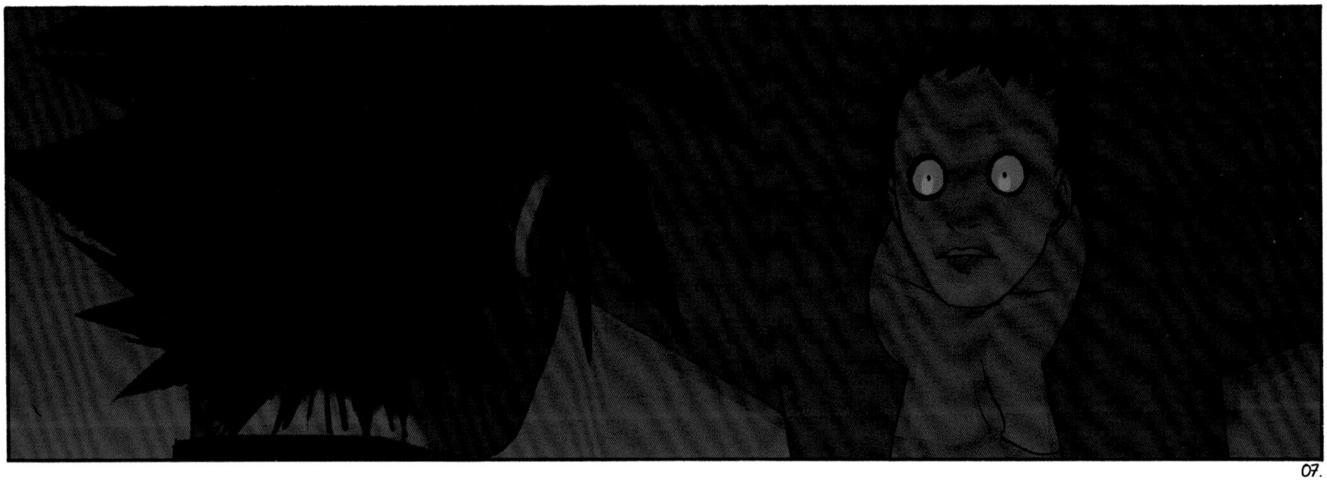

"NUMBER THREE NEARLY KILLED NUMBER ONE.

HE IS SERIOUSLY INJURED."

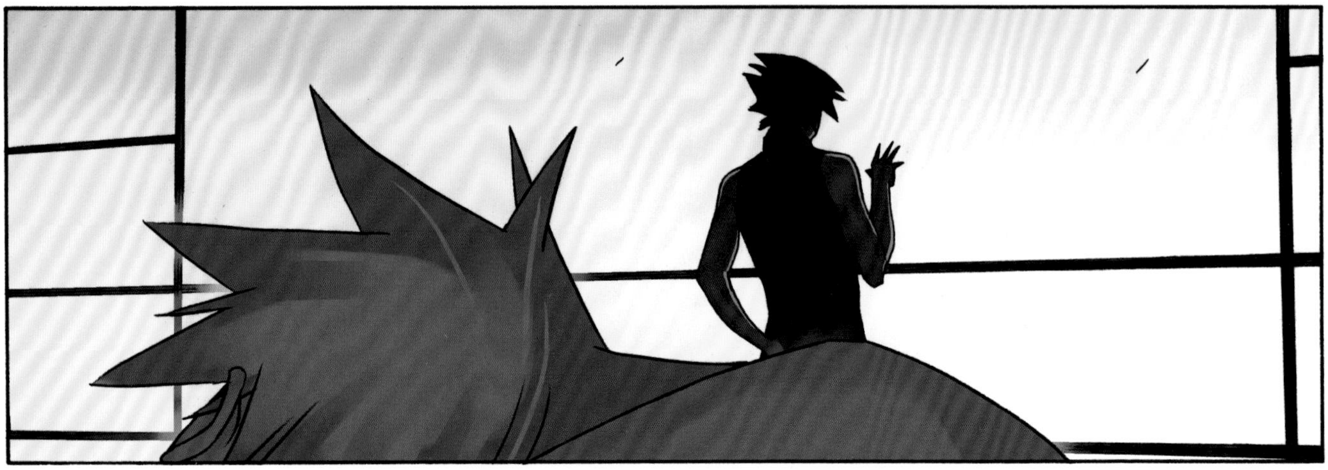

"AND YOU DON'T SEE THIS JOB AS A COMPETITION.
YOU BECAME NUMBER THREE BECAUSE ZERO FELT YOU EARNED IT ..."

"...NOT BECAUSE YOU WANTED IT.
YOU'VE NEVER KILLED ANYONE OUT OF PERSONAL INTEREST."

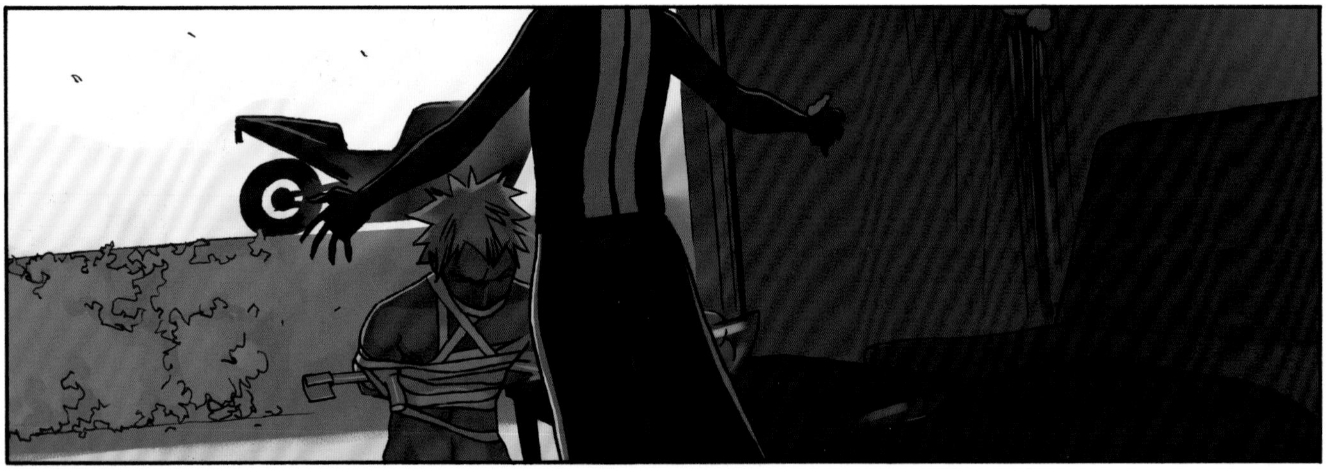

"IT WAS ZERO WHO ORDERED THEM TO GET RID OF YOU.

I THINK YOU SCARE HIM."

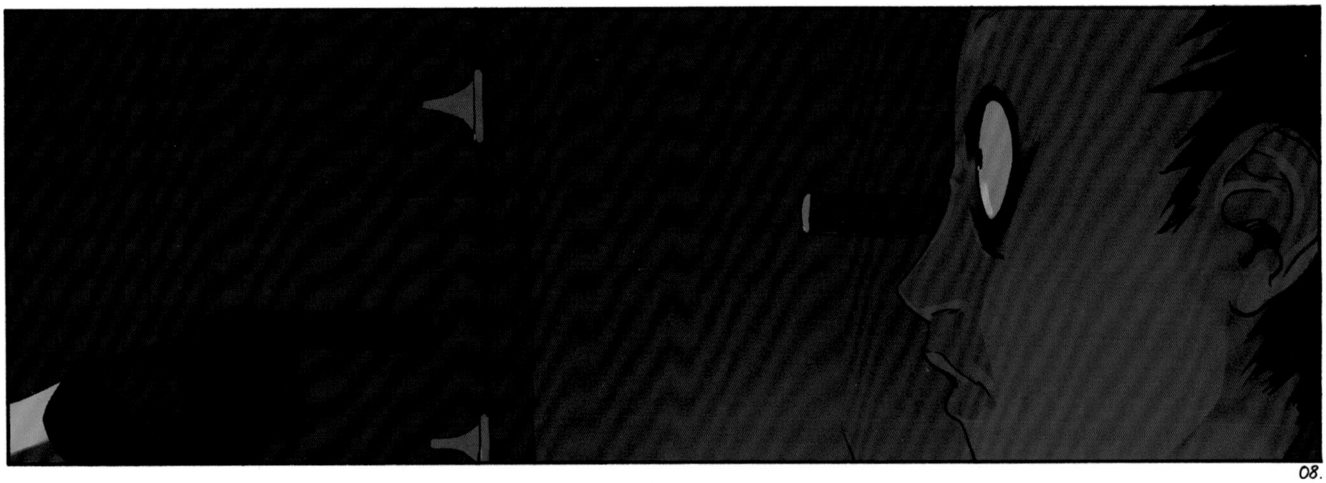

"YOU SHOULD TAKE ADVANTAGE OF THE CHAOS BY SMOKING THEM BOTH.

PROVE TO ZERO THAT YOU DESERVE BETTER THAN SECOND PLACE."

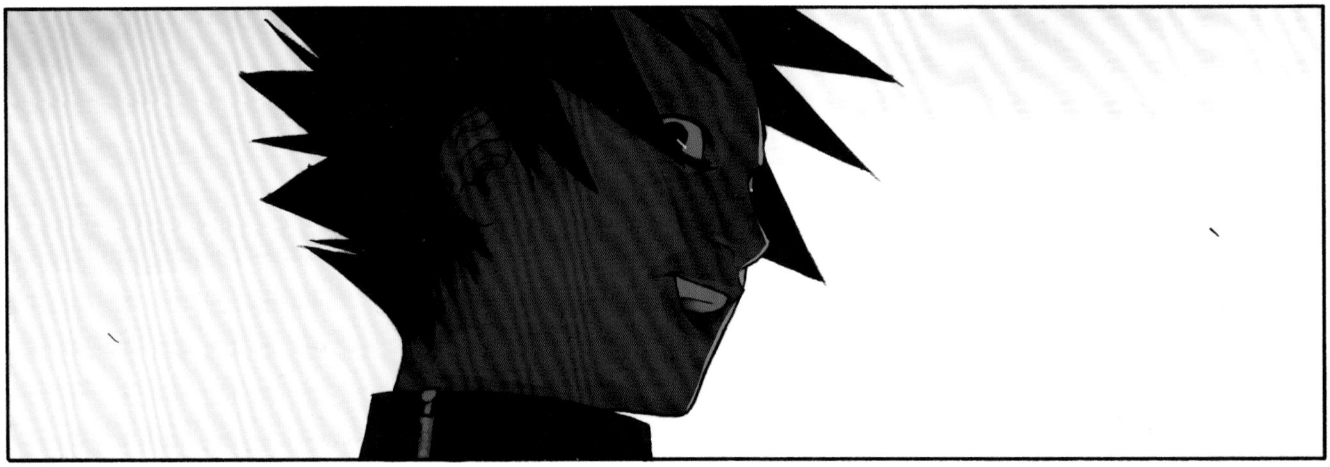

"ONLY WHEN HE DEMANDED IT.
BUT HOW WOULD NUMBER ONE KNOW THAT?"

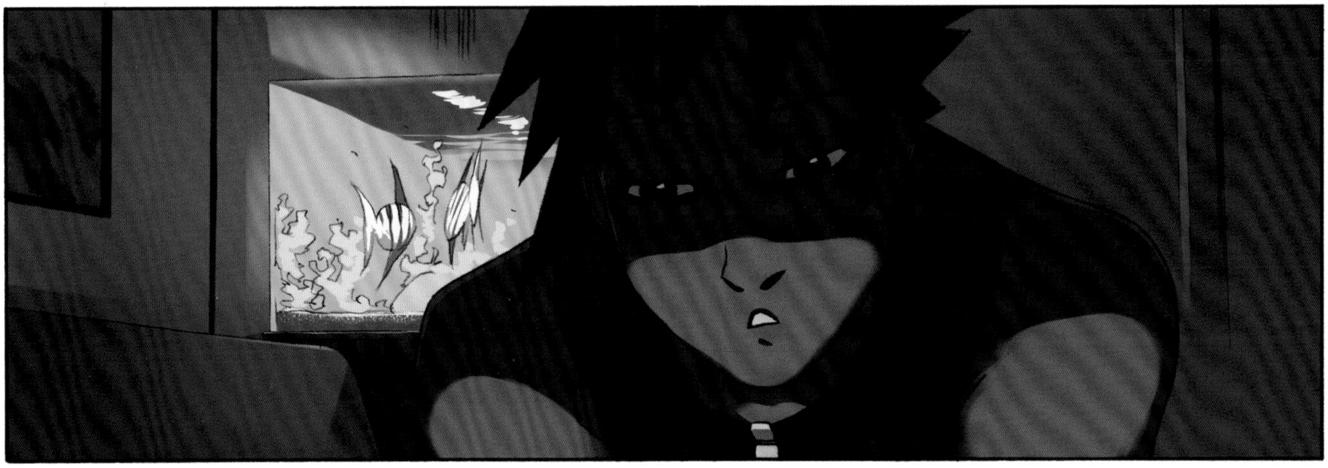

"IT'S NOTHING PERSONAL, MAX. YOU'RE A GOOD GUY.
YOU'RE JUST NOT CUT OUT FOR THIS SORT OF BUSINESS."

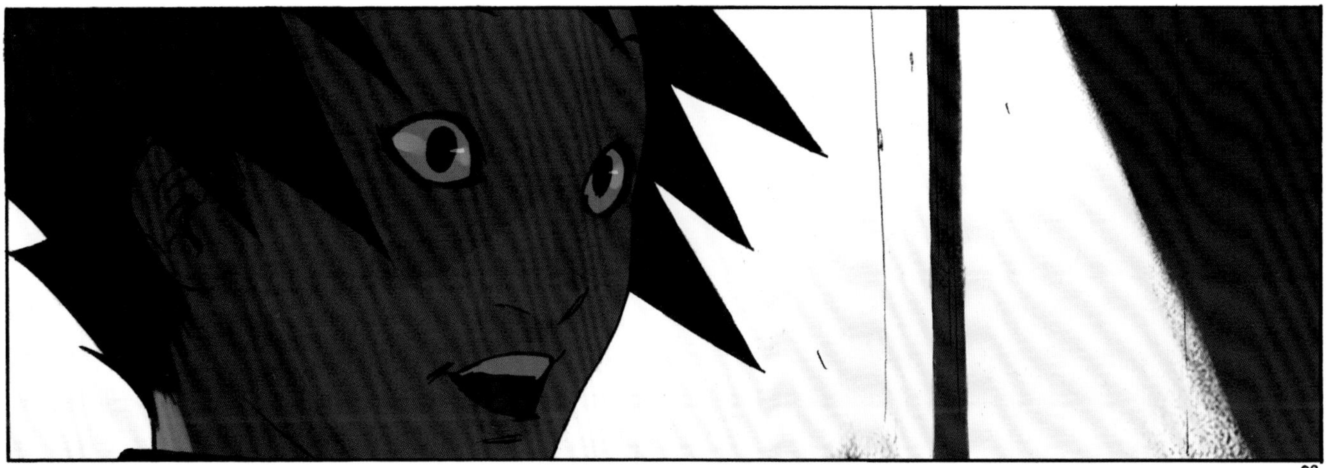

"TO FINALLY BE RECOGNIZED FOR WHAT YOU ARE:
THE VERY BEST!!"

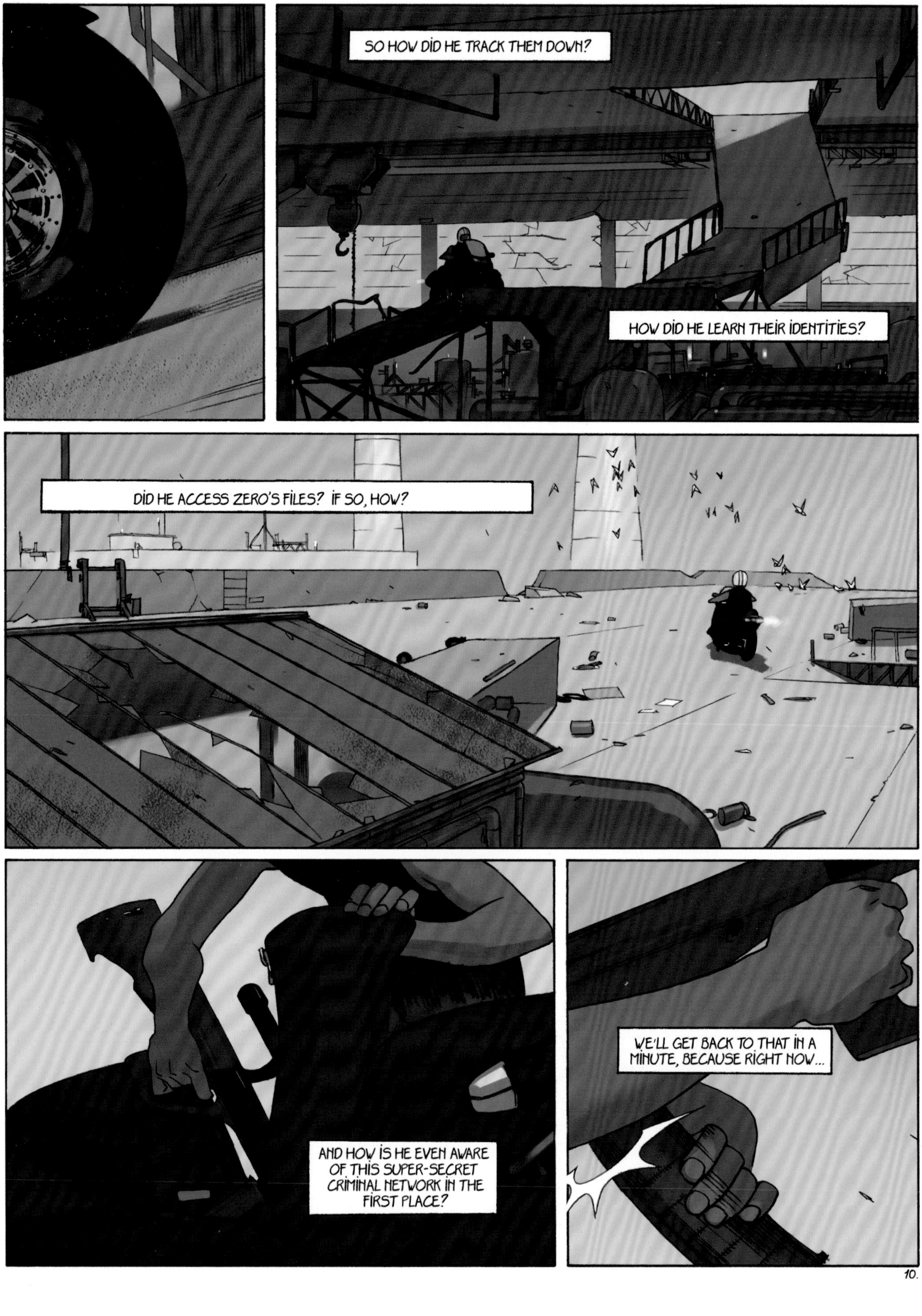
SO HOW DID HE TRACK THEM DOWN?
HOW DID HE LEARN THEIR IDENTITIES?
DID HE ACCESS ZERO'S FILES? IF SO, HOW?
AND HOW IS HE EVEN AWARE OF THIS SUPER-SECRET CRIMINAL NETWORK IN THE FIRST PLACE?
WE'LL GET BACK TO THAT IN A MINUTE, BECAUSE RIGHT NOW...

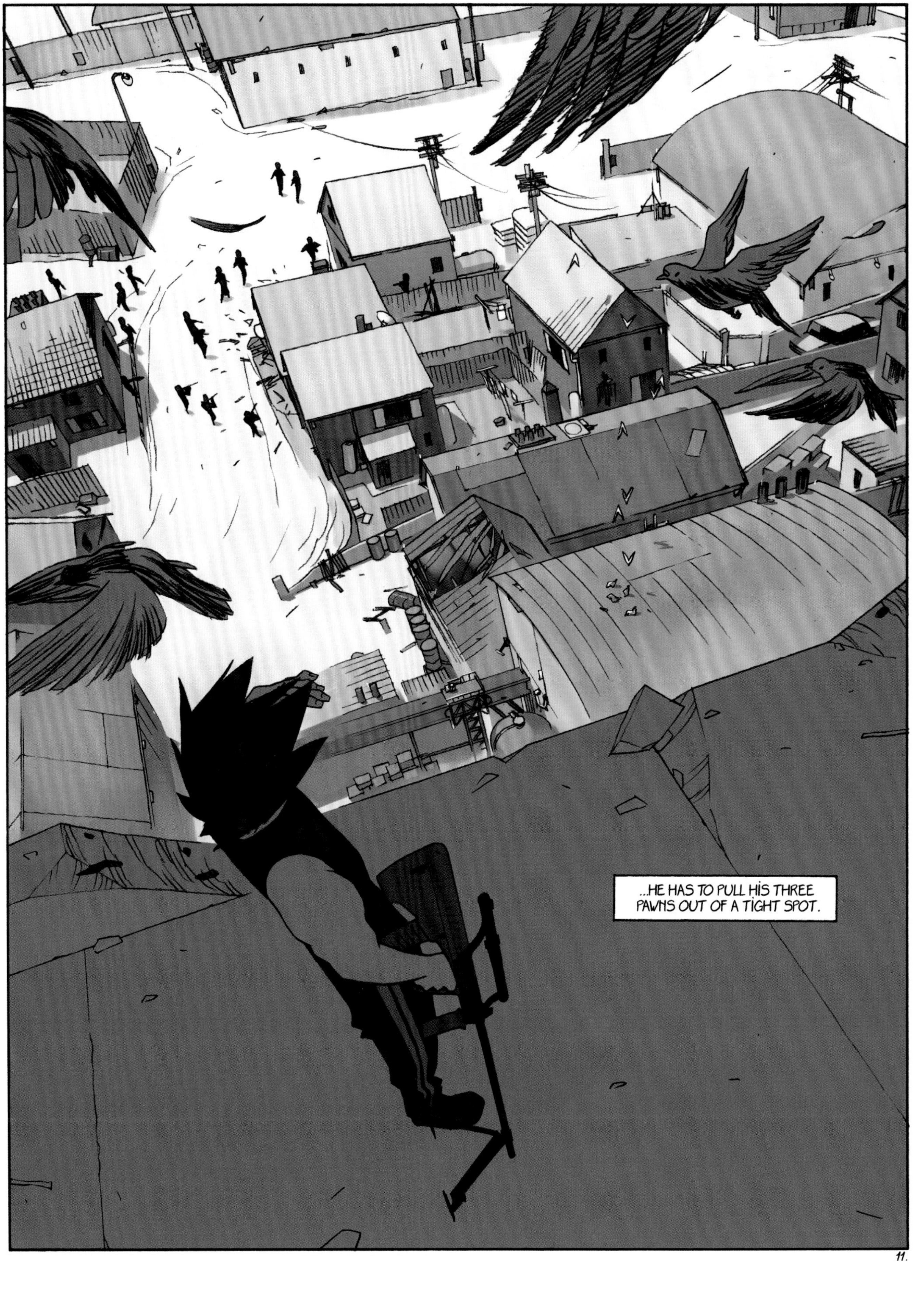
...HE HAS TO PULL HIS THREE PAWNS OUT OF A TIGHT SPOT.

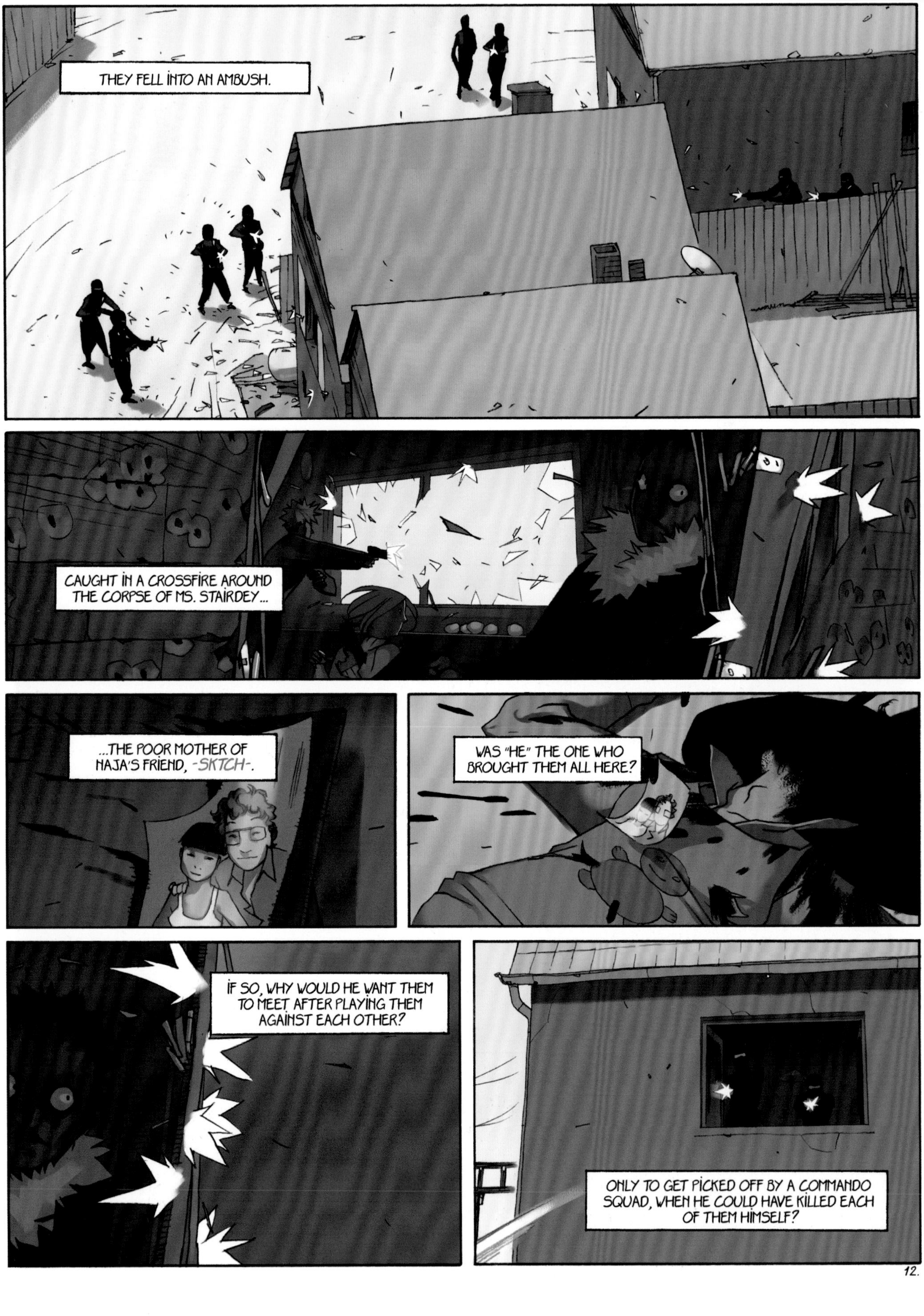
THEY FELL INTO AN AMBUSH.
CAUGHT IN A CROSSFIRE AROUND THE CORPSE OF MS. STAIRDEY...
...THE POOR MOTHER OF NAJA'S FRIEND, -SKTCH-.
WAS "HE" THE ONE WHO BROUGHT THEM ALL HERE?
IF SO, WHY WOULD HE WANT THEM TO MEET AFTER PLAYING THEM AGAINST EACH OTHER?
ONLY TO GET PICKED OFF BY A COMMANDO SQUAD, WHEN HE COULD HAVE KILLED EACH OF THEM HIMSELF?

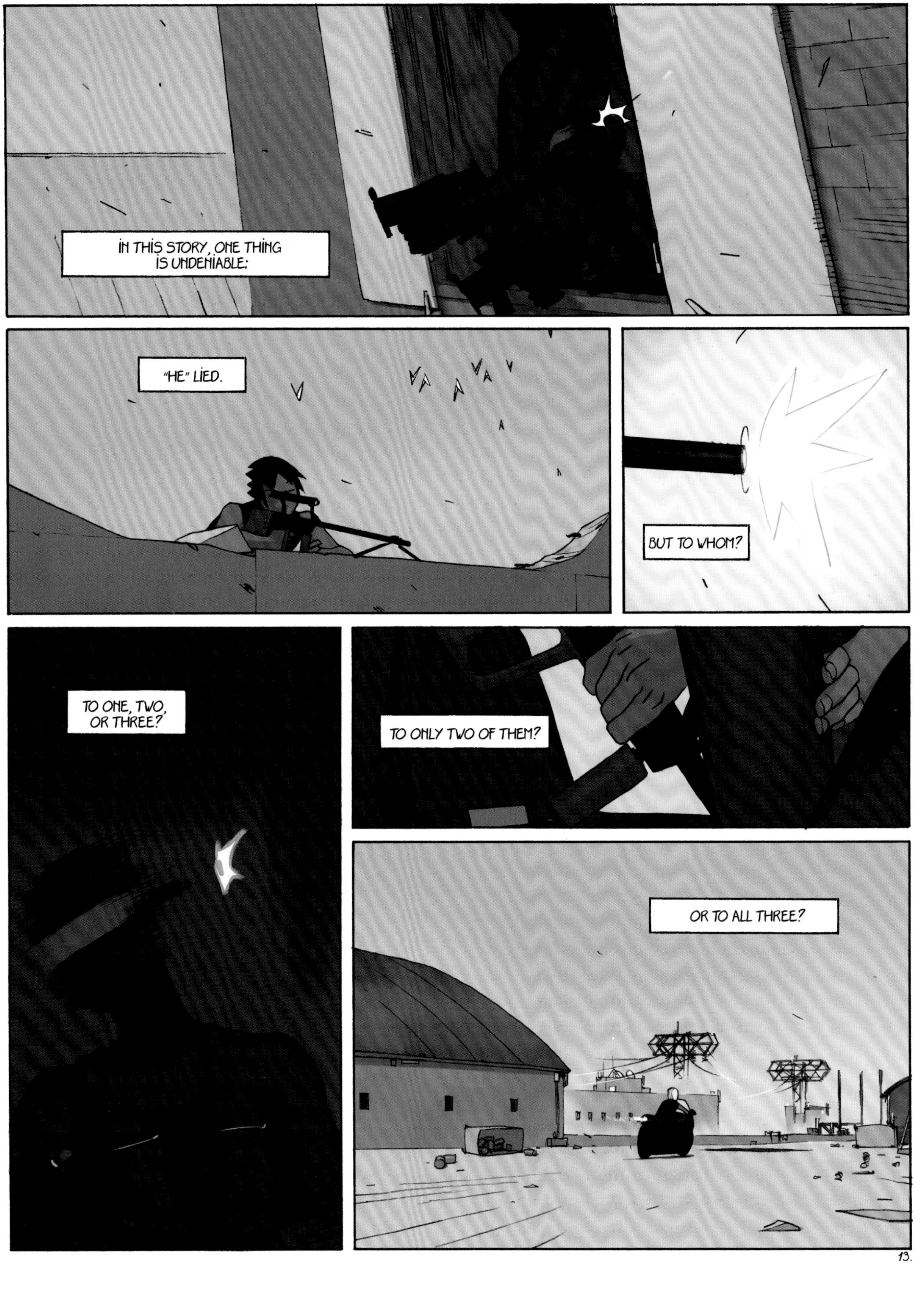
IN THIS STORY, ONE THING IS UNDENIABLE:
"HE" LIED.
BUT TO WHOM?
TO ONE, TWO, OR THREE?
TO ONLY TWO OF THEM?
OR TO ALL THREE?

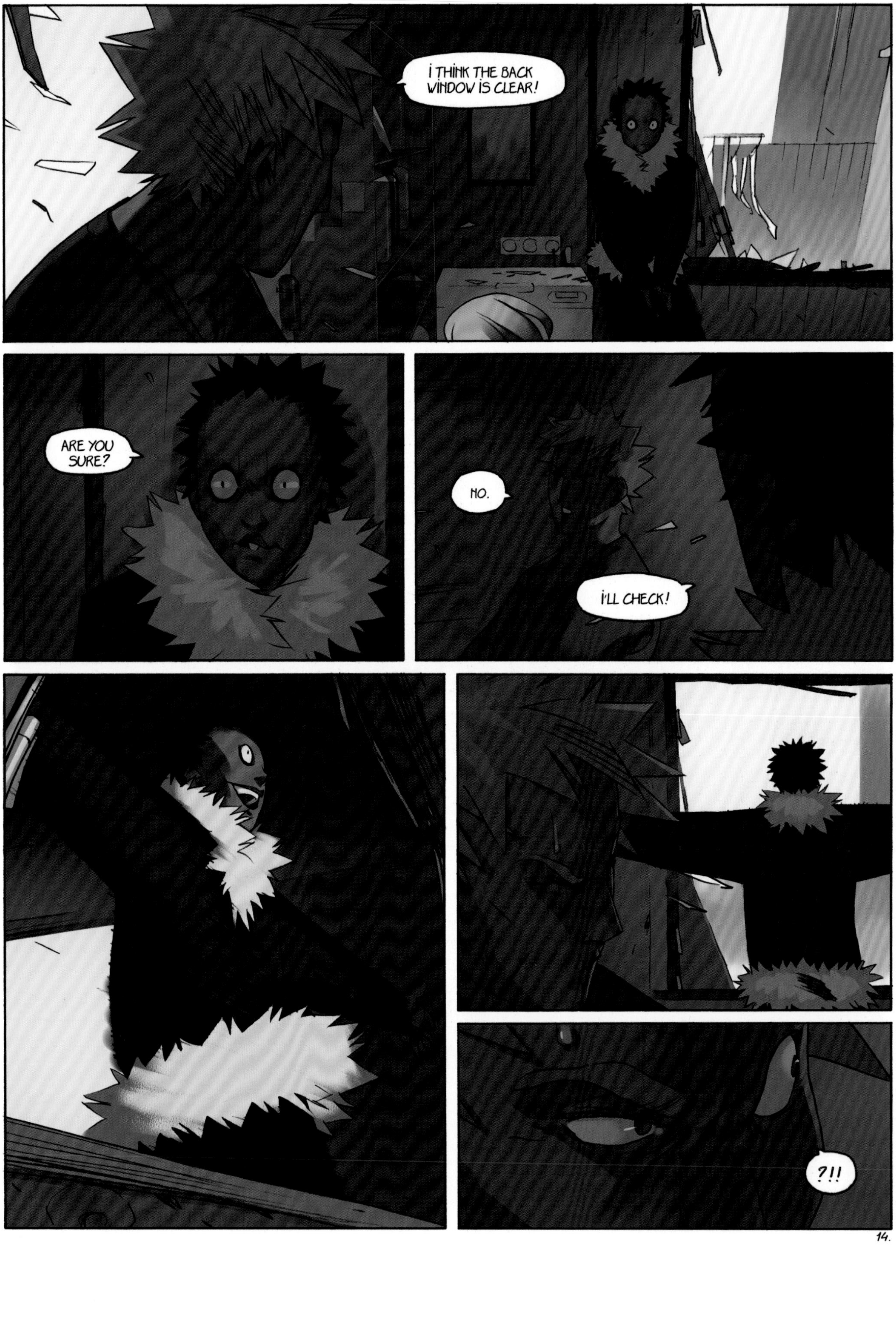

İ THİNK THE BACK WINDOW İS CLEAR!
ARE YOU SURE?
NO.
İ'LL CHECK!
?!!

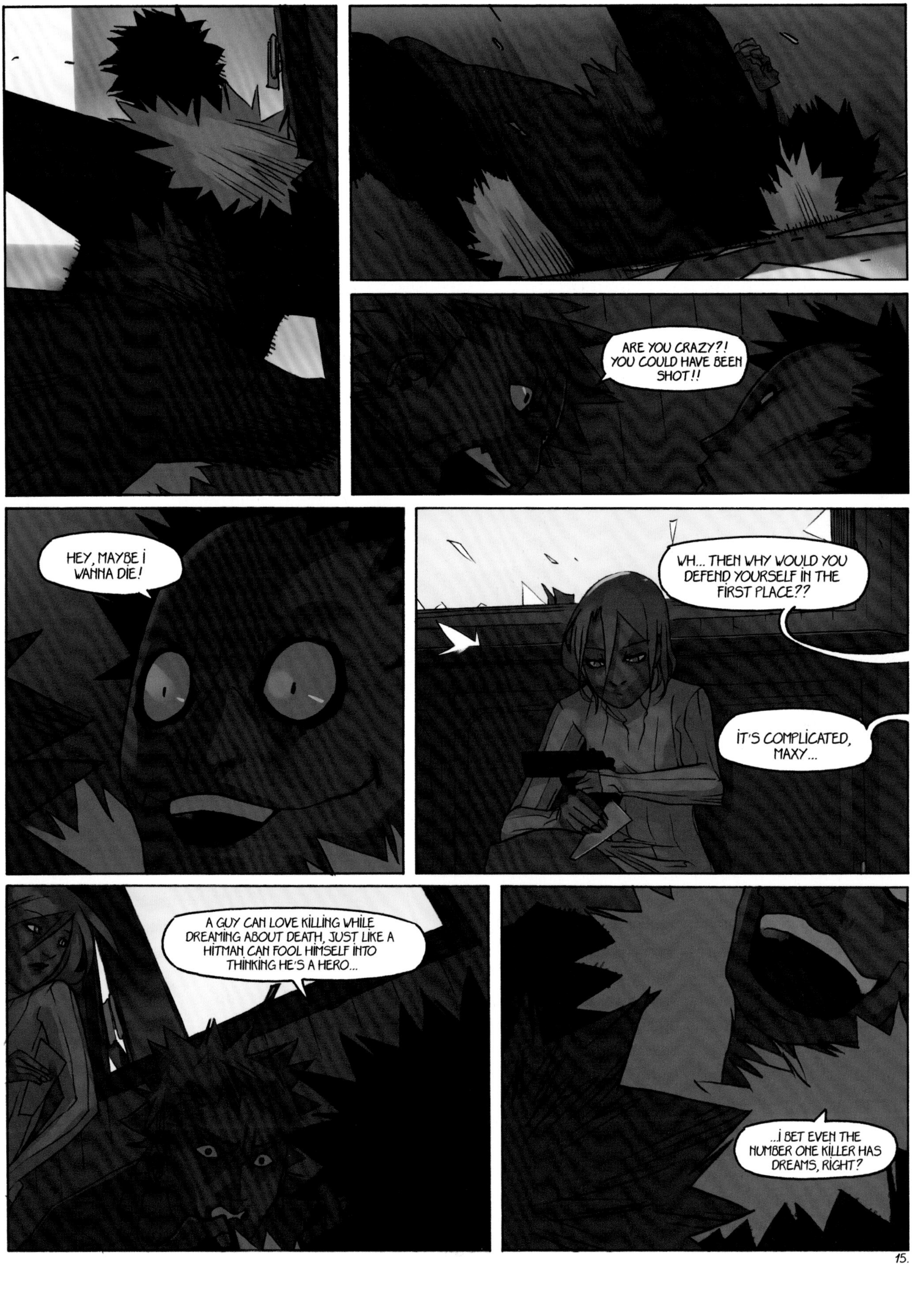
ARE YOU CRAZY?! YOU COULD HAVE BEEN SHOT!!
HEY, MAYBE I WANNA DIE!
WH... THEN WHY WOULD YOU DEFEND YOURSELF IN THE FIRST PLACE??
IT'S COMPLICATED, MAXY...
A GUY CAN LOVE KILLING WHILE DREAMING ABOUT DEATH, JUST LIKE A HITMAN CAN FOOL HIMSELF INTO THINKING HE'S A HERO...
...I BET EVEN THE NUMBER ONE KILLER HAS DREAMS, RIGHT?

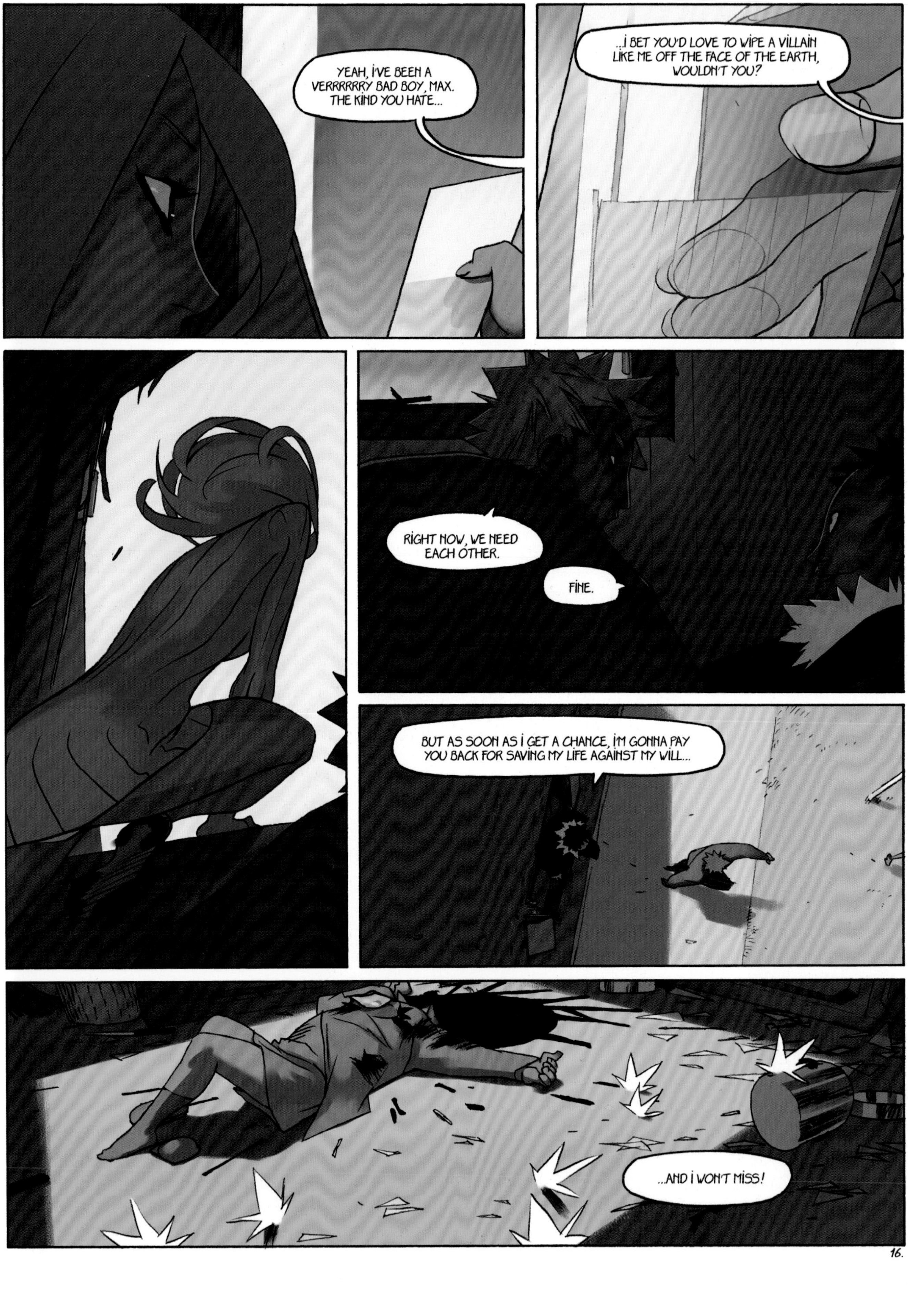
YEAH, I'VE BEEN A VERRRRRRY BAD BOY, MAX. THE KIND YOU HATE...
...I BET YOU'D LOVE TO WIPE A VILLAIN LIKE ME OFF THE FACE OF THE EARTH, WOULDN'T YOU?
RIGHT NOW, WE NEED EACH OTHER.
FINE.
BUT AS SOON AS I GET A CHANCE, I'M GONNA PAY YOU BACK FOR SAVING MY LIFE AGAINST MY WILL...
...AND I WON'T MISS!

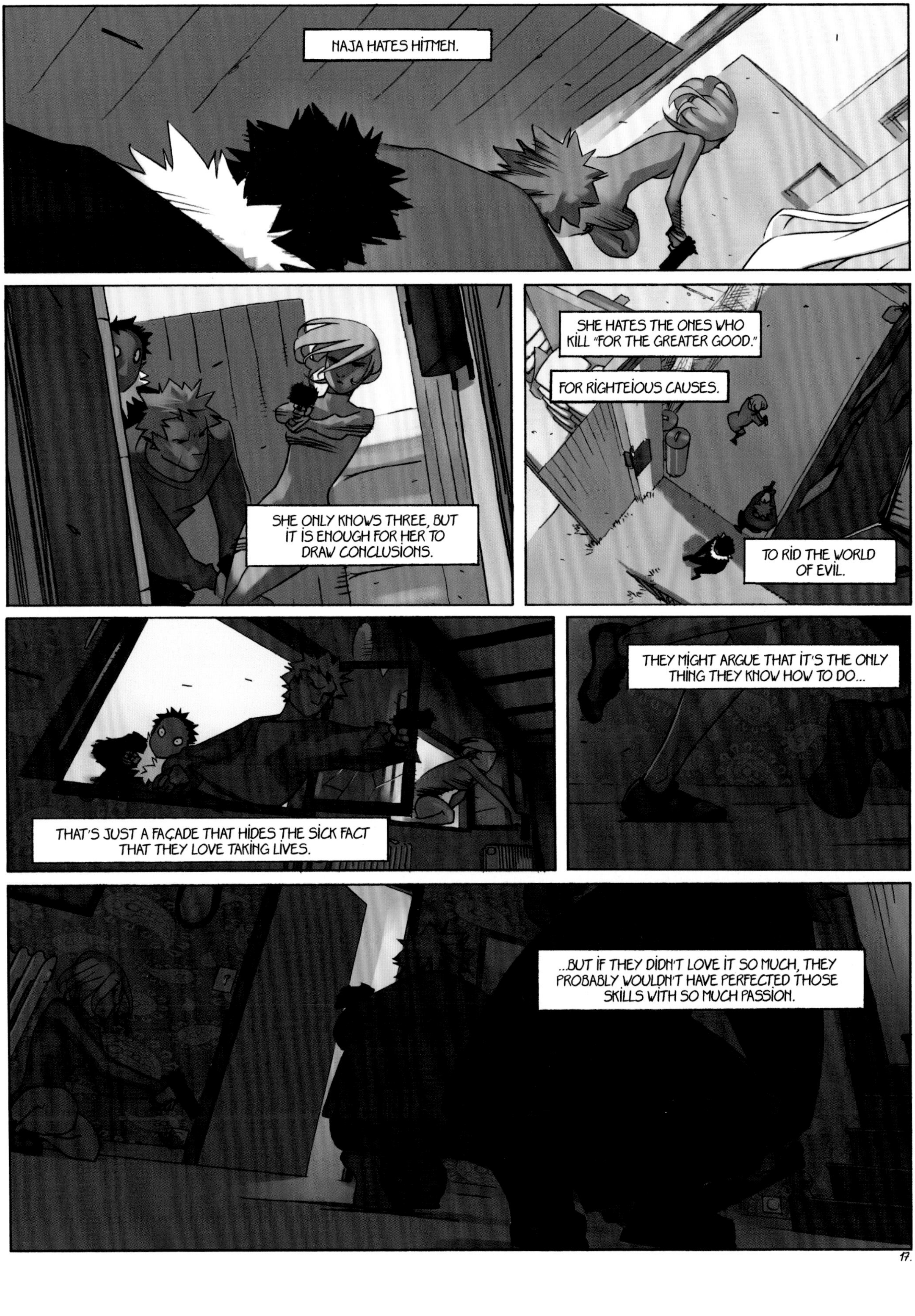
NAJA HATES HITMEN.
SHE ONLY KNOWS THREE, BUT IT IS ENOUGH FOR HER TO DRAW CONCLUSIONS.
SHE HATES THE ONES WHO KILL "FOR THE GREATER GOOD."
FOR RIGHTEOUS CAUSES.
TO RID THE WORLD OF EVIL.
THAT'S JUST A FAÇADE THAT HIDES THE SICK FACT THAT THEY LOVE TAKING LIVES.
THEY MIGHT ARGUE THAT IT'S THE ONLY THING THEY KNOW HOW TO DO...
...BUT IF THEY DIDN'T LOVE IT SO MUCH, THEY PROBABLY WOULDN'T HAVE PERFECTED THOSE SKILLS WITH SO MUCH PASSION.

SHE ALSO HATES THOSE WHO THINK MURDER AND DEATH ARE THE SAME THING --

-- THE INEVITABLE RESOLUTION OF LIFE.

AND SINCE EVERYONE HAS TO DIE EVENTUALLY, IT'S BETTER TO TAKE CONTROL OF THAT DESTINY.

OF COURSE, YOU COULD ARGUE THAT THE KILLER COULD HAVE BEEN GUIDED BY HIS VICTIM'S BAD KARMA, BUT...

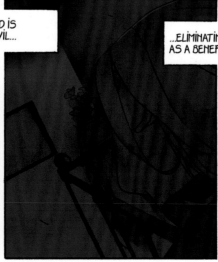

...SINCE MANKIND IS INHERENTLY EVIL...

...ELIMINATING ANYONE COULD BE SEEN AS A BENEFIT TO THE SPECIES, RIGHT?

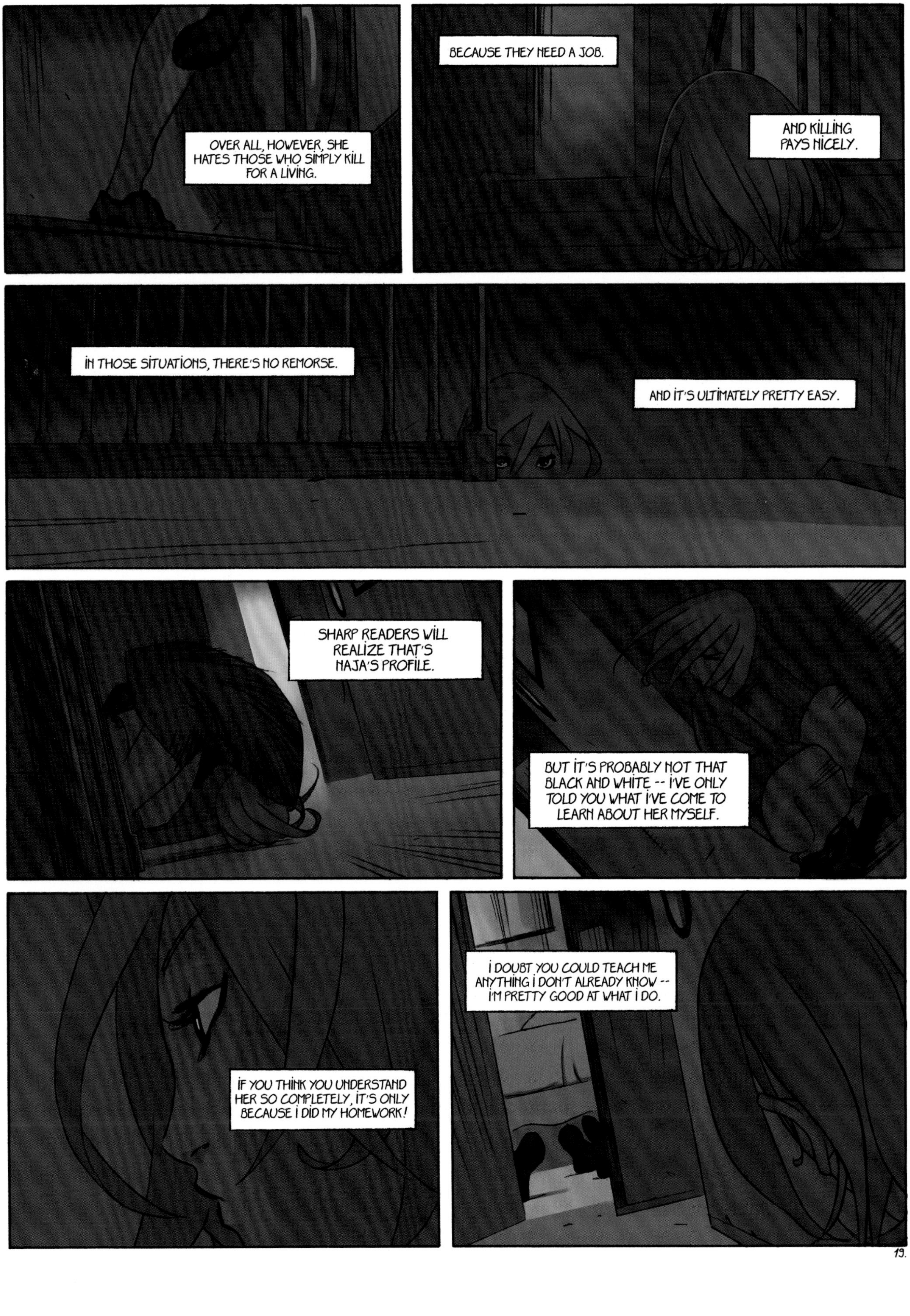
OVER ALL, HOWEVER, SHE HATES THOSE WHO SIMPLY KILL FOR A LIVING.
BECAUSE THEY NEED A JOB.
AND KILLING PAYS NICELY.
IN THOSE SITUATIONS, THERE'S NO REMORSE.
AND IT'S ULTIMATELY PRETTY EASY.
SHARP READERS WILL REALIZE THAT'S NAJA'S PROFILE.
BUT IT'S PROBABLY NOT THAT BLACK AND WHITE -- I'VE ONLY TOLD YOU WHAT I'VE COME TO LEARN ABOUT HER MYSELF.
IF YOU THINK YOU UNDERSTAND HER SO COMPLETELY, IT'S ONLY BECAUSE I DID MY HOMEWORK!
I DOUBT YOU COULD TEACH ME ANYTHING I DON'T ALREADY KNOW -- I'M PRETTY GOOD AT WHAT I DO.

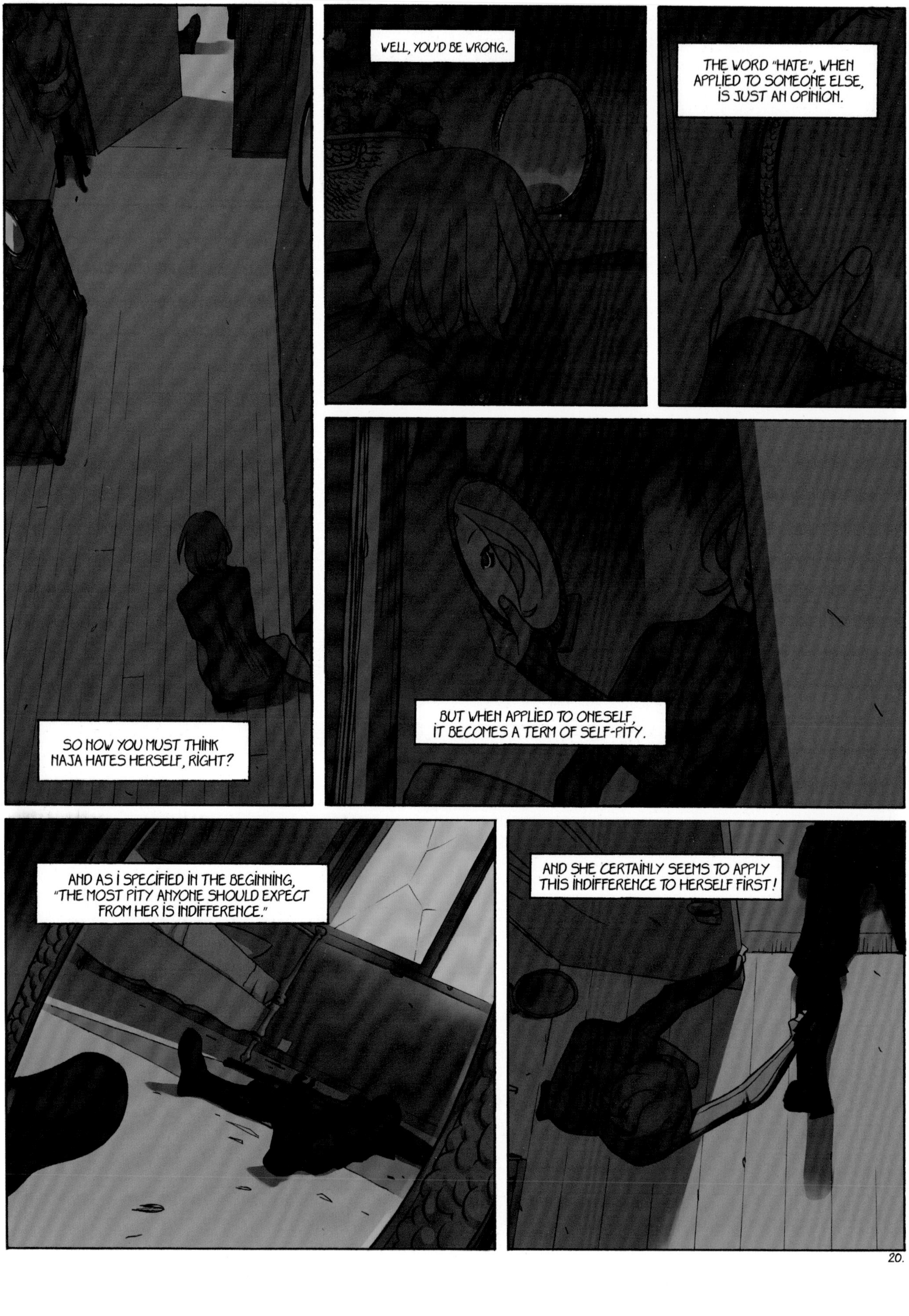
SO NOW YOU MUST THINK NAJA HATES HERSELF, RIGHT?
WELL, YOU'D BE WRONG.
THE WORD "HATE", WHEN APPLIED TO SOMEONE ELSE, IS JUST AN OPINION.
BUT WHEN APPLIED TO ONESELF, IT BECOMES A TERM OF SELF-PITY.
AND AS I SPECIFIED IN THE BEGINNING, "THE MOST PITY ANYONE SHOULD EXPECT FROM HER IS INDIFFERENCE."
AND SHE CERTAINLY SEEMS TO APPLY THIS INDIFFERENCE TO HERSELF FIRST!

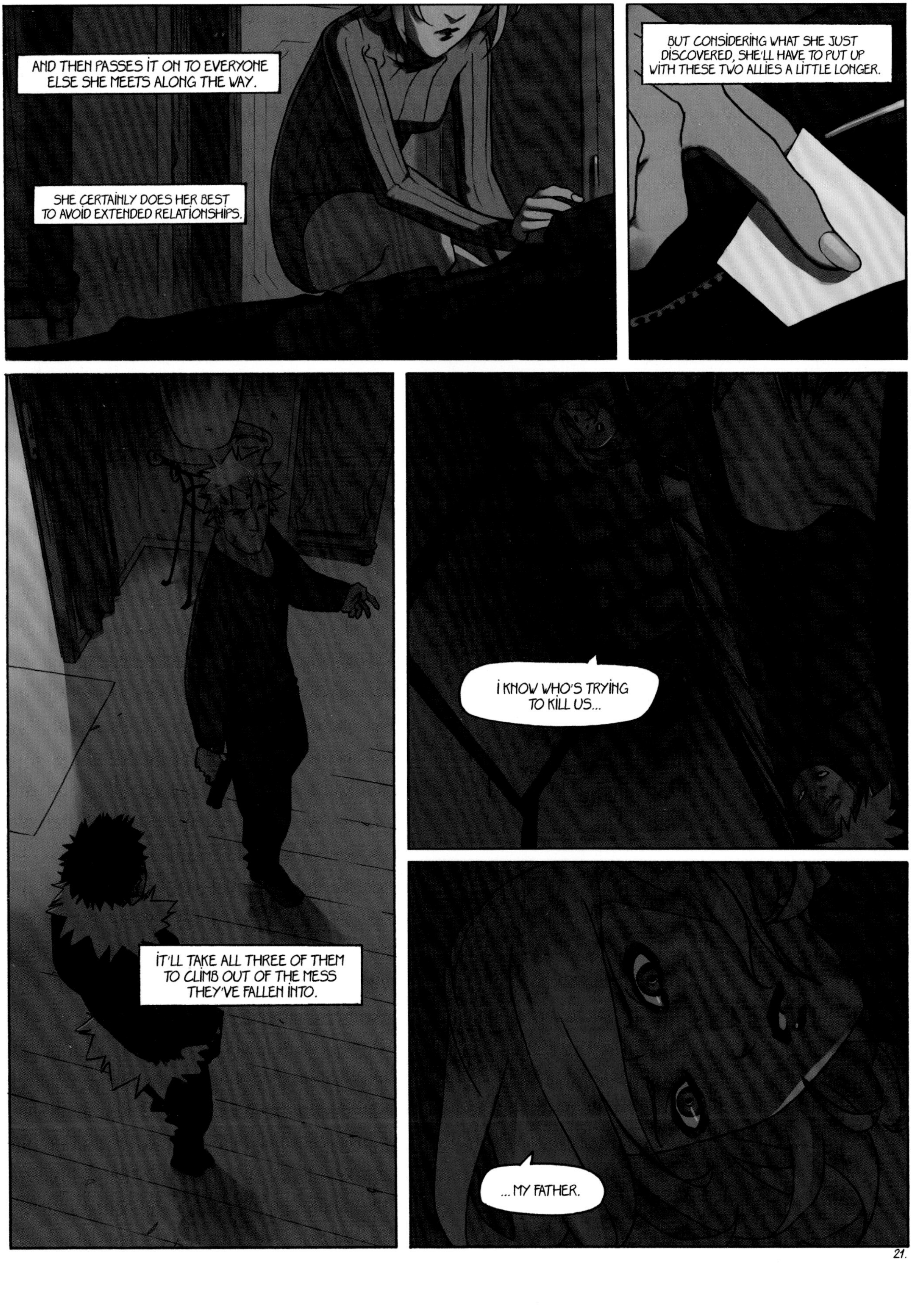
AND THEN PASSES IT ON TO EVERYONE ELSE SHE MEETS ALONG THE WAY.
SHE CERTAINLY DOES HER BEST TO AVOID EXTENDED RELATIONSHIPS.
BUT CONSIDERING WHAT SHE JUST DISCOVERED, SHE'LL HAVE TO PUT UP WITH THESE TWO ALLIES A LITTLE LONGER.
IT'LL TAKE ALL THREE OF THEM TO CLIMB OUT OF THE MESS THEY'VE FALLEN INTO.
I KNOW WHO'S TRYING TO KILL US...
... MY FATHER.

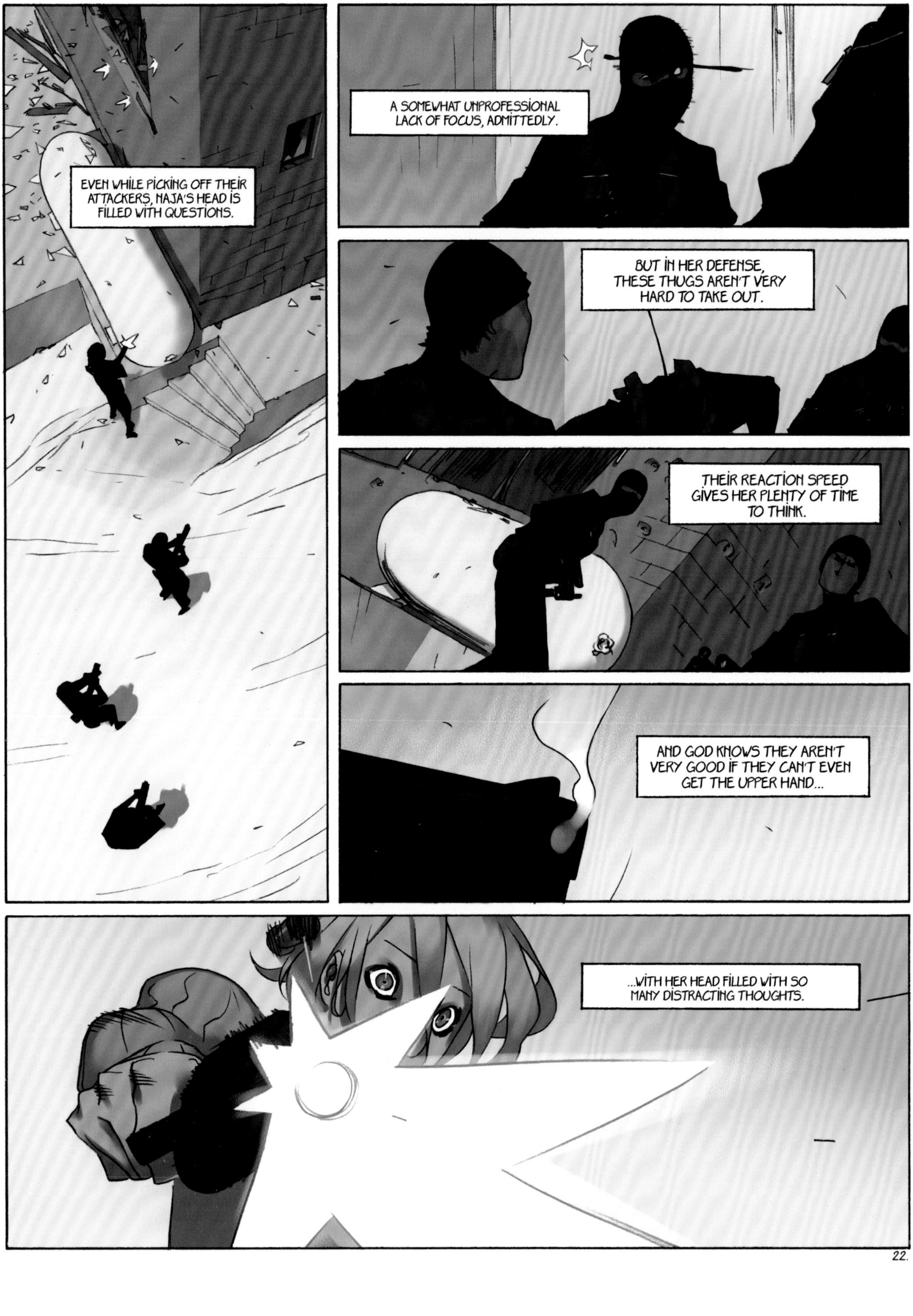
EVEN WHILE PICKING OFF THEIR ATTACKERS, NAJA'S HEAD IS FILLED WITH QUESTIONS.
A SOMEWHAT UNPROFESSIONAL LACK OF FOCUS, ADMITTEDLY.
BUT IN HER DEFENSE, THESE THUGS AREN'T VERY HARD TO TAKE OUT.
THEIR REACTION SPEED GIVES HER PLENTY OF TIME TO THINK.
AND GOD KNOWS THEY AREN'T VERY GOOD IF THEY CAN'T EVEN GET THE UPPER HAND...
...WITH HER HEAD FILLED WITH SO MANY DISTRACTING THOUGHTS.

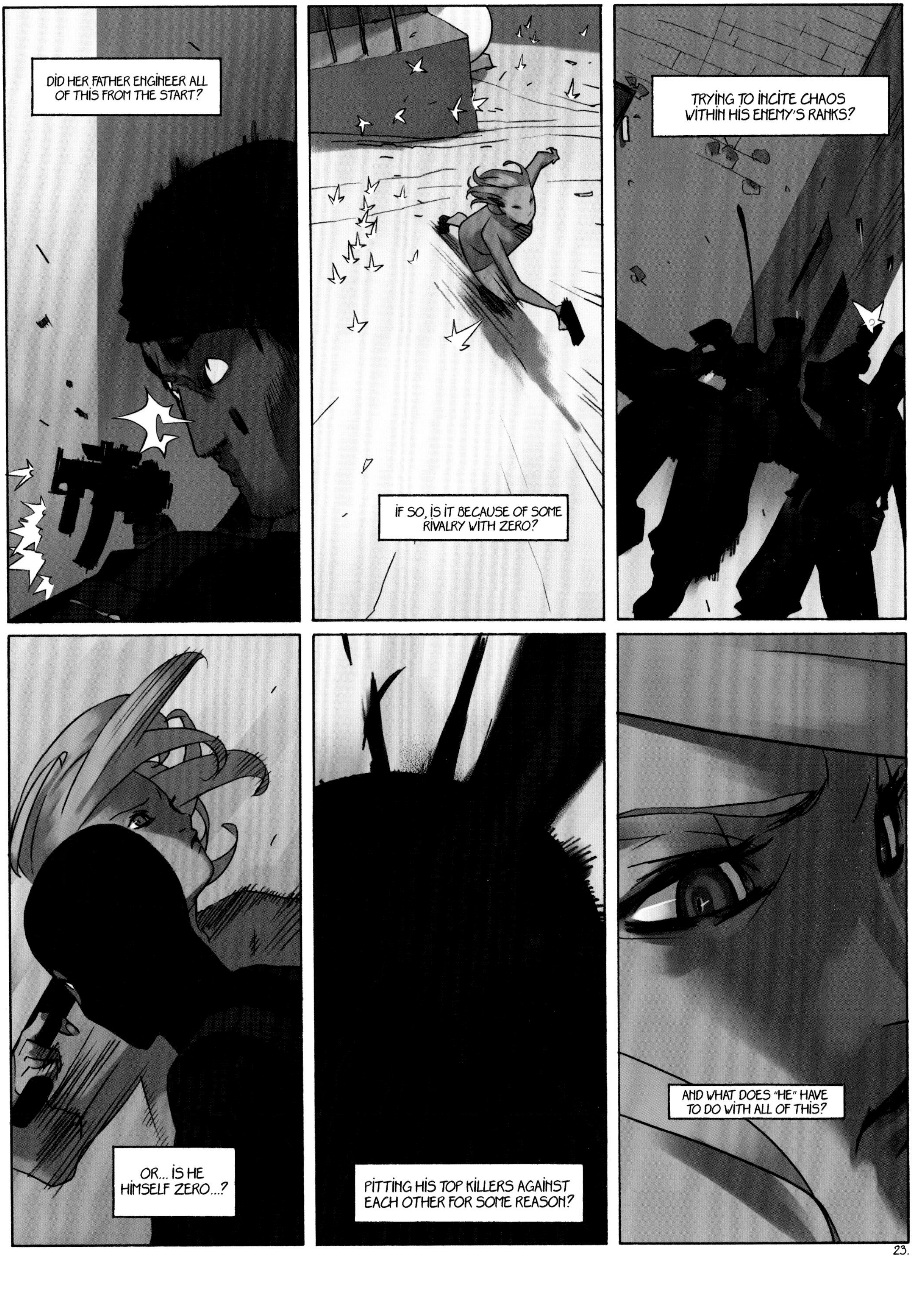
DID HER FATHER ENGINEER ALL OF THIS FROM THE START?
IF SO, IS IT BECAUSE OF SOME RIVALRY WITH ZERO?
TRYING TO INCITE CHAOS WITHIN HIS ENEMY'S RANKS?
OR... IS HE HIMSELF ZERO...?
PITTING HIS TOP KILLERS AGAINST EACH OTHER FOR SOME REASON?
AND WHAT DOES "HE" HAVE TO DO WITH ALL OF THIS?

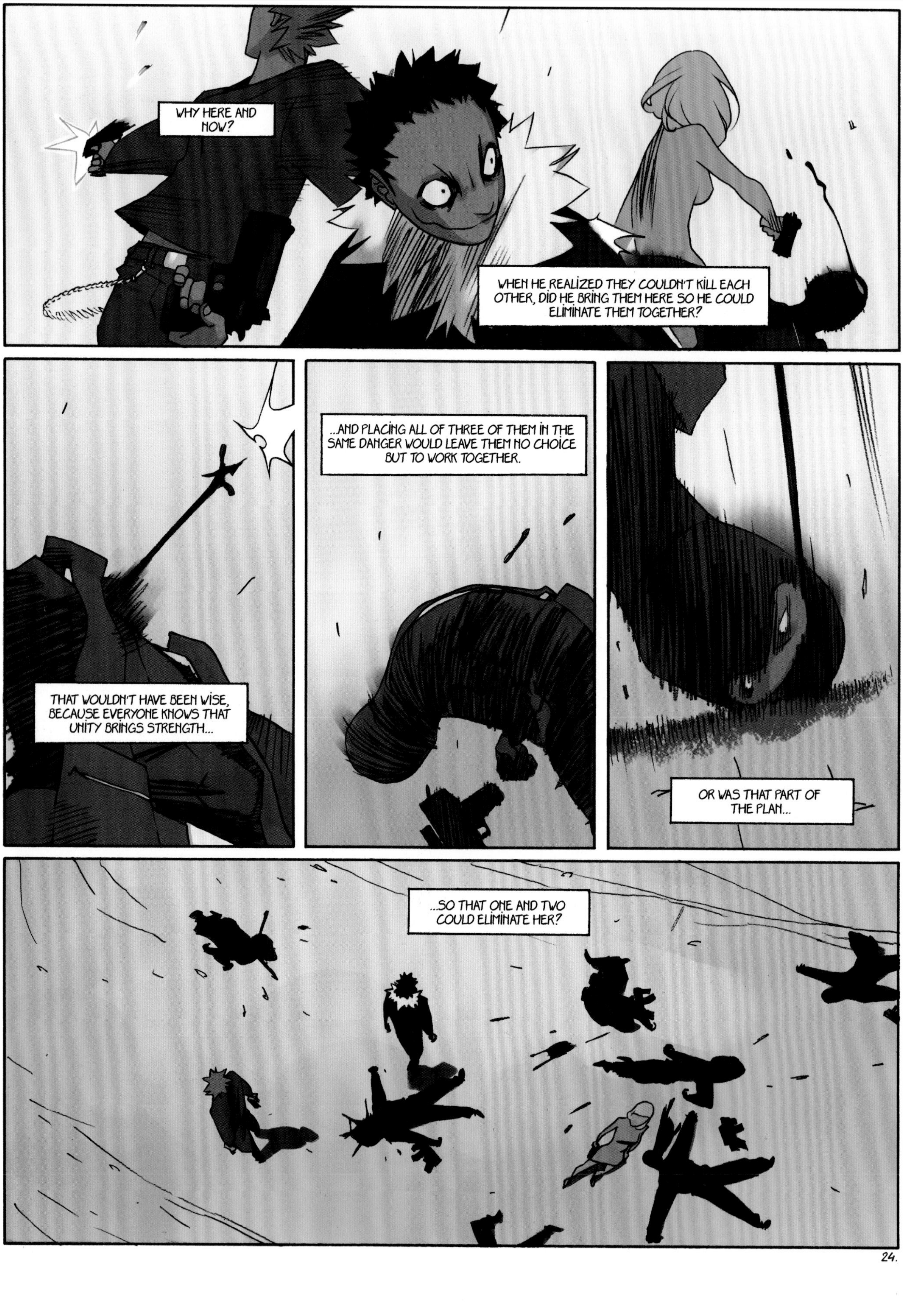
WHY HERE AND NOW?
WHEN HE REALIZED THEY COULDN'T KILL EACH OTHER, DID HE BRING THEM HERE SO HE COULD ELIMINATE THEM TOGETHER?
THAT WOULDN'T HAVE BEEN WISE, BECAUSE EVERYONE KNOWS THAT UNITY BRINGS STRENGTH...
...AND PLACING ALL OF THREE OF THEM IN THE SAME DANGER WOULD LEAVE THEM NO CHOICE BUT TO WORK TOGETHER.
OR WAS THAT PART OF THE PLAN...
...SO THAT ONE AND TWO COULD ELIMINATE HER?

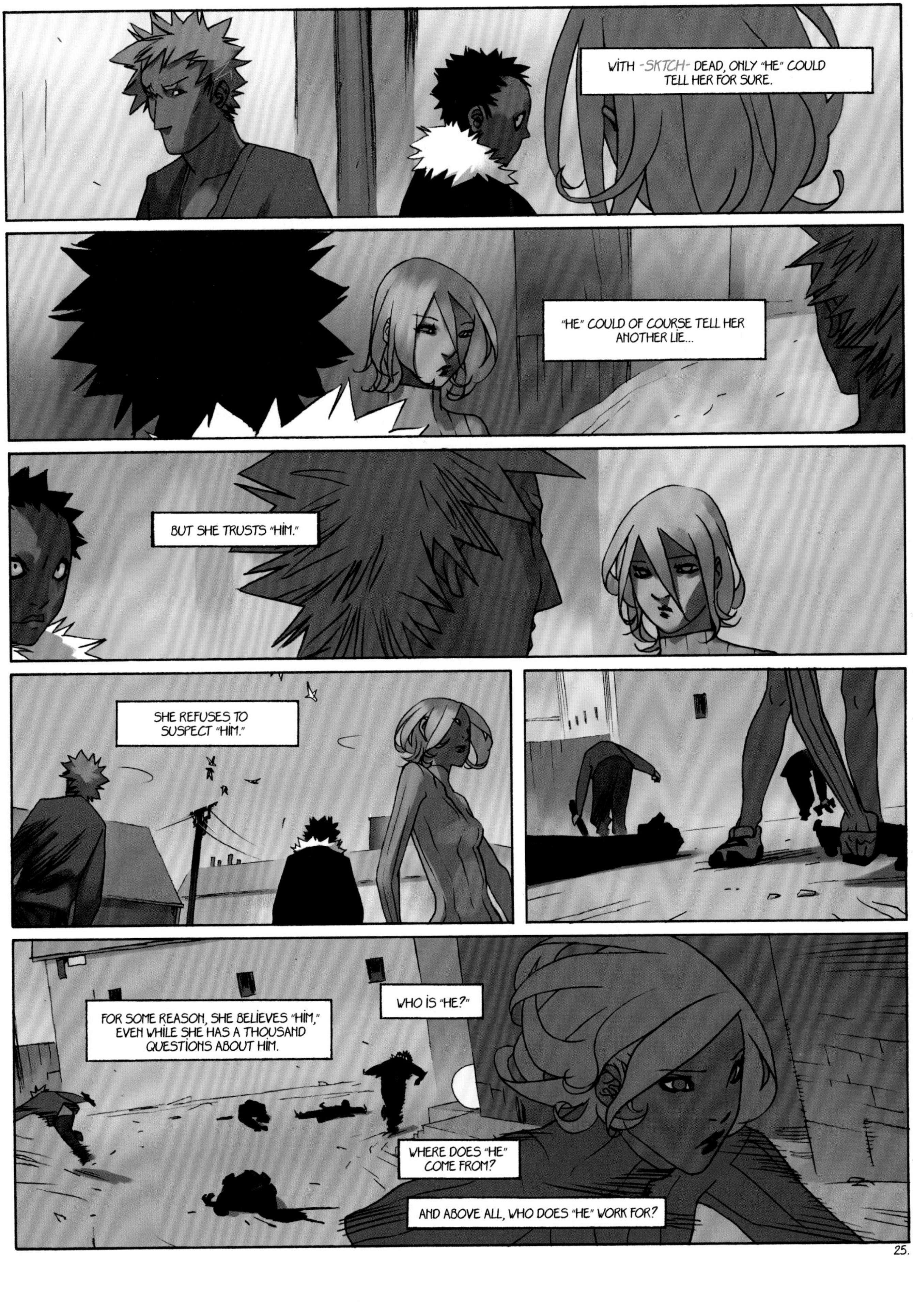
WITH -SKTCH- DEAD, ONLY "HE" COULD TELL HER FOR SURE.
"HE" COULD OF COURSE TELL HER ANOTHER LIE...
BUT SHE TRUSTS "HIM."
SHE REFUSES TO SUSPECT "HIM."
FOR SOME REASON, SHE BELIEVES "HIM," EVEN WHILE SHE HAS A THOUSAND QUESTIONS ABOUT HIM.
WHO IS "HE?"
WHERE DOES "HE" COME FROM?
AND ABOVE ALL, WHO DOES "HE" WORK FOR?

FOR OR AGAINST HER FATHER?

FOR OR AGAINST ZERO?

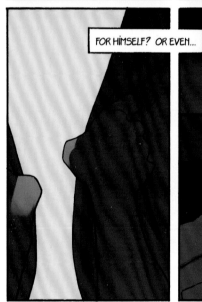

FOR HIMSELF? OR EVEN...

...AGAINST HIMSELF?

IN THIS UNFATHOMABLE BLUR, ANYTHING SEEMS POSSIBLE.

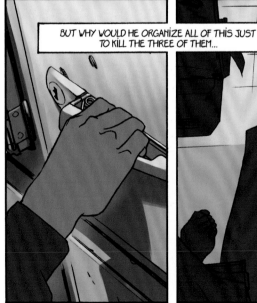

BUT WHY WOULD HE ORGANIZE ALL OF THIS JUST TO KILL THE THREE OF THEM...

...ONE AT A TIME?

A CRAZY THOUGHT OCCURRED TO HER: MAYBE "HE" FELL IN LOVE WITH HER, TOO...

...AND THAT THREW OFF HIS PLANS AT THE LAST MOMENT...

...CAUSING THIS WHOLE MESS.

MAYBE HE BROUGHT THEM TOGETHER SO THAT THEY COULD MAKE PEACE.

BUT NAJA REFUSES TO PUT MUCH STOCK IN THAT HOPE.

SHE'S NOT THE HOPEFUL SORT.

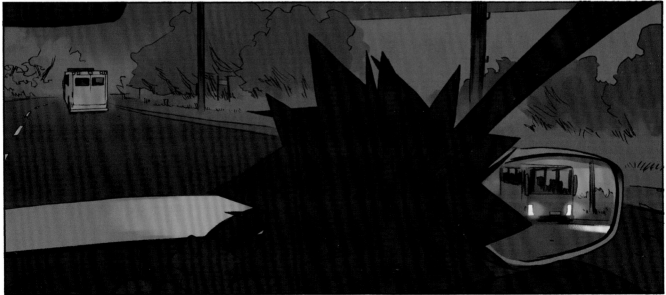

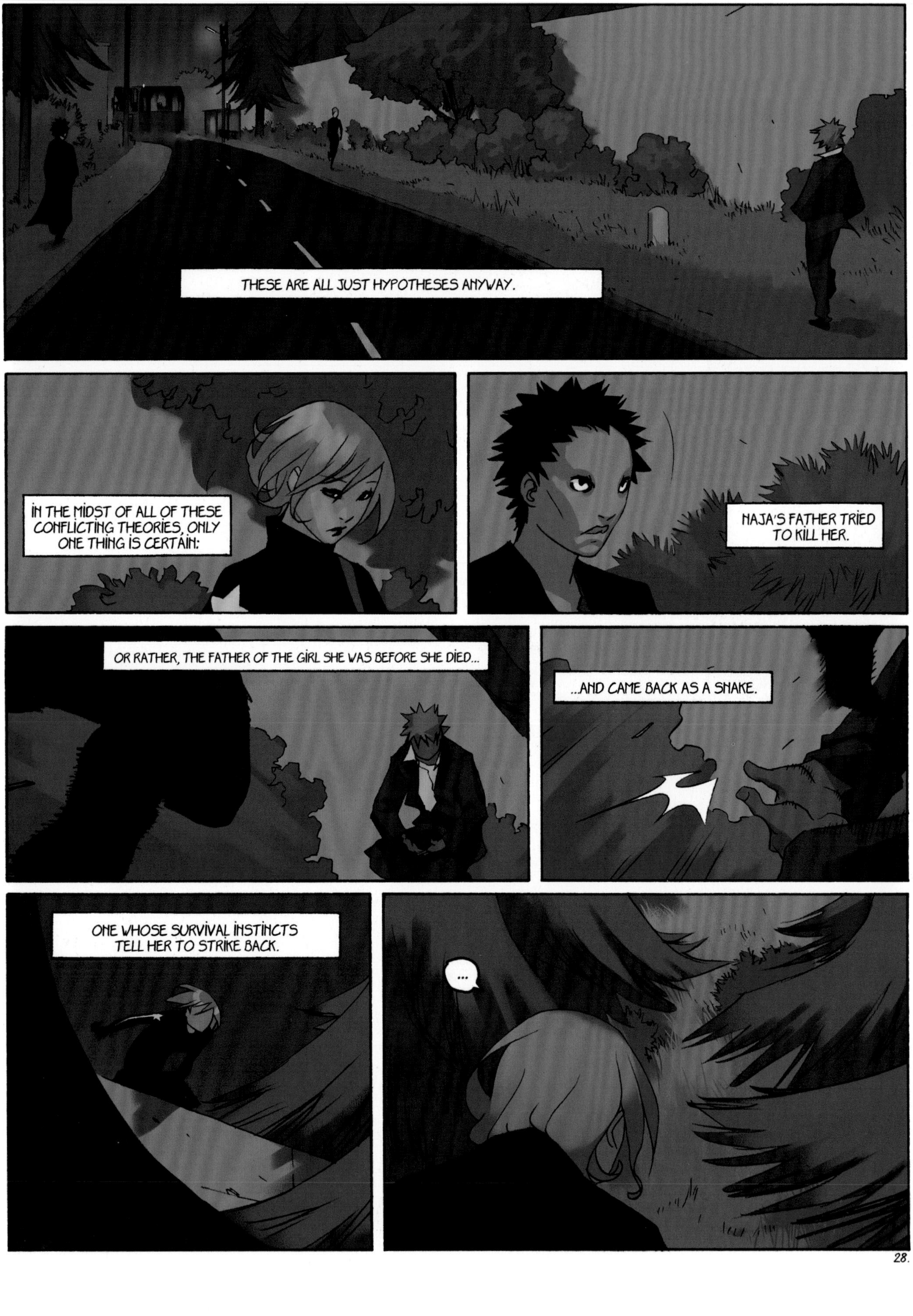
THESE ARE ALL JUST HYPOTHESES ANYWAY.
IN THE MIDST OF ALL OF THESE CONFLICTING THEORIES, ONLY ONE THING IS CERTAIN:
NAJA'S FATHER TRIED TO KILL HER.
OR RATHER, THE FATHER OF THE GIRL SHE WAS BEFORE SHE DIED...
...AND CAME BACK AS A SNAKE.
ONE WHOSE SURVIVAL INSTINCTS TELL HER TO STRIKE BACK.
...

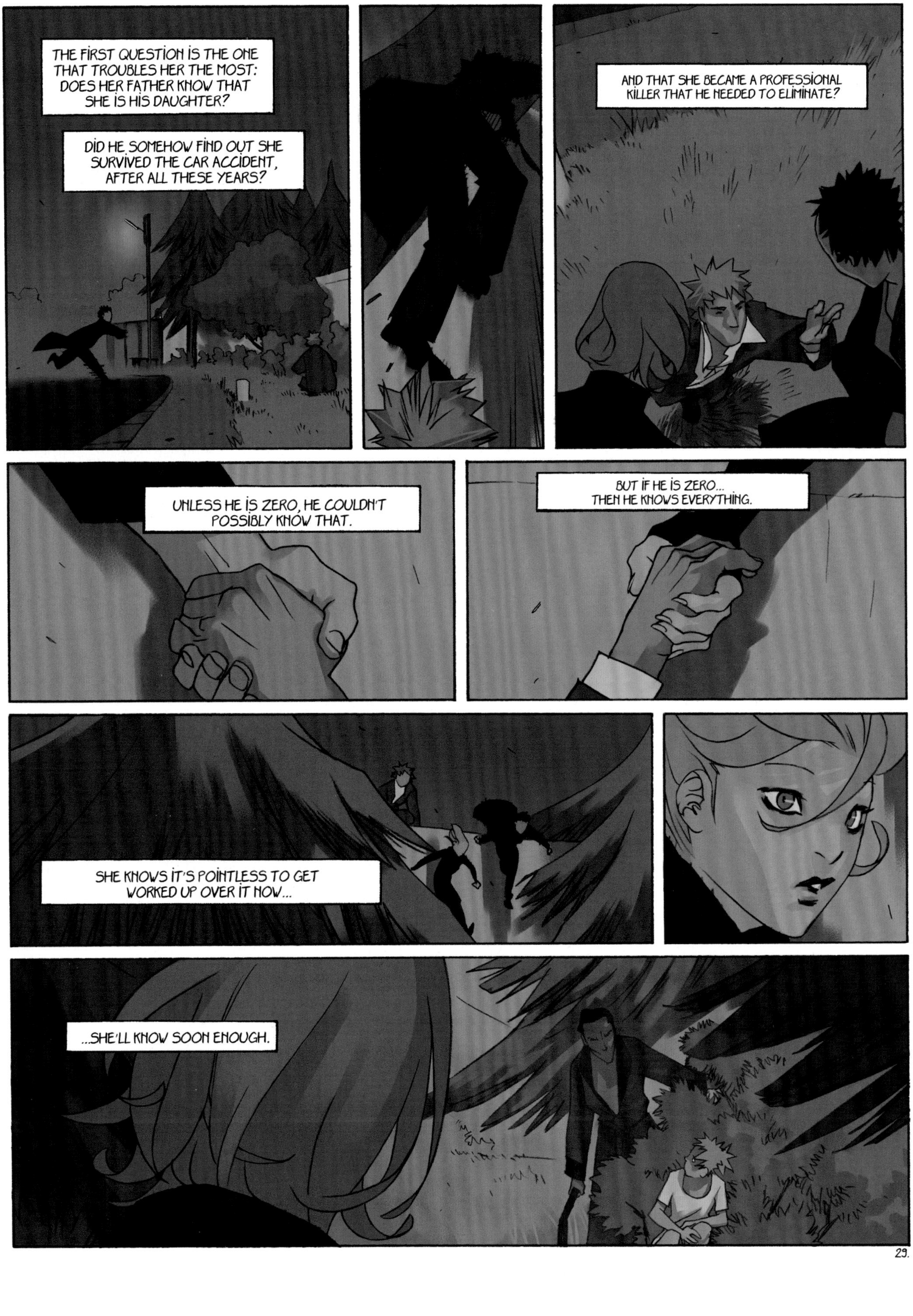
THE FIRST QUESTION IS THE ONE THAT TROUBLES HER THE MOST: DOES HER FATHER KNOW THAT SHE IS HIS DAUGHTER?
DID HE SOMEHOW FIND OUT SHE SURVIVED THE CAR ACCIDENT, AFTER ALL THESE YEARS?
AND THAT SHE BECAME A PROFESSIONAL KILLER THAT HE NEEDED TO ELIMINATE?
UNLESS HE IS ZERO, HE COULDN'T POSSIBLY KNOW THAT.
BUT IF HE IS ZERO... THEN HE KNOWS EVERYTHING.
SHE KNOWS IT'S POINTLESS TO GET WORKED UP OVER IT NOW...
...SHE'LL KNOW SOON ENOUGH.

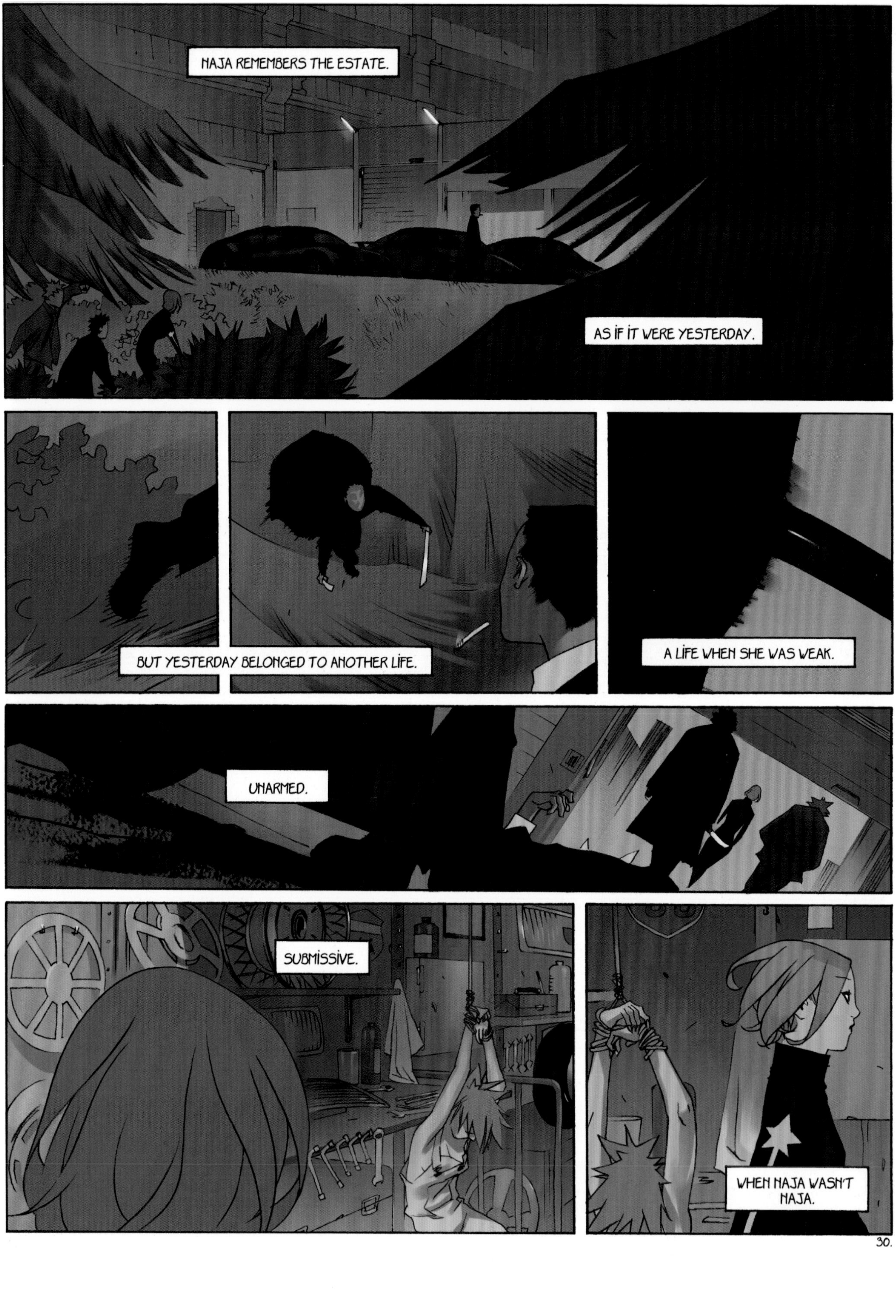
NAJA REMEMBERS THE ESTATE.
AS IF IT WERE YESTERDAY.
BUT YESTERDAY BELONGED TO ANOTHER LIFE.
A LIFE WHEN SHE WAS WEAK.
UNARMED.
SUBMISSIVE.
WHEN NAJA WASN'T NAJA.

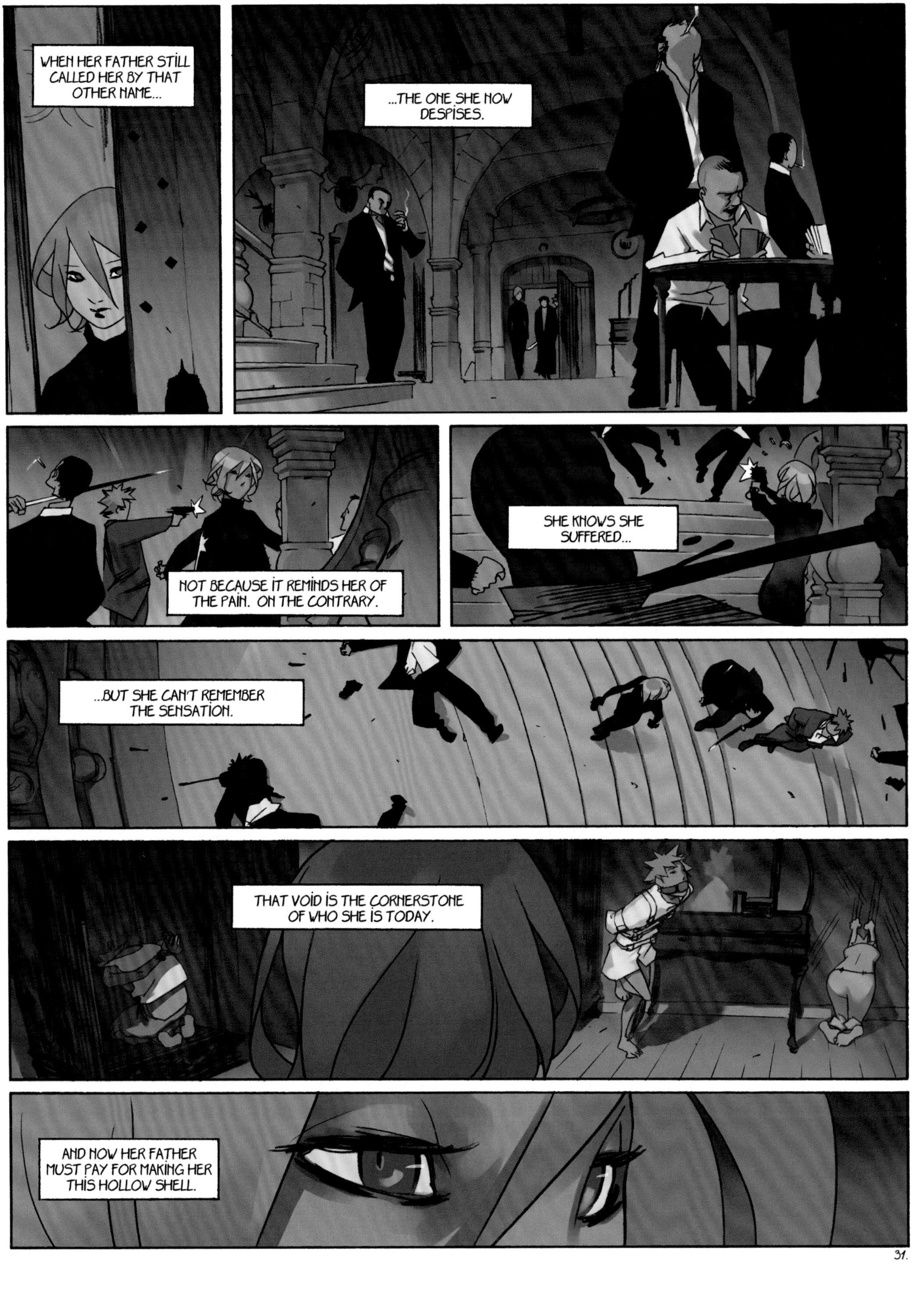
WHEN HER FATHER STILL CALLED HER BY THAT OTHER NAME...
...THE ONE SHE NOW DESPISES.
NOT BECAUSE IT REMINDS HER OF THE PAIN. ON THE CONTRARY.
SHE KNOWS SHE SUFFERED...
...BUT SHE CAN'T REMEMBER THE SENSATION.
THAT VOID IS THE CORNERSTONE OF WHO SHE IS TODAY.
AND NOW HER FATHER MUST PAY FOR MAKING HER THIS HOLLOW SHELL.

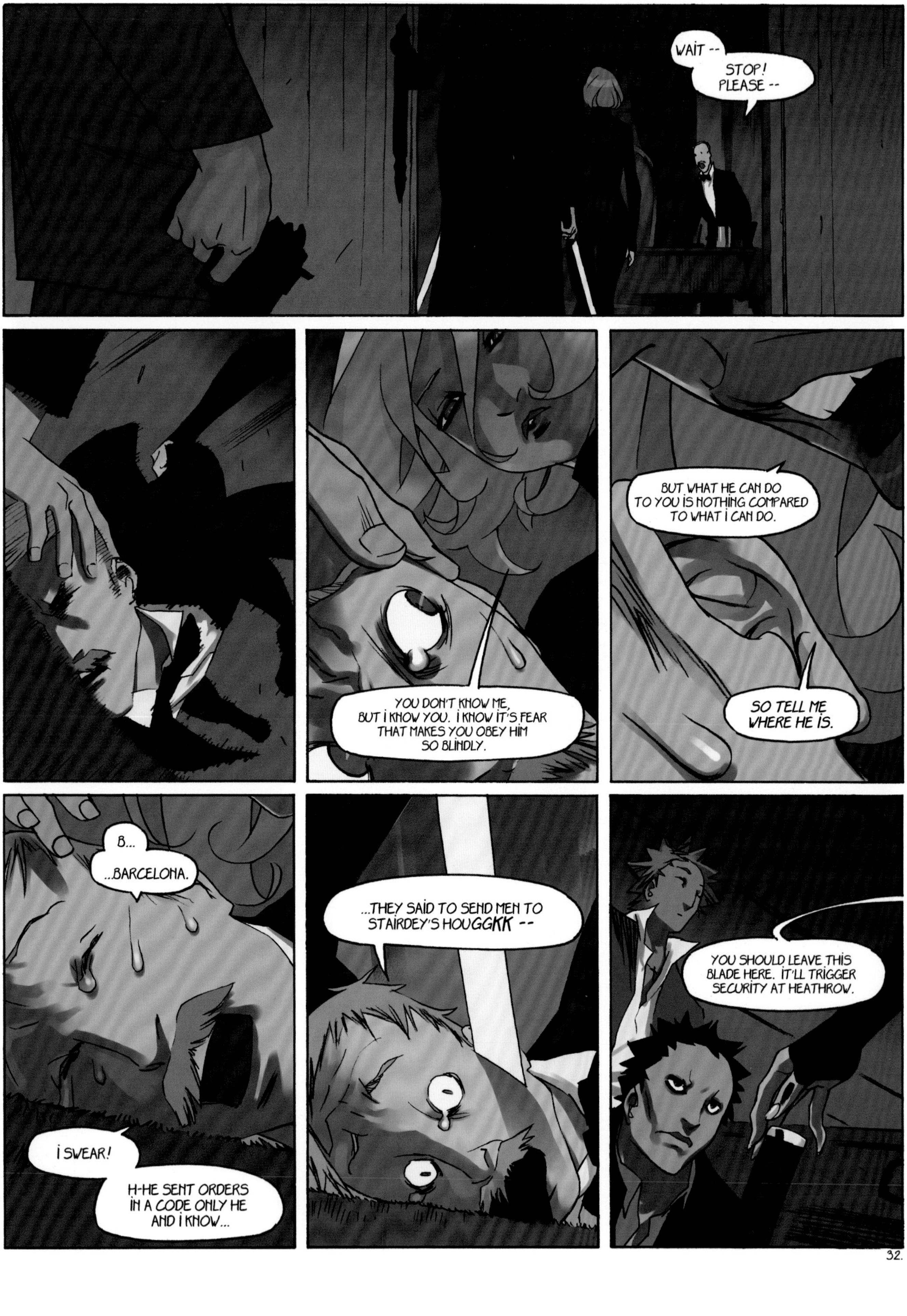
WAIT --
STOP! PLEASE --
YOU DON'T KNOW ME, BUT I KNOW YOU. I KNOW IT'S FEAR THAT MAKES YOU OBEY HIM SO BLINDLY.
BUT WHAT HE CAN DO TO YOU IS NOTHING COMPARED TO WHAT I CAN DO.
SO TELL ME WHERE HE IS.
B...
...BARCELONA.
I SWEAR!
H-HE SENT ORDERS IN A CODE ONLY HE AND I KNOW...
...THEY SAID TO SEND MEN TO STAIRDEY'S HOUGGKK --
YOU SHOULD LEAVE THIS BLADE HERE. IT'LL TRIGGER SECURITY AT HEATHROW.

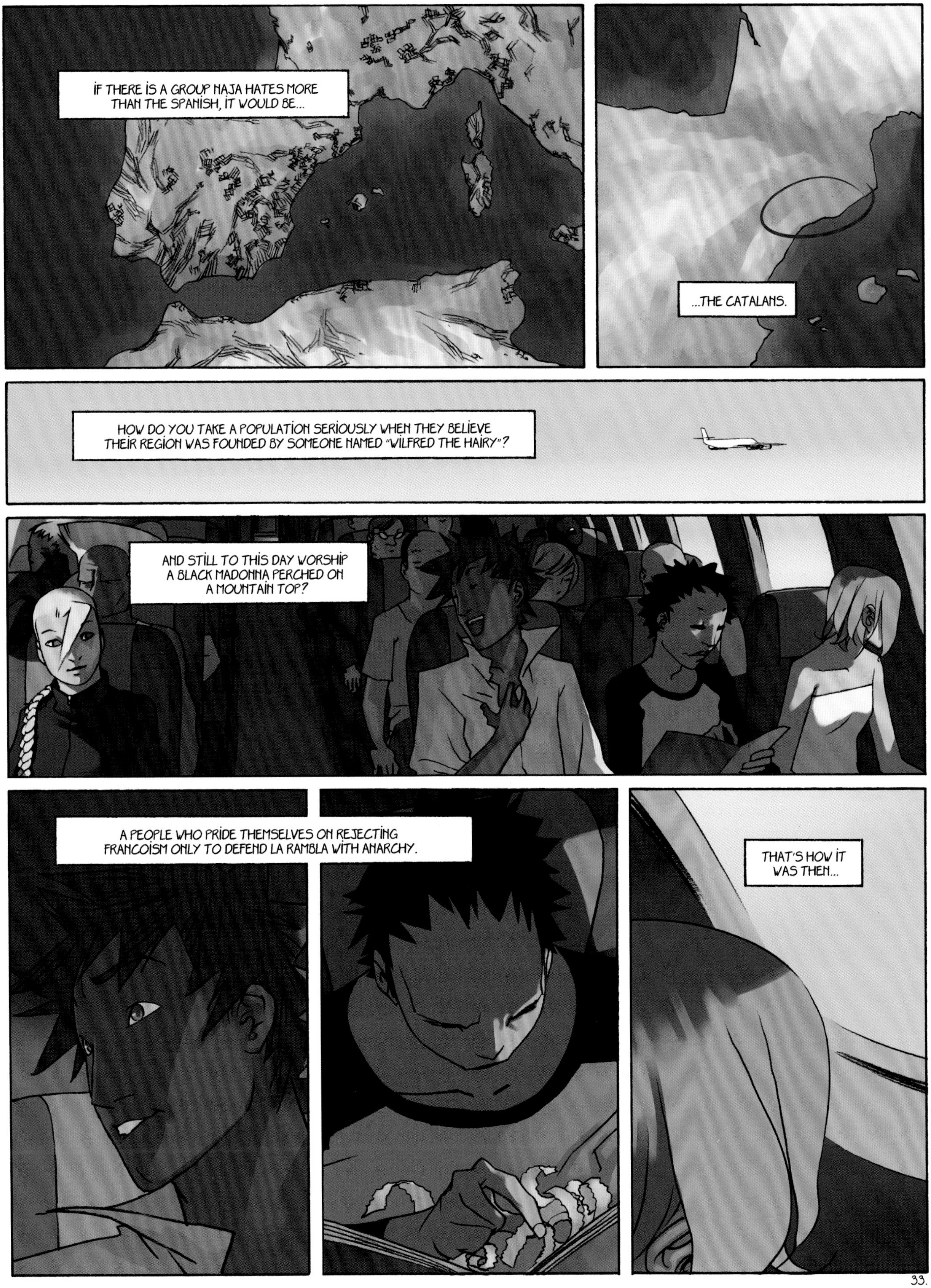
IF THERE IS A GROUP NAJA HATES MORE THAN THE SPANISH, IT WOULD BE...
...THE CATALANS.
HOW DO YOU TAKE A POPULATION SERIOUSLY WHEN THEY BELIEVE THEIR REGION WAS FOUNDED BY SOMEONE NAMED "WILFRED THE HAIRY"?
AND STILL TO THIS DAY WORSHIP A BLACK MADONNA PERCHED ON A MOUNTAIN TOP?
A PEOPLE WHO PRIDE THEMSELVES ON REJECTING FRANCOISM ONLY TO DEFEND LA RAMBLA WITH ANARCHY.
THAT'S HOW IT WAS THEN...

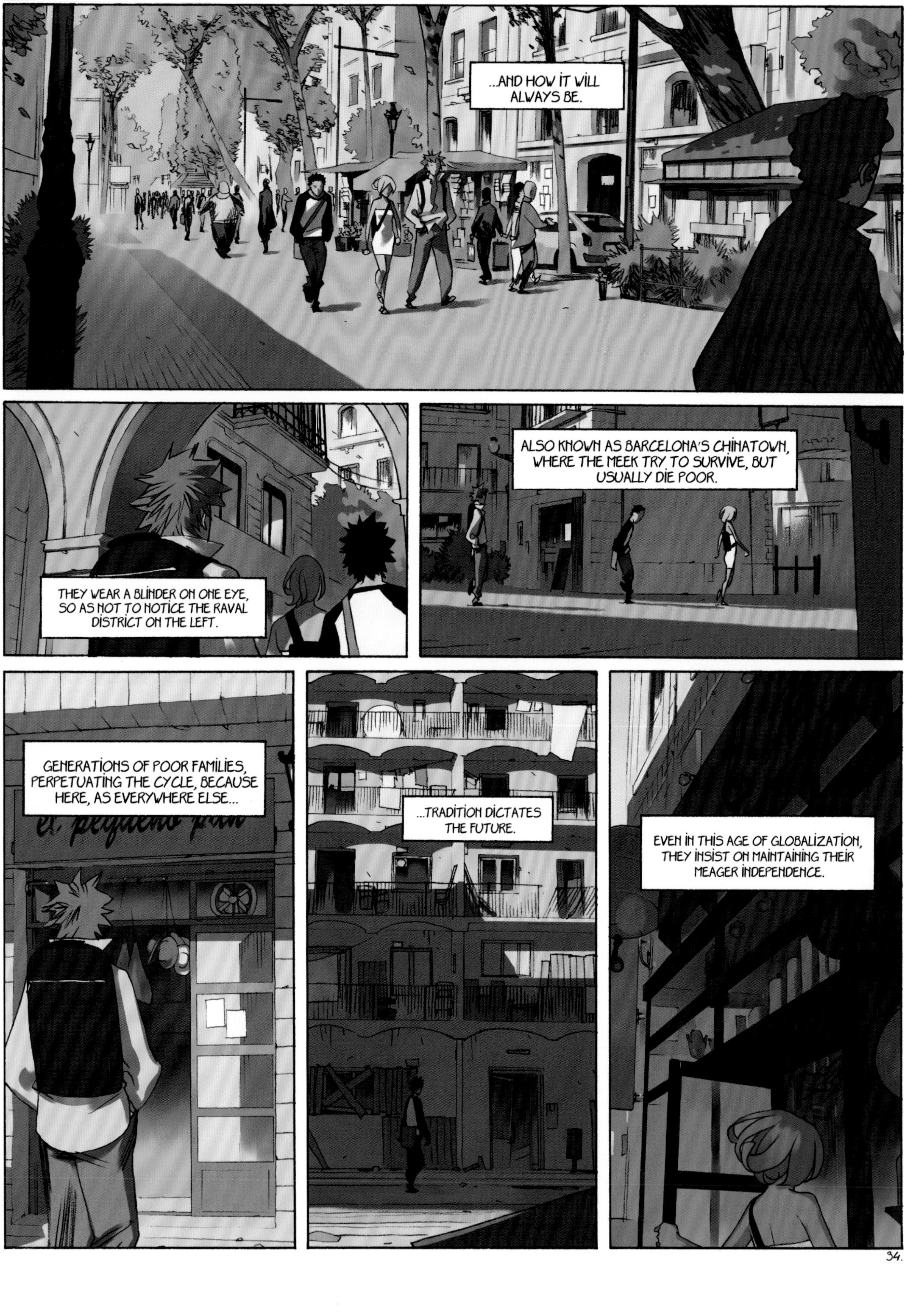
...AND HOW IT WILL ALWAYS BE.
THEY WEAR A BLINDER ON ONE EYE, SO AS NOT TO NOTICE THE RAVAL DISTRICT ON THE LEFT.
ALSO KNOWN AS BARCELONA'S CHINATOWN, WHERE THE MEEK TRY TO SURVIVE, BUT USUALLY DIE POOR.
GENERATIONS OF POOR FAMILIES, PERPETUATING THE CYCLE, BECAUSE HERE, AS EVERYWHERE ELSE...
...TRADITION DICTATES THE FUTURE.
EVEN IN THIS AGE OF GLOBALIZATION, THEY INSIST ON MAINTAINING THEIR MEAGER INDEPENDENCE.

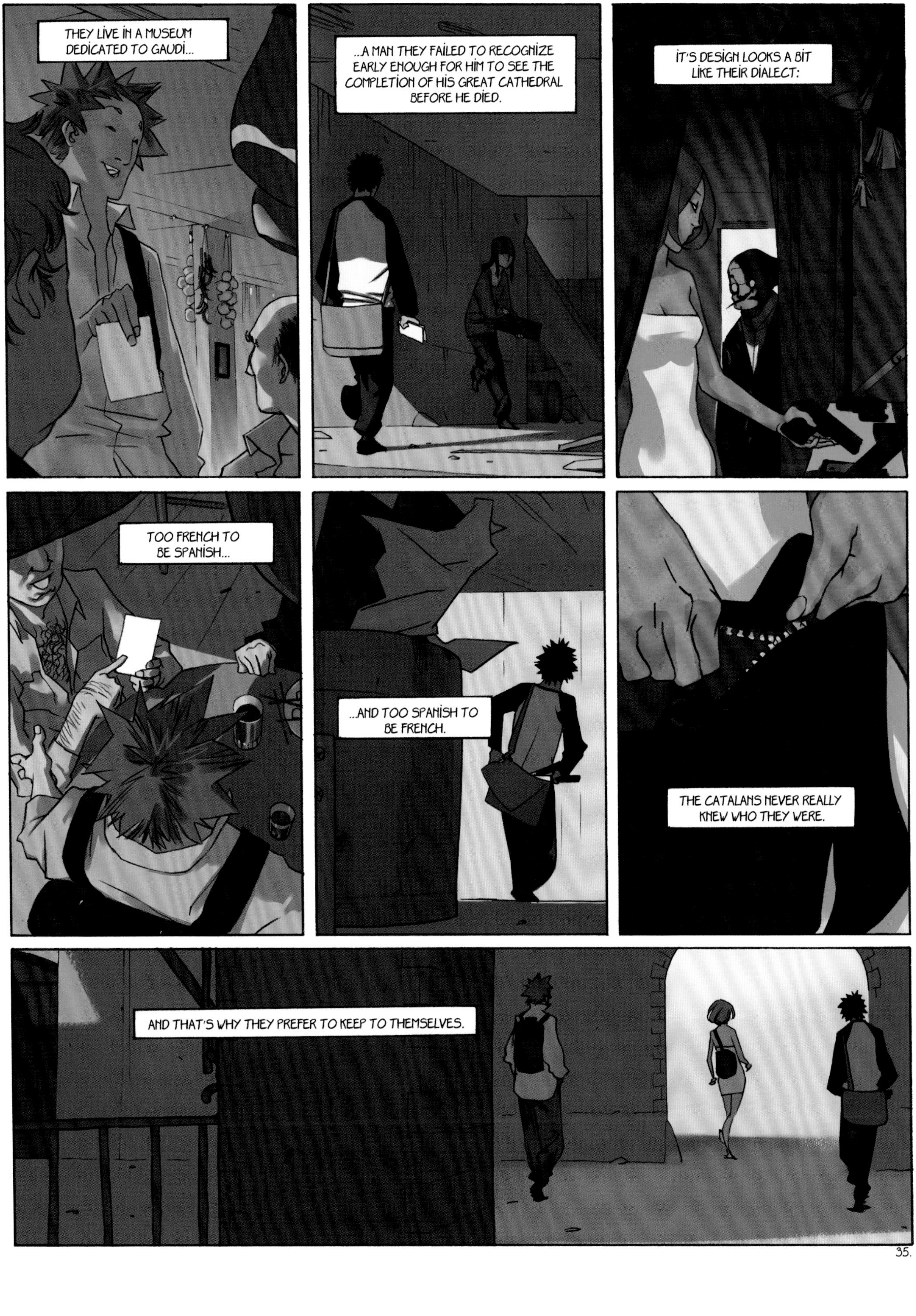
THEY LIVE IN A MUSEUM DEDICATED TO GAUDI...
...A MAN THEY FAILED TO RECOGNIZE EARLY ENOUGH FOR HIM TO SEE THE COMPLETION OF HIS GREAT CATHEDRAL BEFORE HE DIED.
IT'S DESIGN LOOKS A BIT LIKE THEIR DIALECT:
TOO FRENCH TO BE SPANISH...
...AND TOO SPANISH TO BE FRENCH.
THE CATALANS NEVER REALLY KNEW WHO THEY WERE.
AND THAT'S WHY THEY PREFER TO KEEP TO THEMSELVES.

BUT DOES NAJA REALLY
KNOW WHO SHE IS?

OR REMEMBER WHO
SHE USED TO BE?

I DO NOW. PERHAPS EVEN BETTER
THAN SHE KNOWS HERSELF.

LET'S SAY I KNOW WHY SHE DOES CERTAIN THINGS, EVEN
WHEN SHE BELIEVES SHE DOES THEM OUT OF INSTINCT.

I FIND HER SUBCONSCIOUS
TO BE AN OPEN BOOK.

AS IS THAT OF EVERYONE
I'VE TOLD YOU ABOUT SO FAR.

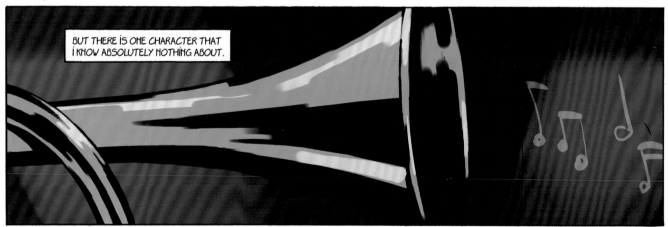
BUT THERE IS ONE CHARACTER THAT
I KNOW ABSOLUTELY NOTHING ABOUT.

FORTUNATELY, IT LOOKS AS IF OTHERS WILL DO A MUCH BETTER JOB OF TELLING YOU ABOUT HIM.

HE HAS A ROLE TO PLAY IN THIS STORY...

...SINCE HE WAS THE FIRST TO FIND NAJA'S TARGET.

ALTHOUGH NOT BY MUCH.

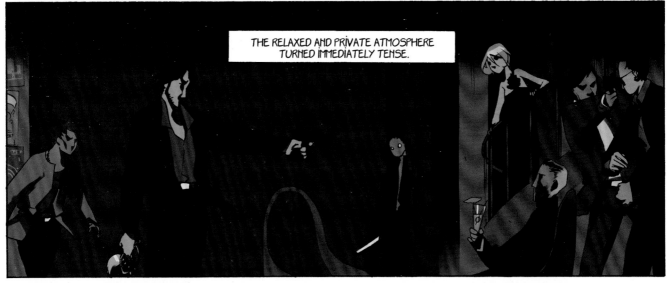

THE RELAXED AND PRIVATE ATMOSPHERE TURNED IMMEDIATELY TENSE.

THEIR EYES CROSSED, AS IF OUT OF RECOGNITION, DESPITE HAVING NEVER MET...

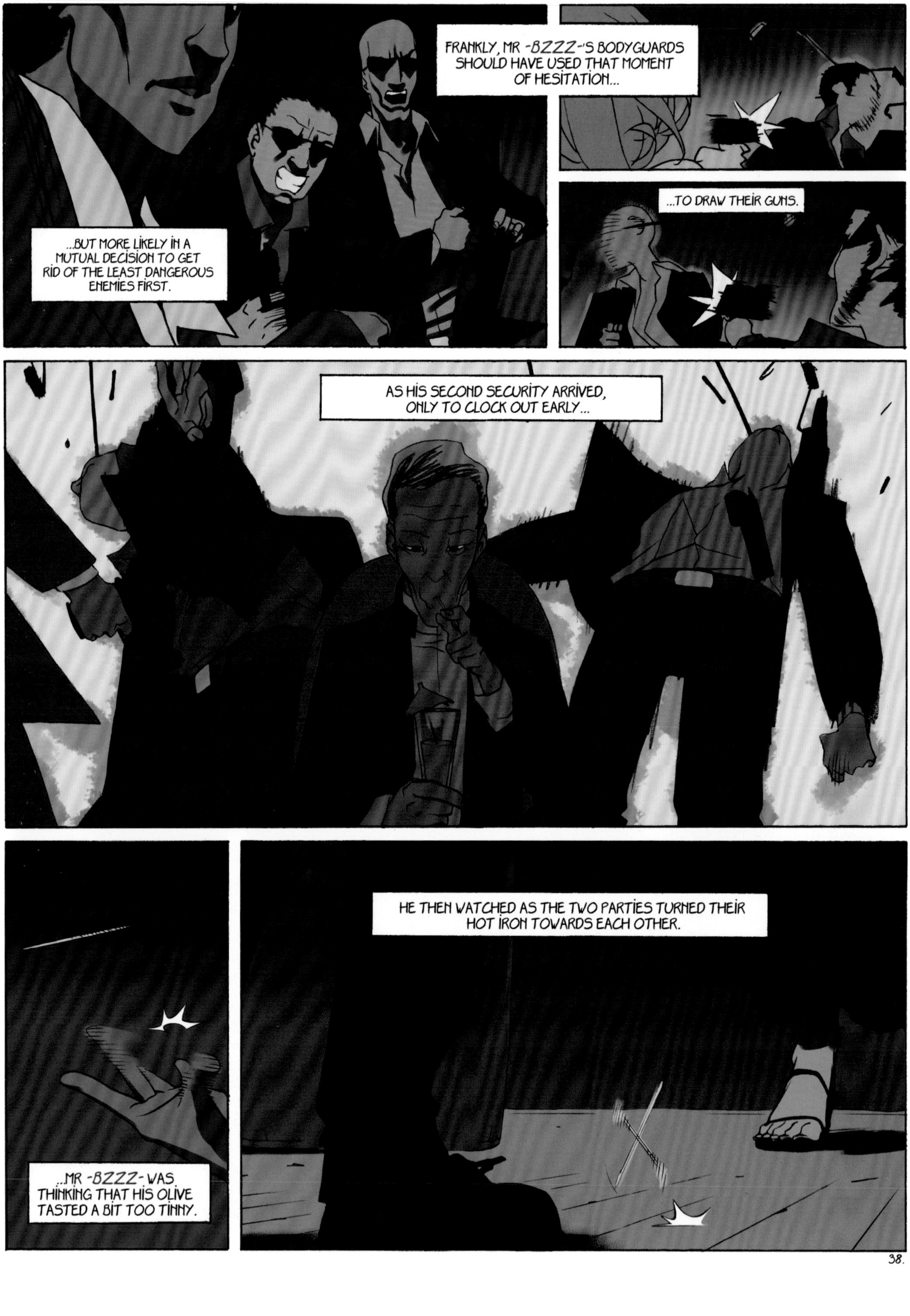
FRANKLY, MR -BZZZ-'S BODYGUARDS SHOULD HAVE USED THAT MOMENT OF HESITATION...
...BUT MORE LIKELY IN A MUTUAL DECISION TO GET RID OF THE LEAST DANGEROUS ENEMIES FIRST.
...TO DRAW THEIR GUNS.
AS HIS SECOND SECURITY ARRIVED, ONLY TO CLOCK OUT EARLY...
...MR -BZZZ- WAS THINKING THAT HIS OLIVE TASTED A BIT TOO TINNY.
HE THEN WATCHED AS THE TWO PARTIES TURNED THEIR HOT IRON TOWARDS EACH OTHER.

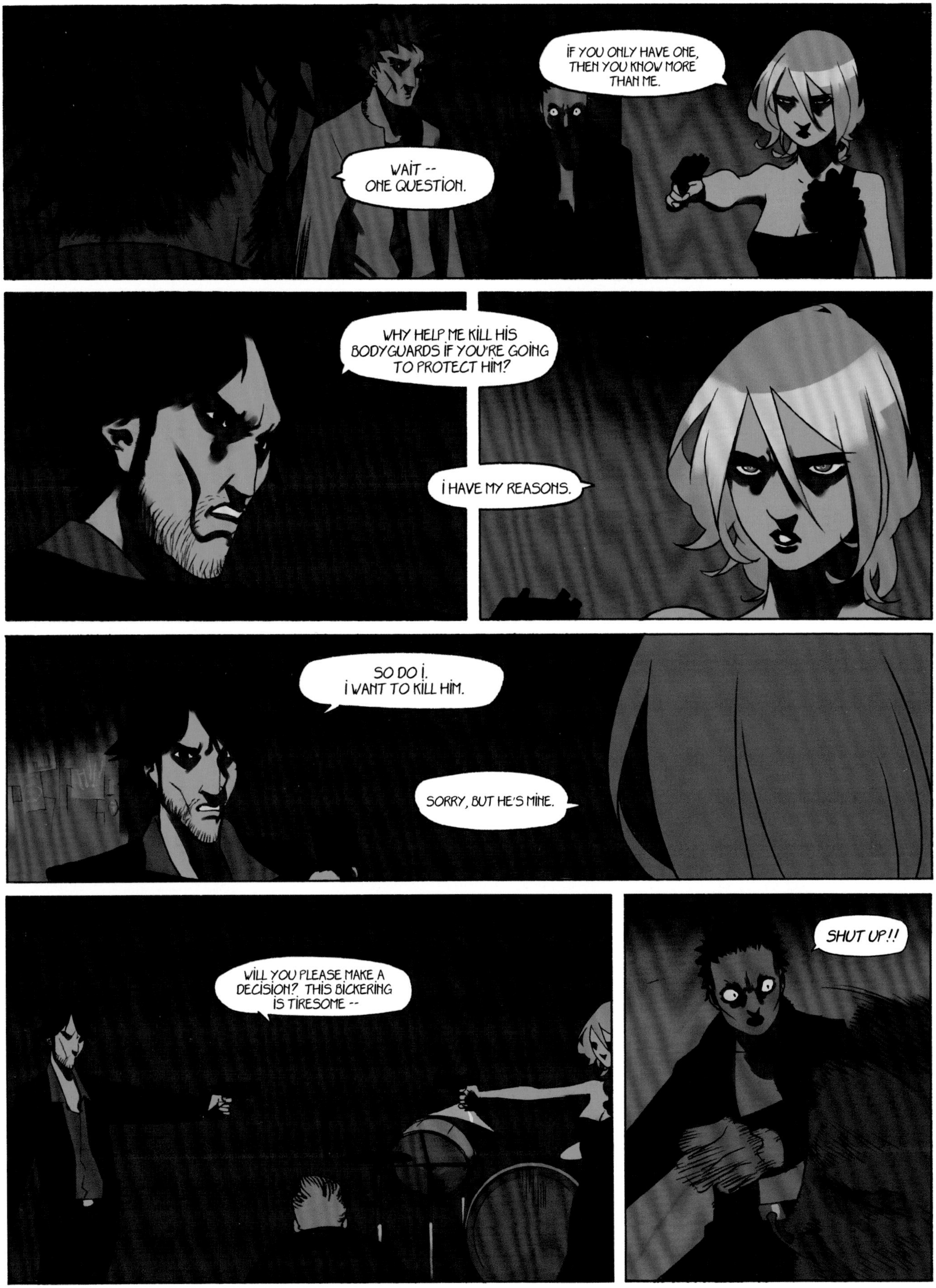
IF YOU ONLY HAVE ONE, THEN YOU KNOW MORE THAN ME.
WAIT -- ONE QUESTION.
WHY HELP ME KILL HIS BODYGUARDS IF YOU'RE GOING TO PROTECT HIM?
I HAVE MY REASONS.
SO DO I. I WANT TO KILL HIM.
SORRY, BUT HE'S MINE.
WILL YOU PLEASE MAKE A DECISION? THIS BICKERING IS TIRESOME --
SHUT UP!!

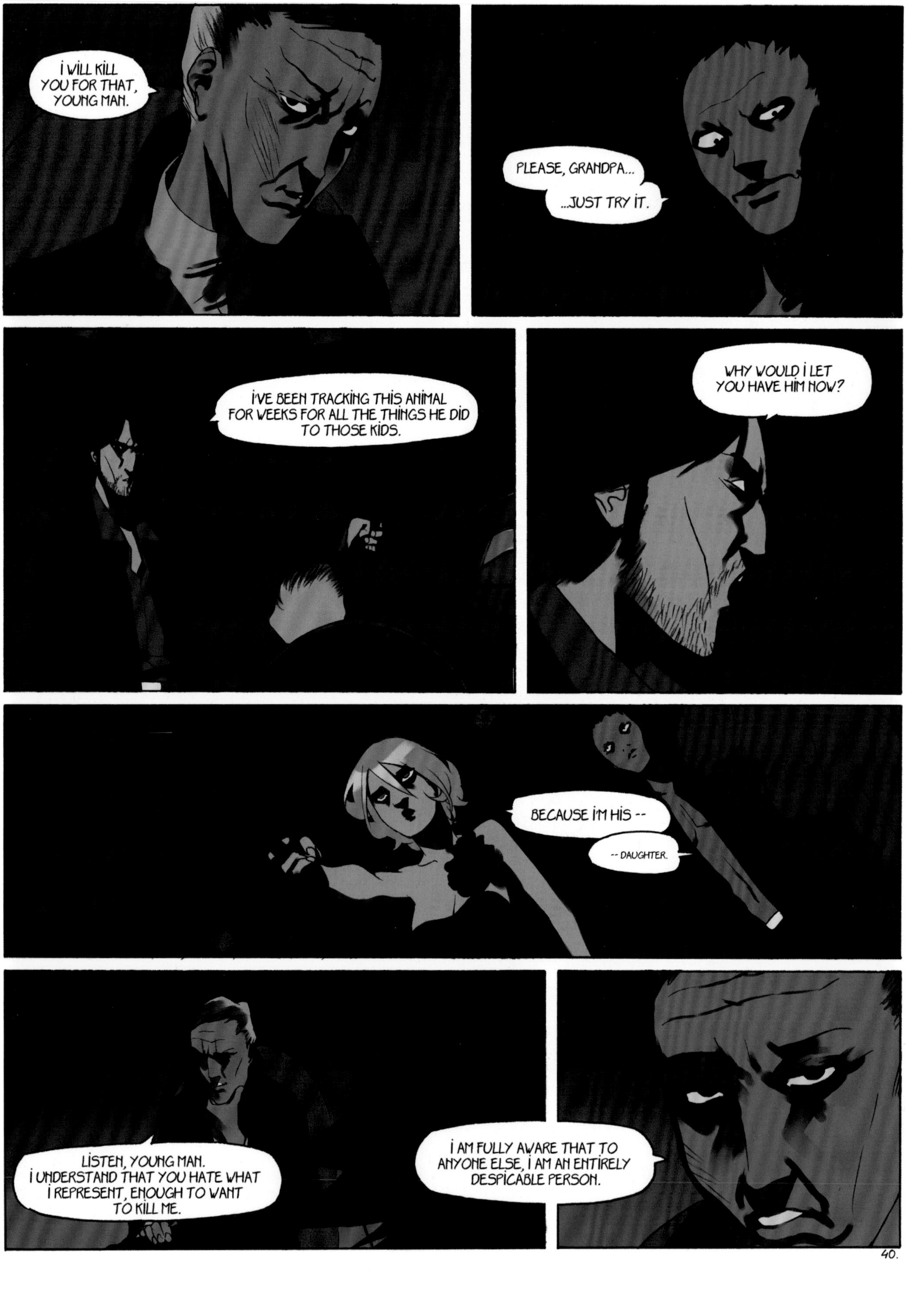
I WILL KILL YOU FOR THAT, YOUNG MAN.
PLEASE, GRANDPA...
...JUST TRY IT.
I'VE BEEN TRACKING THIS ANIMAL FOR WEEKS FOR ALL THE THINGS HE DID TO THOSE KIDS.
WHY WOULD I LET YOU HAVE HIM NOW?
BECAUSE I'M HIS --
-- DAUGHTER.
LISTEN, YOUNG MAN. I UNDERSTAND THAT YOU HATE WHAT I REPRESENT, ENOUGH TO WANT TO KILL ME.
I AM FULLY AWARE THAT TO ANYONE ELSE, I AM AN ENTIRELY DESPICABLE PERSON.

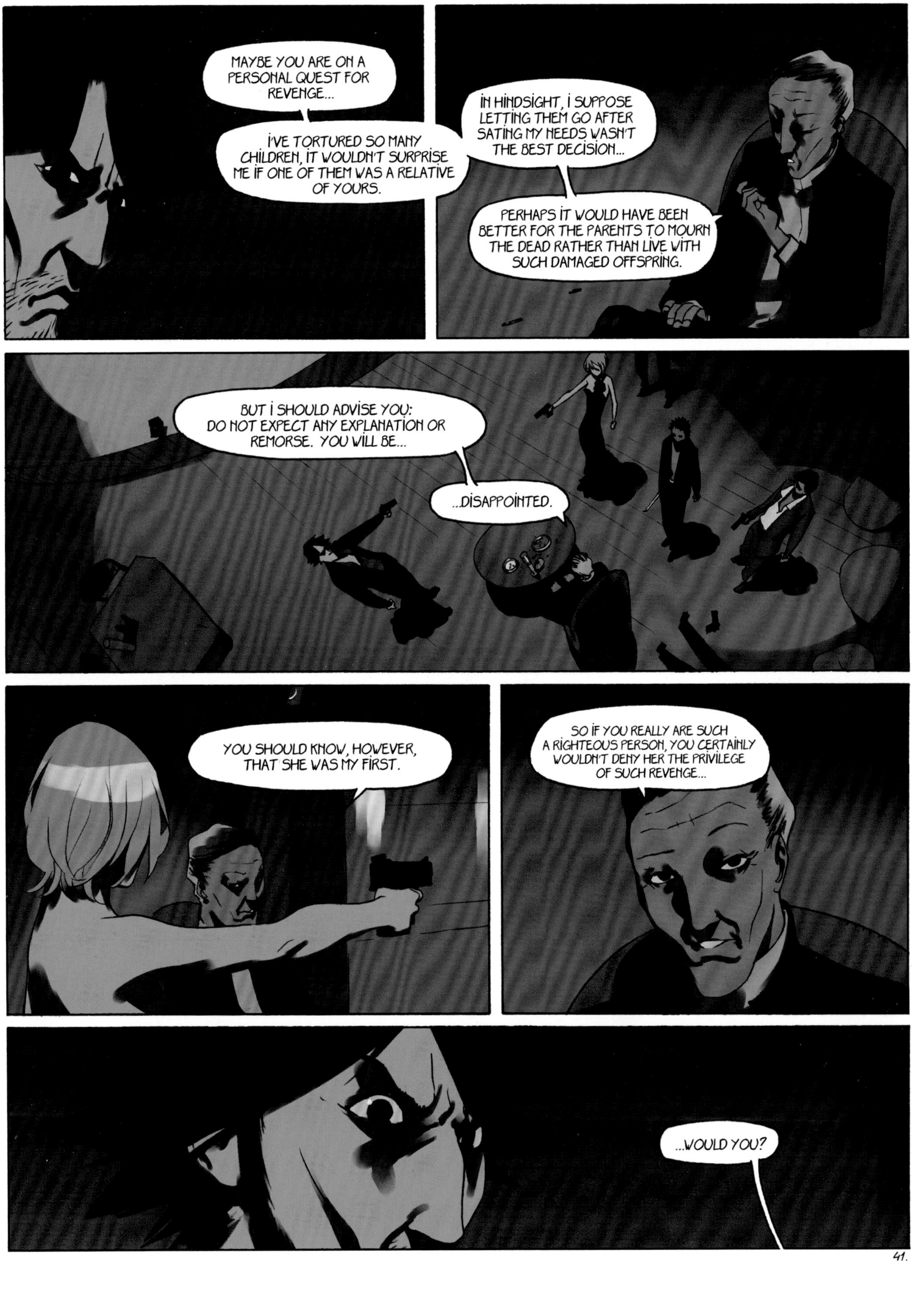
MAYBE YOU ARE ON A PERSONAL QUEST FOR REVENGE...
I'VE TORTURED SO MANY CHILDREN, IT WOULDN'T SURPRISE ME IF ONE OF THEM WAS A RELATIVE OF YOURS.
IN HINDSIGHT, I SUPPOSE LETTING THEM GO AFTER SATING MY NEEDS WASN'T THE BEST DECISION...
PERHAPS IT WOULD HAVE BEEN BETTER FOR THE PARENTS TO MOURN THE DEAD RATHER THAN LIVE WITH SUCH DAMAGED OFFSPRING.
BUT I SHOULD ADVISE YOU: DO NOT EXPECT ANY EXPLANATION OR REMORSE. YOU WILL BE...
...DISAPPOINTED.
YOU SHOULD KNOW, HOWEVER, THAT SHE WAS MY FIRST.
SO IF YOU REALLY ARE SUCH A RIGHTEOUS PERSON, YOU CERTAINLY WOULDN'T DENY HER THE PRIVILEGE OF SUCH REVENGE...
...WOULD YOU?

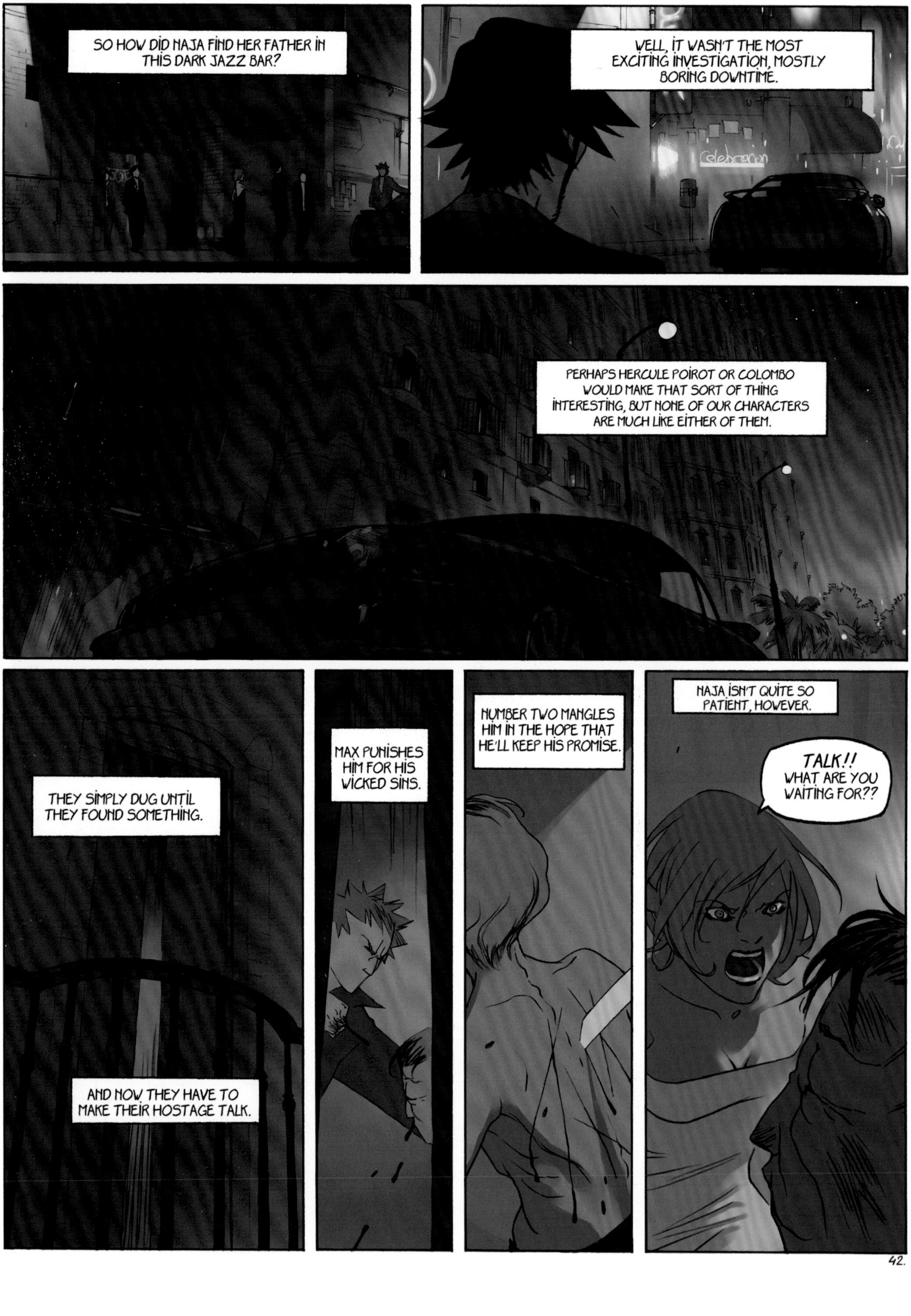
SO HOW DID NAJA FIND HER FATHER IN THIS DARK JAZZ BAR?
WELL, IT WASN'T THE MOST EXCITING INVESTIGATION, MOSTLY BORING DOWNTIME.
Celebration
PERHAPS HERCULE POIROT OR COLOMBO WOULD MAKE THAT SORT OF THING INTERESTING, BUT NONE OF OUR CHARACTERS ARE MUCH LIKE EITHER OF THEM.
THEY SIMPLY DUG UNTIL THEY FOUND SOMETHING.
AND NOW THEY HAVE TO MAKE THEIR HOSTAGE TALK.
MAX PUNISHES HIM FOR HIS WICKED SINS.
NUMBER TWO MANGLES HIM IN THE HOPE THAT HE'LL KEEP HIS PROMISE.
NAJA ISN'T QUITE SO PATIENT, HOWEVER.
TALK!! WHAT ARE YOU WAITING FOR??

WE CAN DO THIS FOREVER!!

WE'LL BREAK YOU PIECE BY PIECE IF WE HAVE TO!

YOUR SILENCE ONLY PROLONGS THE AGONY...

...I'M SORRY, MY CHILD...

...I ENDURE FOR YOUR SAKE.

I THOUGHT THAT'S WHAT YOU WANTED: TO MAKE ME SUFFER AS I MADE YOU SUFFER.

I THOUGHT YOU WANTED TO HAVE YOUR REVENGE, BUT I SUPPOSE THAT WAS ANOTHER OF MY MANY MISUNDERSTANDINGS...

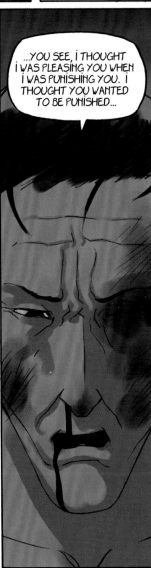

...YOU SEE, I THOUGHT I WAS PLEASING YOU WHEN I WAS PUNISHING YOU. I THOUGHT YOU WANTED TO BE PUNISHED...

...AND WHEN I THOUGHT YOU WERE DEAD, I MISSED YOU SO MUCH.

43.

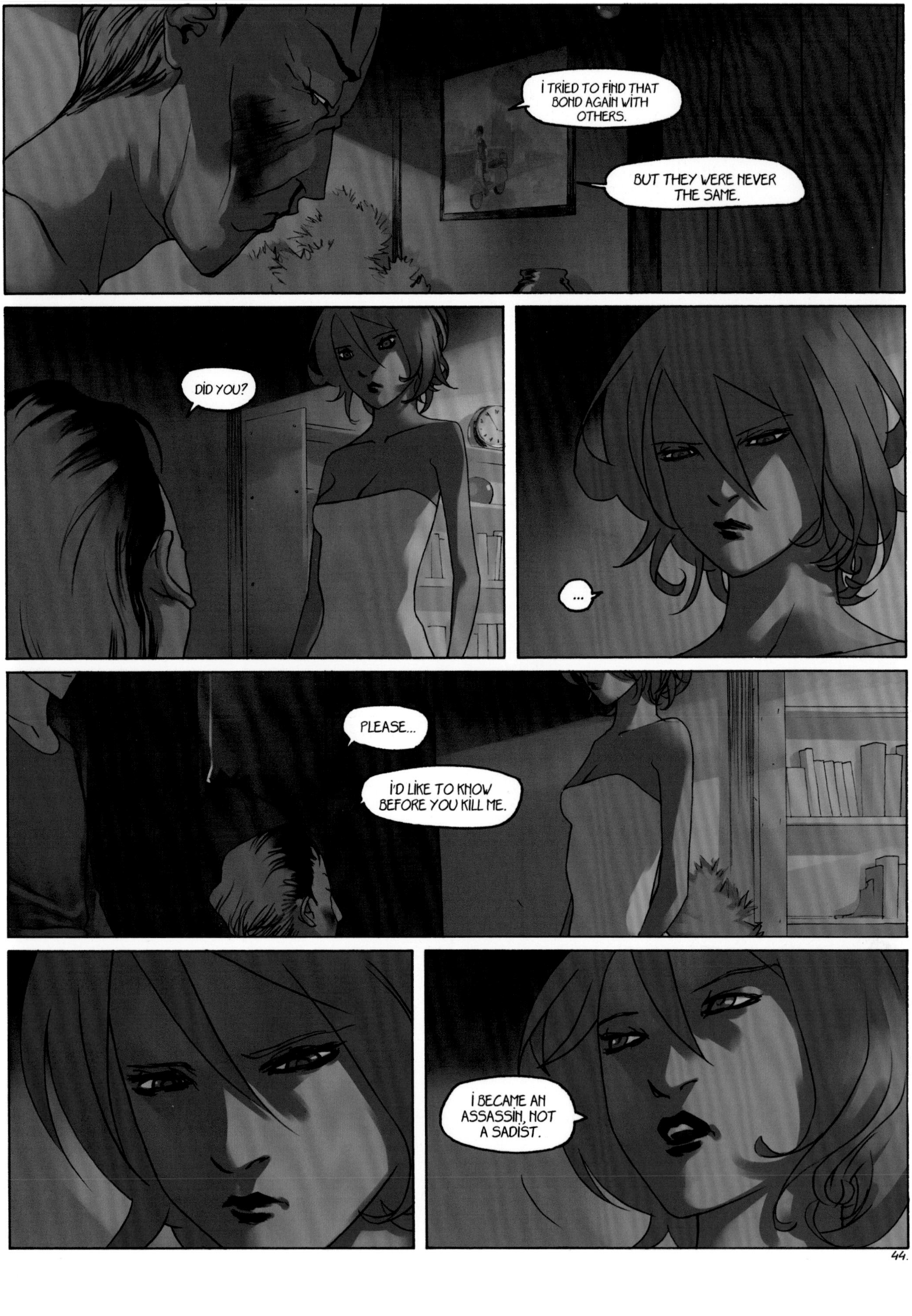
I TRIED TO FIND THAT BOND AGAIN WITH OTHERS.
BUT THEY WERE NEVER THE SAME.
DID YOU?
...
PLEASE...
I'D LIKE TO KNOW BEFORE YOU KILL ME.
I BECAME AN ASSASSIN, NOT A SADIST.

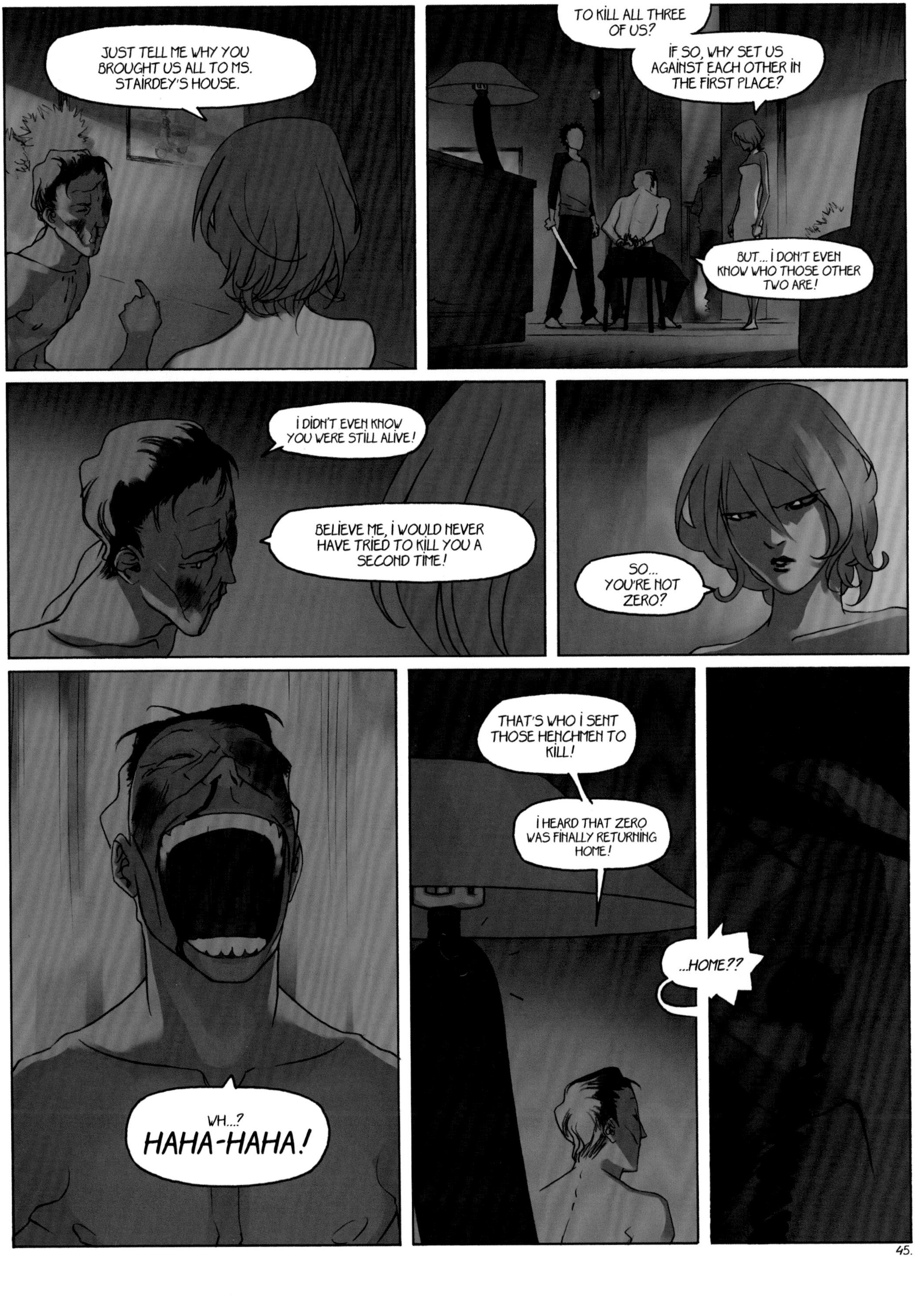

JUST TELL ME WHY YOU BROUGHT US ALL TO MS. STAIRDEY'S HOUSE.
TO KILL ALL THREE OF US?
IF SO, WHY SET US AGAINST EACH OTHER IN THE FIRST PLACE?
BUT... I DON'T EVEN KNOW WHO THOSE OTHER TWO ARE!
I DIDN'T EVEN KNOW YOU WERE STILL ALIVE!
BELIEVE ME, I WOULD NEVER HAVE TRIED TO KILL YOU A SECOND TIME!
SO... YOU'RE NOT ZERO?
WH...? HAHA-HAHA!
THAT'S WHO I SENT THOSE HENCHMEN TO KILL!
I HEARD THAT ZERO WAS FINALLY RETURNING HOME!
...HOME??

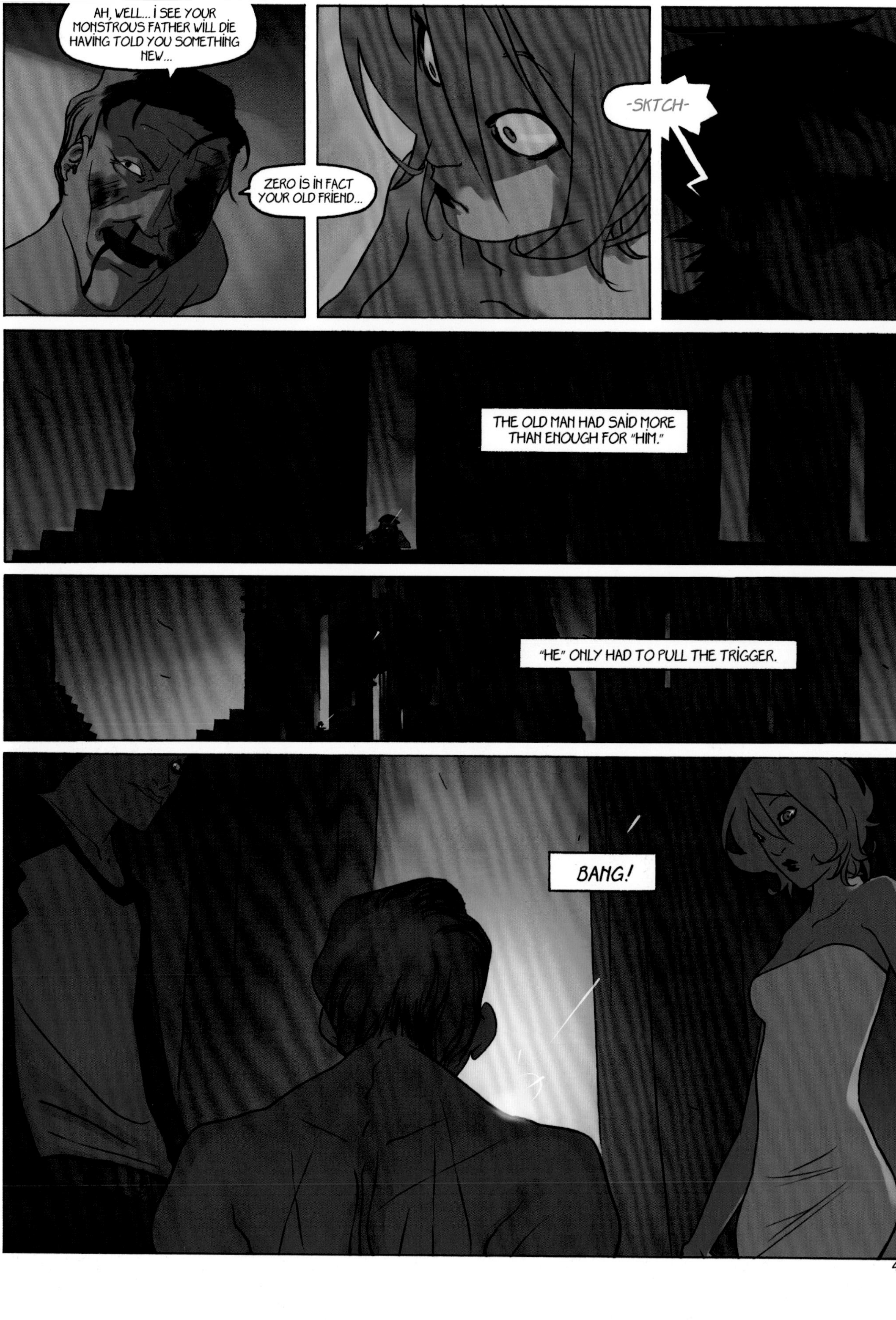
AH, WELL... I SEE YOUR MONSTROUS FATHER WILL DIE HAVING TOLD YOU SOMETHING NEW...
ZERO IS IN FACT YOUR OLD FRIEND...
-SKTCH-
THE OLD MAN HAD SAID MORE THAN ENOUGH FOR "HIM."
"HE" ONLY HAD TO PULL THE TRIGGER.
BANG!

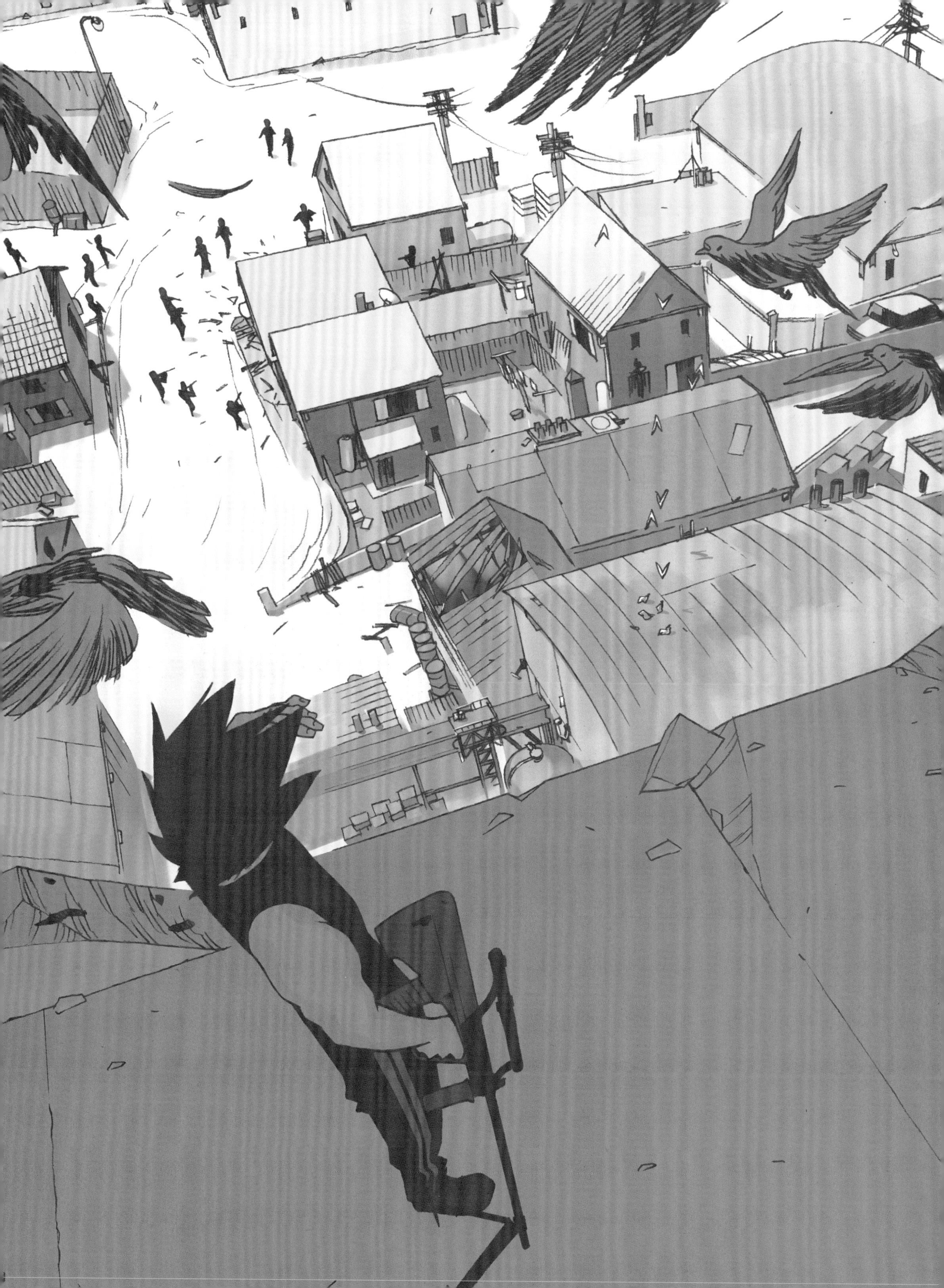

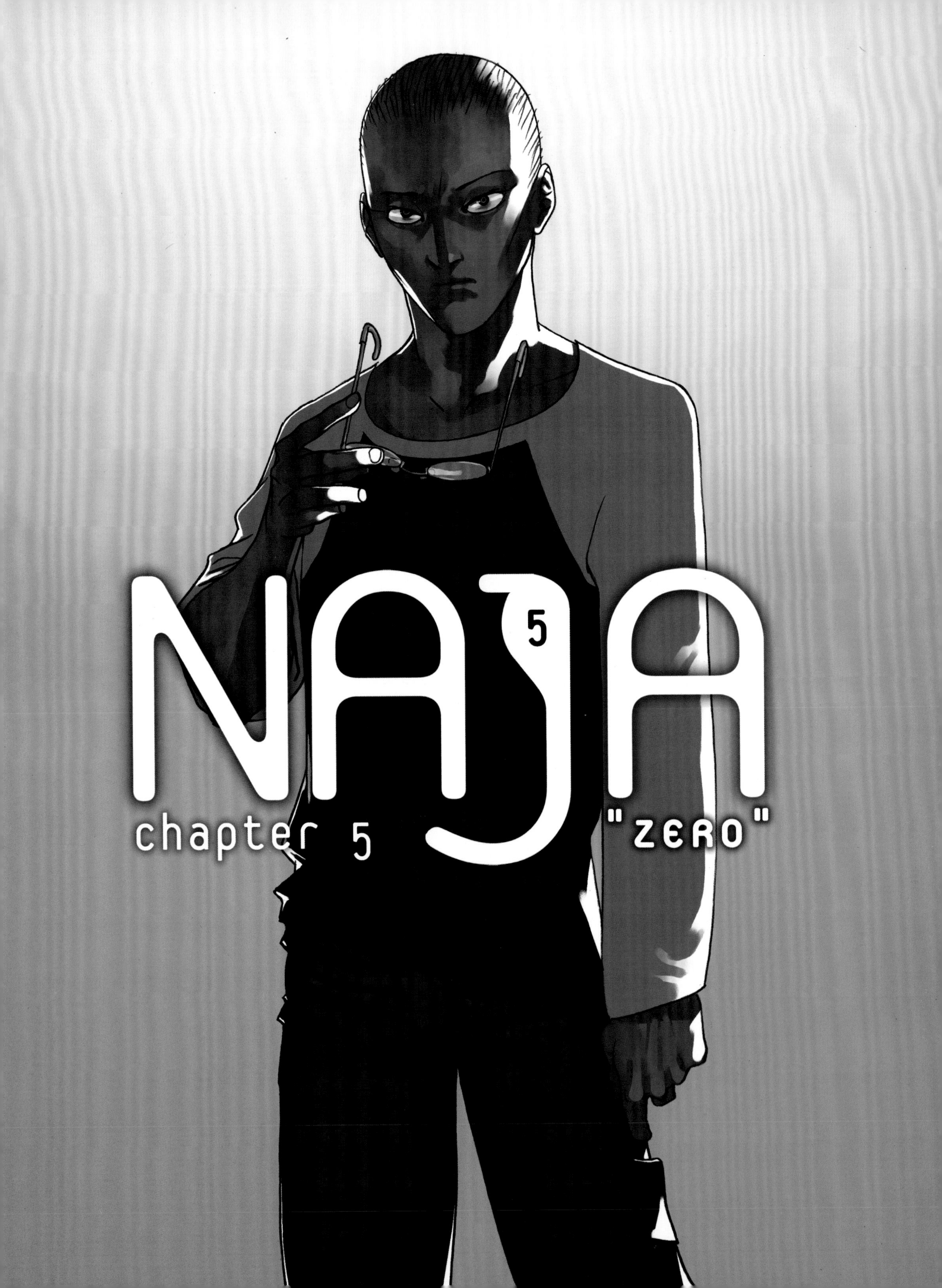
NAJA 5
chapter 5 "ZERO"

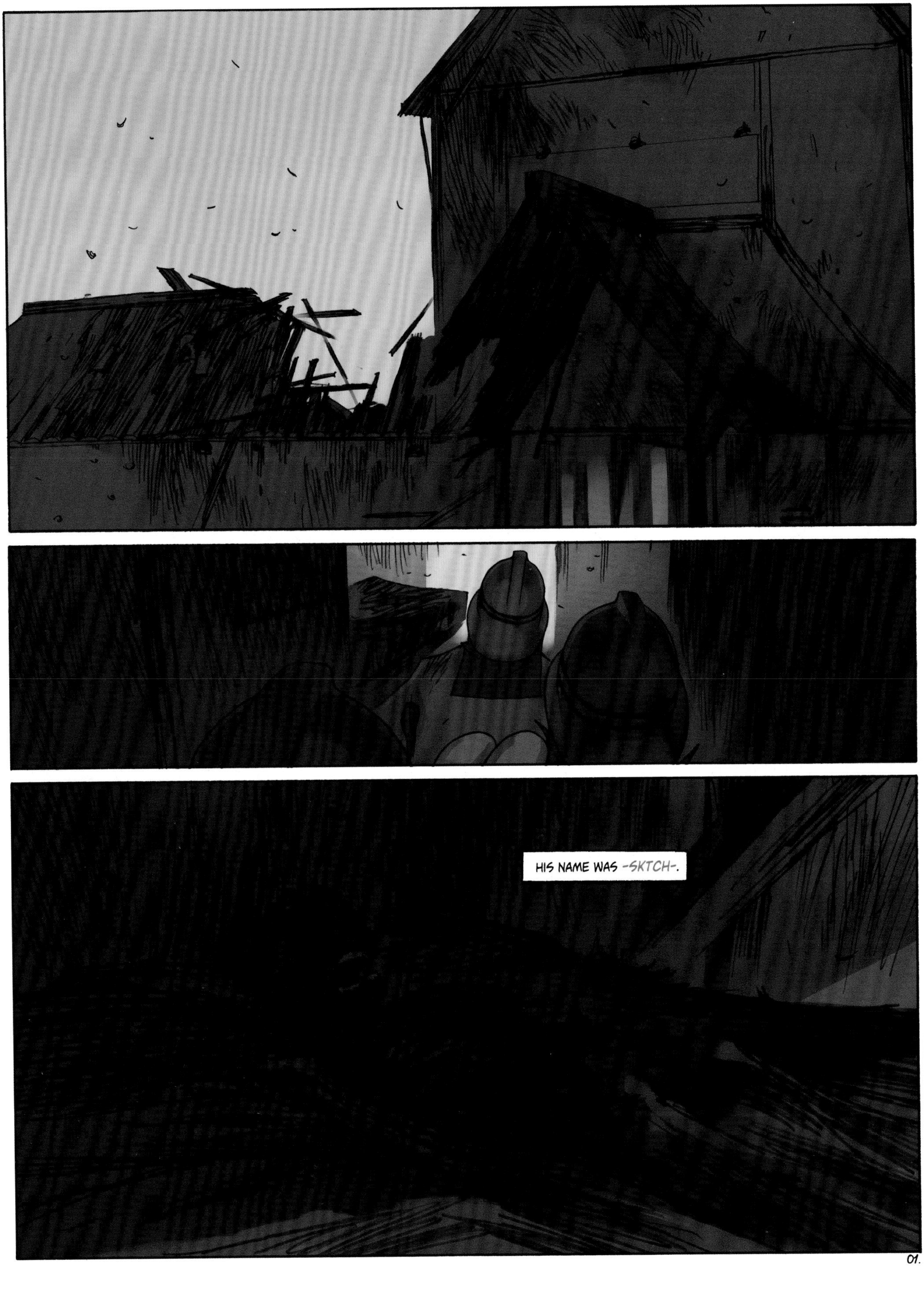
HIS NAME WAS -SKTCH-.

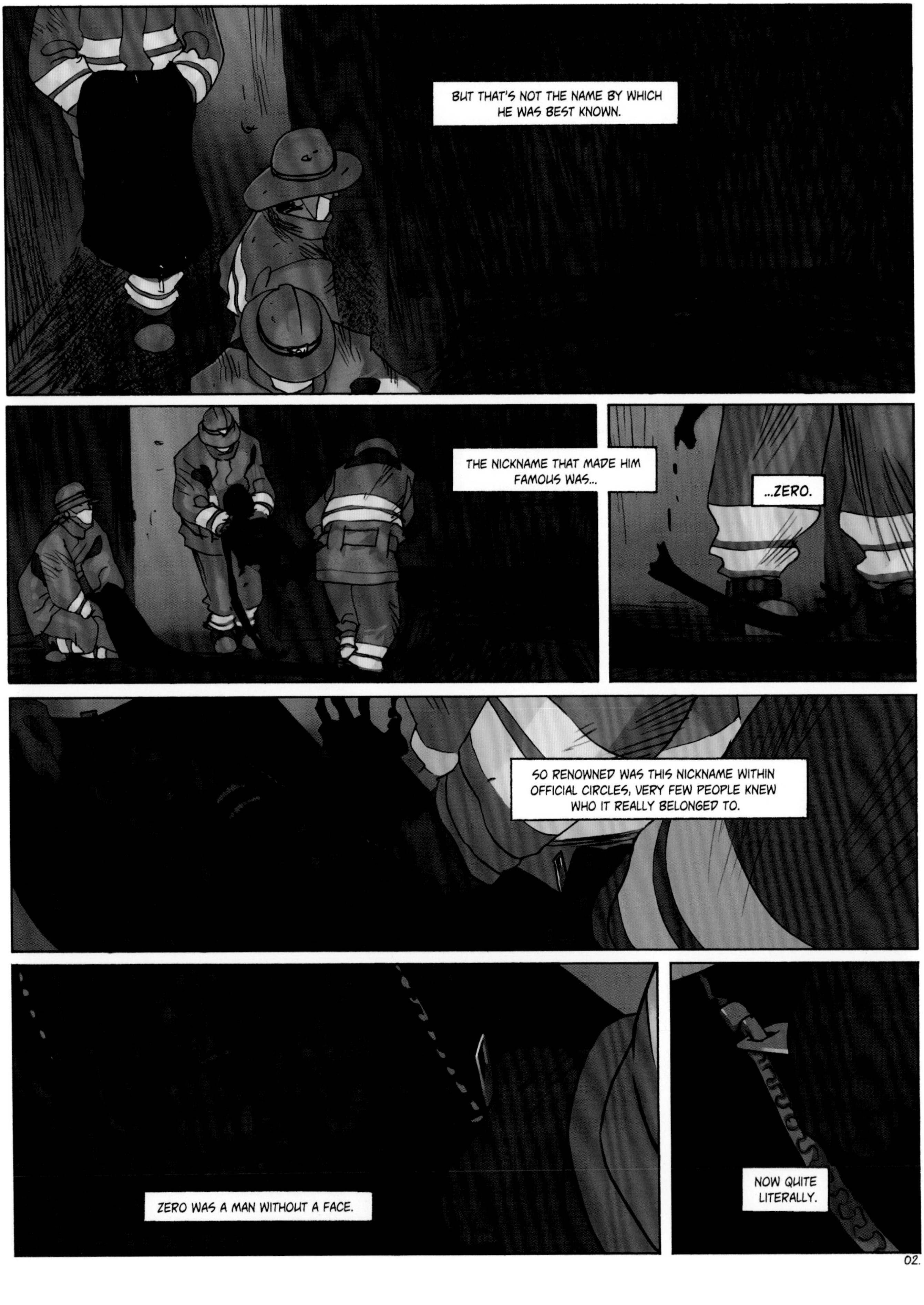

BUT THAT'S NOT THE NAME BY WHICH HE WAS BEST KNOWN.
THE NICKNAME THAT MADE HIM FAMOUS WAS...
...ZERO.
SO RENOWNED WAS THIS NICKNAME WITHIN OFFICIAL CIRCLES, VERY FEW PEOPLE KNEW WHO IT REALLY BELONGED TO.
ZERO WAS A MAN WITHOUT A FACE.
NOW QUITE LITERALLY.

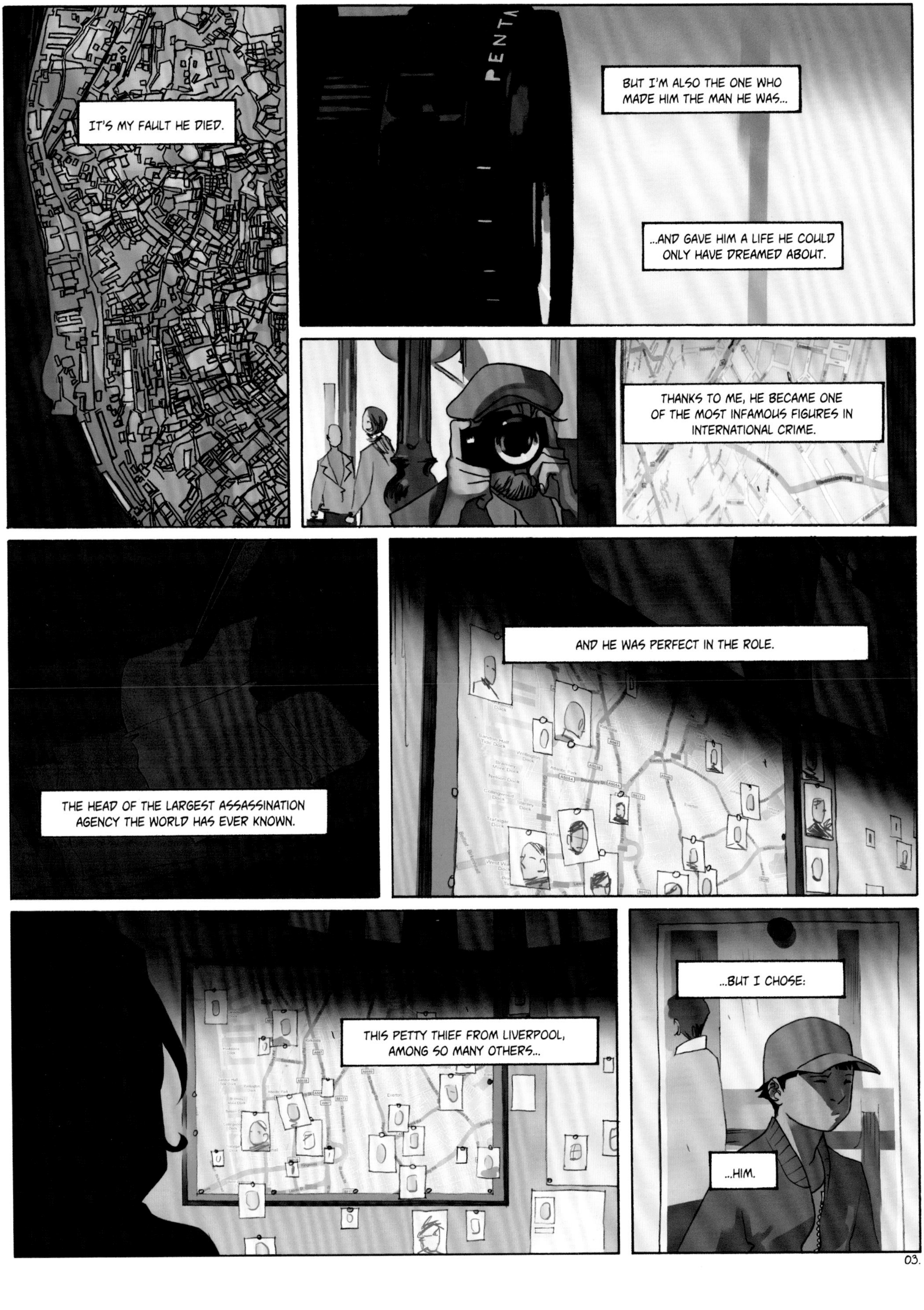

IT'S MY FAULT HE DIED.
BUT I'M ALSO THE ONE WHO MADE HIM THE MAN HE WAS...
...AND GAVE HIM A LIFE HE COULD ONLY HAVE DREAMED ABOUT.
THANKS TO ME, HE BECAME ONE OF THE MOST INFAMOUS FIGURES IN INTERNATIONAL CRIME.
THE HEAD OF THE LARGEST ASSASSINATION AGENCY THE WORLD HAS EVER KNOWN.
AND HE WAS PERFECT IN THE ROLE.
THIS PETTY THIEF FROM LIVERPOOL, AMONG SO MANY OTHERS...
...BUT I CHOSE:
...HIM.

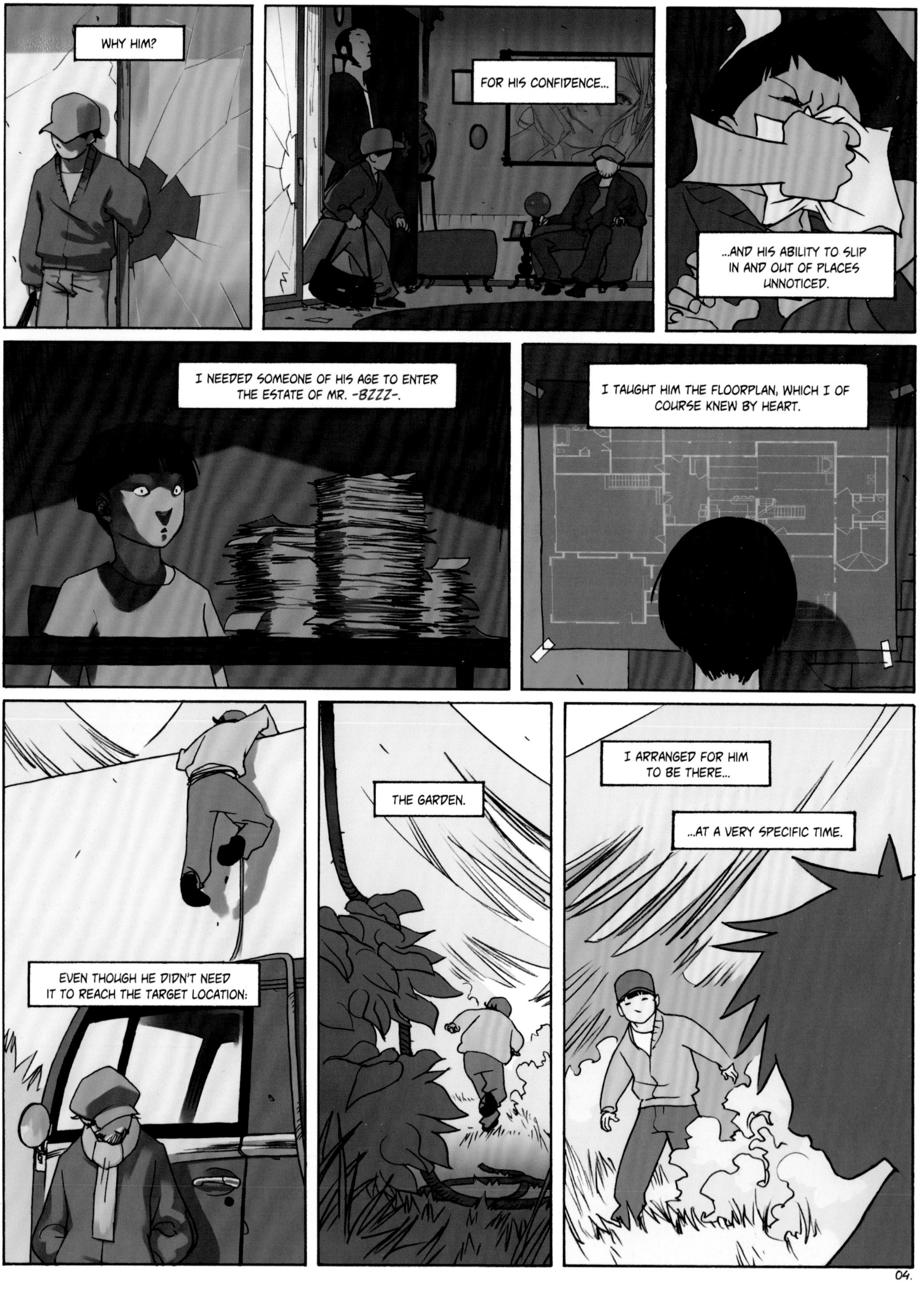
WHY HIM?
FOR HIS CONFIDENCE...
...AND HIS ABILITY TO SLIP IN AND OUT OF PLACES UNNOTICED.
I NEEDED SOMEONE OF HIS AGE TO ENTER THE ESTATE OF MR. -BZZZ-.
I TAUGHT HIM THE FLOORPLAN, WHICH I OF COURSE KNEW BY HEART.
EVEN THOUGH HE DIDN'T NEED IT TO REACH THE TARGET LOCATION:
THE GARDEN.
I ARRANGED FOR HIM TO BE THERE...
...AT A VERY SPECIFIC TIME.

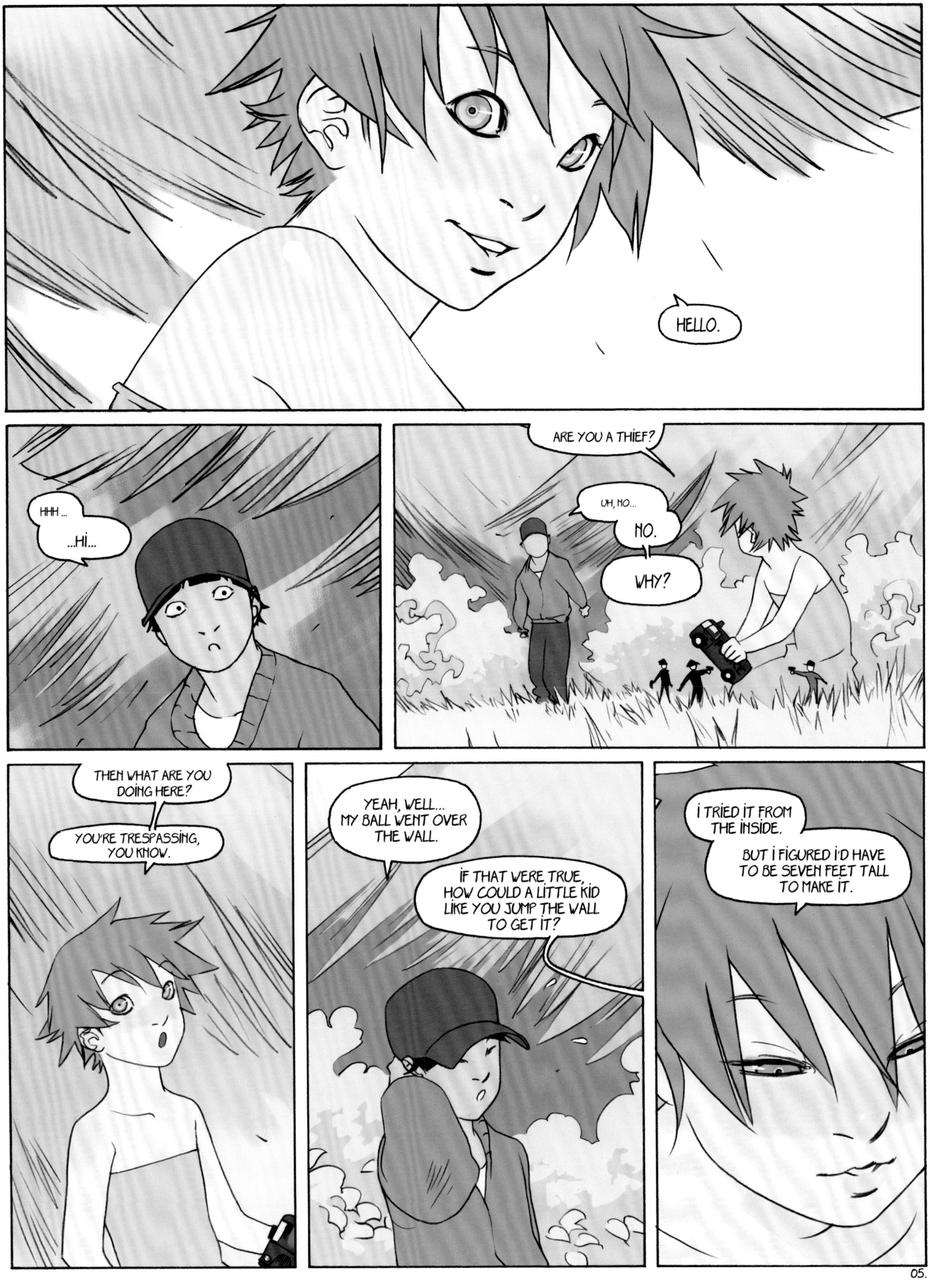
HELLO.
HHH ...
...HI...
ARE YOU A THIEF?
UH, NO...
NO.
WHY?
THEN WHAT ARE YOU DOING HERE?
YOU'RE TRESPASSING, YOU KNOW.
YEAH, WELL... MY BALL WENT OVER THE WALL.
IF THAT WERE TRUE, HOW COULD A LITTLE KID LIKE YOU JUMP THE WALL TO GET IT?
I TRIED IT FROM THE INSIDE.
BUT I FIGURED I'D HAVE TO BE SEVEN FEET TALL TO MAKE IT.

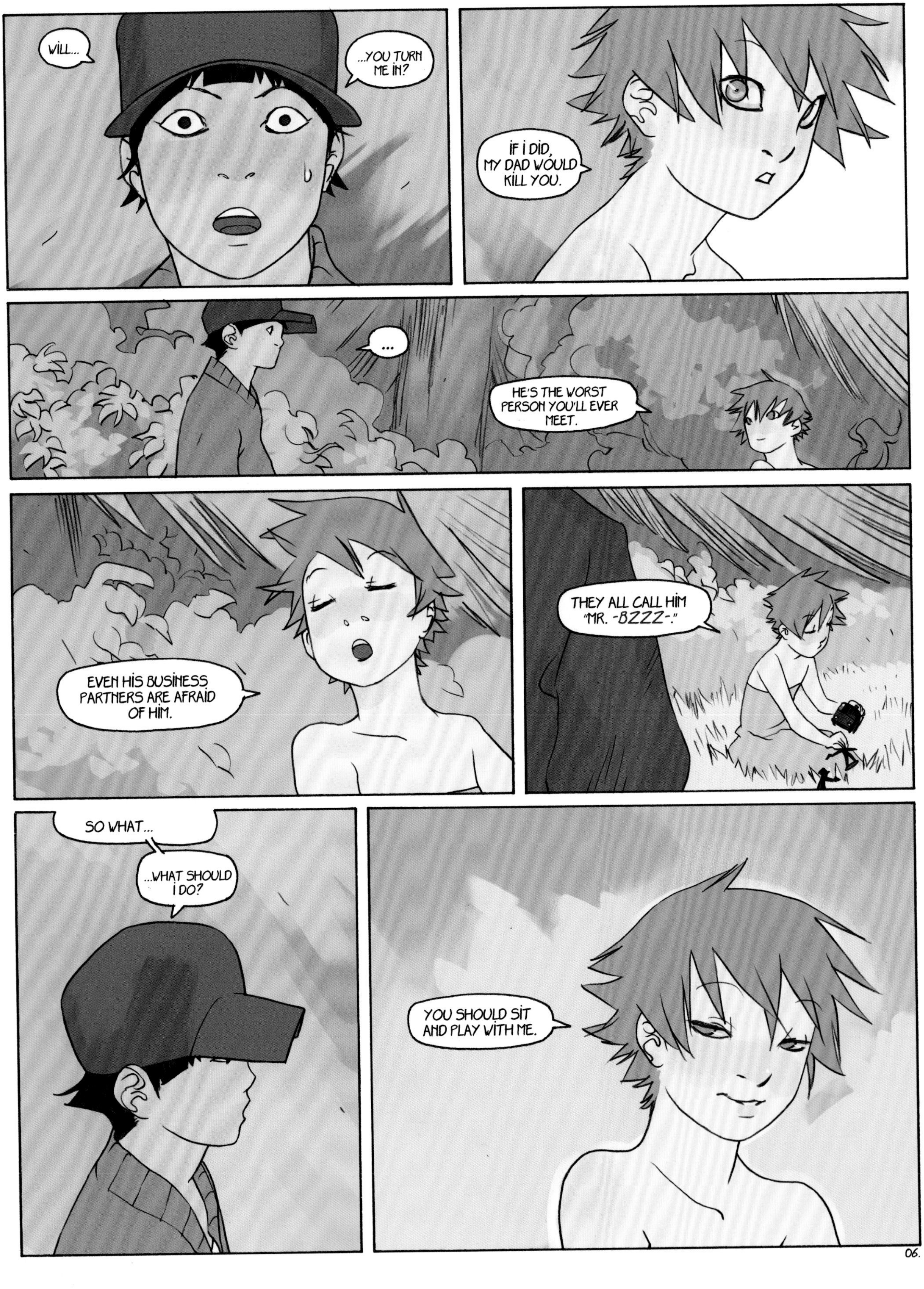
WILL...
...YOU TURN ME IN?
IF I DID, MY DAD WOULD KILL YOU.
...
HE'S THE WORST PERSON YOU'LL EVER MEET.
EVEN HIS BUSINESS PARTNERS ARE AFRAID OF HIM.
THEY ALL CALL HIM "MR. -BZZZ-."
SO WHAT...
...WHAT SHOULD I DO?
YOU SHOULD SIT AND PLAY WITH ME.

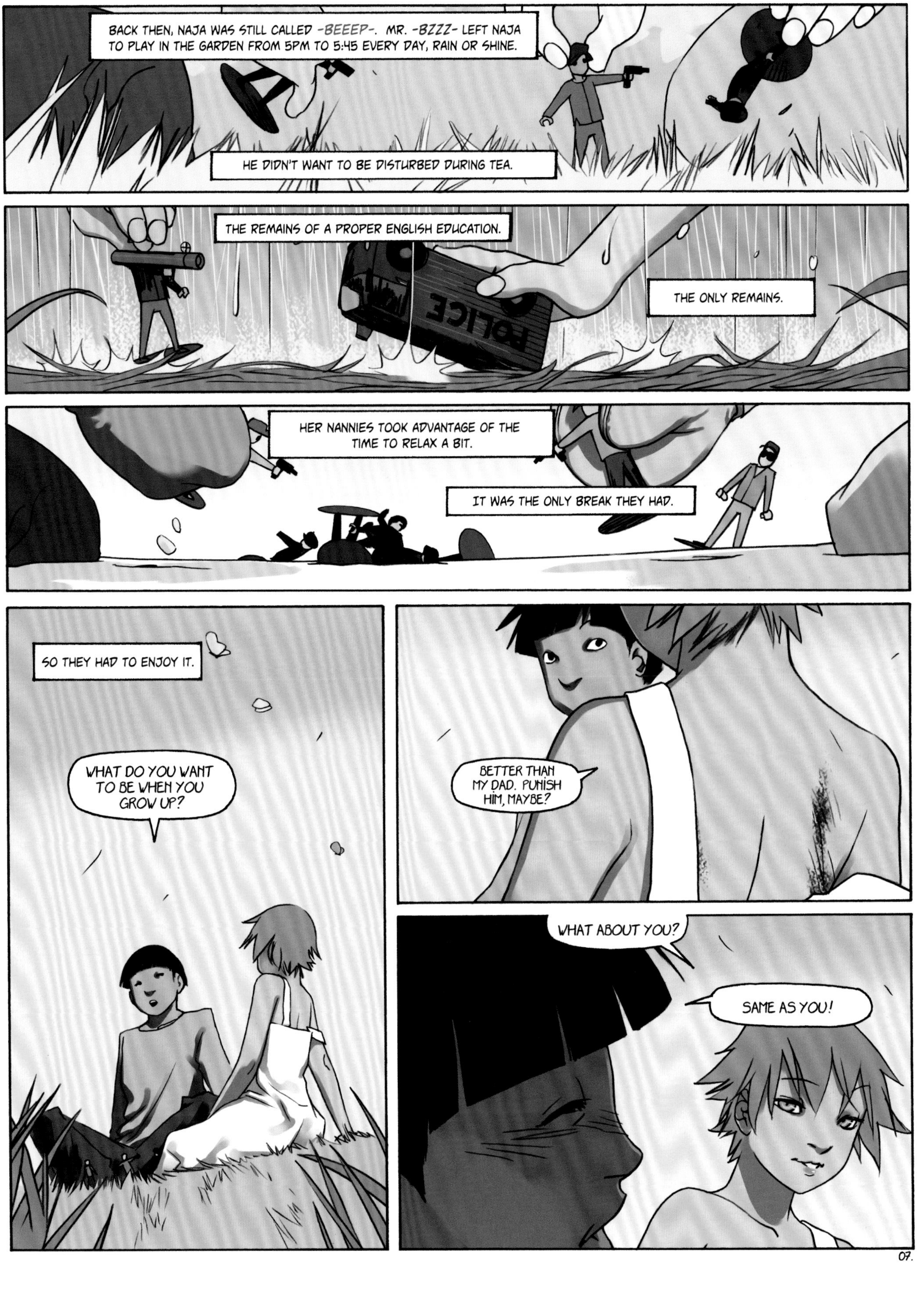
BACK THEN, NAJA WAS STILL CALLED -BEEEP-. MR. -BZZZ- LEFT NAJA TO PLAY IN THE GARDEN FROM 5PM TO 5:45 EVERY DAY, RAIN OR SHINE.
HE DIDN'T WANT TO BE DISTURBED DURING TEA.
THE REMAINS OF A PROPER ENGLISH EDUCATION.
POLICE
THE ONLY REMAINS.
HER NANNIES TOOK ADVANTAGE OF THE TIME TO RELAX A BIT.
IT WAS THE ONLY BREAK THEY HAD.
SO THEY HAD TO ENJOY IT.
WHAT DO YOU WANT TO BE WHEN YOU GROW UP?
BETTER THAN MY DAD. PUNISH HIM, MAYBE?
WHAT ABOUT YOU?
SAME AS YOU!

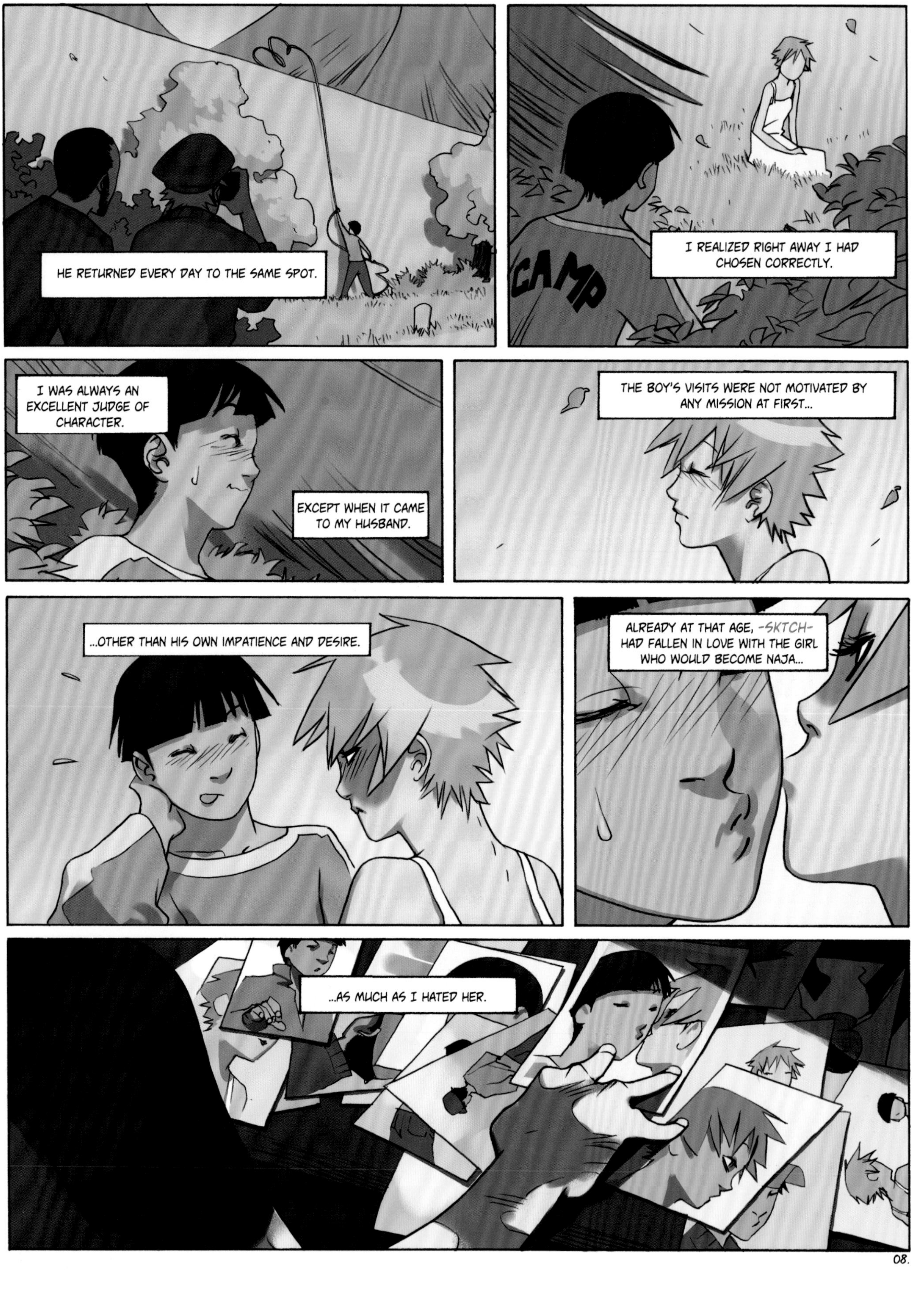

HE RETURNED EVERY DAY TO THE SAME SPOT.
CAMP
I REALIZED RIGHT AWAY I HAD CHOSEN CORRECTLY.
I WAS ALWAYS AN EXCELLENT JUDGE OF CHARACTER.
EXCEPT WHEN IT CAME TO MY HUSBAND.
THE BOY'S VISITS WERE NOT MOTIVATED BY ANY MISSION AT FIRST...
...OTHER THAN HIS OWN IMPATIENCE AND DESIRE.
ALREADY AT THAT AGE, -SKTCH- HAD FALLEN IN LOVE WITH THE GIRL WHO WOULD BECOME NAJA...
...AS MUCH AS I HATED HER.

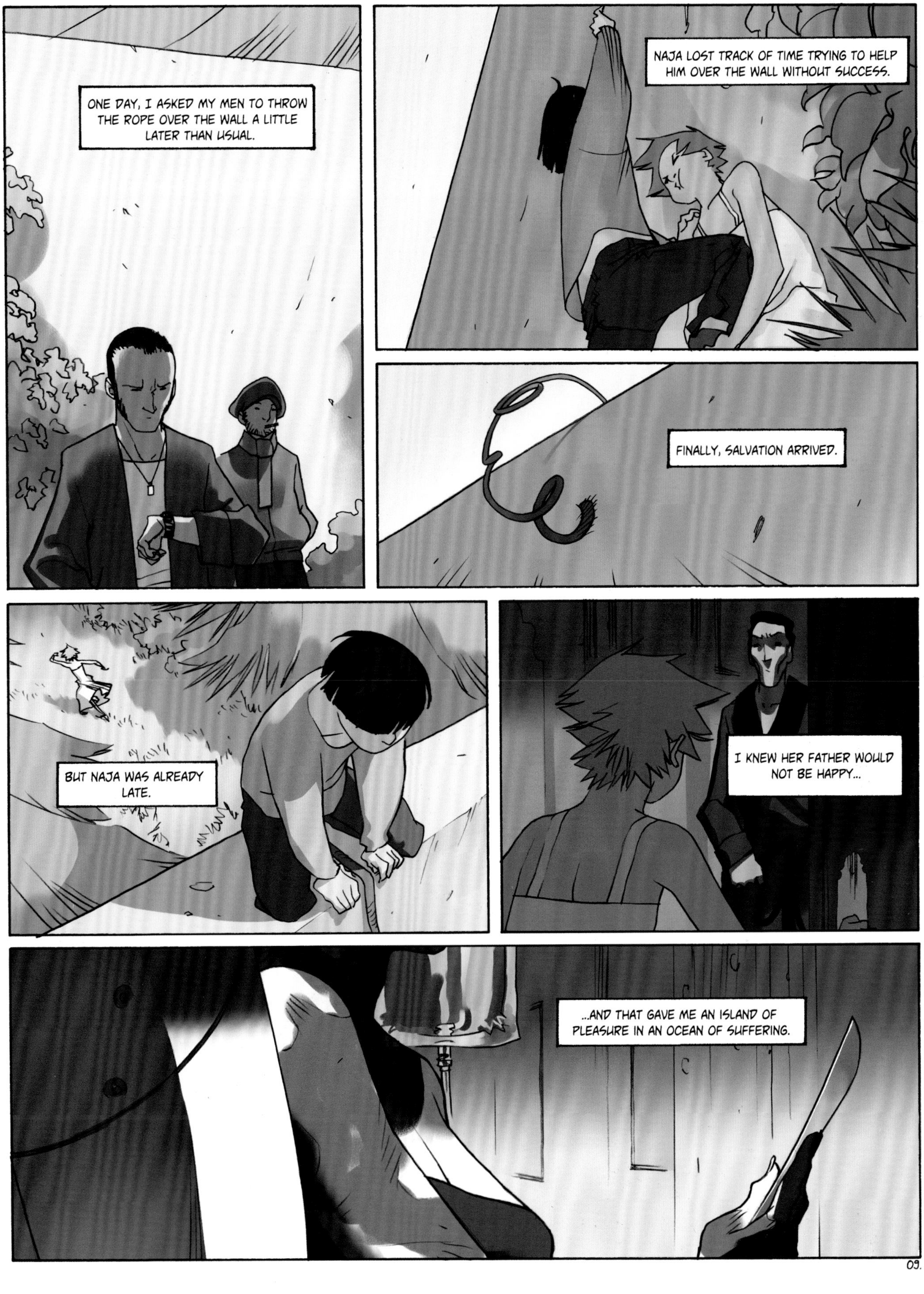
ONE DAY, I ASKED MY MEN TO THROW THE ROPE OVER THE WALL A LITTLE LATER THAN USUAL.
NAJA LOST TRACK OF TIME TRYING TO HELP HIM OVER THE WALL WITHOUT SUCCESS.
FINALLY, SALVATION ARRIVED.
BUT NAJA WAS ALREADY LATE.
I KNEW HER FATHER WOULD NOT BE HAPPY...
...AND THAT GAVE ME AN ISLAND OF PLEASURE IN AN OCEAN OF SUFFERING.

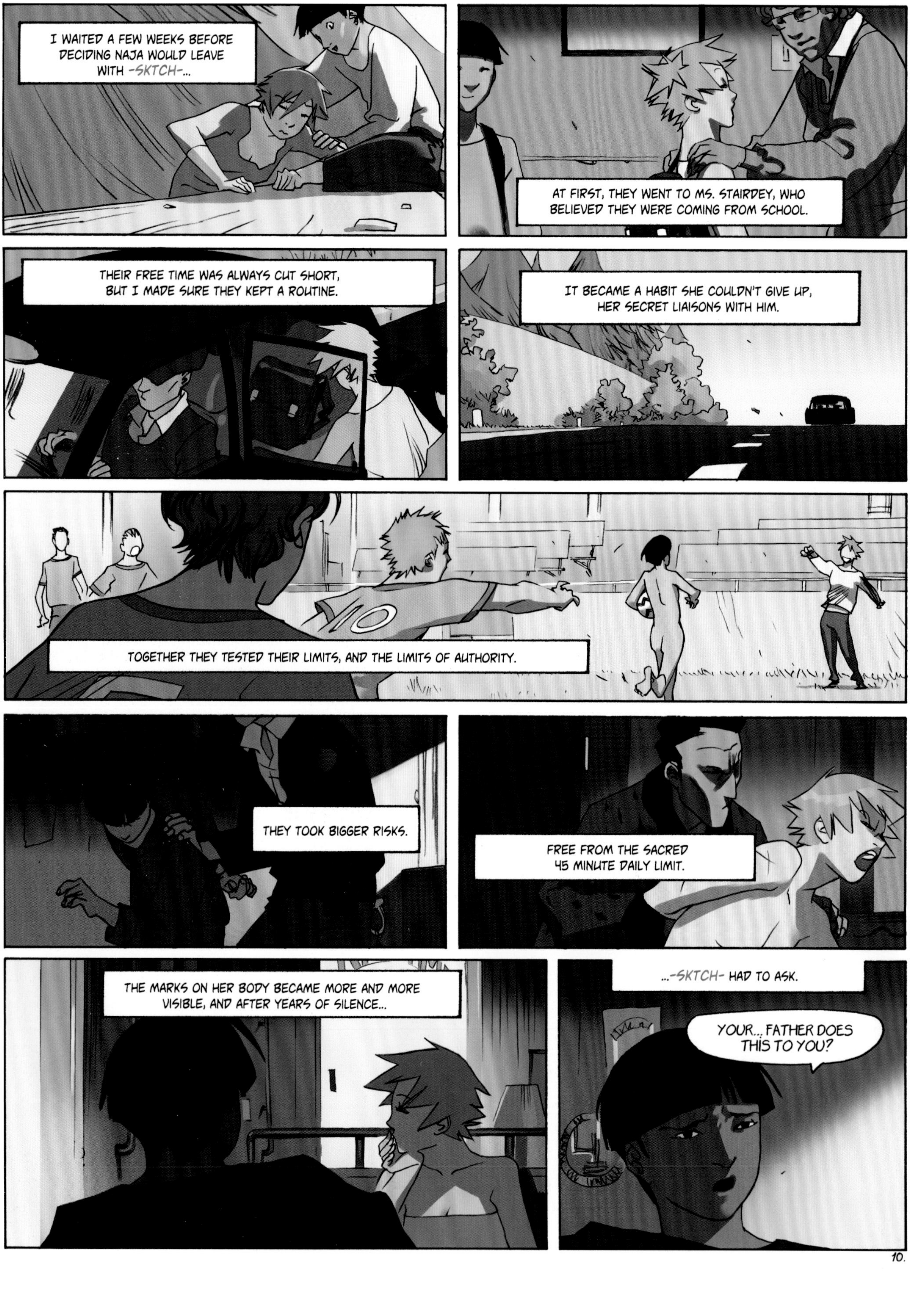
I WAITED A FEW WEEKS BEFORE DECIDING NAJA WOULD LEAVE WITH -SKTCH-...
AT FIRST, THEY WENT TO MS. STAIRDEY, WHO BELIEVED THEY WERE COMING FROM SCHOOL.
THEIR FREE TIME WAS ALWAYS CUT SHORT, BUT I MADE SURE THEY KEPT A ROUTINE.
IT BECAME A HABIT SHE COULDN'T GIVE UP, HER SECRET LIAISONS WITH HIM.
TOGETHER THEY TESTED THEIR LIMITS, AND THE LIMITS OF AUTHORITY.
THEY TOOK BIGGER RISKS.
FREE FROM THE SACRED 45 MINUTE DAILY LIMIT.
THE MARKS ON HER BODY BECAME MORE AND MORE VISIBLE, AND AFTER YEARS OF SILENCE...
...-SKTCH- HAD TO ASK.
YOUR... FATHER DOES THIS TO YOU?

YEAH, BUT IT DOESN'T HURT THAT MUCH.

BUT... THOSE BRUISES ARE FRESH!

AND SOME OF THOSE SCARS LOOK YEARS OLD!

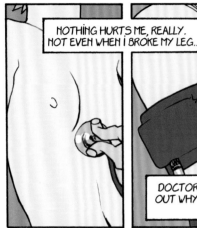

NOTHING HURTS ME, REALLY. NOT EVEN WHEN I BROKE MY LEG...

DOCTORS COULD NEVER FIGURE OUT WHY, BUT I JUST DON'T FEEL PAIN.

THE ONLY PAIN I EVER FEEL IS WHEN MY DAD BEATS ME.

...BUT ONLY BECAUSE I DON'T UNDERSTAND WHY HE HATES ME SO MUCH!

WHAT HE DIDN'T SEE, AND WHAT NAJA STILL DIDN'T KNOW, WAS THAT NO FATHER COULD LOVE HIS DAUGHTER MORE THAN MR. -BZZZ-.

THAT PASSION WAS THE RESULT OF A MADNESS SO POWERFUL AND MORBID THAT IT HAD DESTROYED A LOT OF PEOPLE.

DATING BACK TO WHEN HE WAS ONLY SECOND IN COMMAND.

VIOLENCE WAS THE ONLY MEANS HE KNEW OF EXPRESSING AFFECTION.

AND -BEEEP- WAS DROWNING IN IT.

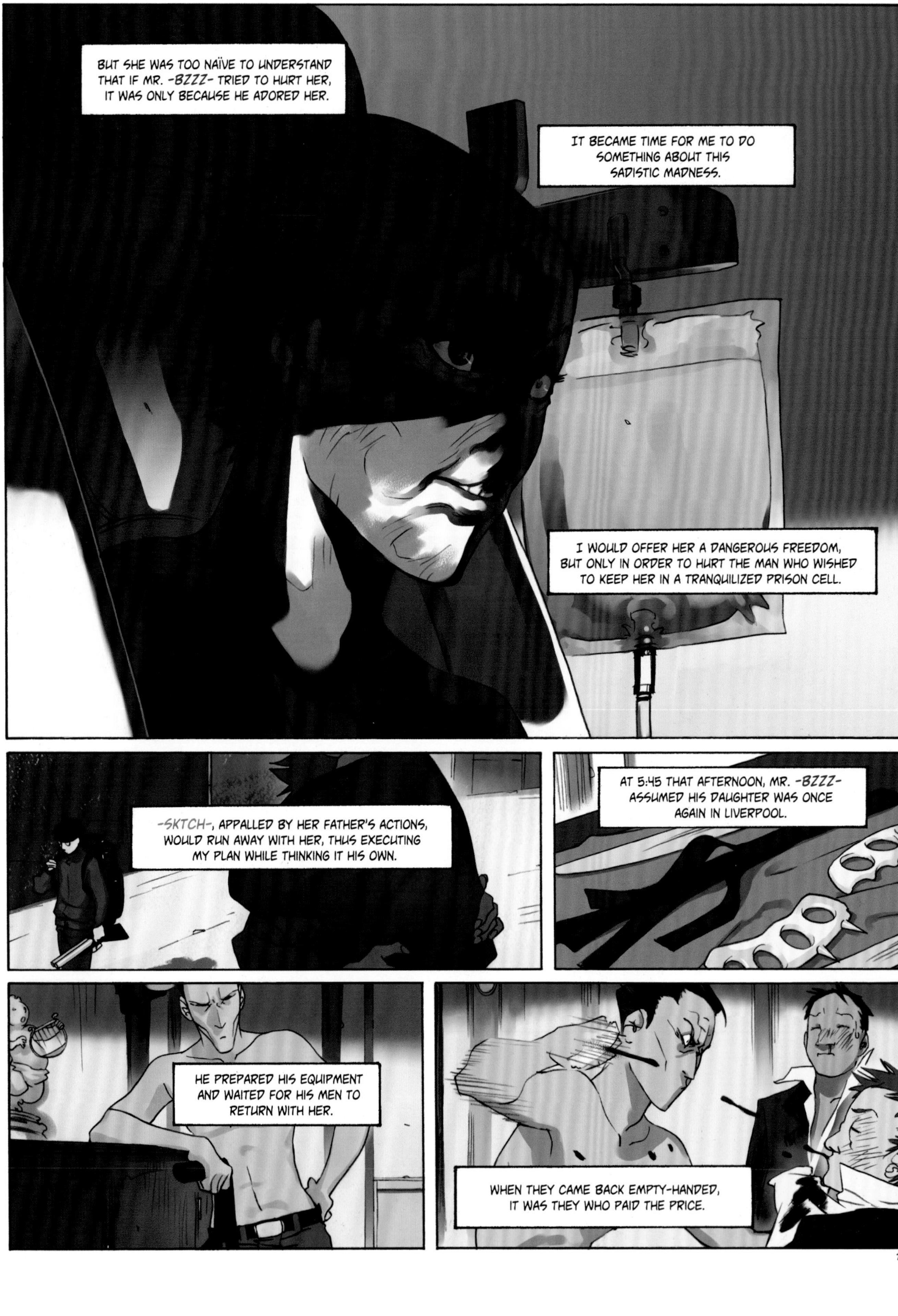
BUT SHE WAS TOO NAÏVE TO UNDERSTAND THAT IF MR. -BZZZ- TRIED TO HURT HER, IT WAS ONLY BECAUSE HE ADORED HER.
IT BECAME TIME FOR ME TO DO SOMETHING ABOUT THIS SADISTIC MADNESS.
I WOULD OFFER HER A DANGEROUS FREEDOM, BUT ONLY IN ORDER TO HURT THE MAN WHO WISHED TO KEEP HER IN A TRANQUILIZED PRISON CELL.
-SKTCH-, APPALLED BY HER FATHER'S ACTIONS, WOULD RUN AWAY WITH HER, THUS EXECUTING MY PLAN WHILE THINKING IT HIS OWN.
AT 5:45 THAT AFTERNOON, MR. -BZZZ- ASSUMED HIS DAUGHTER WAS ONCE AGAIN IN LIVERPOOL.
HE PREPARED HIS EQUIPMENT AND WAITED FOR HIS MEN TO RETURN WITH HER.
WHEN THEY CAME BACK EMPTY-HANDED, IT WAS THEY WHO PAID THE PRICE.

IN TIME, HE SAW HIS DAUGHTER ON THE NEWS.

IF THAT WEREN'T ENOUGH, HE BEGAN TO RECEIVE PHOTOS OF HIS DAUGHTER'S REGULAR ESCAPADES.

IT THRILLED ME TO IMAGINE THE TERROR HE MUST HAVE FELT FOR HER SAFETY!

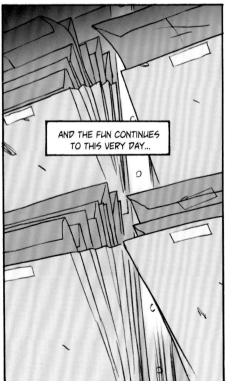

AND THE FUN CONTINUES TO THIS VERY DAY...

...WITH THE ENVELOPE HE RECEIVED JUST BEFORE LEAVING FOR BARCELONA.

YOU HEARD WHAT HE SAID:

WHEN I THOUGHT YOU WERE DEAD, I MISSED YOU SO MUCH.

AND THIS:

I DON'T EVEN KNOW WHO THOSE TWO ARE!

NOR THAT YOU WERE STILL ALIVE!

AND YOU BELIEVED HIM?

HAVE YOU LEARNED NOTHING?

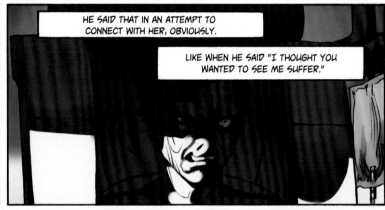

HE SAID THAT IN AN ATTEMPT TO CONNECT WITH HER, OBVIOUSLY.

LIKE WHEN HE SAID "I THOUGHT YOU WANTED TO SEE ME SUFFER."

NO, IN THE GAME OF S&M, MR. –BZZZ– WAS ALWAYS THE "S".

I LEARNED THAT THE HARD WAY.

HE WOULD DO ANYTHING TO SAVE HIS OWN SKIN.

BUT NOTHING CAN SAVE HIS SOUL.

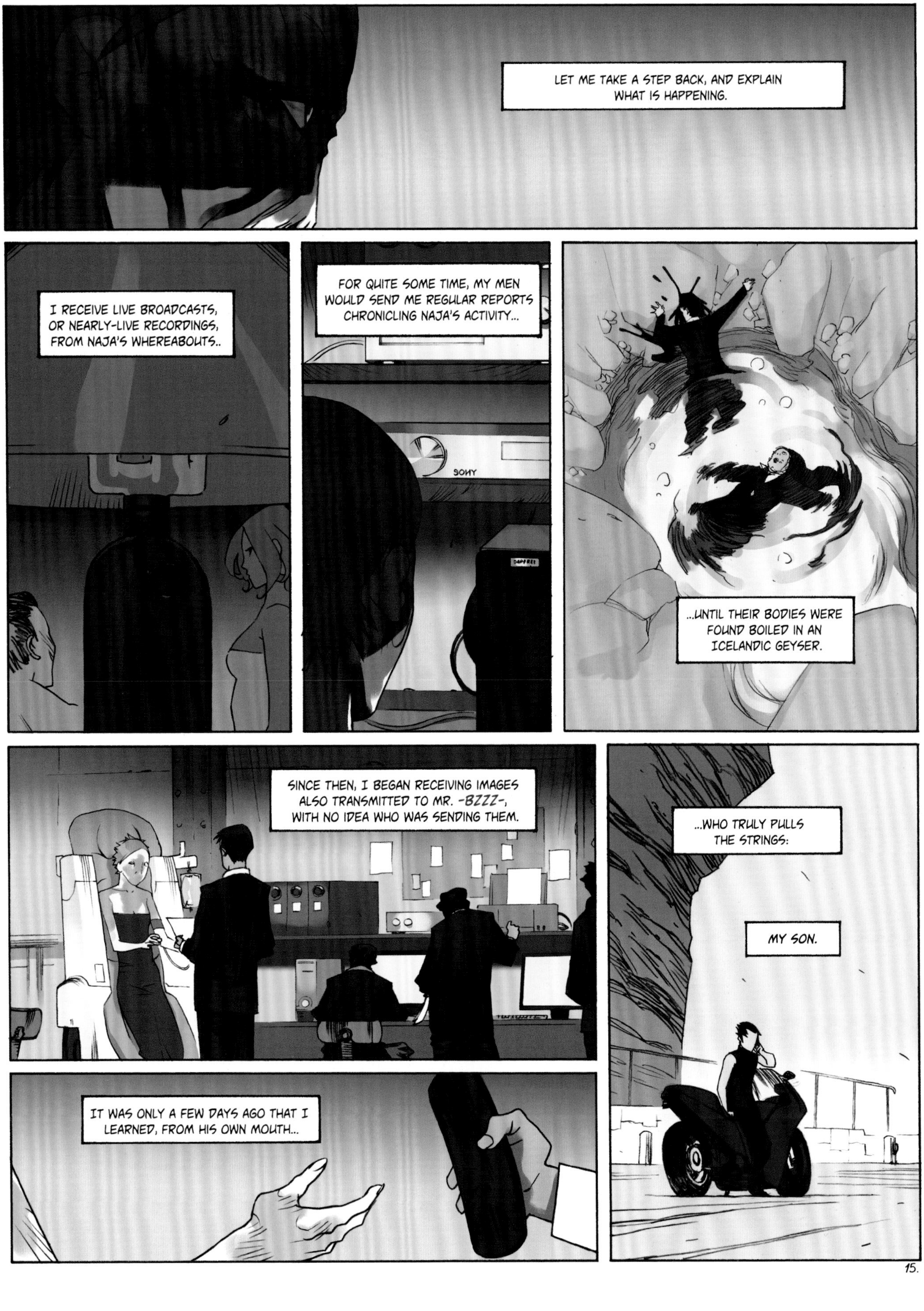
LET ME TAKE A STEP BACK, AND EXPLAIN WHAT IS HAPPENING.
I RECEIVE LIVE BROADCASTS, OR NEARLY-LIVE RECORDINGS, FROM NAJA'S WHEREABOUTS..
FOR QUITE SOME TIME, MY MEN WOULD SEND ME REGULAR REPORTS CHRONICLING NAJA'S ACTIVITY...
SONY
...UNTIL THEIR BODIES WERE FOUND BOILED IN AN ICELANDIC GEYSER.
SINCE THEN, I BEGAN RECEIVING IMAGES ALSO TRANSMITTED TO MR. -BZZZ-, WITH NO IDEA WHO WAS SENDING THEM.
IT WAS ONLY A FEW DAYS AGO THAT I LEARNED, FROM HIS OWN MOUTH...
...WHO TRULY PULLS THE STRINGS:
MY SON.

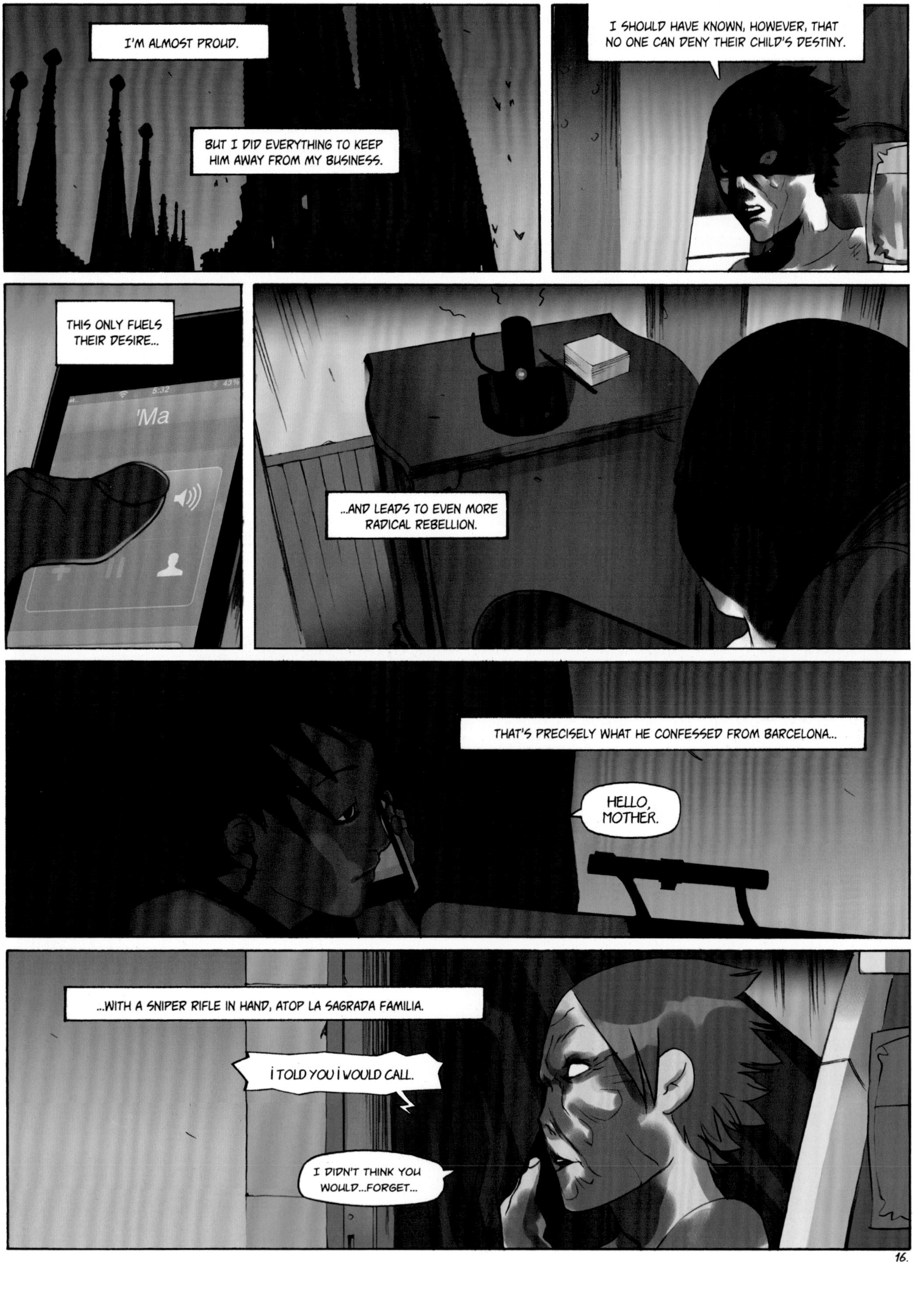
I'M ALMOST PROUD.
BUT I DID EVERYTHING TO KEEP HIM AWAY FROM MY BUSINESS.
I SHOULD HAVE KNOWN, HOWEVER, THAT NO ONE CAN DENY THEIR CHILD'S DESTINY.
THIS ONLY FUELS THEIR DESIRE...
5:32
43%
'Ma
...AND LEADS TO EVEN MORE RADICAL REBELLION.
THAT'S PRECISELY WHAT HE CONFESSED FROM BARCELONA...
HELLO, MOTHER.
...WITH A SNIPER RIFLE IN HAND, ATOP LA SAGRADA FAMILIA.
I TOLD YOU I WOULD CALL.
I DIDN'T THINK YOU WOULD...FORGET...

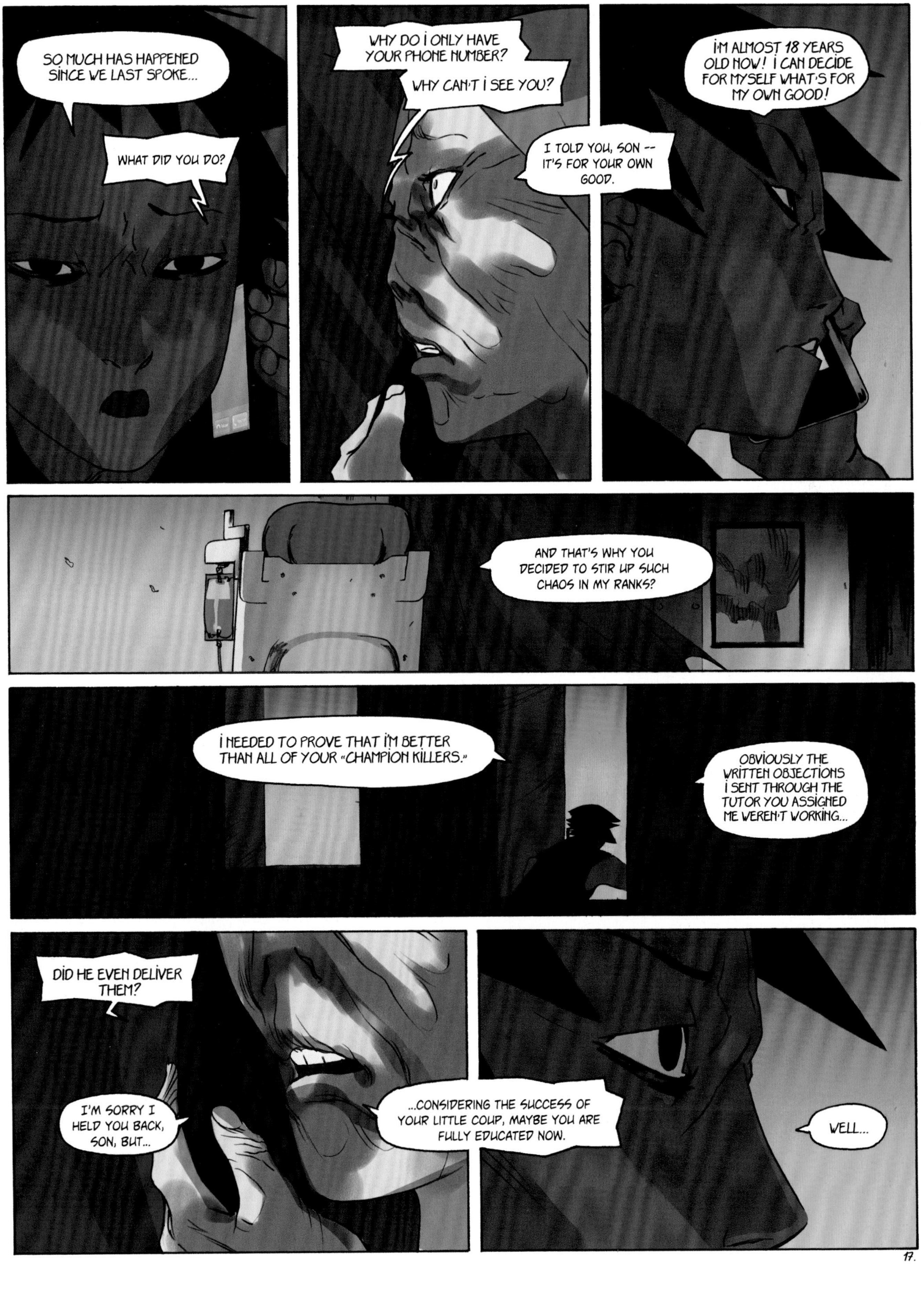
SO MUCH HAS HAPPENED SINCE WE LAST SPOKE...
WHAT DID YOU DO?
WHY DO I ONLY HAVE YOUR PHONE NUMBER?
WHY CAN'T I SEE YOU?
I TOLD YOU, SON -- IT'S FOR YOUR OWN GOOD.
I'M ALMOST 18 YEARS OLD NOW! I CAN DECIDE FOR MYSELF WHAT'S FOR MY OWN GOOD!
AND THAT'S WHY YOU DECIDED TO STIR UP SUCH CHAOS IN MY RANKS?
I NEEDED TO PROVE THAT I'M BETTER THAN ALL OF YOUR "CHAMPION KILLERS."
OBVIOUSLY THE WRITTEN OBJECTIONS I SENT THROUGH THE TUTOR YOU ASSIGNED ME WEREN'T WORKING...
DID HE EVEN DELIVER THEM?
I'M SORRY I HELD YOU BACK, SON, BUT...
...CONSIDERING THE SUCCESS OF YOUR LITTLE COUP, MAYBE YOU ARE FULLY EDUCATED NOW.
WELL...

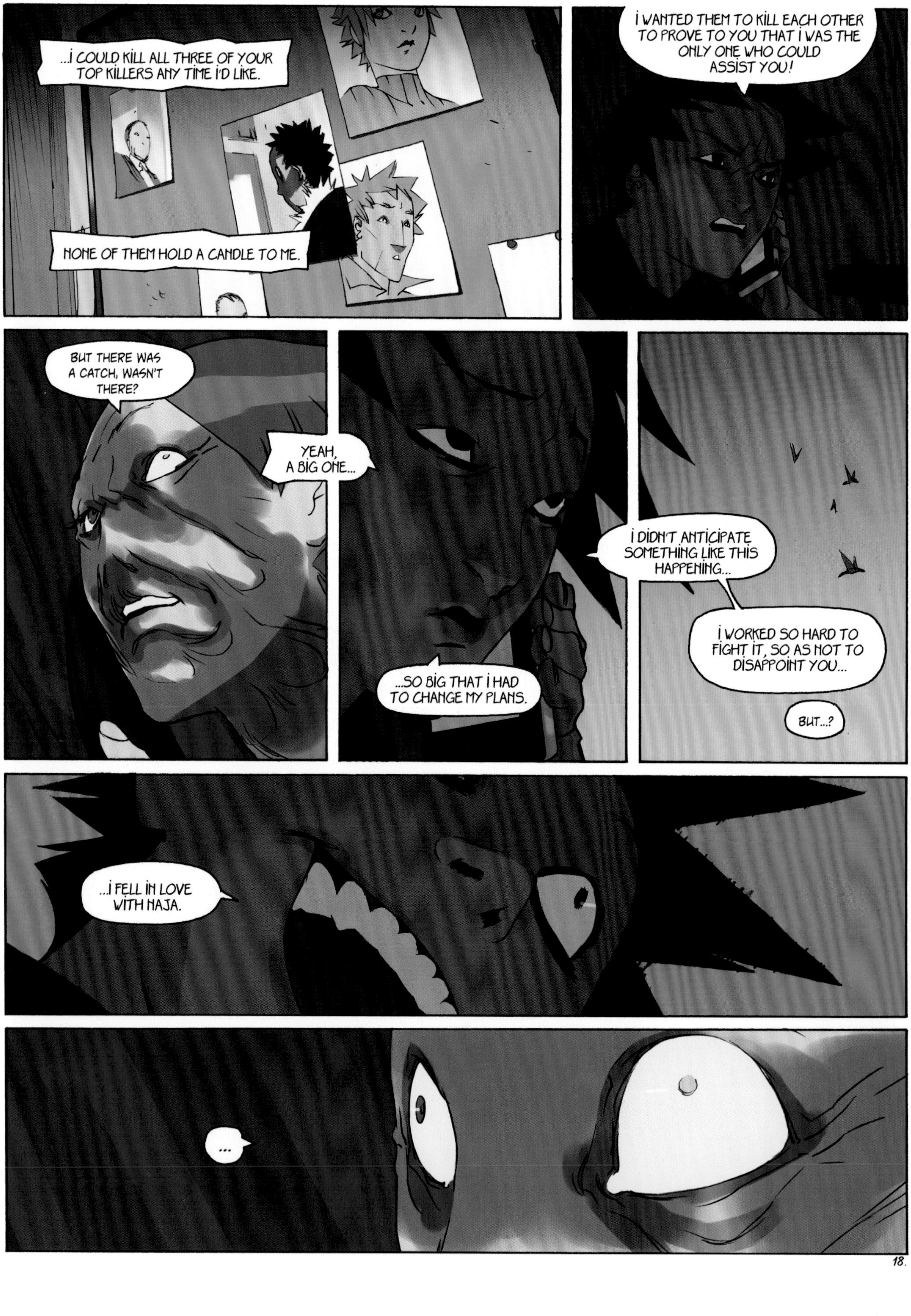

...I COULD KILL ALL THREE OF YOUR TOP KILLERS ANY TIME I'D LIKE.
NONE OF THEM HOLD A CANDLE TO ME.
I WANTED THEM TO KILL EACH OTHER TO PROVE TO YOU THAT I WAS THE ONLY ONE WHO COULD ASSIST YOU!
BUT THERE WAS A CATCH, WASN'T THERE?
YEAH, A BIG ONE...
...SO BIG THAT I HAD TO CHANGE MY PLANS.
I DIDN'T ANTICIPATE SOMETHING LIKE THIS HAPPENING...
I WORKED SO HARD TO FIGHT IT, SO AS NOT TO DISAPPOINT YOU...
BUT...?
...I FELL IN LOVE WITH NAJA.
...

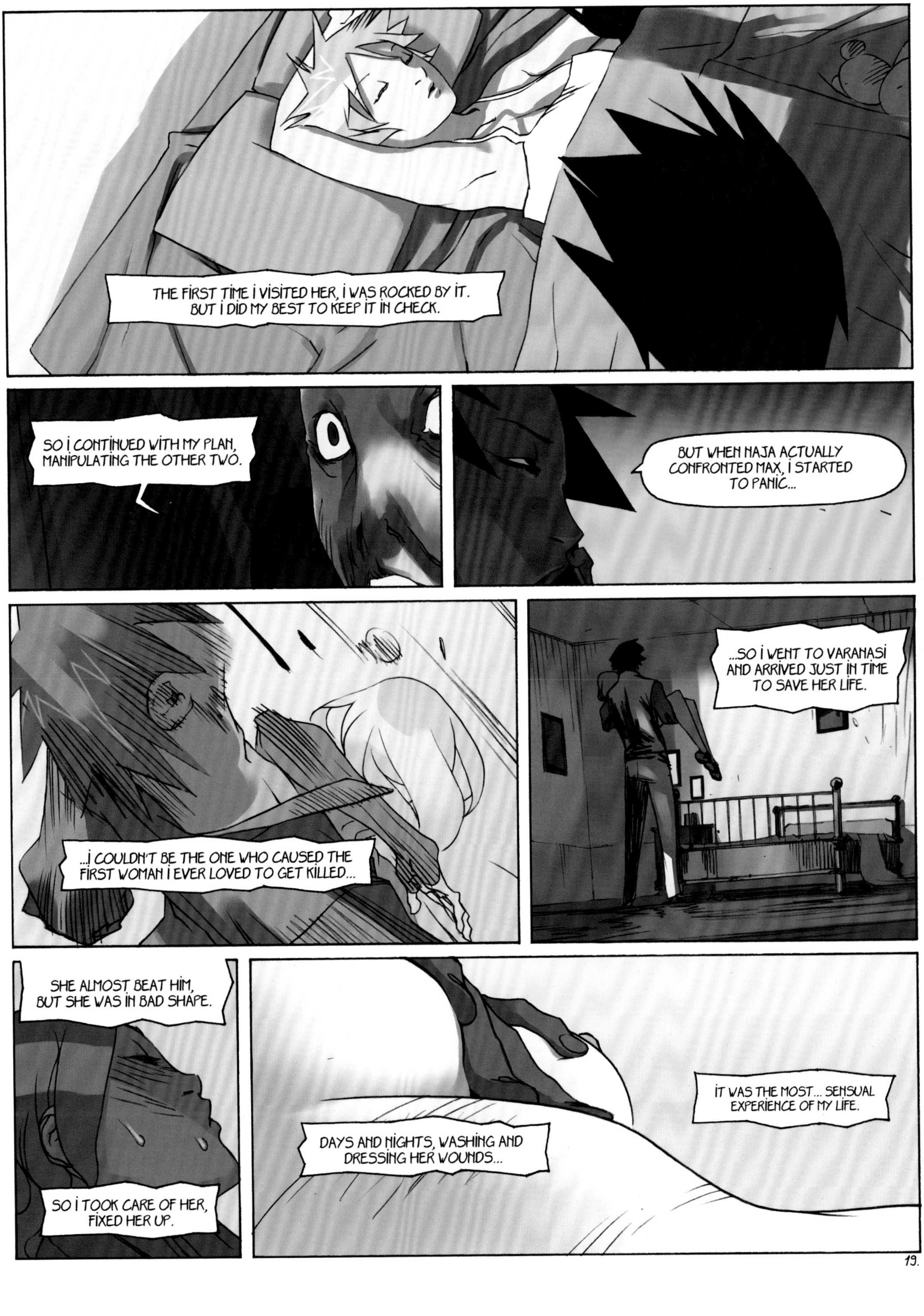
THE FIRST TIME I VISITED HER, I WAS ROCKED BY IT. BUT I DID MY BEST TO KEEP IT IN CHECK.
SO I CONTINUED WITH MY PLAN, MANIPULATING THE OTHER TWO.
BUT WHEN NAJA ACTUALLY CONFRONTED MAX, I STARTED TO PANIC...
...I COULDN'T BE THE ONE WHO CAUSED THE FIRST WOMAN I EVER LOVED TO GET KILLED...
...SO I WENT TO VARANASI AND ARRIVED JUST IN TIME TO SAVE HER LIFE.
SHE ALMOST BEAT HIM, BUT SHE WAS IN BAD SHAPE.
SO I TOOK CARE OF HER, FIXED HER UP.
DAYS AND NIGHTS, WASHING AND DRESSING HER WOUNDS...
IT WAS THE MOST... SENSUAL EXPERIENCE OF MY LIFE.

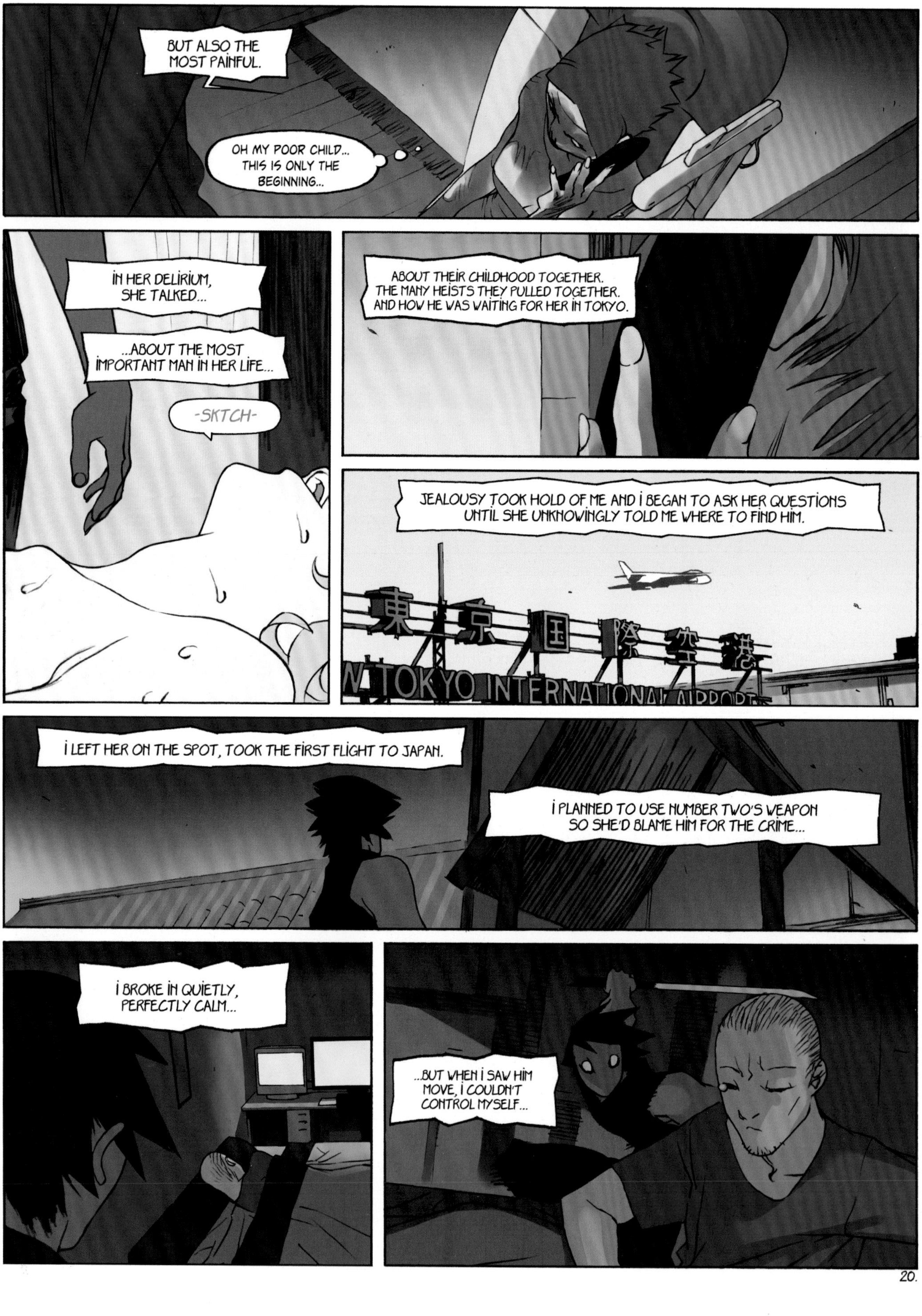

BUT ALSO THE MOST PAINFUL.
OH MY POOR CHILD... THIS IS ONLY THE BEGINNING...
IN HER DELIRIUM, SHE TALKED...
...ABOUT THE MOST IMPORTANT MAN IN HER LIFE...
-SKTCH-
ABOUT THEIR CHILDHOOD TOGETHER. THE MANY HEISTS THEY PULLED TOGETHER. AND HOW HE WAS WAITING FOR HER IN TOKYO.
JEALOUSY TOOK HOLD OF ME AND I BEGAN TO ASK HER QUESTIONS UNTIL SHE UNKNOWINGLY TOLD ME WHERE TO FIND HIM.
東京国際空港
TOKYO INTERNATIONAL
I LEFT HER ON THE SPOT, TOOK THE FIRST FLIGHT TO JAPAN.
I PLANNED TO USE NUMBER TWO'S WEAPON SO SHE'D BLAME HIM FOR THE CRIME...
I BROKE IN QUIETLY, PERFECTLY CALM...
...BUT WHEN I SAW HIM MOVE, I COULDN'T CONTROL MYSELF...

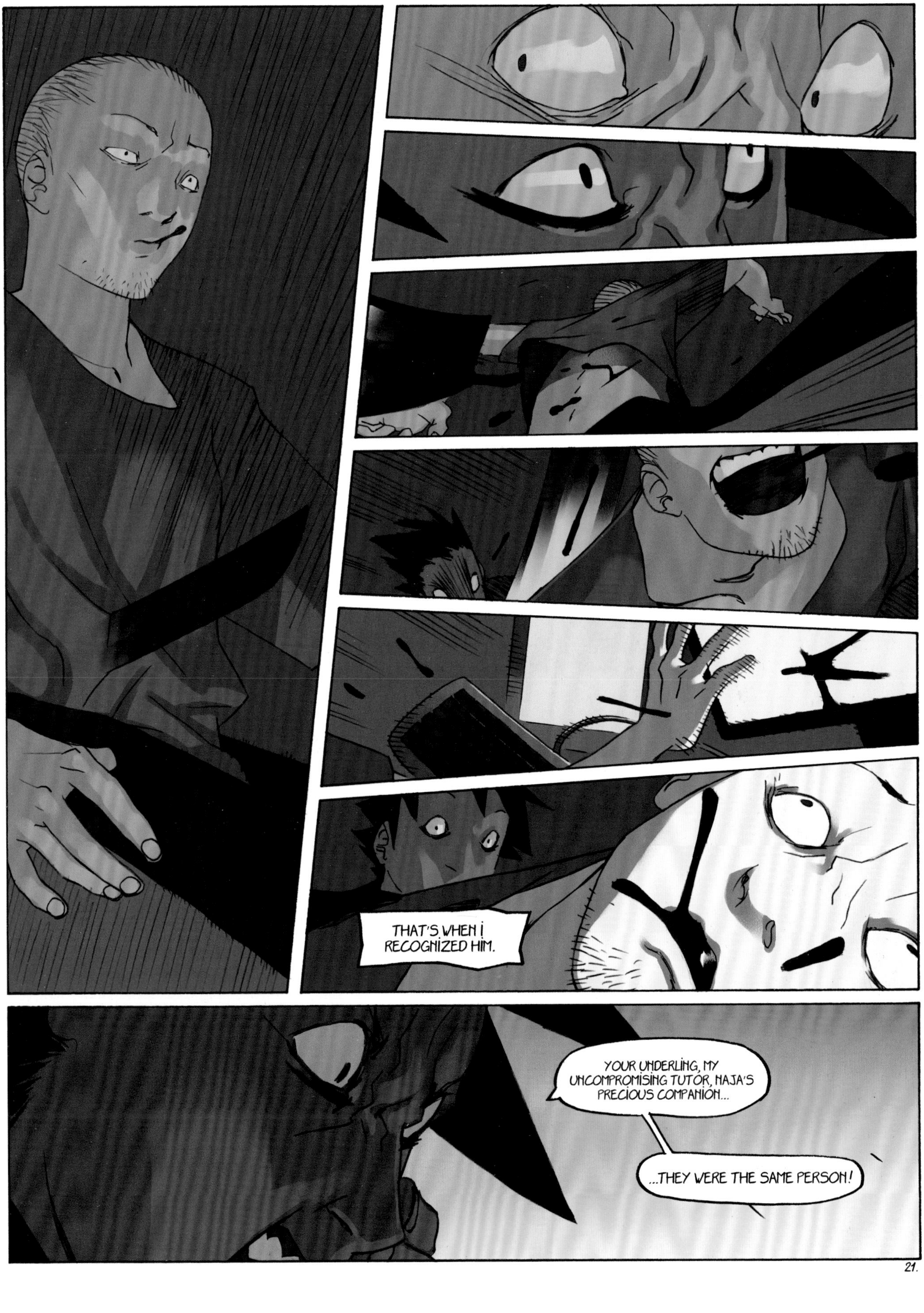
THAT'S WHEN I RECOGNIZED HIM.
YOUR UNDERLING, MY UNCOMPROMISING TUTOR, NAJA'S PRECIOUS COMPANION...
...THEY WERE THE SAME PERSON!

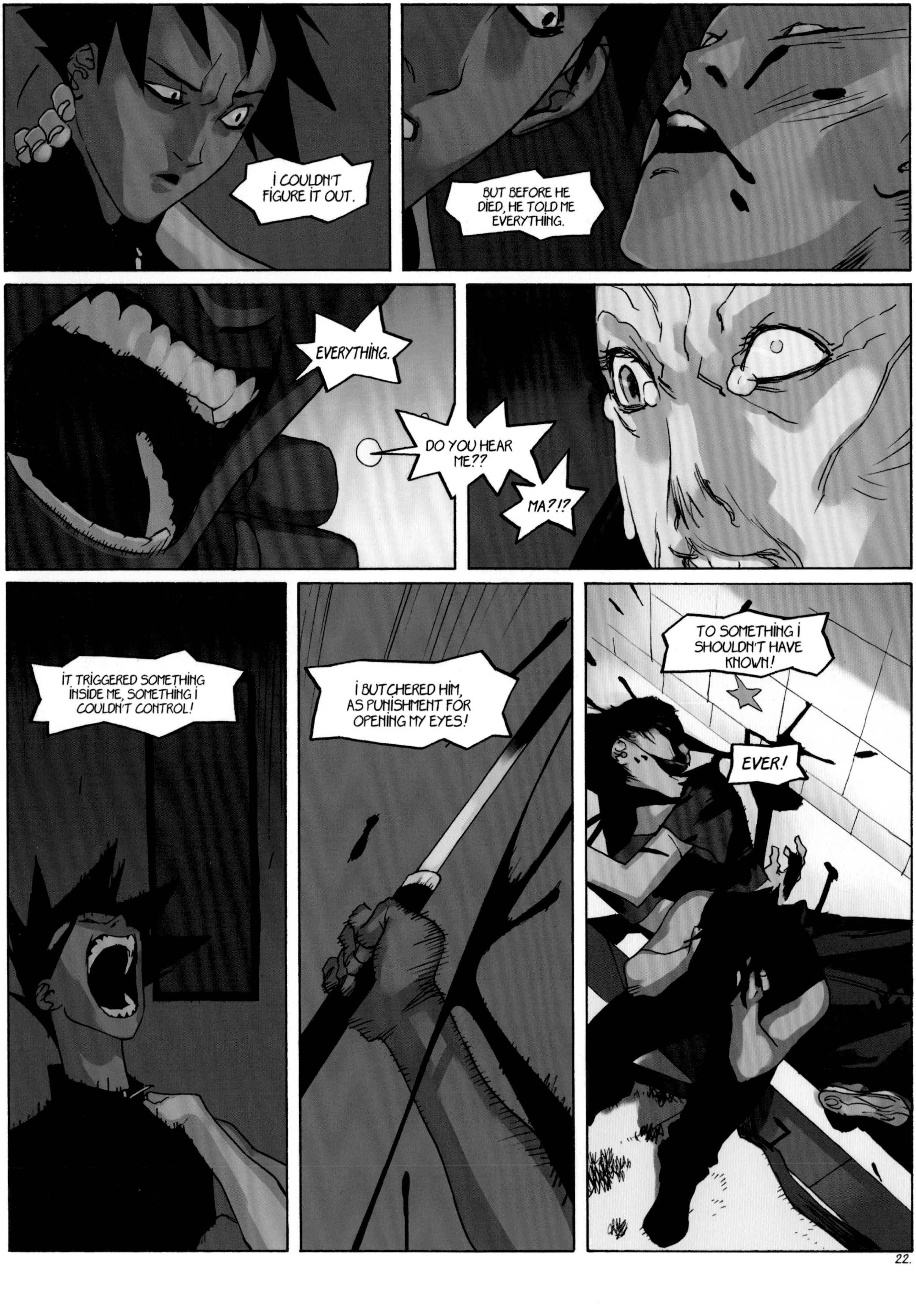

I COULDN'T FIGURE IT OUT.
BUT BEFORE HE DIED, HE TOLD ME EVERYTHING.
EVERYTHING.
DO YOU HEAR ME??
MA?!?
IT TRIGGERED SOMETHING INSIDE ME, SOMETHING I COULDN'T CONTROL!
I BUTCHERED HIM, AS PUNISHMENT FOR OPENING MY EYES!
TO SOMETHING I SHOULDN'T HAVE KNOWN!
EVER!

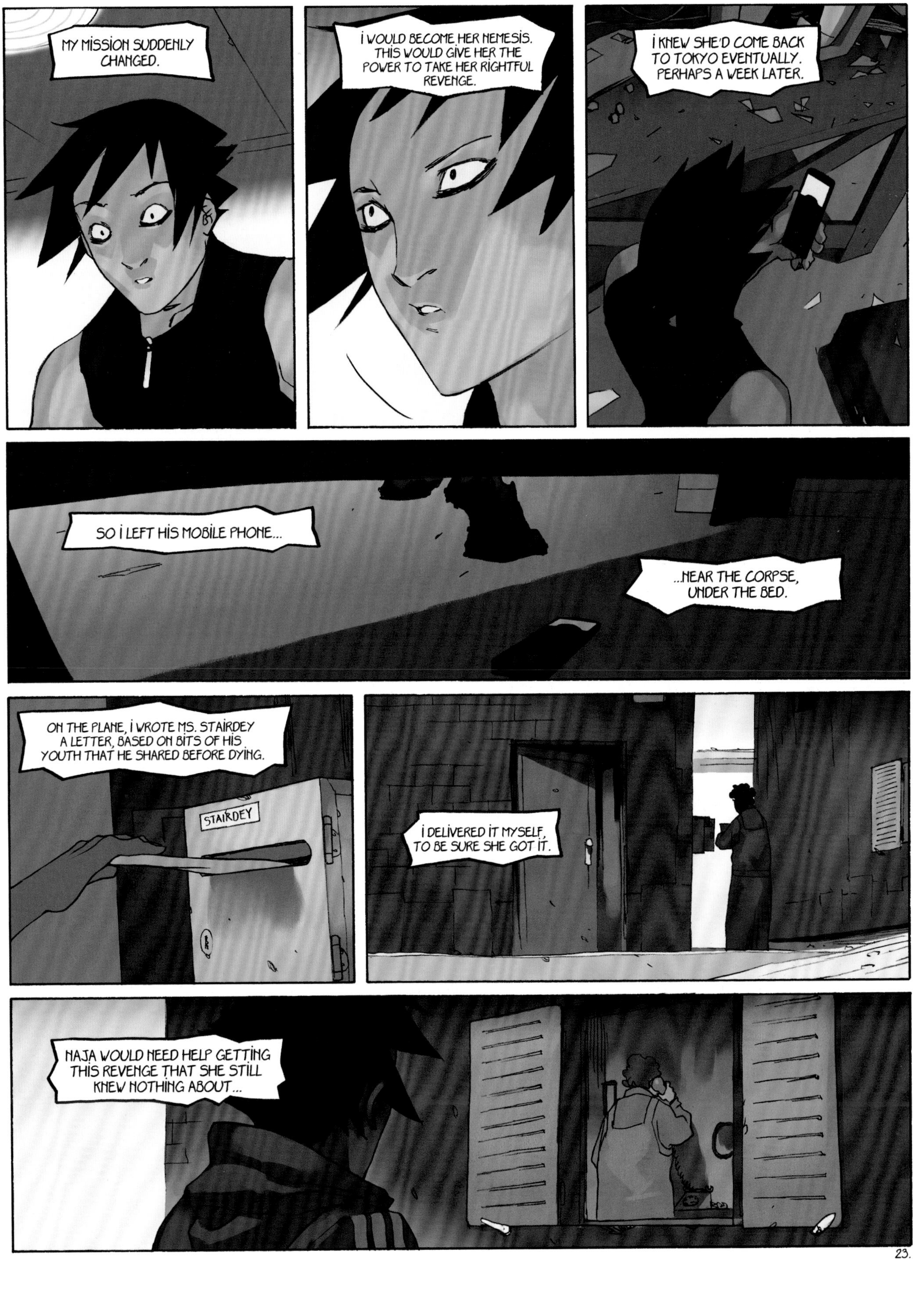
MY MISSION SUDDENLY CHANGED.
I WOULD BECOME HER NEMESIS. THIS WOULD GIVE HER THE POWER TO TAKE HER RIGHTFUL REVENGE.
I KNEW SHE'D COME BACK TO TOKYO EVENTUALLY. PERHAPS A WEEK LATER.
SO I LEFT HIS MOBILE PHONE...
...NEAR THE CORPSE, UNDER THE BED.
ON THE PLANE, I WROTE MS. STAIRDEY A LETTER, BASED ON BITS OF HIS YOUTH THAT HE SHARED BEFORE DYING.
STAIRDEY
I DELIVERED IT MYSELF, TO BE SURE SHE GOT IT.
NAJA WOULD NEED HELP GETTING THIS REVENGE THAT SHE STILL KNEW NOTHING ABOUT...

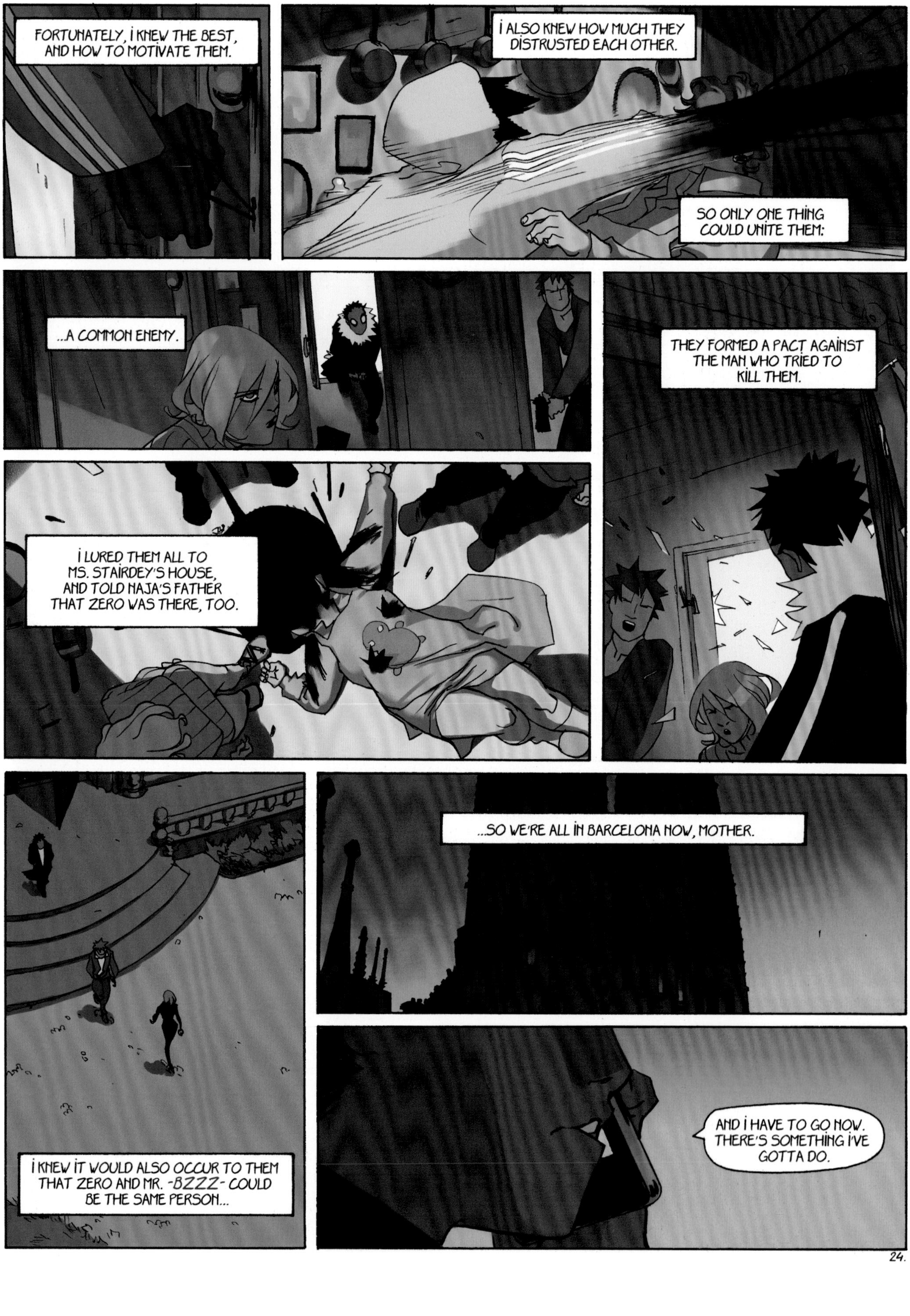
FORTUNATELY, I KNEW THE BEST, AND HOW TO MOTIVATE THEM.
I ALSO KNEW HOW MUCH THEY DISTRUSTED EACH OTHER.
SO ONLY ONE THING COULD UNITE THEM:
...A COMMON ENEMY.
THEY FORMED A PACT AGAINST THE MAN WHO TRIED TO KILL THEM.
I LURED THEM ALL TO MS. STAIRDEY'S HOUSE, AND TOLD NAJA'S FATHER THAT ZERO WAS THERE, TOO.
I KNEW IT WOULD ALSO OCCUR TO THEM THAT ZERO AND MR. -BZZZ- COULD BE THE SAME PERSON...
...SO WE'RE ALL IN BARCELONA NOW, MOTHER.
AND I HAVE TO GO NOW. THERE'S SOMETHING I'VE GOTTA DO.

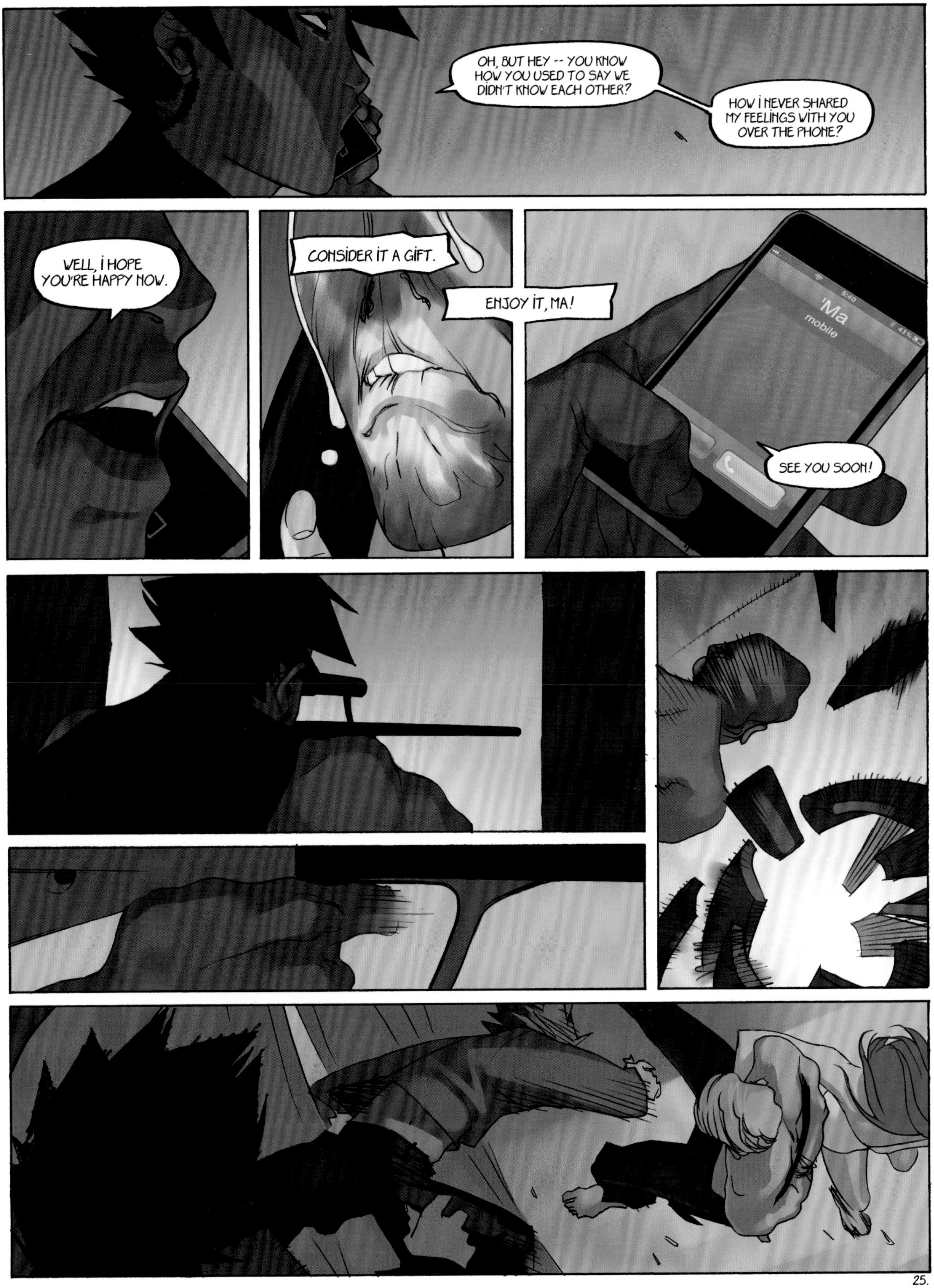
OH, BUT HEY -- YOU KNOW HOW YOU USED TO SAY WE DIDN'T KNOW EACH OTHER?
HOW I NEVER SHARED MY FEELINGS WITH YOU OVER THE PHONE?
WELL, I HOPE YOU'RE HAPPY NOW.
CONSIDER IT A GIFT.
ENJOY IT, MA!
'Ma
mobile
SEE YOU SOON!

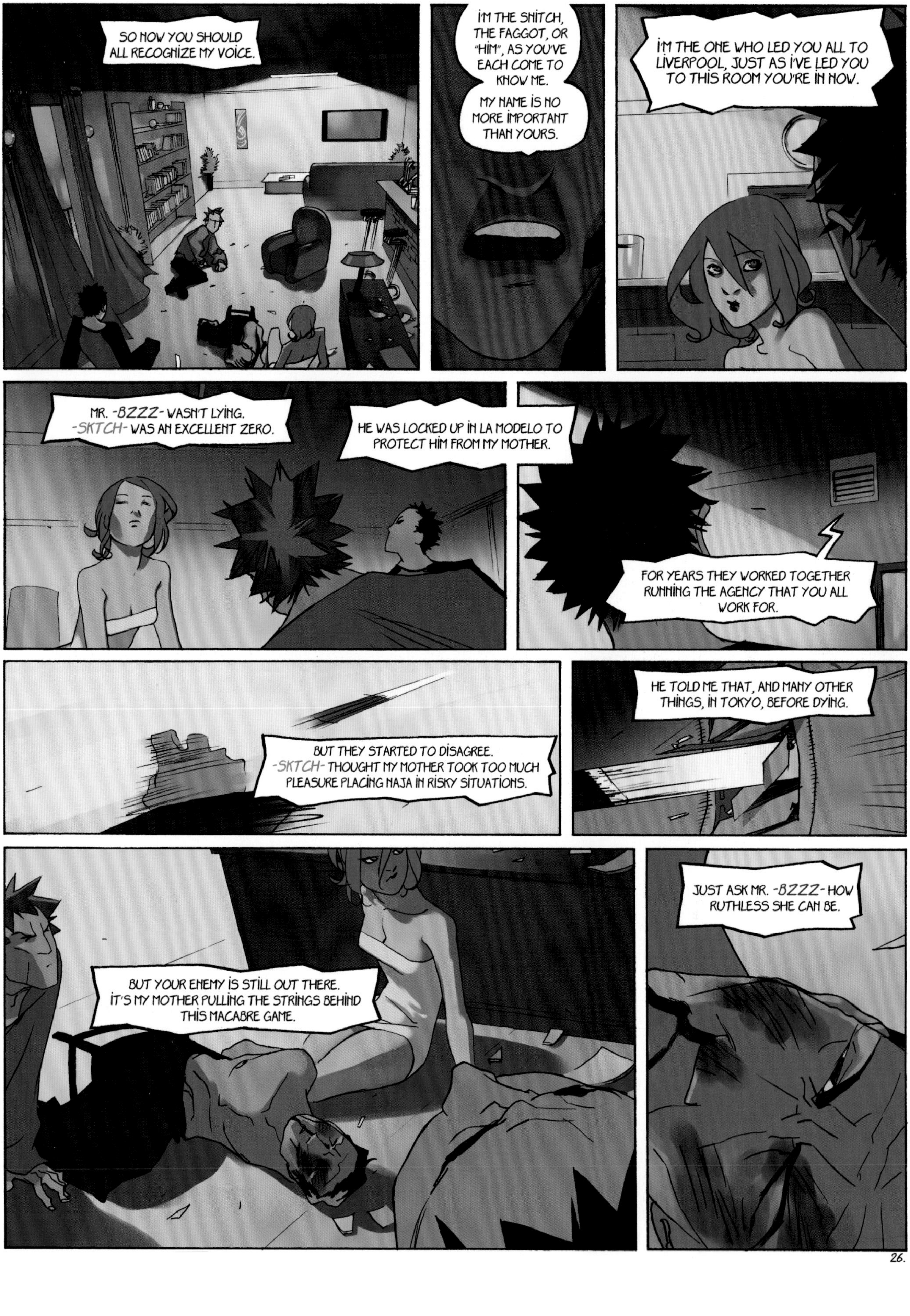
SO NOW YOU SHOULD ALL RECOGNIZE MY VOICE.
I'M THE SNITCH, THE FAGGOT, OR "HIM", AS YOU'VE EACH COME TO KNOW ME.
MY NAME IS NO MORE IMPORTANT THAN YOURS.
I'M THE ONE WHO LED YOU ALL TO LIVERPOOL, JUST AS I'VE LED YOU TO THIS ROOM YOU'RE IN NOW.
MR. -BZZZ- WASN'T LYING. -SKTCH- WAS AN EXCELLENT ZERO.
HE WAS LOCKED UP IN LA MODELO TO PROTECT HIM FROM MY MOTHER.
FOR YEARS THEY WORKED TOGETHER RUNNING THE AGENCY THAT YOU ALL WORK FOR.
BUT THEY STARTED TO DISAGREE. -SKTCH- THOUGHT MY MOTHER TOOK TOO MUCH PLEASURE PLACING NAJA IN RISKY SITUATIONS.
HE TOLD ME THAT, AND MANY OTHER THINGS, IN TOKYO, BEFORE DYING.
BUT YOUR ENEMY IS STILL OUT THERE. IT'S MY MOTHER PULLING THE STRINGS BEHIND THIS MACABRE GAME.
JUST ASK MR. -BZZZ- HOW RUTHLESS SHE CAN BE.

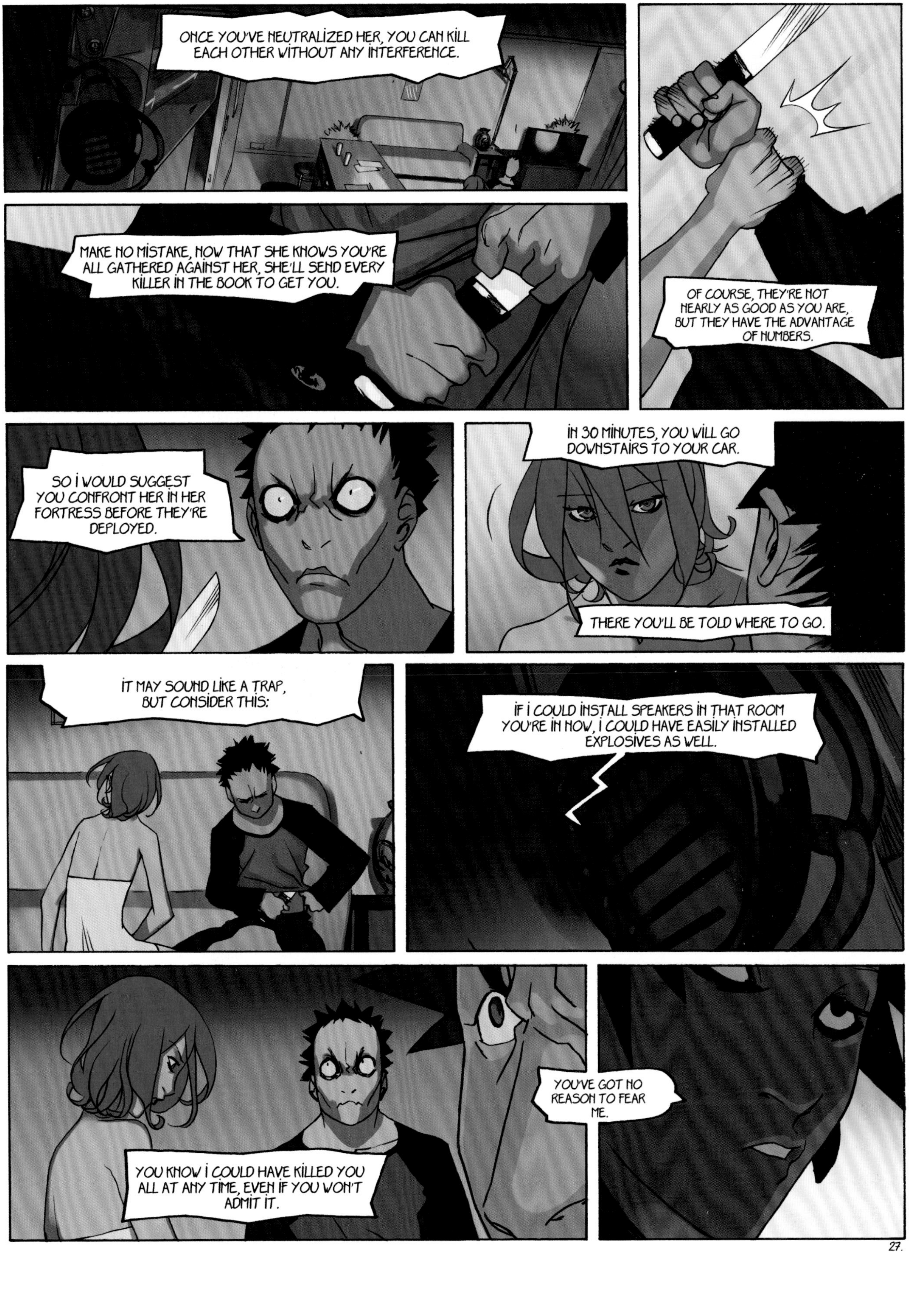
ONCE YOU'VE NEUTRALIZED HER, YOU CAN KILL EACH OTHER WITHOUT ANY INTERFERENCE.
MAKE NO MISTAKE, NOW THAT SHE KNOWS YOU'RE ALL GATHERED AGAINST HER, SHE'LL SEND EVERY KILLER IN THE BOOK TO GET YOU.
OF COURSE, THEY'RE NOT NEARLY AS GOOD AS YOU ARE, BUT THEY HAVE THE ADVANTAGE OF NUMBERS.
SO I WOULD SUGGEST YOU CONFRONT HER IN HER FORTRESS BEFORE THEY'RE DEPLOYED.
IN 30 MINUTES, YOU WILL GO DOWNSTAIRS TO YOUR CAR.
THERE YOU'LL BE TOLD WHERE TO GO.
IT MAY SOUND LIKE A TRAP, BUT CONSIDER THIS:
IF I COULD INSTALL SPEAKERS IN THAT ROOM YOU'RE IN NOW, I COULD HAVE EASILY INSTALLED EXPLOSIVES AS WELL.
YOU KNOW I COULD HAVE KILLED YOU ALL AT ANY TIME, EVEN IF YOU WON'T ADMIT IT.
YOU'VE GOT NO REASON TO FEAR ME.

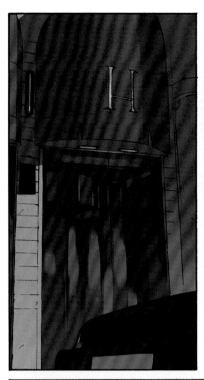

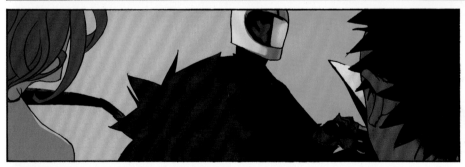

DO YOU KNOW THE TERM "BRUXELISM?"

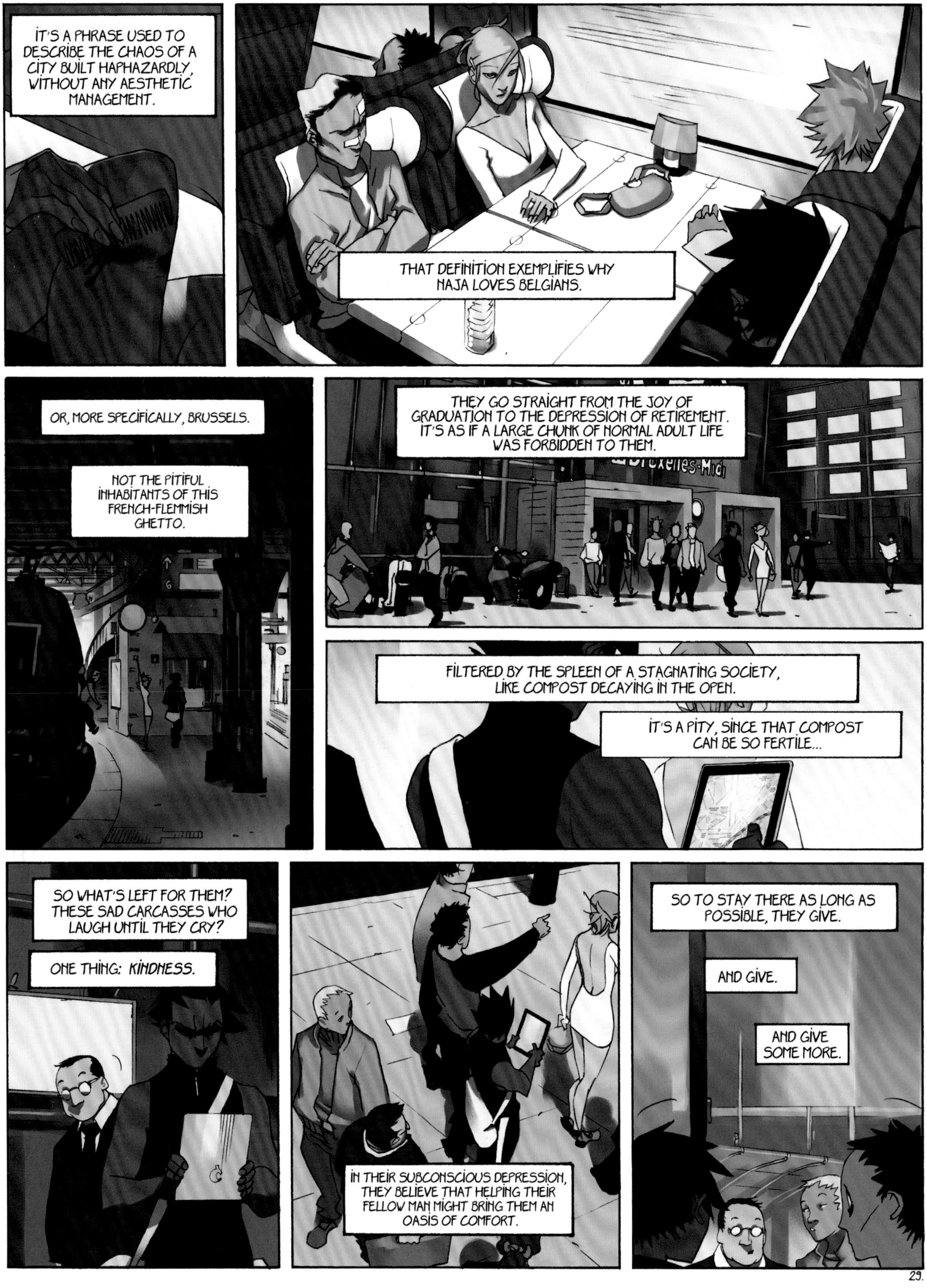
IT'S A PHRASE USED TO DESCRIBE THE CHAOS OF A CITY BUILT HAPHAZARDLY, WITHOUT ANY AESTHETIC MANAGEMENT.
THAT DEFINITION EXEMPLIFIES WHY NAJA LOVES BELGIANS.
OR, MORE SPECIFICALLY, BRUSSELS.
NOT THE PITIFUL INHABITANTS OF THIS FRENCH-FLEMMISH GHETTO.
THEY GO STRAIGHT FROM THE JOY OF GRADUATION TO THE DEPRESSION OF RETIREMENT. IT'S AS IF A LARGE CHUNK OF NORMAL ADULT LIFE WAS FORBIDDEN TO THEM.
Bruxelles-Midi
FILTERED BY THE SPLEEN OF A STAGNATING SOCIETY, LIKE COMPOST DECAYING IN THE OPEN.
IT'S A PITY, SINCE THAT COMPOST CAN BE SO FERTILE...
SO WHAT'S LEFT FOR THEM? THESE SAD CARCASSES WHO LAUGH UNTIL THEY CRY?
ONE THING: KINDNESS.
IN THEIR SUBCONSCIOUS DEPRESSION, THEY BELIEVE THAT HELPING THEIR FELLOW MAN MIGHT BRING THEM AN OASIS OF COMFORT.
SO TO STAY THERE AS LONG AS POSSIBLE, THEY GIVE.
AND GIVE.
AND GIVE SOME MORE.

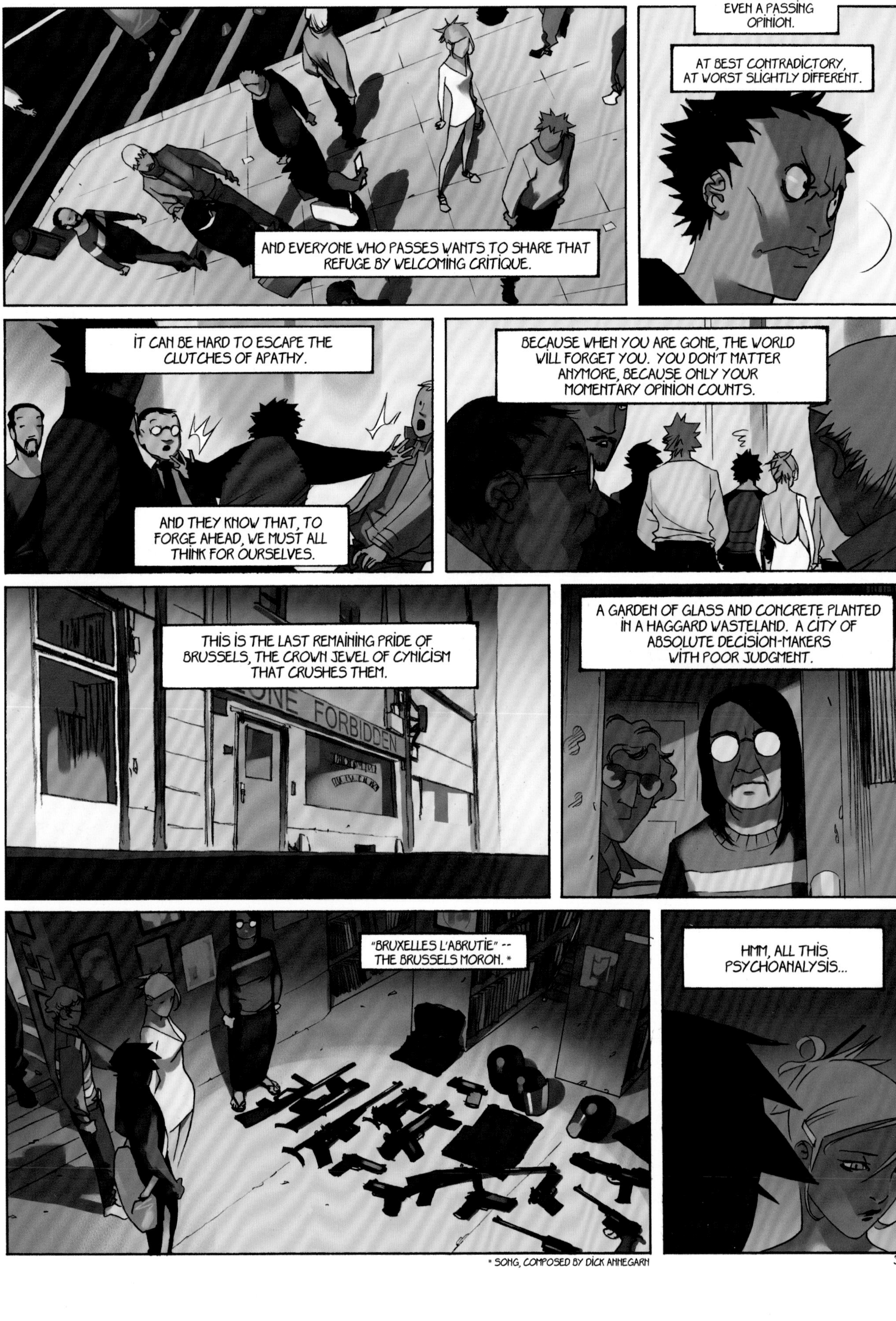
AND EVERYONE WHO PASSES WANTS TO SHARE THAT REFUGE BY WELCOMING CRITIQUE.
EVEN A PASSING OPINION.
AT BEST CONTRADICTORY, AT WORST SLIGHTLY DIFFERENT.
IT CAN BE HARD TO ESCAPE THE CLUTCHES OF APATHY.
AND THEY KNOW THAT, TO FORGE AHEAD, WE MUST ALL THINK FOR OURSELVES.
BECAUSE WHEN YOU ARE GONE, THE WORLD WILL FORGET YOU. YOU DON'T MATTER ANYMORE, BECAUSE ONLY YOUR MOMENTARY OPINION COUNTS.
THIS IS THE LAST REMAINING PRIDE OF BRUSSELS, THE CROWN JEWEL OF CYNICISM THAT CRUSHES THEM.
FORBIDDEN
A GARDEN OF GLASS AND CONCRETE PLANTED IN A HAGGARD WASTELAND. A CITY OF ABSOLUTE DECISION-MAKERS WITH POOR JUDGMENT.
"BRUXELLES L'ABRUTIE" -- THE BRUSSELS MORON. *
HMM, ALL THIS PSYCHOANALYSIS...

* SONG, COMPOSED BY DICK ANNEGARN

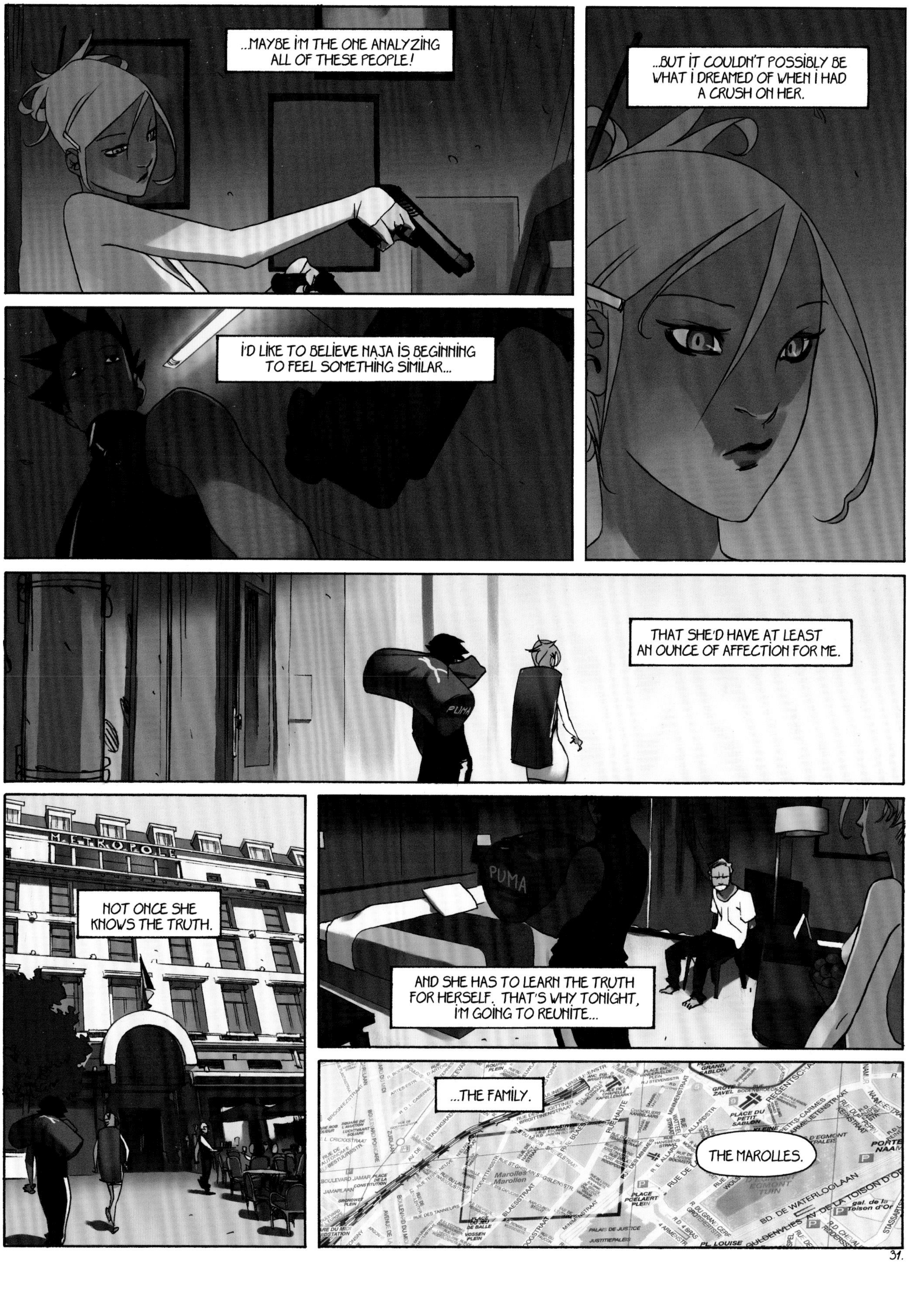
...MAYBE I'M THE ONE ANALYZING ALL OF THESE PEOPLE!
...BUT IT COULDN'T POSSIBLY BE WHAT I DREAMED OF WHEN I HAD A CRUSH ON HER.
I'D LIKE TO BELIEVE NAJA IS BEGINNING TO FEEL SOMETHING SIMILAR...
THAT SHE'D HAVE AT LEAST AN OUNCE OF AFFECTION FOR ME.
PUMA
METROPOLE
NOT ONCE SHE KNOWS THE TRUTH.
PUMA
AND SHE HAS TO LEARN THE TRUTH FOR HERSELF. THAT'S WHY TONIGHT, I'M GOING TO REUNITE...
...THE FAMILY.
THE MAROLLES.

THE TRUE HEART OF BRUSSELS, WHERE THEIR HUMOR, DIALECT, AND LIFESTYLE WERE BORN.

IT'S NOT BY ACCIDENT THAT THE DANTE COURTHOUSE WAS BUILT TO OVERLOOK THE HOUSES OF THE REVOLUTIONARY MASSES.

BUT RATHER THAN BEING IMPOSED BY IT, IT AMUSED THEM, AS IF THEY WERE TICKLING THE FEET OF JUSTICE.

THIS IS WHERE MY PEOPLE ARE FROM.

THEY'VE LIVED IN THIS BUILDING FOR GENERATIONS.

AND FOR GOOD REASON: IT HAS BEEN THE HUB OF ALL EUROPEAN TRAFFIC SINCE THE MIDDLE AGES. MODERN POLITICS HAVE HAD NO EFFECT ON THEIR BUSINESS.

YES, PARADOXICALLY, MORE NEIGHBORHOODS ARE QUIET, WITH MORE POLICE ON PATROL.

BUT REALLY, THEY'RE NOT THE ONES OUR PLAYERS SHOULD FEAR...

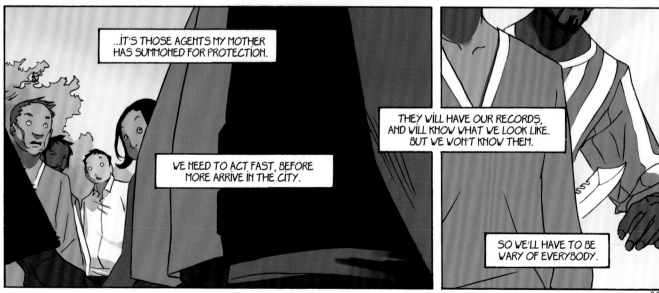

...IT'S THOSE AGENTS MY MOTHER HAS SUMMONED FOR PROTECTION.

WE NEED TO ACT FAST, BEFORE MORE ARRIVE IN THE CITY.

THEY WILL HAVE OUR RECORDS, AND WILL KNOW WHAT WE LOOK LIKE. BUT WE WON'T KNOW THEM.

SO WE'LL HAVE TO BE WARY OF EVERYBODY.

SO HAS YOUR FAMILY ALWAYS BEEN IN THE ASSASSINATION BUSINESS?

NO, NOT EXCLUSIVELY.

IT ALL CAME ABOUT AFTER A LOVE AFFAIR THAT WENT WRONG. IN BRIEF, MY MOTHER FELL IN LOVE WITH THE SON OF A FOREIGN GANGSTER...

LIKE ROMEO AND JULIET, THEY DEFIED THEIR FAMILIES TO LIVE TOGETHER...

...BUT AFTER A FEW YEARS ON THE RUN, HIS FAMILY CAUGHT THEM AND FORCED HIM TO "PUNISH" MY MOTHER BEFORE SENDING HER BACK HOME.

AS THE ONLY HEIRESS, HER CONDITION DID NOT ALLOW HER TO MANAGE THE DAY-TO-DAY BUSINESS. SO SHE SOLD HER SHARES IN GAMBLING, PROSTITUTION, AND DRUGS IN ORDER TO FOCUS ON THIS SECTOR.

SHE FOUND HER NICHE: SHE HAD A NOSE FOR FINDING THE MOST TALENTED KILLERS OF THEIR GENERATION.

AND -SKTCH- HAD ANOTHER, COMPLEMENTARY SKILL: MANAGING THE TROOPS. ERASING THE EXISTENCE OF OTHER AGENTS, SUCH AS YOU.

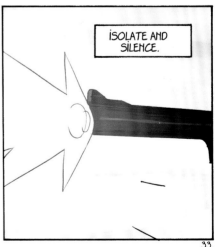

ISOLATE AND SILENCE.

HER COMPANY'S SUCCESS MADE FORMER ADVERSARIES, AS WELL AS CERTAIN GOVERNMENTS, LARGE BUSINESSES, AND POWERFUL INDIVIDUALS, REGULAR CLIENTS.

THERE WAS NOTHING SHE WOULD NOT DO TO SATISFY THEM. IN THIS BUSINESS, MONEY TRUMPS MORALITY.

THAT'S NOT TRUE...

YES, MAX. IT IS. ZERO NEVER APPLIED ETHICAL SCRUPLES AS HER SPOKESMAN, EVEN THOUGH COINCIDENTALLY HE NEVER ASKED YOU TO KILL AN INNOCENT MAN.

KEEP MOVING!

THAT'S WHAT MADE HIM THE PERFECT DIRECTOR. HE SELECTED THE BEST PERSON FOR THE JOB.

SO FOR YOU, MAX, THEY MADE SURE YOU BELIEVED YOUR MISSIONS WERE FOR THE GOOD OF MANKIND.

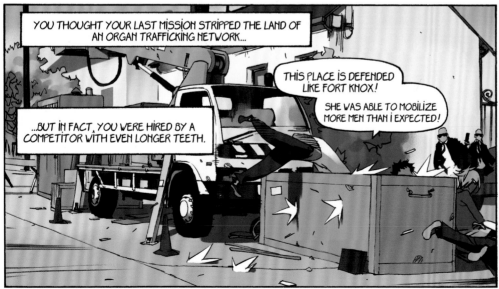

YOU THOUGHT YOUR LAST MISSION STRIPPED THE LAND OF AN ORGAN TRAFFICKING NETWORK...

THIS PLACE IS DEFENDED LIKE FORT KNOX!

SHE WAS ABLE TO MOBILIZE MORE MEN THAN I EXPECTED!

...BUT IN FACT, YOU WERE HIRED BY A COMPETITOR WITH EVEN LONGER TEETH.

THIS IS GOING TO BE MORE COMPLICATED THAN I THOUGHT...

...

34.

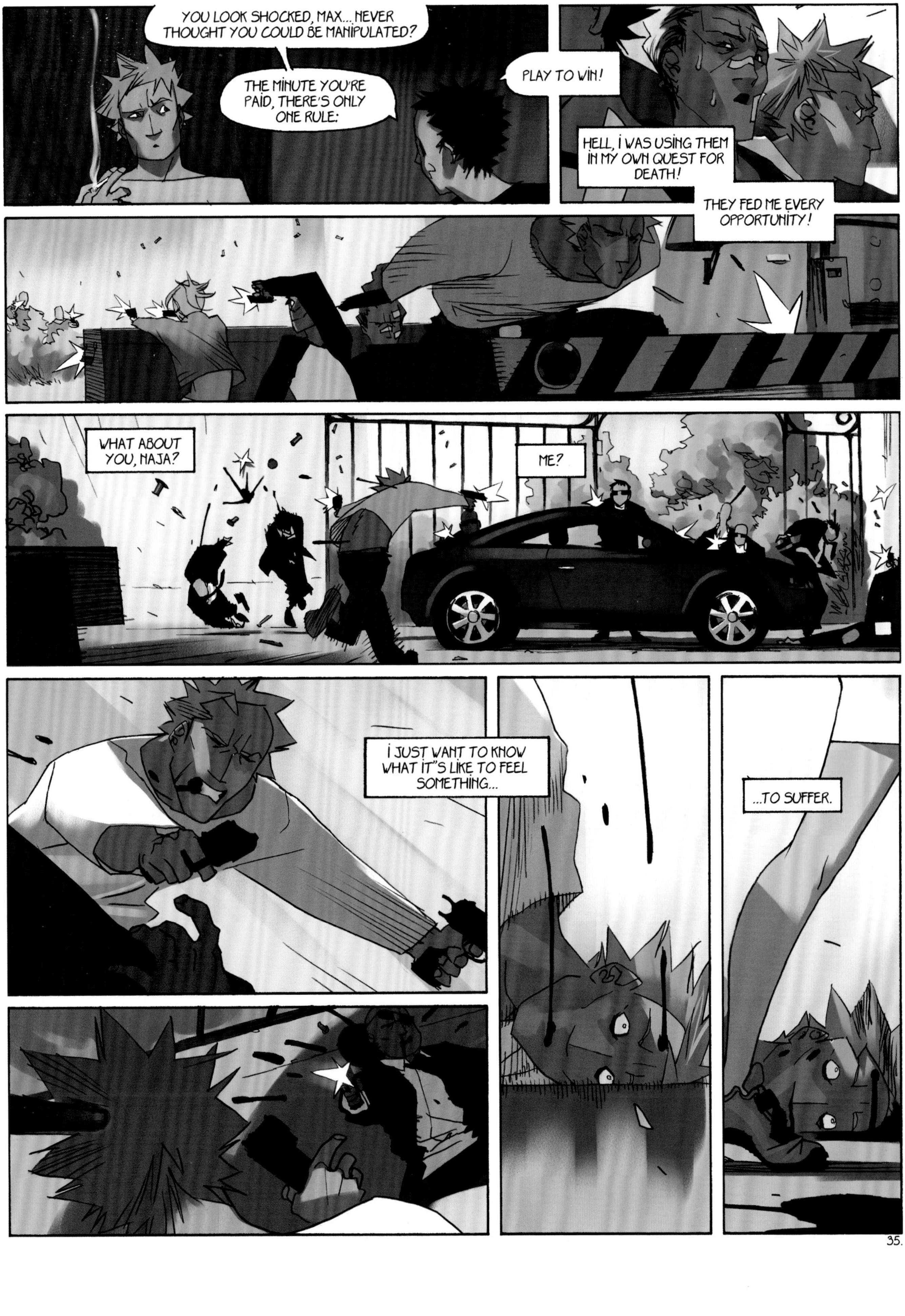

YOU LOOK SHOCKED, MAX... NEVER THOUGHT YOU COULD BE MANIPULATED?
THE MINUTE YOU'RE PAID, THERE'S ONLY ONE RULE:
PLAY TO WIN!
HELL, I WAS USING THEM IN MY OWN QUEST FOR DEATH!
THEY FED ME EVERY OPPORTUNITY!
WHAT ABOUT YOU, NAJA?
ME?
I JUST WANT TO KNOW WHAT IT'S LIKE TO FEEL SOMETHING...
...TO SUFFER.

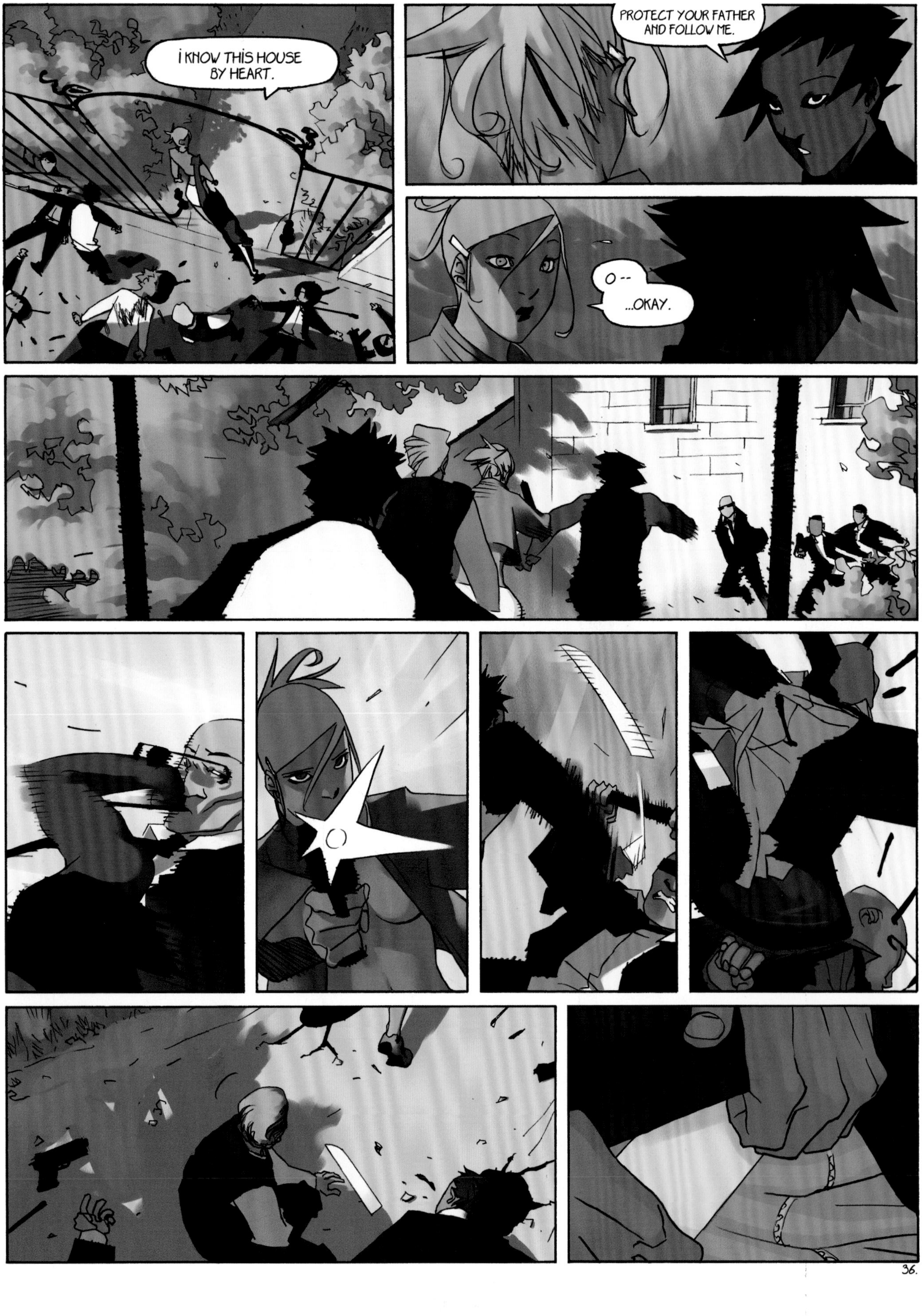
I KNOW THIS HOUSE BY HEART.
PROTECT YOUR FATHER AND FOLLOW ME.
O --
...OKAY.

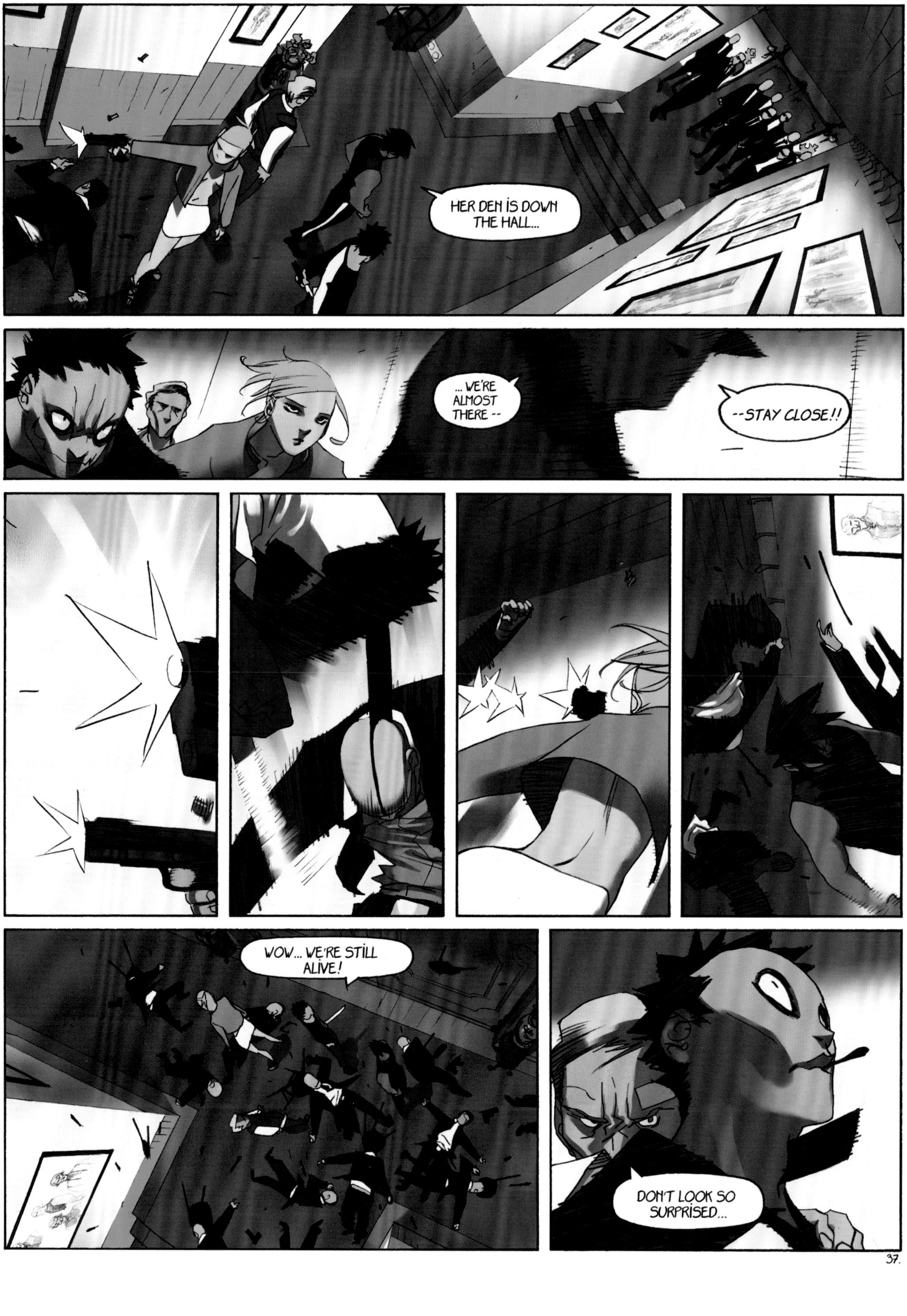
HER DEN IS DOWN THE HALL...
... WE'RE ALMOST THERE --
--STAY CLOSE!!
WOW... WE'RE STILL ALIVE!
DON'T LOOK SO SURPRISED...

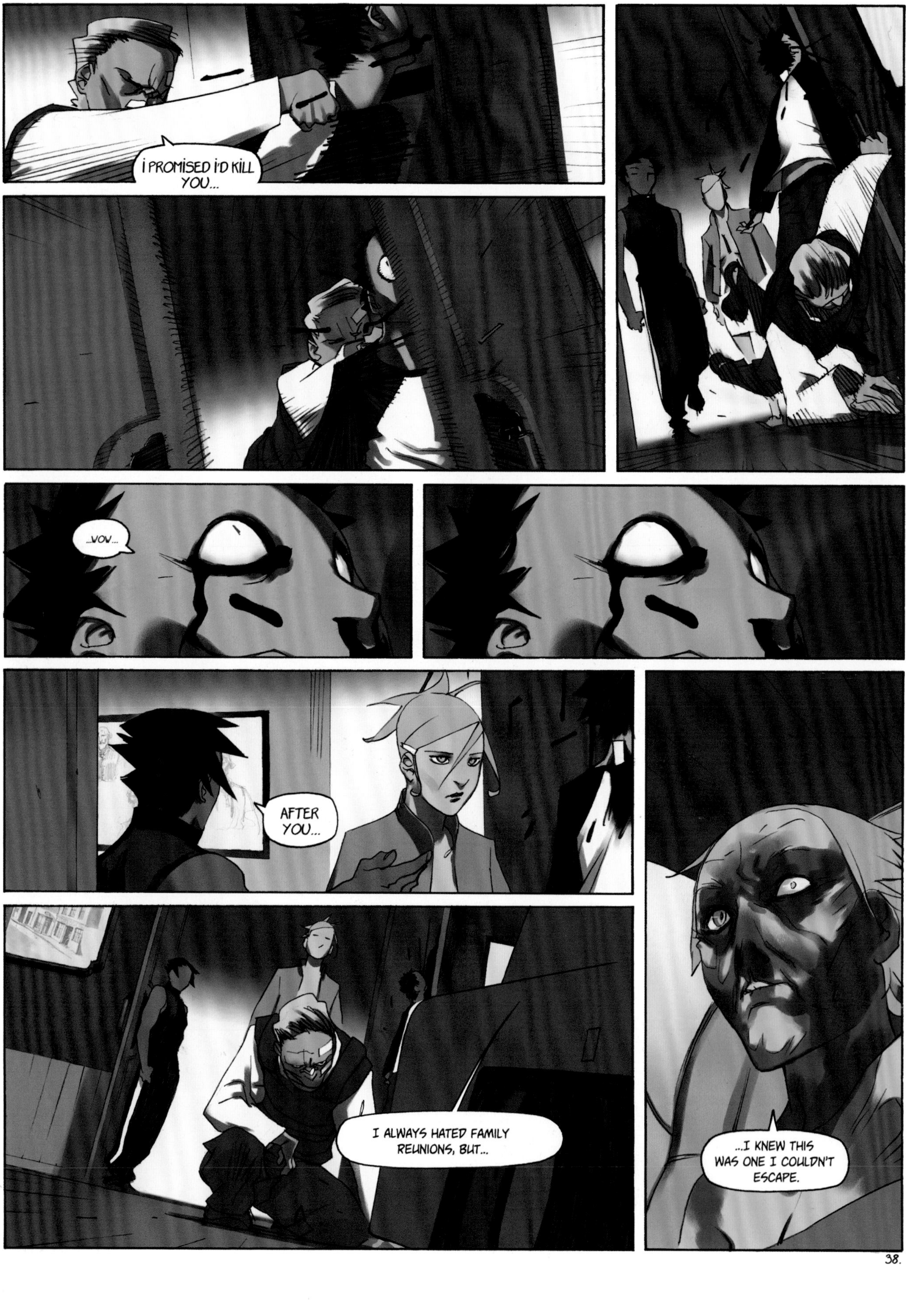
I PROMISED I'D KILL YOU...
...WOW...
AFTER YOU...
I ALWAYS HATED FAMILY REUNIONS, BUT...
...I KNEW THIS WAS ONE I COULDN'T ESCAPE.

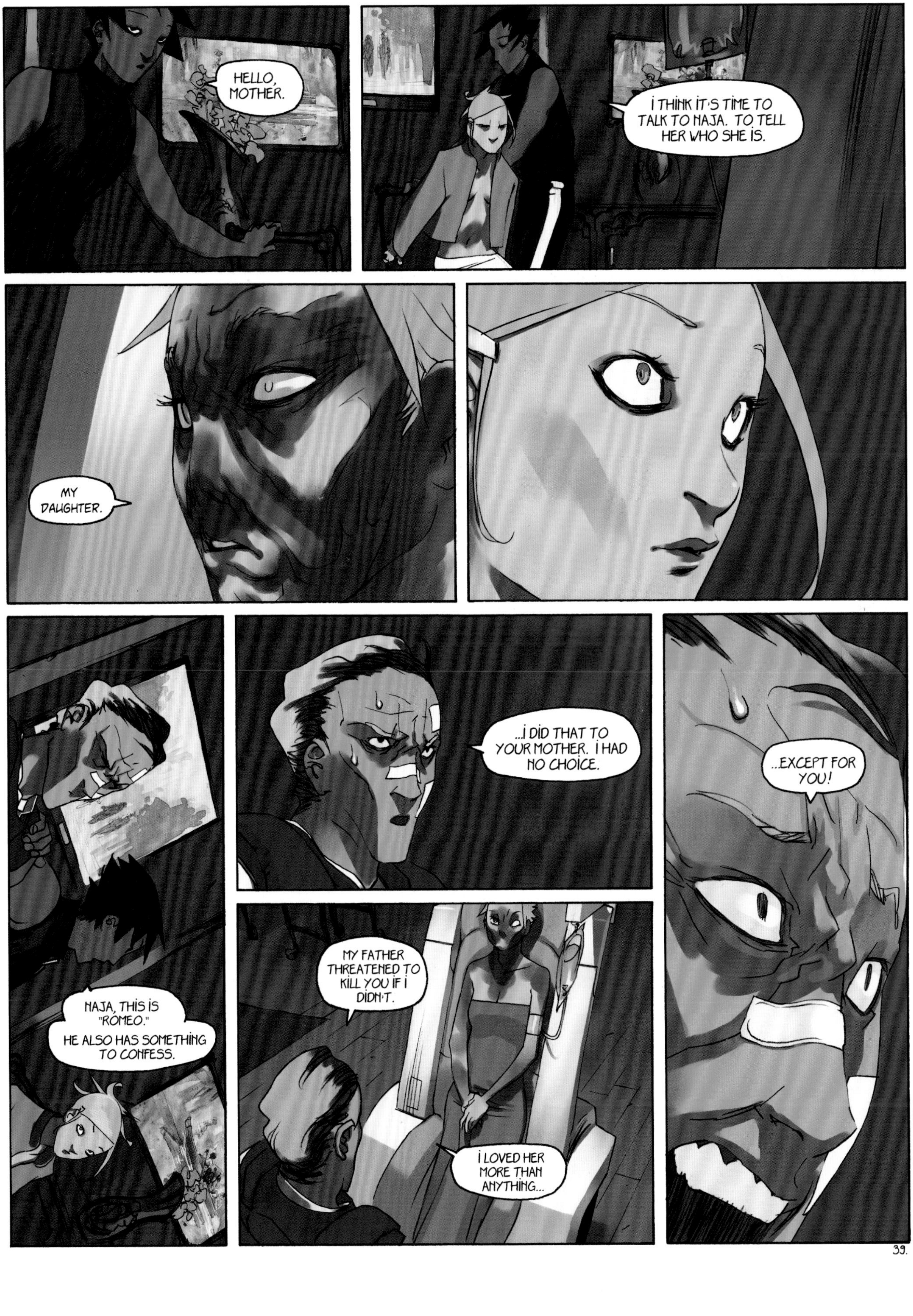
HELLO, MOTHER.
I THINK IT'S TIME TO TALK TO NAJA. TO TELL HER WHO SHE IS.
MY DAUGHTER.
NAJA, THIS IS "ROMEO."
HE ALSO HAS SOMETHING TO CONFESS.
...I DID THAT TO YOUR MOTHER. I HAD NO CHOICE.
MY FATHER THREATENED TO KILL YOU IF I DIDN'T.
I LOVED HER MORE THAN ANYTHING...
...EXCEPT FOR YOU!

HE FORCED ME TO BEAT HER WITHIN AN INCH OF HER LIFE.

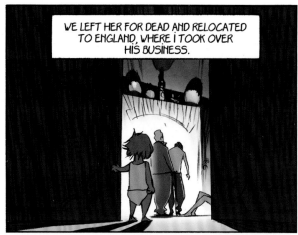

WE LEFT HER FOR DEAD AND RELOCATED TO ENGLAND, WHERE I TOOK OVER HIS BUSINESS.

YOU GREW UP AND...

...SHE TOOK YOU AWAY!

-SKTCH- WAS MY TOY.

BAIT TO LURE YOU AWAY.

I HAD IT ALL PLANNED, EVEN THE CAR ACCIDENT THAT LEFT YOU FOR DEAD.

WHEN YOU AWOKE, YOU CHANGED YOUR LIFE.

AND YOUR NAME.

I WAS ALWAYS SO JEALOUS OF YOU, THE WAY YOU FELT NO PAIN...

THAT DEVELOPED AFTER MY FATHER FORCED YOU TO WATCH ME TORTURE YOUR MOTHER.

YOU WERE ONLY TWO YEARS OLD, AND YOU TOTALLY LOST THE ABILITY TO FEEL.

WHILE I, TO THIS DAY, HAVE BEEN IN CONSTANT PAIN EVER SINCE.

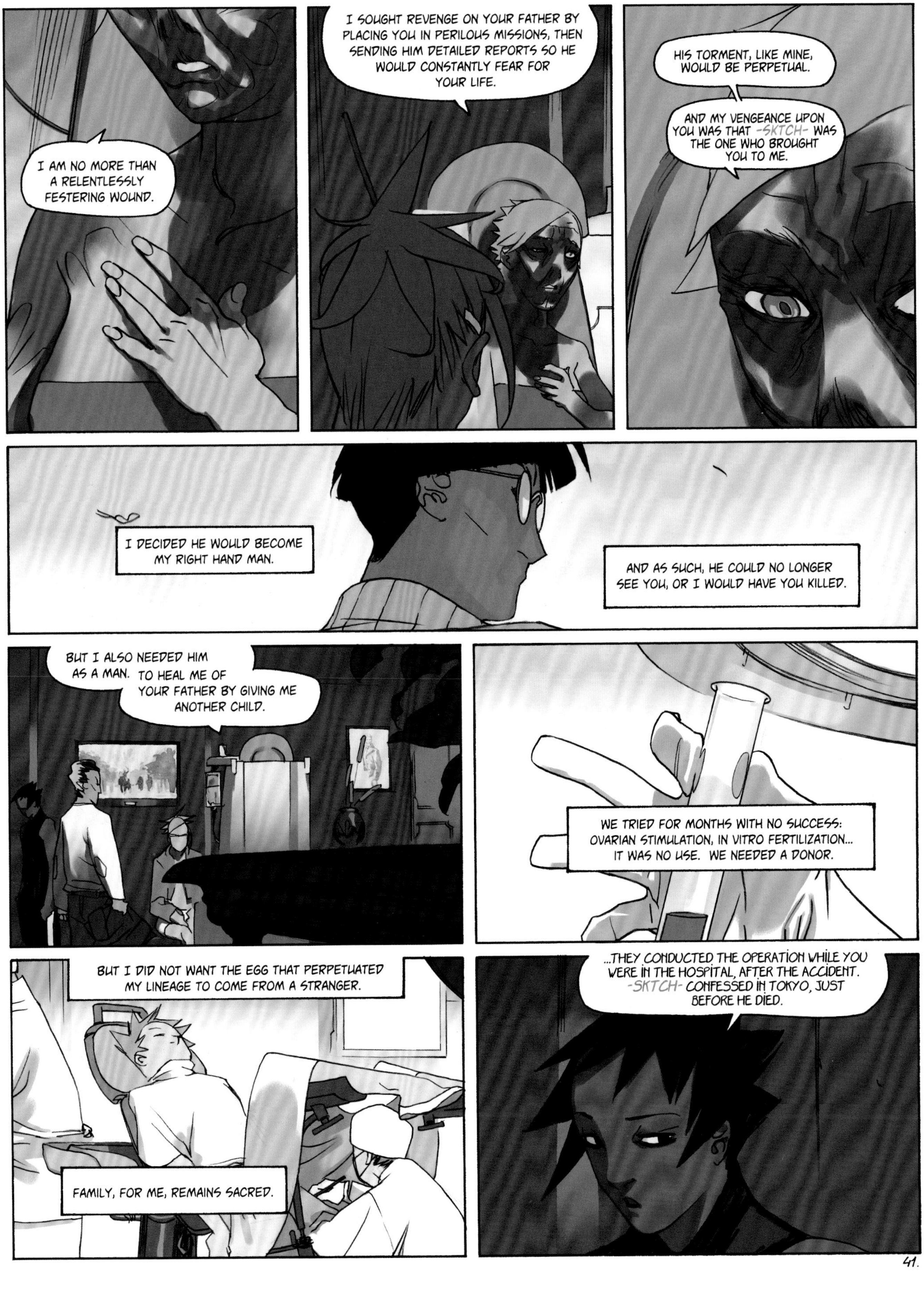
I AM NO MORE THAN A RELENTLESSLY FESTERING WOUND.
I SOUGHT REVENGE ON YOUR FATHER BY PLACING YOU IN PERILOUS MISSIONS, THEN SENDING HIM DETAILED REPORTS SO HE WOULD CONSTANTLY FEAR FOR YOUR LIFE.
HIS TORMENT, LIKE MINE, WOULD BE PERPETUAL.
AND MY VENGEANCE UPON YOU WAS THAT -SKTCH- WAS THE ONE WHO BROUGHT YOU TO ME.
I DECIDED HE WOULD BECOME MY RIGHT HAND MAN.
AND AS SUCH, HE COULD NO LONGER SEE YOU, OR I WOULD HAVE YOU KILLED.
BUT I ALSO NEEDED HIM AS A MAN.
TO HEAL ME OF YOUR FATHER BY GIVING ME ANOTHER CHILD.
WE TRIED FOR MONTHS WITH NO SUCCESS: OVARIAN STIMULATION, IN VITRO FERTILIZATION... IT WAS NO USE. WE NEEDED A DONOR.
BUT I DID NOT WANT THE EGG THAT PERPETUATED MY LINEAGE TO COME FROM A STRANGER.
FAMILY, FOR ME, REMAINS SACRED.
...THEY CONDUCTED THE OPERATION WHILE YOU WERE IN THE HOSPITAL, AFTER THE ACCIDENT. -SKTCH- CONFESSED IN TOKYO, JUST BEFORE HE DIED.

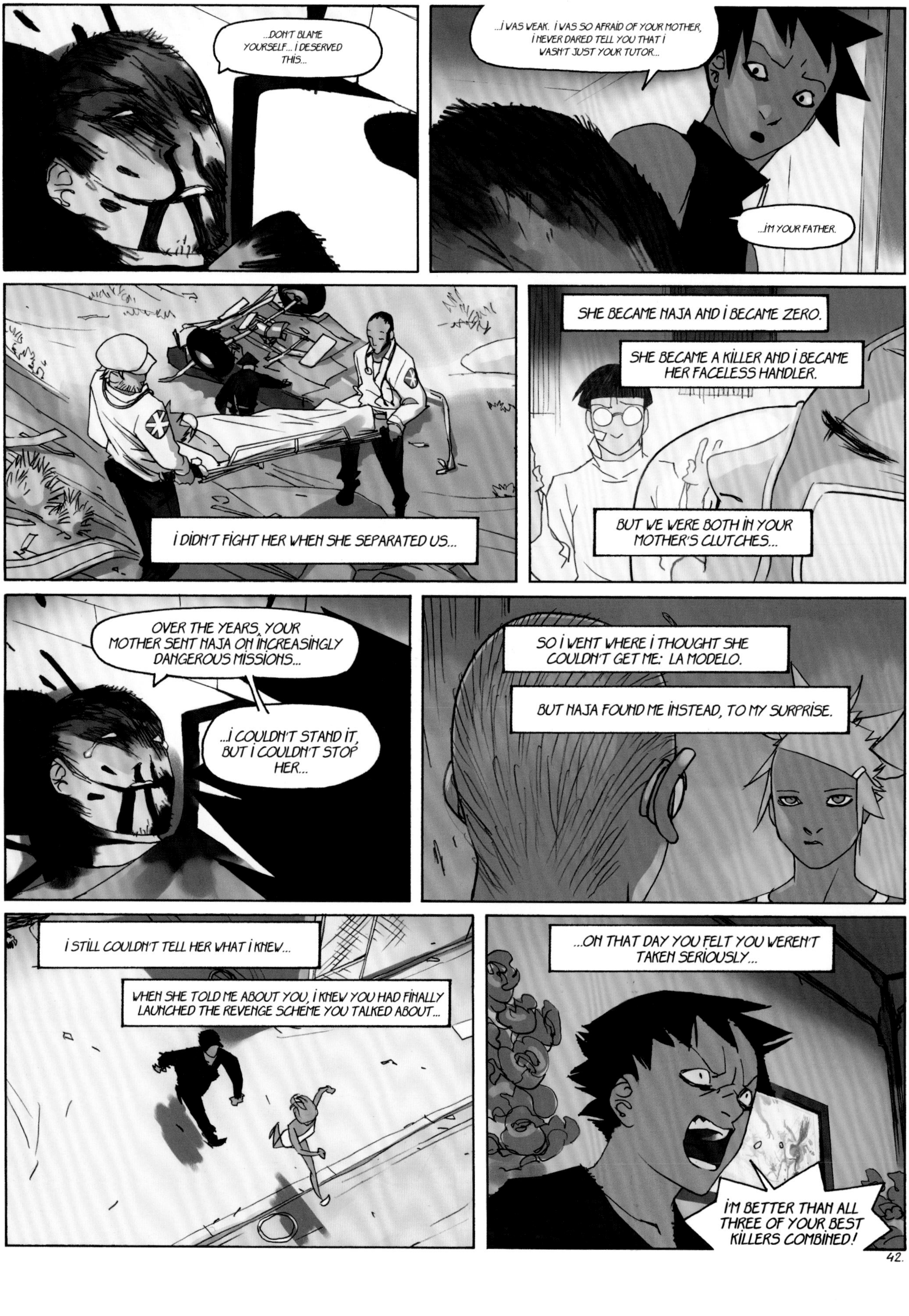
...DON'T BLAME YOURSELF... I DESERVED THIS...
...I WAS WEAK. I WAS SO AFRAID OF YOUR MOTHER, I NEVER DARED TELL YOU THAT I WASN'T JUST YOUR TUTOR...
...I'M YOUR FATHER.
I DIDN'T FIGHT HER WHEN SHE SEPARATED US...
SHE BECAME NAJA AND I BECAME ZERO.
SHE BECAME A KILLER AND I BECAME HER FACELESS HANDLER.
BUT WE WERE BOTH IN YOUR MOTHER'S CLUTCHES...
OVER THE YEARS, YOUR MOTHER SENT NAJA ON INCREASINGLY DANGEROUS MISSIONS...
...I COULDN'T STAND IT, BUT I COULDN'T STOP HER...
SO I WENT WHERE I THOUGHT SHE COULDN'T GET ME: LA MODELO.
BUT NAJA FOUND ME INSTEAD, TO MY SURPRISE.
I STILL COULDN'T TELL HER WHAT I KNEW...
WHEN SHE TOLD ME ABOUT YOU, I KNEW YOU HAD FINALLY LAUNCHED THE REVENGE SCHEME YOU TALKED ABOUT...
...ON THAT DAY YOU FELT YOU WEREN'T TAKEN SERIOUSLY...
I'M BETTER THAN ALL THREE OF YOUR BEST KILLERS COMBINED!

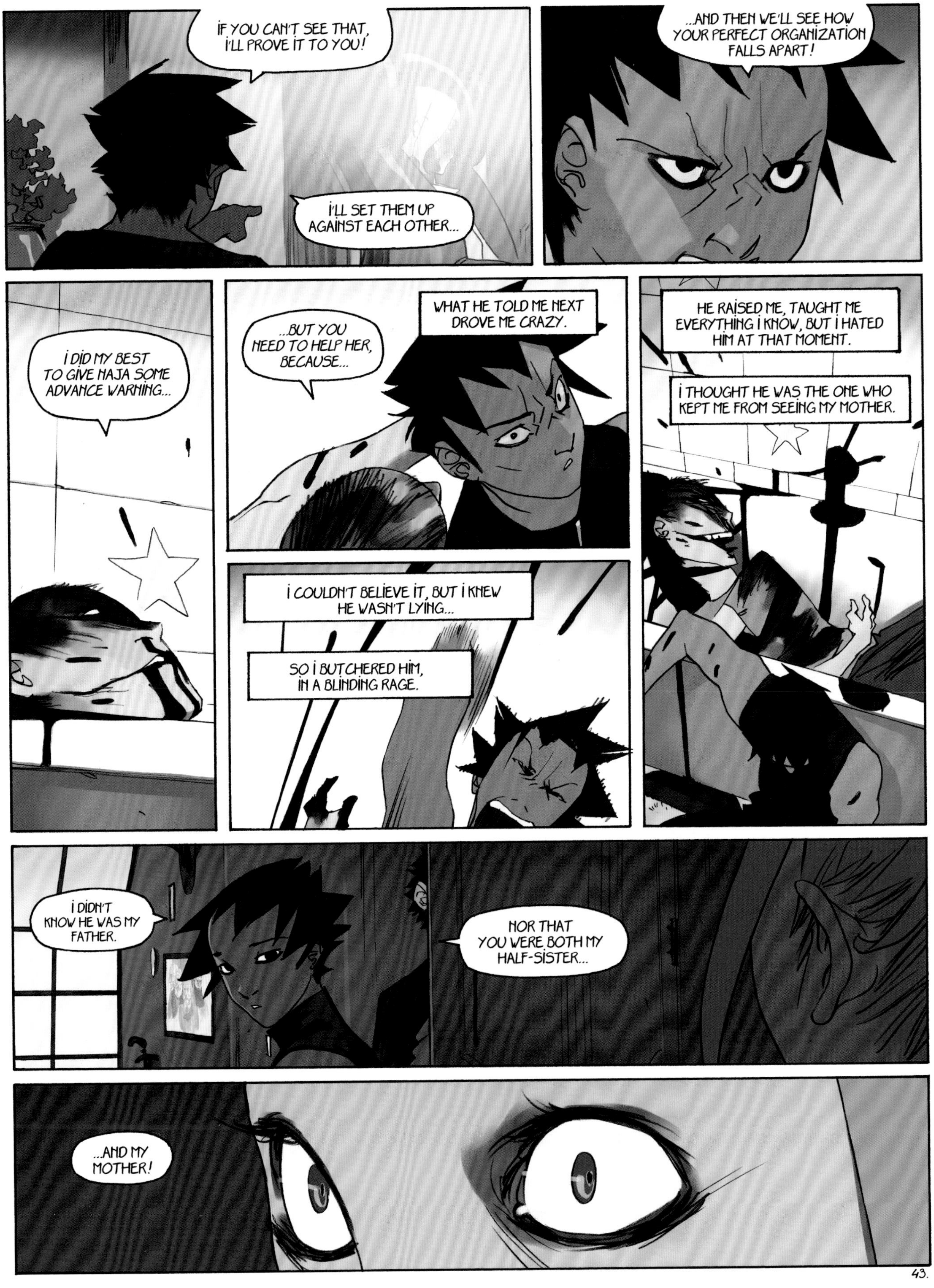
IF YOU CAN'T SEE THAT, I'LL PROVE IT TO YOU!
I'LL SET THEM UP AGAINST EACH OTHER...
...AND THEN WE'LL SEE HOW YOUR PERFECT ORGANIZATION FALLS APART!
I DID MY BEST TO GIVE NAJA SOME ADVANCE WARNING...
WHAT HE TOLD ME NEXT DROVE ME CRAZY.
...BUT YOU NEED TO HELP HER, BECAUSE...
HE RAISED ME, TAUGHT ME EVERYTHING I KNOW, BUT I HATED HIM AT THAT MOMENT.
I THOUGHT HE WAS THE ONE WHO KEPT ME FROM SEEING MY MOTHER.
I COULDN'T BELIEVE IT, BUT I KNEW HE WASN'T LYING...
SO I BUTCHERED HIM, IN A BLINDING RAGE.
I DIDN'T KNOW HE WAS MY FATHER.
NOR THAT YOU WERE BOTH MY HALF-SISTER...
...AND MY MOTHER!

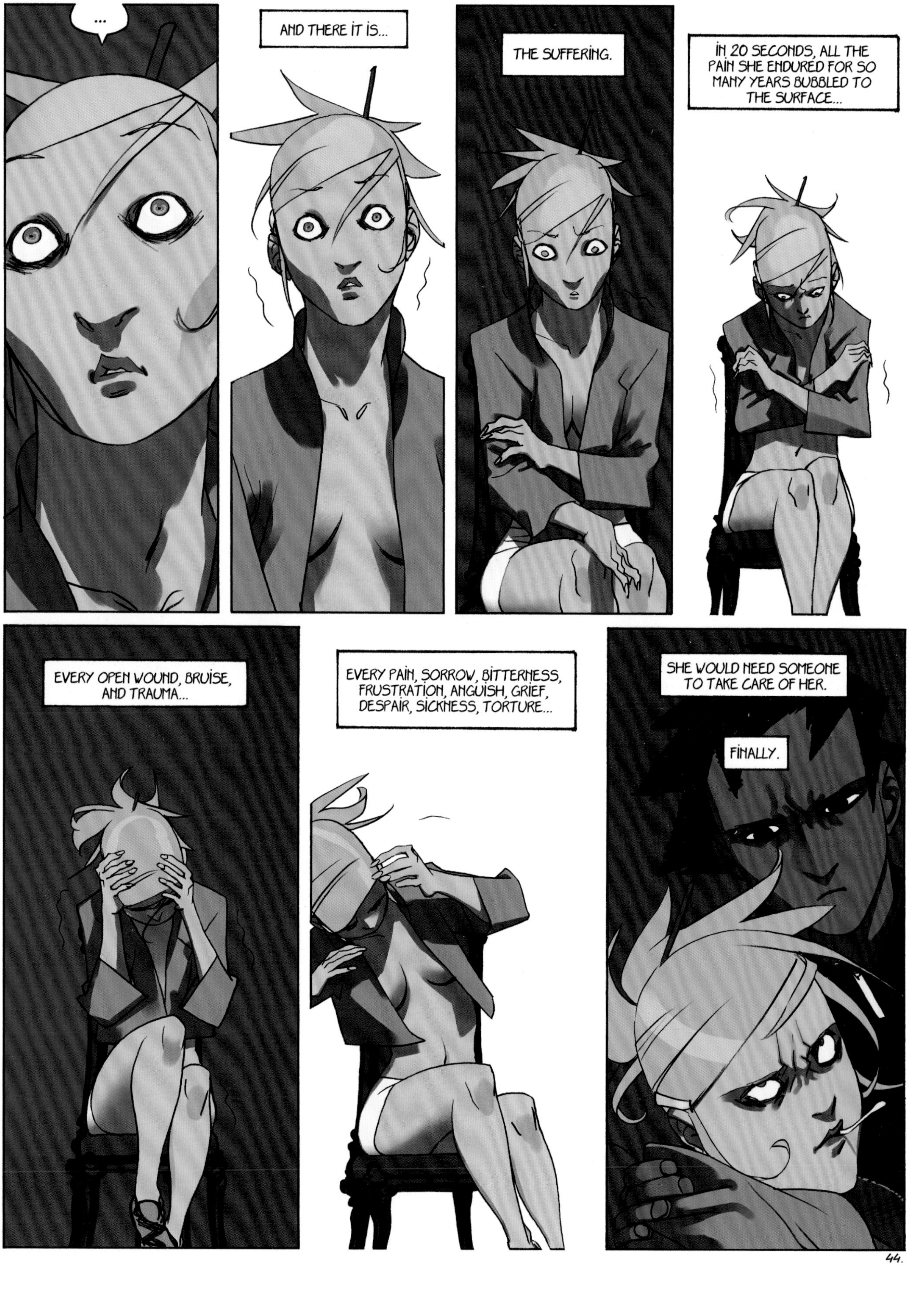
...
AND THERE IT IS...
THE SUFFERING.
IN 20 SECONDS, ALL THE PAIN SHE ENDURED FOR SO MANY YEARS BUBBLED TO THE SURFACE...
EVERY OPEN WOUND, BRUISE, AND TRAUMA...
EVERY PAIN, SORROW, BITTERNESS, FRUSTRATION, ANGUISH, GRIEF, DESPAIR, SICKNESS, TORTURE...
SHE WOULD NEED SOMEONE TO TAKE CARE OF HER.
FINALLY.

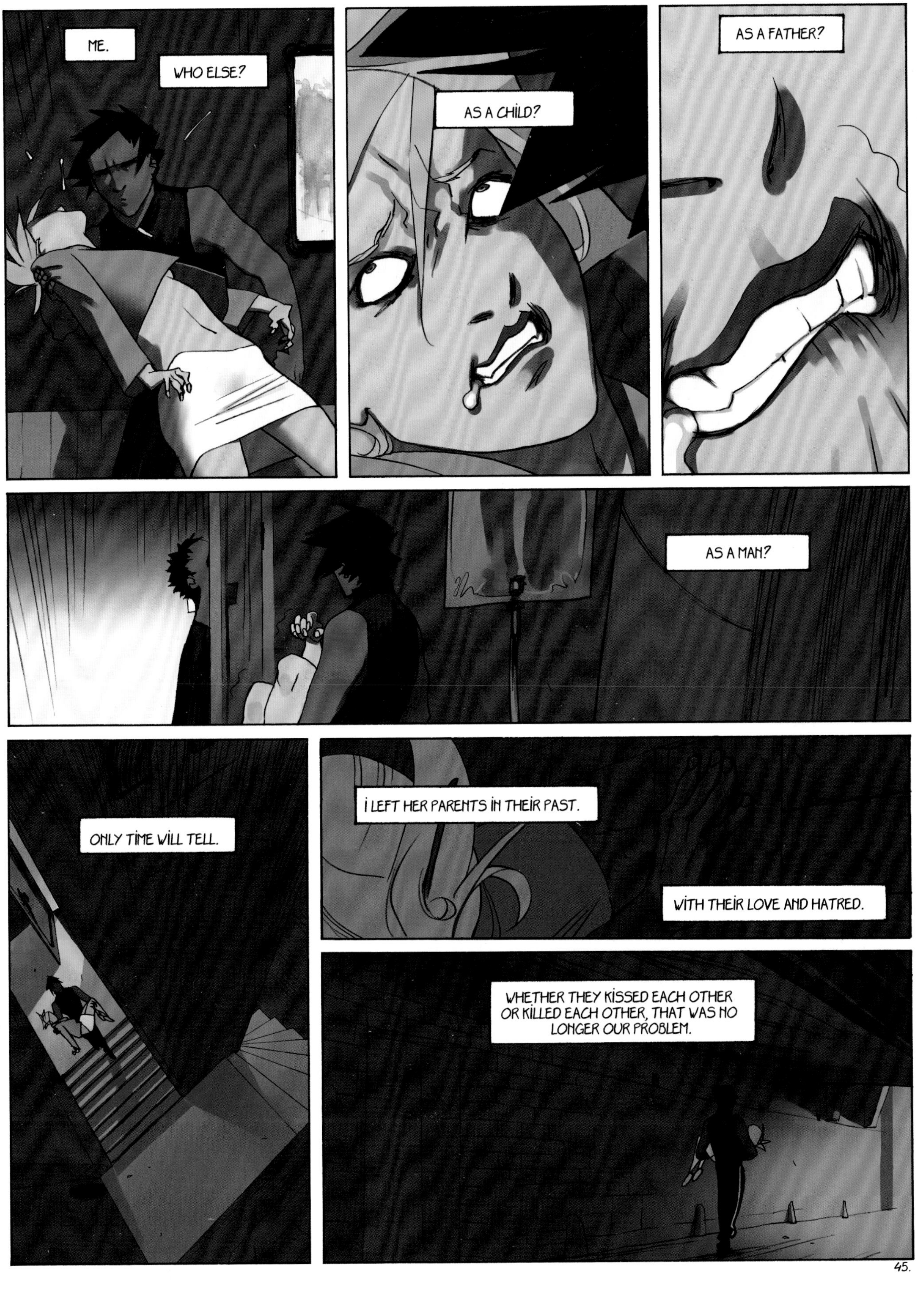
ME.
WHO ELSE?
AS A CHILD?
AS A FATHER?
AS A MAN?
ONLY TIME WILL TELL.
I LEFT HER PARENTS IN THEIR PAST.
WITH THEIR LOVE AND HATRED.
WHETHER THEY KISSED EACH OTHER OR KILLED EACH OTHER, THAT WAS NO LONGER OUR PROBLEM.

BECAUSE FRANKLY...

...NAJA ALWAYS HATED FAMILY.

I NO LONGER NEED TO TELL YOU WHY.

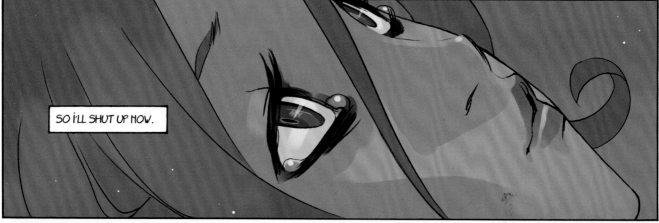

SO I'LL SHUT UP NOW.

FIN.

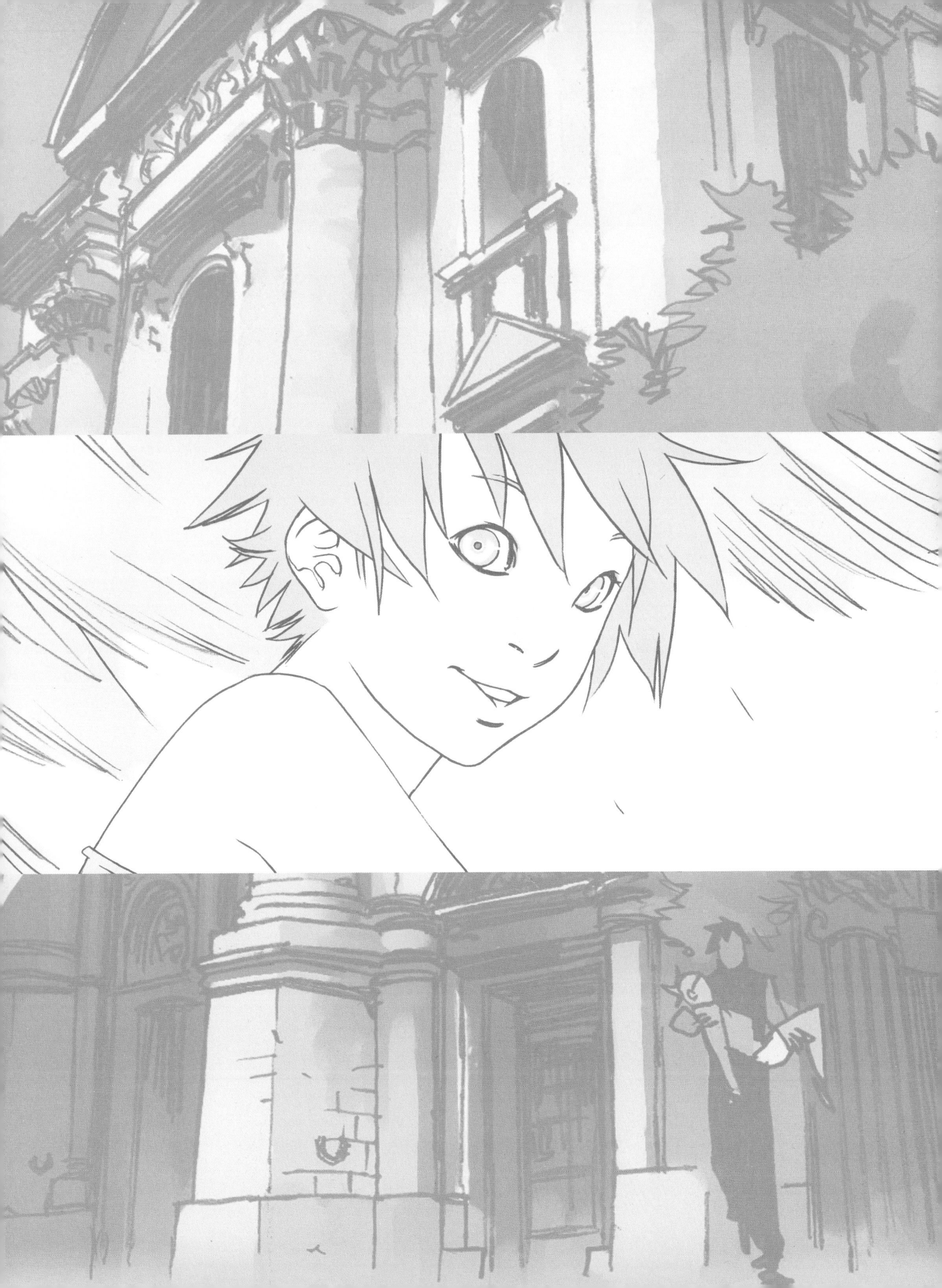

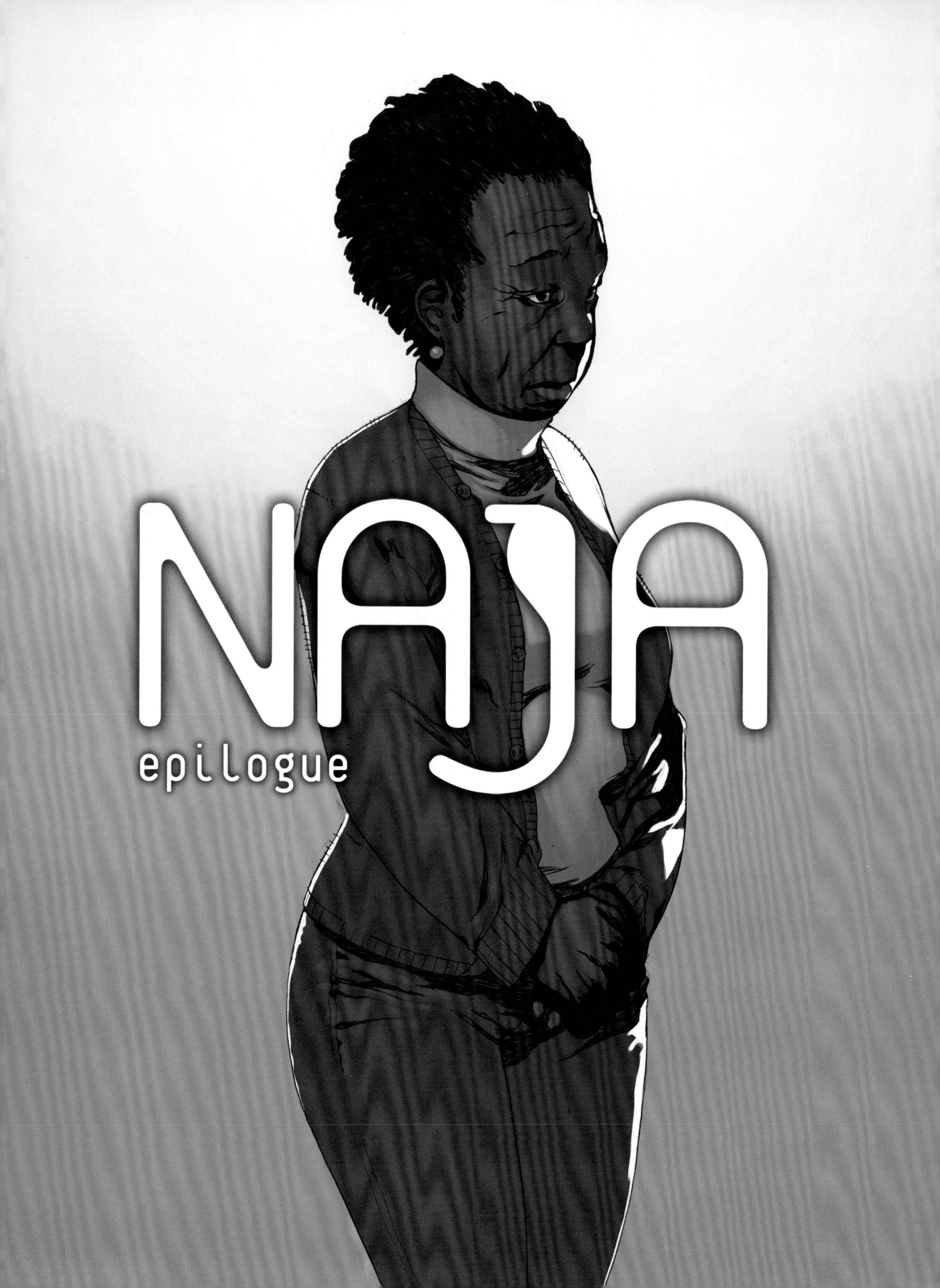
NAJA
epilogue

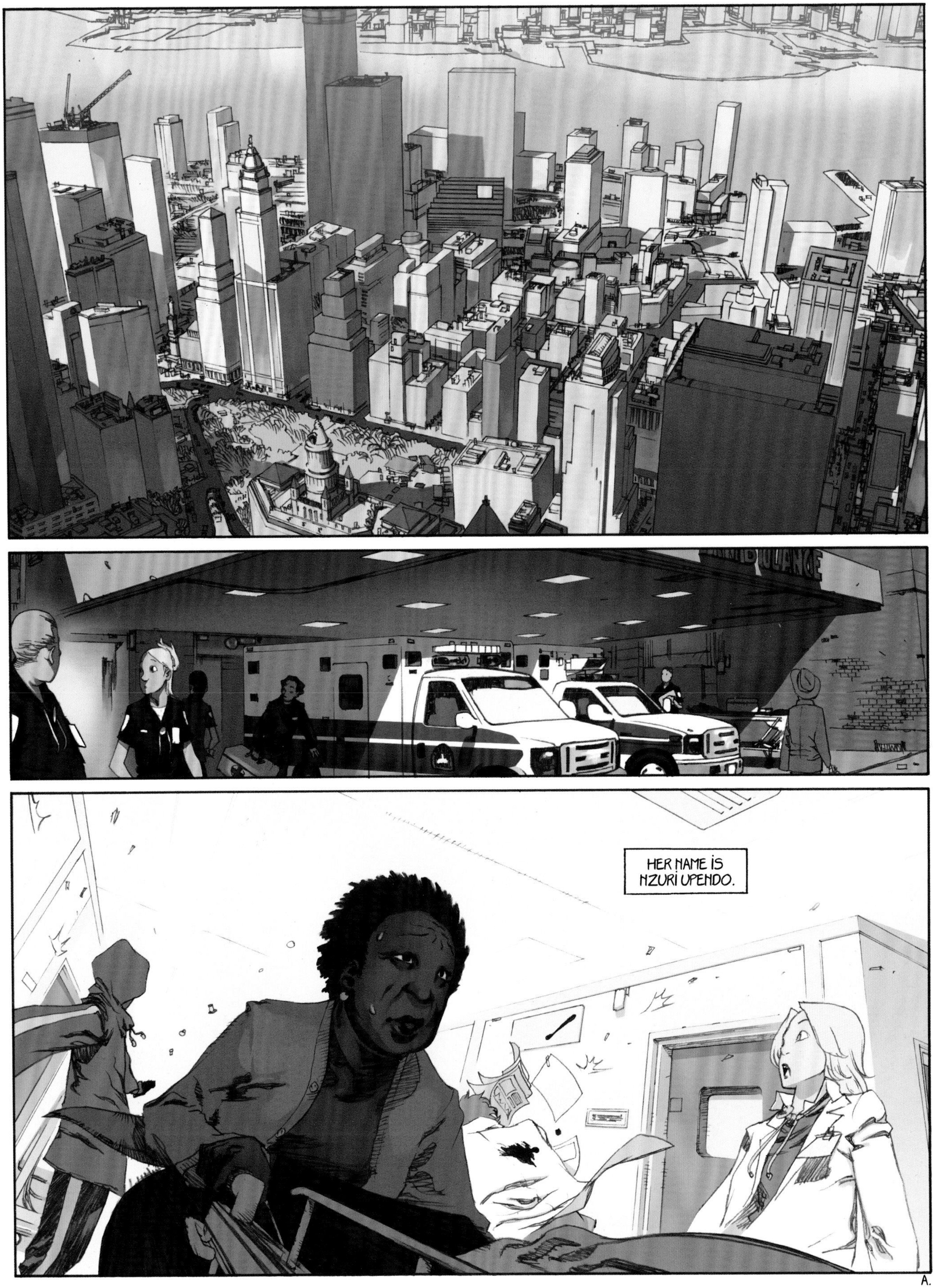
HER NAME IS
NZURI UPENDO.

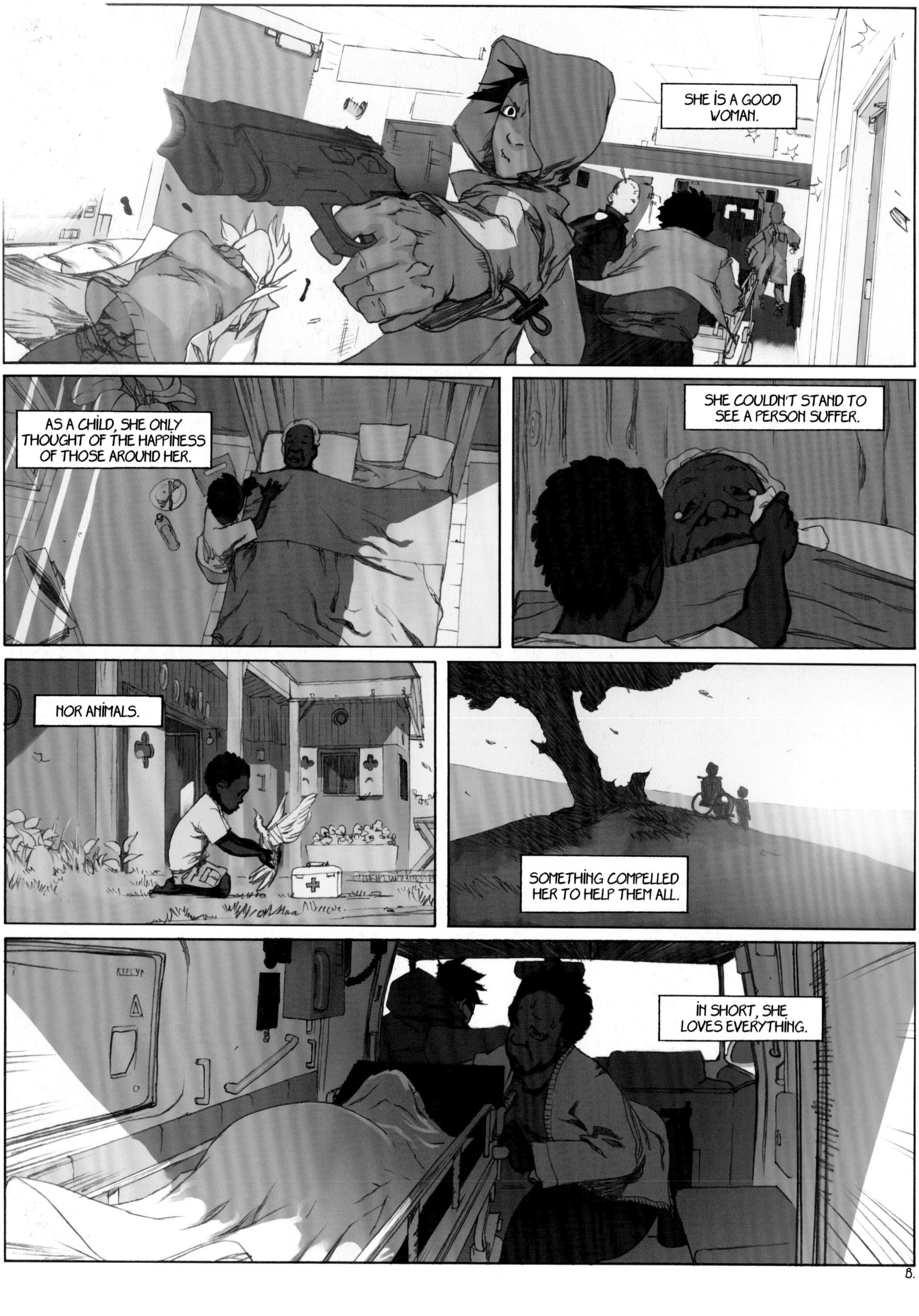
SHE IS A GOOD WOMAN.
AS A CHILD, SHE ONLY THOUGHT OF THE HAPPINESS OF THOSE AROUND HER.
SHE COULDN'T STAND TO SEE A PERSON SUFFER.
NOR ANIMALS.
SOMETHING COMPELLED HER TO HELP THEM ALL.
IN SHORT, SHE LOVES EVERYTHING.

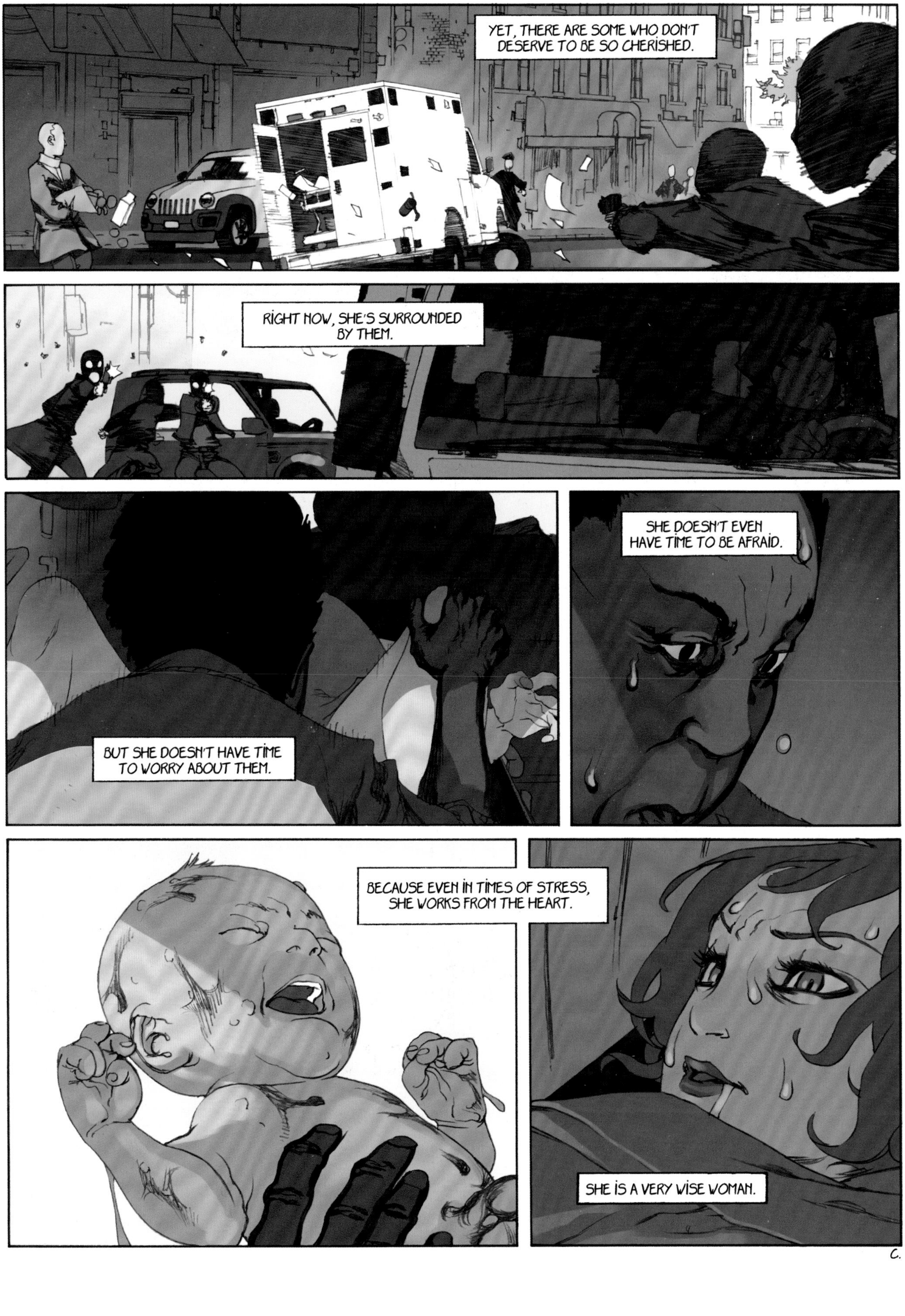
YET, THERE ARE SOME WHO DON'T DESERVE TO BE SO CHERISHED.
RIGHT NOW, SHE'S SURROUNDED BY THEM.
BUT SHE DOESN'T HAVE TIME TO WORRY ABOUT THEM.
SHE DOESN'T EVEN HAVE TIME TO BE AFRAID.
BECAUSE EVEN IN TIMES OF STRESS, SHE WORKS FROM THE HEART.
SHE IS A VERY WISE WOMAN.

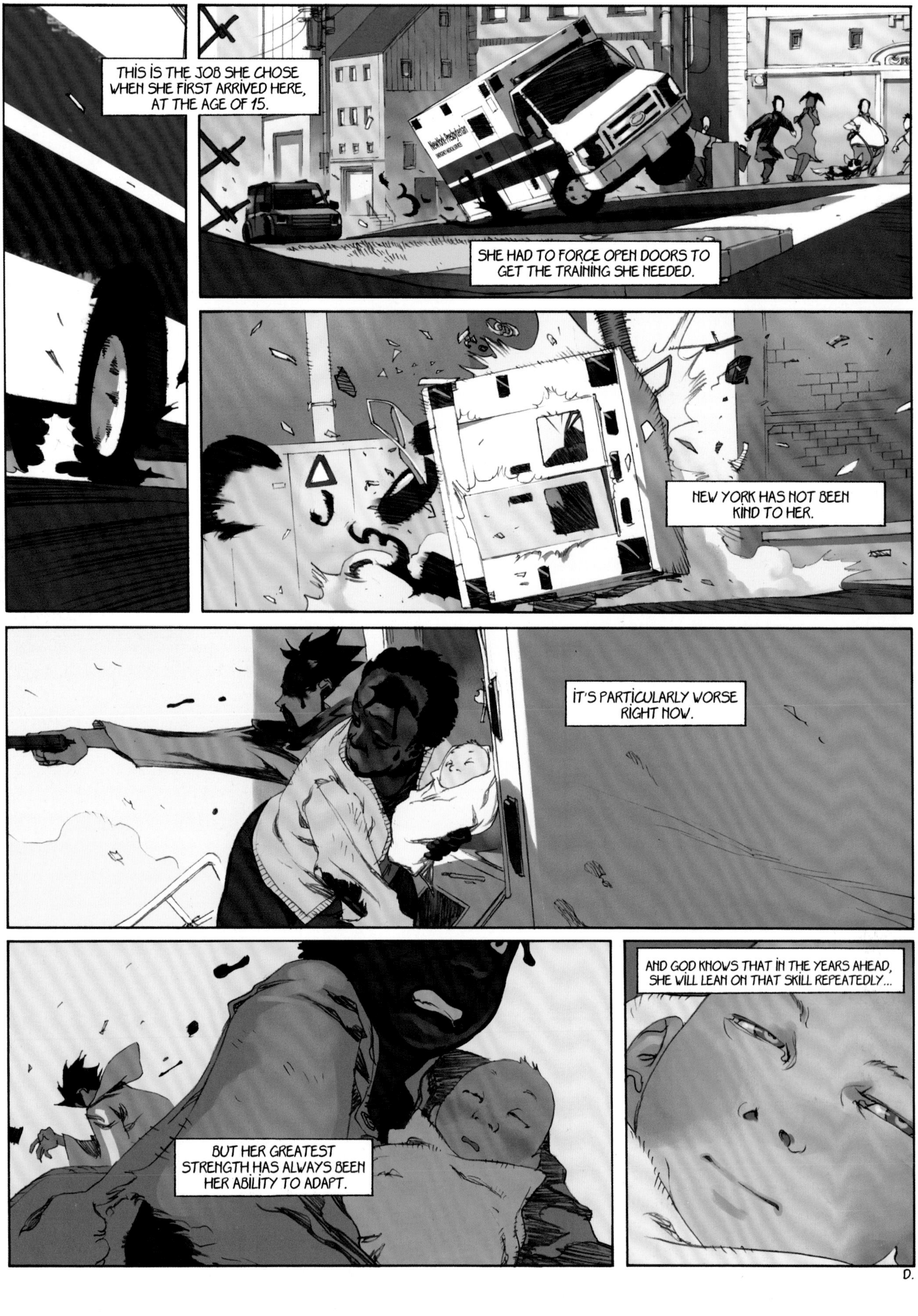
THIS IS THE JOB SHE CHOSE WHEN SHE FIRST ARRIVED HERE, AT THE AGE OF 15.
SHE HAD TO FORCE OPEN DOORS TO GET THE TRAINING SHE NEEDED.
NEW YORK HAS NOT BEEN KIND TO HER.
IT'S PARTICULARLY WORSE RIGHT NOW.
BUT HER GREATEST STRENGTH HAS ALWAYS BEEN HER ABILITY TO ADAPT.
AND GOD KNOWS THAT IN THE YEARS AHEAD, SHE WILL LEAN ON THAT SKILL REPEATEDLY...

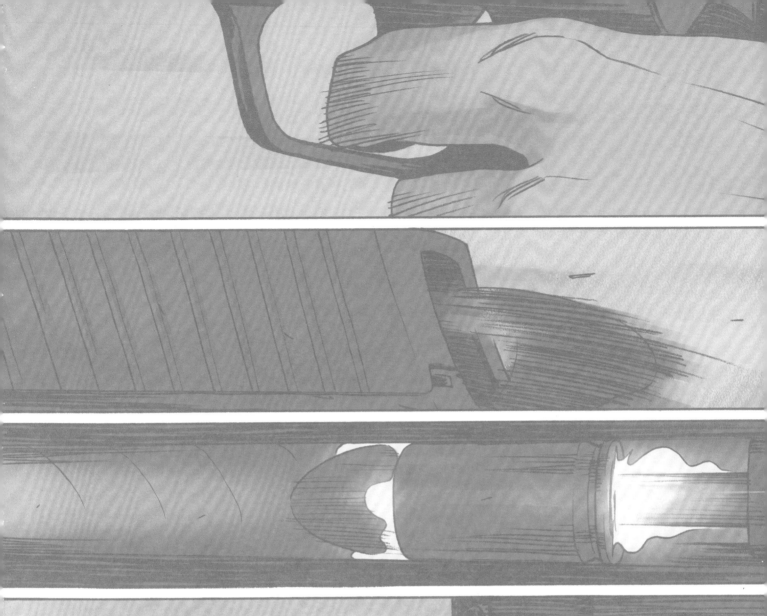

J.D. MORVAN

BORN IN REIMS, FRANCE, IN 1969, J.D. MORVAN TOOK THE LITTLE WORLD OF FRENCH COMICS BY STORM. HE GRADUATED FROM THE INSTITUT SAINT-LUC IN BRUSSELS, WHERE HE FIRST ASPIRED TO BE AN ILLUSTRATOR, THOUGH HE WAS CONVINCED THAT HE'D ACTUALLY END UP BEING A WRITER. AFTER PENNING SEVERAL MAJOR TITLES, INCLUDING NOMAD AND HK FOR GLÉNAT, HE CREATED THE WILDLY POPULAR SERIES SILLAGE FOR DELCOURT, ESTABLISHING HIMSELF AS ONE OF THE MOST SOUGHT AFTER WRITERS IN "BD" (OR BANDE DESSINEE, THE FRENCH TERM FOR 'COMIC BOOKS'). EXTREMELY PROLIFIC, HE HAS CREATED SEVERAL SERIES FOR DARGAUD, INCLUDING MON ANNEE WITH JIRO TANIGUCHI, AL'TOGO, LE PETIT MONDE, REALITY SHOW AND NAJA. HE ALSO AUTHORED A NUMBER OF VOLUMES OF SPIROU & FANTASIO, WITH ILLUSTRATOR JOSE-LUIS MUNUERA, AS WELL AS THE MERLIN SERIES, CO-CREATED WITH JOANN SFAR AND MUNUERA. IN 2011, HE CREATED CRIME SCHOOL, A MANGA-FLAVORED SERIES FOR KIDS, WHICH WAS NOMINATED FOR AN AWARD AT THE ANNUAL BD FESTIVAL IN ANGOULEME. IN 2012, HE CREATED ZAYA WITH CHINESE ARTIST HUANG JIA WEI, AND HE IS CURRENTLY WORKING ON A NEW SERIES WITH KOREAN ARTIST KIM JUNG GII.

BENGAL

BENGAL CHOSE TO BECOME AN AUTHOR AND AN ILLUSTRATOR IN THE LATE 90S. AS AN AVID READER OF BD, MANGA, AND COMICS BOOKS, AS WELL AS DIGITAL PAINTING, VIDEO GAMES, ANIMATION, AND FILM, HE RECEIVED HIS FIRST PROFESSIONAL WORK IN 1998 WITH HIS PUBLISHED WORK, "THE ONLY ONE", PUBLISHED BY GLÉNAT. BETWEEN 1999 AND 2003, HE WORKED IN PARIS AS AN ILLUSTRATOR AND DESIGNER FOR VIDEO GAME DEVELOPER DARKWORKS. HE RETURNED TO COMICS WITH THE DYPTIC SERIES MEKA, WRITTEN BY JD MORVAN AND PUBLISHED BY DELCOURT, WHILE SIMULTANEOUSLY WORKING ON SEVERAL SHORT STORIES FOR VARIOUS ANTHOLOGIES, INCLUDING FLIGHT FROM IMAGE COMICS AND SPIROU MAGAZINE FROM DUPUIS. HE ALSO CONTRIBUTED TO THE POPULAR FRENCH SERIES SILLAGE FROM DELCOURT AND SKYDOLL SPACESHIP COLLECTION FROM SOLEIL. IN 2008, HE CO-CREATED NAJA WITH JEAN-DAVID MORVAN FOR DARGAUD. HE RECENTLY COMPLETED THE TWO-PART SERIES LUMINAE FOR ANKAMA, AND HAS STARTED HIS NEXT PROJECT WITH JEAN-DAVID MORVAN, BIEN DU MAL. HE ALSO CO-FOUNDED THE ONLINE ARTIST COMMUNITY CFSL (OR "CAFÉ SALE"), ESTABLISHED TO GIVE EUROPEAN ARTISTS A DIGITAL FORUM TO SHARE THEIR WORK, MUCH LIKE DEVIANTART IN THE US. (WWW.CFSL.NET)

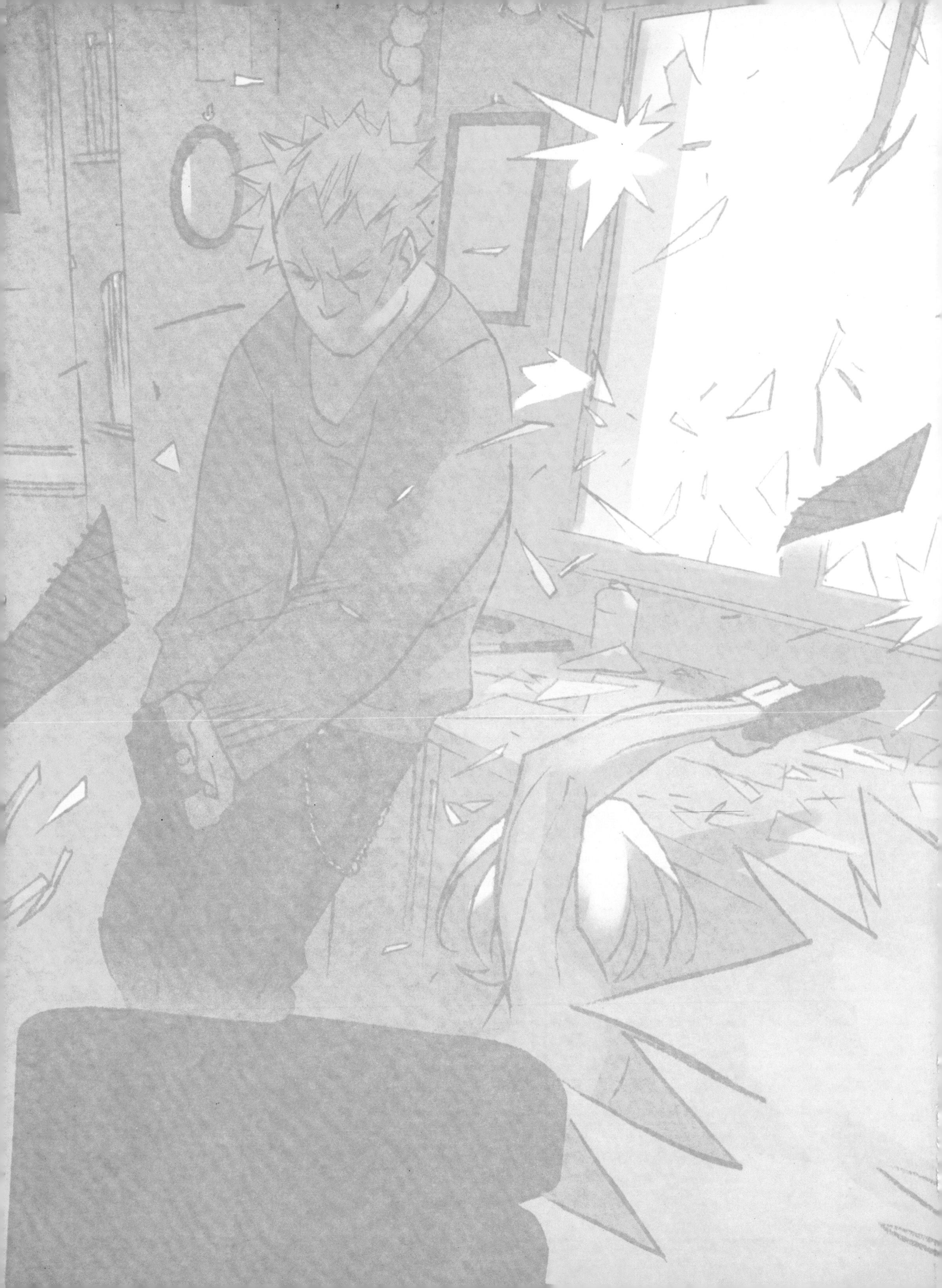